FOOD AND POVERTY

FOOD
AND POVERTY

Food Insecurity
and Food Sovereignty
among America's
Poor

Edited by Leslie H. Hossfeld, E. Brooke Kelly, Julia F. Waity

Vanderbilt University Press
Nashville

© 2018 by Vanderbilt University Press
Nashville, Tennessee 37235
All rights reserved
First printing 2018

This book is printed on acid-free paper.

Library of Congress Cataloging-in-Publication Data on file
LC control number 2017044692
LC classification number HV696.F6 F63145 2018
Dewey classification number 363.80973—dc23
LC record available at *lccn.loc.gov/2017044692*

ISBN 978–0-8265–2203–0 (cloth)
ISBN 978–0-8265–2204–7 (paperback)
ISBN 978–0-8265–2205–4 (ebook)

To all those who struggle with food,
life's most basic necessity.

CONTENTS

ACKNOWLEDGMENTS

Editing a book of this scope necessitates help from many people. We are particularly grateful to the authors who contributed such meaningful and insightful chapters. We also appreciate the endless support from Michael Ames at Vanderbilt University Press, who early on believed in this project and knew immediately of its importance. We are also grateful to the anonymous reviewers who provided supportive feedback on the manuscript.

INTRODUCTION

The Mississippi Delta is a remote part of the United States. Rural, isolated, and poor, the delta has a long history of significant social inequalities of all types, including race, class, and gender. Issaquena County is a small county in the Mississippi Delta with a population of about thirteen hundred people, 40 percent of whom live in poverty. The county is about 65 percent African American. There is no grocery store. There is no place to buy food in the routine sense of "going to the grocery store to buy food," no place to get your vegetables and fruit—your fresh meat or frozen foods—or simple household supplies that keep your house going on a daily basis. Imagine navigating this basic need—food—and trying to meet this daily need for yourself, for your family.

Imagine not being able to get to a grocery store to purchase something for dinner. Imagine not having access to a *real* grocery store. Added to this puzzlement of no access to healthy food through a conventional grocery store, it turns out Issaquena County has one of the highest obesity rates in the nation, with 38 percent of adults in the county considered obese.

While the Mississippi Delta may represent an extreme case in the United States, having access to healthy, affordable food is a very real problem in America, not just in remote, poor counties. We may ask, "How can this be? How can this exist in the United States?" Unfortunately this may be a more common problem than most people realize. Neighborhoods and cities, rural communities, and entire counties often have little to no access to healthy, affordable food.

We may also ask, "How can poor counties have such high obesity rates? Isn't poverty related to being underweight and malnourished?" If we think about poverty and hunger in developing nations, we often draw on images of starving children who are thin and underweight. Yet, increasingly, the growing problem in the United States in terms of health has to do with food and the food environment in which people live. The type of food we eat, the food that is cheap and plentiful and easy to access, is often food that has little to no nutritional value, and is high in calories and fat.

The Great Recession catapulted the poor into the forefront of America's conscience in ways not seen since the war on poverty began fifty years ago. With the increased focus on the poor came stories about the newly poor who were turning toward assistance for the first time in their lives, assistance they never thought they were going to need. There are also those in persistent poverty whose circumstances may have been exacerbated by the economic downturn. Food insecurity, or hunger, skyrocketed as did the number relying on federal food assistance programs like the Supplemental Nutrition Assistance Program (SNAP). There has been a growing focus on issues of obesity and access to healthy food.

The story of food and poverty in the United States is a complex and compelling story with many moving parts, many of which focus on the way in which food production has changed significantly in a fairly short amount of time. Indeed there have been dramatic shifts in food production since World War II, changes to meet the increased needs of families and a growing population, and changes due to new technology. Since the 1940s there has been a marked decrease in the number of small family farms, once the mainstay of US food production, to a notable increase in commodity production (soy and corn) together with an increase in large-scale agricultural production. US farm policy since WWII has also changed significantly, with an increased focus on supporting commodity production, and in turn, driving down the costs of commodities such as corn and soybean through government subsidies and support. One of the results of these changes has been the introduction of fructose corn syrup and hydrogenated vegetable oils into the American diet, products that make snacks, soda, candy, and fats very inexpensive, and indeed economical. Farm policy that buttresses the cheap production of these products in recent years has, at the very same time, had very few subsidies to support the costs of fruits and vegetables. Indeed since World War II, we have seen a steady, noticeable increase in the price of fruits and vegetables. It has become easier, and indeed cheaper, to buy "junk food"—the low-nutritional, low-cost, long-shelf-life, mass-produced food that is found at every corner store, at every convenience store, and on grocery store shelves. In short, farm policy and food policy is not health policy.

If we look at data from the Centers for Disease Control we see that American adults are twenty-four pounds heavier today than they were in 1960. In direct relationship with the mass production of cheap, high-fat, high-caloric food, obesity rates for American adults have skyrocketed since World War II. If we simply look at high poverty counties and neighborhoods in the United States and overlay these data with obesity rates, we see a striking pattern emerge: the higher the poverty, the higher the obesity rate.

This book is about the complex and perplexing issue of food and poverty in America. There are indeed paradoxes between food and poverty in the United States: paradoxes such as the land of plenty with vast food supplies, juxtaposed with hunger and food insecurity—a lack of food; and the overwhelming paradox of obesity co-existing with hunger.

PART ONE

CONCEPTS

Around 1990, the US Department of Agriculture (USDA) began measuring household *food security*, a concept centered on understanding whether households have enough consistent food to live a healthy, active life. Food *insecure* households, conversely, have difficulty and uncertainty in meeting these basic food needs. The development of this measure emanated from the 1984 US Presidential Task Force on Food Assistance, which drew attention to the lack of a good measure of hunger. The USDA has refined the measure over the years to capture the range of severity of food insecure households and their relationship to *hunger*.

The concept of food sovereignty is a concept about the right to food, more specifically about the right of people to *define* their own food and agricultural production. The idea arose in the 1990s in response to policies and practices around food security and large-scale agribusiness production of food globally, and the immiseration of small family farmers and producers. Food sovereignty has grown into a global movement about how and where food is produced and who benefits when people are in control of "healthy and culturally appropriate food produced through ecologically sound and sustainable methods, and their right to define their own food and agriculture systems" (Declaration of the Forum for Food Sovereignty 2007).

The chapters in this first section examine these concepts in greater detail. While this book focuses primarily on food and poverty in the United States, we begin this section with a discussion of food security and food sovereignty from the Global South. The contrast to, and comparison of, experiences and policy development around food insecurity in developing nations provides a rich context to begin an examination of these very issues here in the United States. This is followed by two innovative chapters, one that considers rethinking *food* as a measure of *poverty*, and another that examines cultural factors—like foodways and lifestyle patterns—that mediate food and poverty.

1

Security via Sovereignty
Lessons from the Global South

MYRIAM PAREDES AND MARK EDWARDS

The American shopper walking down a grocery store aisle naively participates in a food system full of ironies and unintended consequences. If asked to interpret the contrast between great volumes of food on the shelves and the request at the cash register for contributions to the food bank, a thoughtful person will quickly recognize the most blatant of ironies—a country that produces mass quantities of food and pays farmers to stop producing too much is also a country with 17.4 million food insecure households (Coleman-Jensen, Rabbitt, Gregory, and Singh 2015). But beyond this glaring contradiction, the complexities and frequent dysfunctions of the country's provisioning remain a mystery. One reason for shoppers' naiveté is the dominance of food security "thinking" about the feeding of populations and the lack of awareness of an alternative food sovereignty theoretical framework. In this chapter we highlight the distinctions, connections, and implications of these frameworks, advocating for a more thoughtful approach to understanding the feeding of the United States by incorporating the strengths of food sovereignty, a concept embraced by South Americans in their constitutions.

Consider another apparent contradiction. From a food security point of view, high rates of obesity and diabetes among poor Americans are nonintuitive, especially given that in other countries poverty can lead to stunted growth and gaunt faces. But a food sovereignty lens brings into focus the fact that powerful interests arrange for government-subsidized commodities that keep prices low on calorie-intensive, nutrition-poor diets, while healthy fruits and vegetables remain unsubsidized, more expensive, and therefore more accessible to middle and upper classes.

The sovereignty lens also reveals ironies inherent in the production and delivery components of the food system. For example, sometimes, the same trucks that transport organic produce from the rural "salad-bowl" areas to the cities are the same ones that bring back from port cities the less expensive canned produce gathered and processed elsewhere, at times from halfway around the world. So, rural farmworkers in the United States use their meager wages *not* to purchase the food they cultivated and harvested, but instead to buy food that other farmworkers produced more cheaply elsewhere. Even stranger, low-income workers and the unemployed, both in remote rural and in densely urban places, often find themselves in the midst of food deserts; that is, they live in places that lack a wide variety of affordable, quality foods and instead are full of cheap, highly processed foods. Supermarkets may choose to avoid urban ghettos, or not stock their stores with the same quality produce owing to economic and transportation obstacles, while little country stores are often so remote that food distribution companies decide not to deliver fresh dairy, bread, or produce to such small markets.

Further ironies appear when a sovereignty lens is used to consider the food access concerns of low-wage, working Americans. For example, many of the low-income inhabitants of these urban food deserts work in "food service" while low-income workers in rural places are often engaged in cultivating, harvesting, and packing food. In both rural and urban areas of the northwestern United States, food service workers have been among the highest represented workers among food insecure households (Grussing and Edwards 2006). Meanwhile, at the end of the food chain, consumers who work in retail (such as Walmart) often earn wages so low that they must turn to federal assistance (Supplemental Nutrition Assistance Program—SNAP), providing them modest funds to purchase food, often from the very employers who pay them low wages.

The computer-precise and remarkably organized food-delivery system that daily feeds multitudes with safe, if not always healthy, food also displays occasional unintended consequences that achieve notoriety in the media. For example, the same amazingly efficient industrial food complex that distributes massive quantities to most parts of the country and the world also produces large outbreaks of food-borne illnesses when food safety is compromised. One bad crop of cantaloupes or batch of ice cream contaminated with Listeria (Centers for Disease Control and Prevention 2015b) or one side of beef infected with "mad cow disease" (Centers for Disease Control and Prevention 2015a) can put at risk thousands of consumers because indeed millions of consumers partake of the rationalized system that so widely distributes cantaloupes, ice cream, and hamburger from and to all parts of the country. From a food security point of view, such problems may be regarded as unavoidable collateral damage that can be minimized with ever-greater technological improvements. With a food sovereignty lens, one may instead ask if perhaps there are alternate possibilities to access more localized food via community or family gardens, relying on closer providers or markets that need little to no public intervention.

Finally, federal public policy focused on food systems in the United States (a country whose constitution emphasizes the separation of powers) has ironically placed one agency (the US Department of Agriculture, USDA) in charge of advocating for both producers and consumers. Because food industry companies are organized and resource rich, they can influence decision makers more readily than can the poor, leading to a situation akin to putting foxes in charge of the hen house (to borrow a food metaphor). Agribusiness and the food industry spend tens of millions of dollars each year on campaign contributions (for candidates sympathetic to the industry) and on lobbyists. The result is pressure on the USDA for subsidies on corn and beef and resistance to efforts to raise nutrition standards on school lunches. Debates over whether ketchup is a vegetable, and less silly but nonetheless contentious wrangling over revising the USDA's food pyramids, reveal how the USDA faces often irreconcilable goals and competing pressures from unequally matched constituents. So, one part of the USDA favors commodity producers (e.g., dairy industry) while another part of the agency is questioning the healthfulness of all that cheese on lunchroom pizza. A food security lens does not address such questions about who is deciding the menu of the poor but rather focuses on making sure that food is distributed widely. The sovereignty lens brings into relief these discontinuities and could remind Americans (a) that what they eat is largely determined by much bigger forces and vested interests and (b) that they could actively support their own interests regarding feeding their families.

American eaters of any class, but especially of working and lower classes, need not invent the critique and the questions on their own. They can learn from the efforts, successes, and failures of international movements seeking to ask these uncomfortable questions in countries where economic and political circumstances have made it possible to give voice to them. We focus on two South American examples. First, Ecuador, where unlike in the United States, the constitution of the country addresses food rights for producers and consumers, and the food system is explicitly called out as a vital part of society to be evaluated and debated through a deeply democratic process that creates new institutions of deliberation. The concept of food sovereignty plays a central role in the polity of the country although not without problems. Second, in Brazil, a food sovereignty framework takes center stage in that country's integrated, multipronged approach to creating food security for the population, while taking seriously the structural reasons for hunger. Brazil's Zero Hunger policy, like Ecuador's policy, includes the creation of institutions that allow the participation of the wider public in the design and implementation of local programs that include the support of local and regional producers. We begin by first elaborating on the food security and food sovereignty frameworks, describing how conflicting and/or compatible they are, before turning attention to these two South American examples and some of the lessons US eaters can learn from them.

Food Security and Food Sovereignty
Food Security: A Dominant but Incomplete Narrative

The concept of food security is almost as intuitive as hunger. No one wants to be hungry, and everyone wants the security of knowing that their next meal is assured. And most would likely wish for food security for their community, region, or country as well—a condition where there is plenty for all and assured access to that plenty in the future. Yet, as intuitive as this understanding of food security may be, there has remained a surprising amount of debate about, and number of differences in, definitions of food security.

In 1974, before food security in America was being widely discussed, growing international concern over world hunger led professional development bureaucrats and academics to establish a food security framework at the World Food Congress in Rome. Over the subsequent decades, the concept evolved as consensus grew that there should be internationally shared responsibility for national-level hunger, recognizing that the Green Revolution (i.e., large-scale technical improvements in agriculture that dramatically increased world production of crops) was not rapidly or automatically leading to reductions in poverty or malnutrition. Indeed, in some cases, that revolution may have increased hunger vulnerability in some countries (McIntyre et al. 2009). By

1996, at the World Food Congress, there was international acknowledgement of the *social* causes of hunger and an emerging recognition that access to food is a "universal right." Even with these changes, food security as the end goal remained and continues as the dominant framework for understanding the feeding of the world's population.

Examining official definitions of food security reveals the primary elements of a food security framework for understanding the feeding of countries. The Food and Agricultural Organization (FAO) of the United Nations World Health Organization declared that "food security, at the individual, household, national, regional and global levels [is achieved] when all people, at all times, have physical and economic access to sufficient, safe and nutritious food to meet their dietary needs and food preferences for an active and healthy life" (Food and Agriculture Organization 2003, 28). This definition describes a condition where access is never in question, where quality is assured, and where culture is taken into account ("preferences"). Parsing the sentence reveals that "access" is what people have, and the remainder of the definition describes "what" they have access to. Note that it does not address production, processing, manufacturing, and sourcing of foods, leaving open the debate as to whether this condition of constant access is achievable through the current international food system. Some critics argue that this definition predisposes actions to be the development of technical solutions for production and delivery but without illuminating the sources of food insecurity, and hence the root causes of it.

In the United States, the concept of food security was introduced to decision makers in the mid-1990s by the USDA. The USDA continues to use a minimalist definition of food security that ignores many of the elements found in the FAO definition, describing it as "access by all people at all times to enough food for an active, healthy life" (Coleman-Jensen, Rabbitt, Gregory, and Singh 2015). Issues related to food preference, nutrition, safety, and means by which food is obtained are not explicitly included in the USDA definition nor in the official measure of food security used by the agency. The measure focuses primarily on respondents having enough money for purchasing food and ignores receipt of SNAP, food boxes, school breakfasts and lunches, or congregant meals. The definition emphasizes purchase rather than production or even eating, which, while shallow, is not unreasonable given the fact that most people do not produce any of their own food anyway.

But definitions of problems are not neutral. They are reflective of assumptions about the way the world works. When those assumptions are hidden, they exert power in unexamined ways. This is true of the international and domestic definitions of food security. The absence of attention to where food comes from, who decides what will be produced, who produces it, and at what cost hides issues that are ignored, yet deeply relevant to the low-income shopper, the diabetic, the child eating free and reduced-price lunch, the local grocer, and the small farmer. Evidence of just how shallow has been the food security framework, on its own, can be seen in the US response to growing rates of officially measured "food insecurity."

If contributions to food banks are any indication, the American public has increasingly come to believe that domestic hunger exists. Since the early 1990s, the collective response from citizens has not been to question the systems that provide food to the population, but rather it has been to give food and money to regional and local food banks (Poppendieck 1999). Initially, the USDA also responded by distributing agricultural excess through this same emergency food system. Further expansion of SNAP (Supplemental Nutritional Assistance Program) also prioritizes money-for-food approaches without interrogating the processes that make some groceries more expensive than others, or that make some people more likely to be low income than others. These incomplete and narrow responses reflect what is possible with only a food security lens, which gives emphasis to making sure that low-income people have food in the cupboard but without evaluating the means by which the food is obtained, the quality of the food, and the larger vested interests that put low-income people into this situation.

Similarly, the food security framework's incomplete narrative about food and the systems that produce and deliver it sometimes positions antihunger workers and activists at cross-purposes, or at least having to navigate complicated food politics. For example, the nationwide organization Feeding America begins with a food security framework and impressively organizes the delivery of millions of pounds of donated food to people who are left hungry in the current system. While they are deeply engaged in research and advocacy that informs government decisions, they must refrain from directly criticizing large food producers and distributors who contribute to their hunger-relief efforts. (Imagine the public relations quandary of wishing to advocate for local, sustainably grown produce, instead of relying on canned, high-sodium vegetables from another country, when an industrial canner and distributor is willing to donate tons of canned produce.) Other advocacy organizations such as FRAC (Food Research and Action Center) more obviously lobby and advocate within the political system, but faced with resistance to food sovereignty critiques of the existing food production and delivery systems, they primarily focus on existing food security policies such as support for child nutrition services or protecting SNAP benefits.

The food security framework in the United States has achieved two important things while leaving unexamined others that we have previously mentioned. First, in the raising of public awareness of the extent of domestic hunger, the effort to measure food insecurity has made it possible to document annual federal and state rates of food insecurity, thus lending scientific credibility to claims that economic and policy changes may be impacting families' material well-being. In a country where obvious malnutrition is not evident to people and where shelves are full, having trustworthy statistics to document the number of struggling families has assisted advocates in making the case to decision makers and the public that a problem exists. Second, the concept of food security is not inherently partisan (compared to "food sovereignty," which immediately elicits questions of power). By focusing on provision of sufficient calories, this framework permits people on the political left and right to seek to address it, whether through defending government programs on the left or advocating for more private charity on the right. However, this framing has left unexamined the influence of vested interests, has individuated the problem rather than addressed structural reasons for it, and has ignored nonmarket solutions.

Food Sovereignty: An Emerging but Contested Approach

In part a response to the perceived shortcomings of food security for seriously addressing recurring food shortages as well as to the tenacity of rural poverty and the international rise of corporate influence over food, peasant movement representatives participating in a 1996 international meeting of La Vía Campesina made an international call for "food sovereignty" (Vía Campesina 1996). The definition emerged as "the right of the populations to food which is culturally adequate and nutritious, accessible and produced in a sustainable and ecological way, and the right to decide their own food and production system" (Nyéléni Declaration 2007). They asserted that food insecurity must be resolved by the affected people themselves in a favorable policy environment supported by governments and international organizations.

The food sovereignty framework demands the direct participation of food insecure persons in local food policy and program design and implementation, letting them take an active part in influencing the quantity, quality, and price of food available to them. This approach contradicts the notion of the consumer as simple receptor of food and food aid, an approach that tends to favor opinions and plans of food corporations, investors, and government experts. Embracing food sovereignty means the creation of institutions that support and enhance the quality of participation as well as public (state) support for food insecure consumer organizations (e.g., training about their rights, about nutrition, etc.). Although there are organized groups of food insecure consumers in the United States, these tend to be focused on adjusting or improving current food aid programs with little or no say in the way such programs are organized, and without institutionalized and/or public mechanisms to support their organizations. With different mechanisms for participation, they could effectively ensure that programs that target food insecure people would become more integrated with other policies and programs such as labor and housing programs. Currently, in the United States, there is no such effective space to debate the role of huge food corporations in maintaining the status quo, to challenge the way they affect public policies, or to discuss how they market and promote low-quality, highly processed and sugary food.

Contradictory, Corrective, yet Complementary

Critics of the food sovereignty framework argue that it is naive in its emphasis on small farms and urban gardening for feeding the world and its rejection of many modern agricultural practices (Bernstein 2013; Southgate 2011). Others argue that it confronts more than cooperates "on the ground" (Aerni 2011) and that the food sovereignty movement has been unclear about the nature of sovereignty (Hospes 2014). Some of these critics appear to dismiss out of hand the sovereignty approach, with the same vigor with which food sovereignty advocates criticize the food security framework.

While the food security framework emphasizes the importance of technology, food sovereignty prioritizes the "rule of the people." We argue that the food sovereignty approach improves a food security approach, showing that these are complementary approaches that in practice do not need to be set up as hostile to one another. Indeed, the food sovereignty lens for understanding food systems has been a response to the failures of the food security approach to solving nutritional problems in the world. Instead of being proposed by government experts or international organizations, the food sovereignty response has come from the very populations that have been affected by the experience of food insecurity. This development is both historic and highly unusual, with affected populations of the Global South identifying a concept that resonates with them in terms of the definition of the problem and possible ways out. Perhaps because it does not come from scientific/academic or governmental domains as such it has been the cause of much debate.

We identify three ways that food sovereignty improves the food security framework. First, the food sovereignty approach reclaims the right to decide for the most affected people regarding the ways to solve their daily problems of food insecurity. It does not supplant the food security framework for another one to be implemented by governments or international organizations. This observation highlights the "sovereignty" part of the term. In other words, while the food security framework implies plenty of calories for everyone, food sovereignty implies that people exert control over what they eat and how it is produced and distributed. Process becomes as important as final outcome.

Second, unlike food security's technical, scientific approach to measuring deficits and inequalities, food sovereignty focuses on (a) making visible existing solutions already embraced by millions of people around the world and (b) addressing root systemic causes that lead to food insecurity. Among these root causes are: (1) distancing and disconnection from the production of one's own food (e.g., most people do not know where their food comes from or how it is produced), (2) turning all processes involved in food production and distribution into a money-making proposition ("commoditization"), and (3) depending on knowledge external to the community (i.e., quality certification comes from bodies unfamiliar with local practices of production). Presently many countries in the world produce enough food for their populations but have uneven distribution, thus the food sovereignty approach questions the assumption that "more production is needed for a growing world population."

Third, the food sovereignty approach gives new vision and purpose for the existing structures that have emerged in a food security framework. Governments and international organizations that have implemented the current food security system still have an important albeit different role within the food sovereignty approach. From the food sovereignty point of view, these entities would support the different deliberative institutions and implement policies that reflect people's positive experiences in accessing food in sustainable ways. The likely heterogeneity of these various solutions (such as producing food in urban and rural areas in family or community gardens; supporting producer-to-consumer markets; bartering and many other localized and creative ways of production, distribution, and consumption) around the world is certainly a challenge for policy making and implementation.

The transformation of today's reality of food insecurity, according to the core proposal of food sovereignty, means transforming our personal and collective approach to accessing food every day. Such changes may include: expanding food production as a responsibility of more families either in rural or urban areas; actively choosing direct contact and thus mutual responsibilities with the producers of our food and their realities; and decommoditizing as much as possible the relations around food so that food quality and quantity would be a right to everybody and not something that relates to income level, race, class, gender, and the like. (Can one really argue that some people are more deserving of healthy food than are others?) To further illustrate these possibilities, we turn attention to two examples from the Global South that provide lessons for how eaters of all classes in the United States may critique and influence the food systems they are a part of.

Learning from the Global South

The cases from Ecuador and Brazil illustrate how the broader population may more actively influence and participate in how food is produced, delivered, and consumed, sometimes integrating existing practices and ideas into a national strategy.

Social Participation for Food Sovereignty in Ecuador

In 2008 the Ecuadorian Constitution was changed in ways considered among the most inclusive and innovative in terms of the rights of people and nature. An important section of the constitution relates to a mandate for food sovereignty, establishing a specific law and its regulations so that a food sovereignty regime could be put in practice. Before this constitutional change, different social movements in Ecuador had been working toward food sovereignty for more than a decade. So, the inclusion of this new framework reflects the pressures and contributions of these movements prior to and during the constitutional assembly. For the first time in Ecuadorian history, wide participation was encouraged in the constitutional process in an attempt to end a decade of social, economic, and political turmoil in which citizens nearly constantly expressed dissatisfaction with the performance of the Ecuadorian government.

Food sovereignty was thus legally instituted through the Organic Law for the Food Sovereignty Regime (Spanish acronym LORSA), which also enabled the formal participation of different groups for changing other related laws and policies. Such participation was pursued by the creation of an entity called Plurinational and Intercultural Conference for Food Sovereignty (Spanish acronym COPISA). The members of COPISA are nine representatives of different collectives and organizations of the civil society related to the LORSA (different producers, consumers, universities, indigenous, and Afro-Ecuadorian groups) and selected through a democratic process every four years in order to promote debate, deliberation, monitoring, and proposal generation. Participation is encouraged through processes of public deliberation organized by the state and by various advocacy groups and is articulated through the Food Sovereignty and Nutrition System (Spanish acronym SISAN), an entity that includes representatives of four related ministries, the national planning secretariat, the decentralized local governments, and the members of COPISA, whose president is also the coordinator of SISAN.

In their first year of functioning, these newly created organizations and institutions faced numerous challenges. The most significant problem was that civil society participation through these newly formed institutions was new for everyone, especially for state ministries and local governments now required to listen attentively to nongovernmental groups. Meanwhile, in spite of hundreds of debates promoted throughout the country regarding the content of various food policy innovations, different members of SISAN and the various movements and collectives in COPISA often would go "their own way," developing independent and uncoordinated versions of the same law, sending them for approval to the National Congress. As a result, the members of the National Congress who were from the dominant political party tended to approve proposals that most aligned with government objectives rather than giving full consideration to new and alternative policy innovations.

In spite of such difficulties, social movement organizations working on food sovereignty found that the LORSA was a legal endorsement of their practices and activities. Legitimated by this new law, one movement called the Colectivo Agroecologico del Ecuador initiated various campaigns in 2011 that for the first time focused on consumers. The three hundred individuals and organizations that composed the Colectivo Agroecologico came from throughout the country and represented diverse practices and areas of focus. Yet they unified around the idea of a food sovereignty campaign that would target the consumer-citizen, meaning that all people who had a concern about the sustainability of the food system (not just producers and distributors) were relevant to debates about food, food practices, and food policies. This development shows a wider and more integrative understanding of how food sovereignty applies. The idea of the campaign was to mobilize Ecuadorians to express themselves with sustainable food practices that would enable a transition toward food sovereignty. This transition would be financed by consumers themselves by way of actively choosing sustainable food practices. These practices included participating in local and agroecological production in the country and, in cities, direct marketing and purchasing, cooked and fresh food at school cafeterias, and so on. The objective of the campaign was to reach 250,000 families that would actively participate with their own practices while also informing others. With this kind of mobilization, the goal was that one-third of the population in Ecuador would begin pressing for changes toward food sovereignty.

The Ecuadorian example illustrates the ability of individuals and organizations to promote food sovereignty in ways that surpass the simple vision of participation within the state and its institutions. To American ears, this suggestion means new forms of deliberation and "lobbying"—not just asking one's congressional representative to vote a certain way on the "Farm Bill"—but actually communicating with all forms of government leaders and with other mobilized citizens about food production, distribution, consumption, and so on.

Zero Hunger in Brazil

In 2003 the Brazilian government initiated its Zero Hunger state policy, which set food security for all the population as the main objective to be reached through interrelated policies in all sectors of society (policies that tackle structural causes of hunger such as employment and specific policies that covered emergent situations such as food subsidies, food cards, food banks etc.). Veiga explains: "Since the hunger problem in Brazil was not being caused by insufficient food supply but rather by difficulties in accessing food, the concept adopted by the Brazilian government was based on the assumption that eradicating hunger entailed fighting extreme poverty and social inequality, which in turn required combining actions against hunger with a food and nutrition security policy that took into account the human right to food and Brazil's food sovereignty" (2011, 90).

The Zero Hunger policy combines policies needed for immediate access and provision of food for the poorest residents (resonating with a food security framework), together with strategic policies that would (from a food sovereignty perspective) redistribute income, promote production, generate jobs, foster agrarian reform, increase the minimum wage, and expand the social security system (Da Silva et al. 2011). The design of this policy was based on recognition that there was a vicious cycle between hunger in the country, "excessive income concentration, low wages, high unemployment levels and low growth rates," which are not merely connected but are "endogenous to the current growth pattern and, therefore, inseparable from the prevailing economic model" (Da Silva et al. 2011, 19). This diagnosis of the problem motivated the aims of the policy to change the model and not just the food insecurity situation. However, according to policy makers, this was not possible without the participation of "society at large," an observation consistent with a food sovereignty framework.

Veiga summarizes the policy like this:

[In Brazil] food and nutrition security policy involves four dimensions. The first one refers to the quantity of food, which can be characterized by the quantity of calories, proteins, vitamins and minerals consumed by human beings. The second one refers to the quality of the food that is consumed, which can be translated by the nutritional balance of food and its sanitary quality. The third one refers to the regularity at which a person consumes food, which can be translated by eating at least three times a day every day. The fourth one refers to dignity, which can be translated into the freedom of people to choose their own food without dependence. (Veiga 2011, 91)

In practice, the Brazilian policy went beyond food security by focusing on social justice with citizen participation. Evaluations of these efforts show that this last element has been one of the main factors of early success with this policy. Takagi (2011, 62) describes the program as having three axes: "implementation of public policies; participatory building of the food and nutrition security policy; and self-help action against hunger." This means that formal and nonformal spaces for those affected by food insecurity and those who had been working with them were created in the decision-making processes. As a result, projects and programs throughout the country reflect people's experiences and struggles to ensure their own provision and access to food.

A remarkable result of Brazil's Zero Hunger policy is that it reduced the poverty rate from 28.1 percent (44 million) in 2003 to 15.4 percent (29.6 million) by 2009, with the majority of these people living in urban areas (Da Silva et al. 2011). Considering that poverty reduction has a strong connection to reduction of food insecurity, this is a huge advance in the right direction. In addition to reduction of food insecurity, the policy appears to have led to other important developments consistent with food sovereignty. For example, all Brazilian children and adolescents who attend public schools now have better access to a nutritious meal every day in their day care center, preschool, or elementary school. After almost doubling the funds allocated to each participant, the National School Meal Program (PNAE) expanded opportunities to improve the quality of the food served in schools. Some initial efforts were made for meals served in schools to use items purchased locally from family farmers, for education on nutrition to be included in the curriculum of primary education, and for special attention to be paid to the diet needs of indigenous populations in order to respect their food habits and expand the program's social impact. Moreover, urban programs were designed to improve nutritional standards among poorer groups through partnerships with local authorities, NGOs, and private companies including subsidized restaurants, community kitchens, food banks, and urban agriculture schemes.

More than a decade after the Zero Hunger policy was put in place, the most interesting lessons emerge around the practices to ensure civil society participation in as many instances of decision making as possible. Supporting this policy was a vision that food insecurity could be tackled only when people had more decision-making power about not only food but other aspects of their lives as well. The Brazilian government's strategy was based mostly on structural and strategic measures to reduce poverty, inequality, and lack of social security and access to jobs, along with efforts to increase immediate access to food.

Given the recent recession in Brazil, it remains to be seen which of these positive outcomes will persist. However, there is little reason to believe that genuine and institutionalized citizen participation, public-private cooperation, and program attentiveness to root causes of food insecurity need be threatened, even as unemployment and loss of confidence in the government rise.

Opportunities for Applying These Lessons in the United States

Some of the most important lessons from food sovereignty in South America have to do with the inclusive, democratic, and holistic approaches to deliberating about how food is produced and consumed. The example of Ecuador and Brazil shows food insecure people being guaranteed the right to influence the conditions under which they access food and, as importantly, the ways in which they can get out of dependency on food aid. Apart from occasional poor people's protests or testimony given to Congress, with few exceptions SNAP participants in the United States rarely deliberate with state agencies, nonprofits, and producer distributors to decide how SNAP recipients could escape dependency on food aid. The Ecuadorian and Brazilian cases also alert us to what can happen when new forms of deliberation are made possible. In the United States, food councils are the most closely related form of organization that resembles the new deliberative bodies described in Ecuador and Brazil. Indeed, food councils vary in their resiliency and effectiveness, but their potential for impacting policy within the fifty states is reasonable to expect, if state legislatures were to more consistently rely on them for policy development (see Chen, Clayton, and Palmer 2015).

Movements that are already working on food sovereignty like the Colectivo Agroecologico in Ecuador are a rich source of solutions that are being put in practice. In the United States, many policies can start from grassroots activities instead of coming only from technocratic experts. In the United States, grassroots organizing, such as through FEAST (Food, Education, Agriculture Solutions Together), a community-organizing approach initiated in rural Oregon by the Oregon Food Bank and now spreading through other states, has produced dozens of examples of substate regions solving local food problems, with some of their solutions likely to be reproducible in other parts of the United States. Such new efforts for mobilizing citizens through community food security efforts are promising.

Finally, the effort to make legal changes in Brazil and Ecuador point to the potential for better "local" legislation within states, some of which can and will be emulated across the country. For example, recent cottage food laws (which empower small producers of processed, cooked foods in home kitchens) and farm direct laws (which strengthen connections between smaller farmers and local institutions such as hospitals and schools) provide new opportunities for substate regions to grow in the direction of food security through food sovereignty.

REFERENCES

Aerni, Philip. 2011. "Food Sovereignty and Its Discontents." *African Technology Development Forum Journal* 8 (1): 23–40.

Bernstein, Henry. 2013. "Food Sovereignty: A Skeptical View." ICAS Review Paper Series No. 4. *www.iss.nl/fileadmin/ASSETS/iss/Research_and_projects/Research_networks/ICAS/ICAS_Review_Paper_4_Bernstein.pdf*.

Centers for Disease Control and Prevention. 2015a. "About Bovine Spongiform Encephalopathy." *www.cdc.gov/ncidod/dvrd/bse*.

———. 2015b. "Listeria Outbreaks." *www.cdc.gov/listeria/outbreaks*.

Chen, Wei-ting, Megan L. Clayton, and Anne Palmer. 2015. "Community Food Security in the United States: A Survey of the Scientific Literature Volume II." Johns Hopkins Center for a Livable Future. *assets.jhsph.edu/clf/mod_clfResource/doc/CFS%20Lit%20Review-II-final%20for%20printer-1-29-15.pdf*.

Coleman-Jensen, Alisha, Matthew Rabbitt, Christian Gregory, and Anita Singh. 2015. "Household Food Security in the United States in 2014." Economic Research Service No. 194. *www.ers.usda.gov/media/1896841/err194.pdf*.

Da Silva, Jose Graziano, Mauro Eduardo Del Grossi, and Ciao Galvao de Franca. 2011. "The Fome Zero (Zero Hunger) Program: The Brazilian Experience." Food and Agriculture Organization of the United Nations. *www.fao.org/docrep/016/i3023e/i3023e.pdf*.

Food and Agriculture Organization. 2003. "Trade Reforms and Food Security: Conceptualizing the Linkages." Commodities and Trade Division. *www.fao.org/3/a-y4671e.pdf*.

Grussing, Jay, and Mark Edwards. 2006. "Non-metropolitan Hunger and Food Insecurity in the Northwest." Rural Studies Program: Oregon State University. *ruralstudies.oregonstate.edu/sites/default/files/pub/pdf/rsp_reports/rsp06–02.pdf*.

Hospes, Otto. 2014. "The Debate, the Deadlock, and a Suggested Detour." *Agriculture and Human Values* 31: 119–30.

McIntyre, Beverly, Hans Herren, Judi Wakhungu, and Robert Watson. 2009. "Agriculture at a Crossroads: International Assessment of Agricultural Knowledge, Science and Technology for Development." *www.unep.org/dewa/agassessment/reports/IAASTD/EN/Agriculture%20at%20a%20Crossroads_Synthesis%20Report%20%28English%29.pdf*.

Nyéléni Declaration. 2007. Food Sovereignty International Forum, Sélingué, Mali. *nyeleni.org/spip.php?article291*.

Poppendieck, Janet. 1999. *Sweet Charity: Emergency Food and the End of Entitlement*. New York: Penguin.

Southgate, Douglas. 2011. "Food Sovereignty: The Ideas Origins and Its Dubious Merits." *African Technology Development Forum Journal* 8 (1): 18–22.

Takagi, Maya. 2011. "Food and Nutrition Security and Cash Transfer Programs," in Da Silva, Jose Graziano, Mauro Eduardo Del Grossi, and Ciao Galvao de Franca.

Veiga, Adriana. 2011. "Zero Hunger: A Project Turned into a Government Strategy," in Da Silva, Jose Graziano, Mauro Eduardo Del Grossi, and Ciao Galvao de Franca.

Vía Campesina. 1996. "The Right to Produce and Access to Land." Vía Campesina, November 11–17, Rome, Italy.

2

Can You Put Food on the Table?
Redefining Poverty in America

MAUREEN BERNER AND ALEXANDER VAZQUEZ

W e are obsessed with numbers in the United States.[1] We listen to updates on gross national product or the unemployment rate without understanding what is included and what is not, what represents good news or bad, these being test items in long-forgotten social studies or economics classes. They represent how well we are doing as a nation, and, by association, we translate those numbers into hope for our own future. Policy makers examine data in detail for support or criticism of various government programs in our new evidence-based decision-making culture. And researchers often rely on these easily and quickly tracked data.

But what if those numbers thrown around on news shows and blogs are basically flawed? What information can give us the best understanding of our economic condition—at the community level, as a region, or as a nation? We argue there is not a "link" between food and poverty, but access to sufficient healthy food for a family *is* the best, direct definition of poverty. If you can't put healthy, sufficient food on the table for your family on a predictable, regular basis, you are poor. When measuring poverty with access to food, as we do here, we discover poverty is far worse than official statistics recognize, and it has been getting worse for decades, even during the 1990s "go-go" years of strong economic growth. A large portion of society that had once been considered middle class now finds itself searching for food to meet basic family needs.

Government data do not capture the extensive work done by the nonprofit sector in meeting basic human needs—needs not met by the traditional social safety net. Research using standard government program data to the exclusion of parallel data from the nonprofit sector is recommending policy choices with only half the picture. Could a different approach provide the missing half of the picture, allowing us to better understand the history and extent of economic hardship overall, an approach that is not self-limiting? What we need to know is, can people meet basic household needs?

This information is vital for national policy makers. Poverty is a term now relegated to well-intentioned nonprofits and social scientists, but income inequality has taken on a new status of national importance with the recognition by the business sector that it is impacting national growth and tax revenues across the board (Standard and Poor's Rating Services 2014). Economic hardship is not just for the poor to worry about anymore.

Traditional Measures of Poverty

The Poverty Line

Most public policy conversations around poverty default to the federal definition without establishing an independent assessment of what it means to be "poor." Our government measures poverty via income, using a fifty-year-old measure called the poverty line.[2] It represented three times what a family would pay for the least expensive ("economy") food plan, as defined by the USDA in 1963. There is a separate poverty line ("threshold") for each family size, indexed for inflation annually. The federal government designated the Census Bureau the official determiner of the poverty thresholds. Annual guidelines used for administrative purposes are then established by the US Department of Health and Human Services in line with those thresholds.[3] Depending on household composition, a family's income must fall beneath the designated threshold to be considered in poverty.

The official poverty line is the strictest measure in common use. Interestingly, according to its developer, Molly Orshansky, it was not meant as a measure of adequate income, but a measure of inadequacy of income—rather than a measure of what is enough, she sought to measure what was *clearly not enough* to maintain a household. The official poverty line is often the default used by lower levels of government for their own purposes, although there can be exceptions. Additional efforts have been made to develop state or local specific measures (Chung, Isaacs, and Smeeding 2013). However, despite the need for an improved measure for poverty, "the technical difficulties involved, such as the lack of data and techniques needed to identify accurate information about comprehensive needs and resources, make the analysis expensive and impede research on this topic" (526).

This measure has been criticized for decades (Ricketts and Sawhill 1988) but remains in use because there is no readily acceptable alternative. The main criticism is that the official line is too low, but researchers also emphasize that by focusing on income, the measure doesn't take into account the actual cost of living for poor families, such as rapidly escalating health and child care costs, and basic expenses that impact the family budget for poorer families more than others. In "Lies, Damn Lies, and Poverty Statistics: The Census Bureau Is Right to Reconsider the Official Poverty Line," Jeannette Wicks-Lim, writes, "Without revising the official poverty line to reflect the actual costs of families' basic needs, the key statistic we use to understand economic deprivation in the United States will not only undercount the poor, but it will do so by a larger margin every passing year."[4]

The Census "New Approach" and Federal Programs

A true government-wide attempt to revise the poverty definition did not take place until 1995 with a National Academy of Science panel study (Citro and Michael 1995). As a result, experimental poverty measures have been tested (Olsen 1999) and a supplemental poverty measure, which included the impact of government assistance, was finally produced by the Census Bureau in 2012. It is being tracked alongside the official version, but it is important to recognize the supplementary measure is also based on income, and carries with it the same problems.[5] It is also unclear what exactly the new poverty measure will be used for other than to point out how the official measure is incomplete. According to the Census Bureau, "The new measure will be a more complex statistic incorporating additional items such as tax payments and work expenses in its family resource estimates. Thresholds used in the new measure will be derived from Consumer Expenditure Survey expenditure data on basic necessities (food, shelter, clothing and utilities) and will be adjusted for geographic differences in the cost of housing. Unlike the official poverty thresholds, the new thresholds are not intended to assess eligibility for government programs. Instead, the new measure will serve as an additional indicator of economic well-being and will provide a deeper understanding of economic conditions and policy effects."[6]

The Census Bureau uses the poverty line definition when reporting on the levels of poverty in any geographic area, such as cities, counties, and states. However, poverty is also defined by participation in programs targeting the needy. These programs often use an eligibility criterion higher than the official poverty line, but generally a multiplier of it. A common example is eligibility for the National School Lunch (free and reduced-price lunch) and related federal programs. Children can participate if they come from a household with income up to 185 percent of the federal poverty line, as listed below. The percentage of children in schools who qualify for free and reduced-price lunch is probably the most common measure of childhood poverty used in program administration decisions.

Being deemed "poor" or "needy" by the free and reduced-price lunch or similar program standard often serves as the criteria for other programs—in other words, if a child is eligible for free and reduced-price lunch, he or she may be automatically eligible for other assistance. The same logic applies with other programs targeting poor communities, which may base area eligibility on the percentage of children in the school system who qualify for the free and reduced-price lunch program.

In this way, the poverty line definition is the fundamental building block on which most other definitions are based. And in turn, the entire conversation around poverty in the United States—trends, programs, and who is affected—is based fundamentally on how much income is coming into a household. Recent discussion and research has considered income inequality, or the distribution of income and/or relative income growth or decline. While such measures consider relative income in a community over time, they by definition remain fundamentally focused on income levels.

Where Are We in Terms of Poverty According to These Measures?

To see how our view of poverty changes using these different measures, let's look at the picture of poverty in a single state, North Carolina. Using the official poverty line, North Carolina has a higher portion of its population living in poverty, at around 18 percent, than the US average, approximately 16 percent. Figure 2.1 shows the percentage of the population living in different poverty ranges in each North Carolina county according to 2012 census data. Poverty rates range from around 10 percent in the wealthier counties to at least three having 30 percent or more of the population living at or below the poverty line. A clear pattern of high poverty in the eastern rural and western mountain areas of the state emerges.

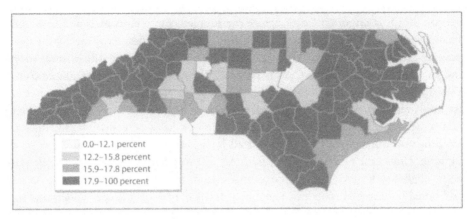

FIGURE 2.1. Percentage of population living in poverty, North Carolina, 2012.

North Carolina is a majority poor state, compared to national averages. The lighter colored areas include several of the larger cities, so the political debate in North Carolina is often characterized by an urban/rural split focused on the poorer rural areas, understandable given the decline in rural tobacco and furniture production. However, within some of the relatively better-off counties, an analysis using more precise data by the University of North Carolina–Chapel Hill's Center for Urban and Regional Studies showed county averages often mask pockets of deep poverty.[7] To be considered severely distressed, census tracts, usually representing an area of approximately four thousand people, must meet three criteria: unemployment equal to 14.5 percent, annual per capita income in the tract that is at least one-third less than statewide per capita income, and a poverty rate of greater than or equal to 24 percent. This report showed that even in the wealthier counties, parts of well-to-do urban areas were sometimes much worse off than those found in broader rural poor areas.

Over the past fifteen years, the percentage of individuals in poverty in North Carolina has been rising in fits and starts. The general trend over the past two decades has been rising levels of poverty, even with some annual drops. The poverty rate in North Carolina for 2015 was estimated at 15.3 percent, a drop from 2013. Yet, while there have finally been some signs of recovery in terms of wages and jobs nationally, real median household income was still lower than in 2007. We are still behind, a decade from the start of the recession.

Using the percentage of children who qualify for free and reduced price lunch (185 percent of the poverty line) as a measure of poverty, we see the same pattern, but much higher numbers. Approximately 60 percent of all public school children are enrolled in the program, a record high. A majority of North Carolina children live in poor households. If one looks at county-by-county data, it is shocking to realize some counties are close to having every school-aged child living in a poor household.

What about Income Inequality?

The national conversation and academic research has shifted in recent years to changes in household status across the whole economy, going beyond the traditional question of how many people were "poor." This research tends to be on economic inequality, or the distribution of income and/or relative income growth or decline. It asks where income is concentrated across the economic spectrum, and whether or not people are worse off or better off than they were over time, relative to everyone else. In terms of poverty, the focus tends to be on whether or not people are climbing out of poverty, and thus whether the share of the population who are poor is decreasing, or whether more are falling into it, and thus the share of the population who are poor is growing. As in other states, there has been downward pressure in income distribution in North Carolina. In 2005, those making $100,000 or more comprised 12.1 percent of the population, but that amount increased to 17.2 percent by 2013.

Proposed Alternative Measures for Poverty

The traditional concept of poverty based on income is being challenged in academic research. Income measures account only for resources available, not whether those resources are sufficient. And the poverty line does not account for costs of housing, food, transportation, and so on. How can we define poverty to inform policy and services in a way that more accurately matches the experiences of people in or near poverty? If the main measure is accepted as wrong, what is the alternative?

A growing body of work around multidimensional measures of poverty, particularly from an international perspective, provides possible answers to how we can improve a definition of poverty within the United States. One of the most important contributions is included in *Counting the Poor: New Thinking about European Poverty Measures and Lessons for the United States* (Besharov and Couch 2012), especially the material addressing the idea of poverty through a lens of resources (income, US-based conceptualization) versus social exclusion (European-based conceptualization).[8]

Meyer and Sullivan (2012) present an important alternative to traditional research using poverty rates by a consumption-based approach. Using their approach, poverty in the United States has declined. Like income, however, the consumption-based model falls short because it measures what is actually consumed, not what is *still needed*.

What is important now is a growing emphasis on living conditions. Material well-being is the key, as was discussed twenty years ago in the Measuring Poverty study (Citro and Michael 1995, 212). We have measures that use resources or document consumption, but not the gap preventing individuals and families from a particular acceptable standard of living. The international community in this regard, primarily in Western, developed countries such as Canada and in northern Europe, and Western-based international organizations are starting to define poverty as material deprivation. These measures revolve around whether a household can meet its basic needs such as housing, food, water, and energy. These measures by definition account for differences in cost of living across geography.

Meyer and Sullivan (2012) present an important alternative to traditional research using poverty rates by a consumption-based approach. Using their approach, poverty in the United States has actually declined! Like income, however, the consumption-based model falls short because it measures what is actually consumed, not what is *still needed*.

Food Insecurity

If understanding poverty is about a basic living standard, and having sufficient food is a basic feature of that standard, food insecurity is an effective measure of poverty.

It moves the concept of poverty to material deprivation.[9] Food insecurity means a household cannot provide sufficient, predictable food to maintain an active, healthy life,[10] and it is officially measured in the United States through a series of eighteen questions on an annual federal survey on purchasing or preparing food (Bartfeld and Dunifon 2006). How does this measure poverty? It is likely that a struggling family will skip meals before allowing power to be cut off or eviction from a home. A parent will skip lunch to provide a meal for the children. Food becomes the expendable item when a family can't meet all its needs day to day. Usually, it is not a family showing up at a soup kitchen. It is much more likely to be skimping or scraping by until the next paycheck or benefit or pension check, when a full meal can be served. It is therefore one of the earliest and the most direct measures of economic hardship in a household.

Generally, food insecurity estimates show higher levels of need than poverty rates. In fact, analyses show a significant portion, approximately a third, of those considered food insecure have an income too high to quality for US federal benefits. Yet food insecurity alone may not be showing the complete picture. All these measures seem to underestimate poverty. So what provides a better picture of need? Craw (2010) states, "Poverty in the United States is as much a local problem as a national one" (906). To understand a local problem, we turn to the local providers in the nonprofit sector, food pantries and food banks.

When households are unable to meet current need, they turn to food pantries and banks to fill the gap, an institutionalized means to address hunger (Wakefield et al. 2013; Fiese et al. 2014). Therefore, demand on food pantries reflects true need better than either income- or consumption-based approaches. Using pounds of food distributed by these organizations indirectly incorporates both differences in cost of living and income as well as other financial resources in an area. It also avoids the problem of uncertainty of "poverty versus preference" plaguing consumption-based models (Hick 2013). It is relatively comparable across geography and time and already gathered by the nonprofit agencies involved without the need for additional surveys or tools. Food banks and pantries track demand in terms of pounds of food distributed in day-to-day inventory management, relatively consistent and easy to understand and record, regardless of location. A family needs a certain amount of food whether it resides in Santa Monica, California; Athens, Georgia; or Marfa, Texas.

Issues of stigma, lack of transportation, limited food quality and choice, paperwork, and other barriers exist for those seeking nonprofit food assistance. These individuals are clearly seeking such aid because of poverty—a need that is not met through personal means or government social safety net programs—rather than simply opting for a low-consumption lifestyle.

There are two main limitations to this measure. As need has grown, evidence is also growing that the food supply on which the food banks and pantries rely is running out. With a limited supply, assistance is rationed by either reducing the amount of food each family receives at each visit or reducing the number of visits allowed. If there is regional variation in the supply of food, the reliability of food supply as a generalizable measure is reduced. In areas with stronger donation systems, increases in food distribution reflect true community needs, while those areas that run out of food would show a flattening of demand that is masking true need.

Second, at this time there is no systematic poundage reporting structure above the pantry level, so widespread use of this measure depends on such a system being established or on individual efforts to gather such data directly. And while pounds of food distributed is a fairly clear measure, there will naturally be variation in the quality, consistency, and accessibility in how each pantry records the data. Many food pantries do not keep electronic records—according to one study only about one half of pantries in North Carolina, for example, have access to a computer at all. However, the same study shows pantries do keep records, historically on paper but more often now electronically (Paynter and Berner 2014).

Nonprofit Food Assistance

A general description of the nonprofit food assistance system will help frame the opportunity for moving from food insecurity as a concept to an implementable measure of poverty. In the United States, food banks serve as central food distribution centers for member agencies that include pantries, homeless shelters, soup kitchens, after-school and day care programs, summer meal programs, domestic violence shelters, nonprofit nursing homes, and other community-based agencies. They receive food items, farm produce, and money from a variety of sources, including all levels of government. The food bank serves as a warehouse for a region. Small nonprofits are members, purchasing food for pennies on the dollar. Van Steen and Pellenbarg (2014) provide a wonderful concise history of food banks:

> The first so-called "food bank" was founded in 1967 in the United States by John van Hengel. . . . Inspired by a mother of 10 children that pointed out there should be a "bank of food" to deposit and take out food, he established the "St. Mary's Food Bank" in Phoenix, Arizona. . . . Quickly, more food banks were started. . . . However, with severe budget cuts for social policies implemented by the Reagan administration in the early 1980s, hunger again came to the forefront and many new food banks were founded. . . . Holt-Giménez and Patel (2012, 9) speak of an "explosion of . . . food banks and food pantries" in the late 2000s. (370)

Today's food banks typically follow the same process. A representative of a member pantry might come from a small town to the food bank once a month with a truck, select items from what the food bank has available in its warehouse, and pay by the pound. The pantry supplements what the food bank sold with local donations and may even use financial contributions to purchase food directly from a local grocery store to fill in gaps. The local pantry would be open a day or two a week. Clients come to the pantry, often lining up early to ensure they can receive food before supplies run out, or if given the opportunity to choose food themselves, they will want to be first to choose key desirable items (meat, bread, produce) before they are gone. They are checked in, the vast majority with some form of eligibility paperwork, referral system, or application process, and are often required to prove after the initial visit that they have applied for government assistance.

Most community-level nonprofit agencies such as food pantries are established and run independently of significant government oversight, involvement, or formal coordination and are religiously affiliated. They may belong to larger professional associations. Some pantries are large and sophisticated organizations; most are small, volunteer-only organizations (Fiese et al. 2014).

Food pantries are invisible in policy and academic research. While well known to the local social services providers in communities, there is little academic research on the local-level nonprofit food assistance network (an exception might be Downing and Kennedy 2013). Research is growing primarily through public health work focused on nutrition and food access, which calls for better understanding their impact (see, for example, Collins et al. 2014; Kuhls et al. 2012; and Neter et al. 2014). Yet the pantry network is huge. A recent study by Feeding America, the national nonprofit representing food banks and their member agencies, reports over forty thousand community pantries nationwide, compared to the over twenty-five hundred municipal governments reporting providing any direct social welfare program in 2002 (Craw 2010). In 2009, thirty-three million individuals used food pantries in the United States (Fiese et al. 2014).

Clients may or may not get additional benefits from other government programs. In fact, prior research demonstrates less than half of food pantry clients were eligible for government programs, and a measurable number of pantry clients or those deemed food insecure are employed (Berner et al. 2008; McIntyre et al. 2014).

The Pattern of Economic Hardship in the United States Prior to and after the Great Recession

The data trends in Figures 2.2 and 2.3 represent the level of service provided by the Food Bank of Central and Eastern North Carolina (FBCENC) on the US East Coast and one of its member pantries, the CORA food pantry in Pittsboro, North Carolina, a small town in a rural area located approximately thirty miles from the university town of Chapel Hill. The FBCENC data represents the total food dispersed across its approximately 450 member pantries in thirty-four counties, a full population of its membership, covering over a third of the state, some of the most populous areas with major universities (Duke, University of North Carolina–Chapel Hill, North Carolina State University, North Carolina Central University) and the state capital, as well as extensive rural areas with extreme poverty in former tobacco-dependent areas that are now home to major chicken- and pork-processing industries.

In both cases, demand rose dramatically well before the current recession, in the late 1990s, and continues to grow at relatively high rates. In a 2012 article in *Brookings Papers on Economic Activity*, Meyer and Sullivan argue, using consumption-based measures of poverty, "We may not yet have won the war on poverty, but we are certainly winning" (177). These data contradict that view.

In the case of CORA, the smaller food pantry in rural North Carolina, demand has risen almost 500 percent in the past decade. In the case of the Food Bank of Central and Eastern North Carolina, starting from a larger base, in the same time period, demand doubled. It is important to note the overall growth pattern is continuous, not leveling off for any significant time period. Based on discussions with the pantry and food bank director involved, indications of slower growth recently may also be due to a lack of supply rather than a slow-down in growth in demand. Service delivery

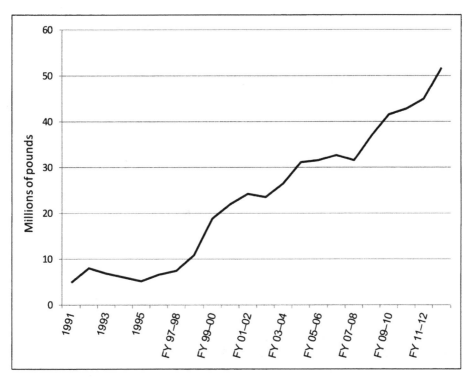

FIGURE 2.2. FBCENC total food distribution.

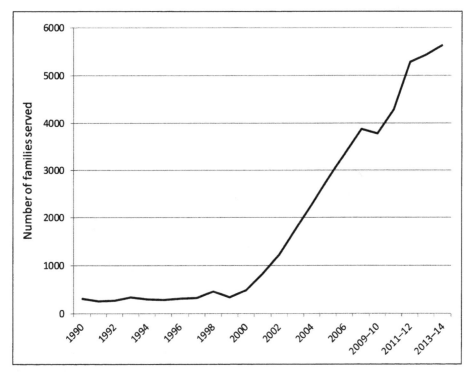

FIGURE 2.3. CORA food pantry, Pittsboro, North Carolina.

has slowed because across nonprofits, and capacity is limited. While they don't like to describe the situation as such, the organizations are running out of food, turning to rationing by reducing the amount of food each family can receive per visit or limiting service area or days of operation. CORA now relies on cash purchases of discounted foods for 60 percent of its food delivered because actual food donations are insufficient to meet demand.

Both nonprofits have increased capacity at times over the years to make up for unmet demand, but there appears to be a constant supply constraint. More compelling are data on per capita food distribution, in pounds, across the thirty-four member counties of the FBCENC from six years prior to the Great Recession to the present.

The average doubled between 2002 and 2014. Not only is more food being distributed, but more food per person, indicating not just a higher level of need overall in terms of *more* families, but a higher level of need *within* the families.

A Nonprofit Poverty Line

Food bank officials state member pantries will not turn away anyone seeking assistance the first time. However, most pantries apply established eligibility criteria before distributing food to individual client households on a regular basis, and in some cases, even at the time of a first visit. In many cases, this means the client must provide either a referral from an established social service agency already checking for eligibility for government assistance or from a church or trusted community organization who conducts a screening process. This does not mean households must actually qualify for government assistance. In fact, many pantry clients do not qualify for government assistance but still need help. However, overall, pantries want to see evidence clients are seeking official assistance before turning to the nonprofits as a regular supplement.

Is there a common "poverty line" across the disparate pantries? Pantries are independent, and each has its own policies and criteria. However, informal interviews with food banks and selected pantries over the past decade suggest community nonprofits tend to settle on a point equivalent to approximately 180 percent of the US federal poverty line. The interviews focused on what seemed to be an appropriate income for survival for the community in which the pantry existed, thus indirectly acknowledging the local cost of living. At the time of this research, the amount equaled about 180 percent of the federal poverty line—and thus it becomes our nonprofit poverty line.

This is based on North Carolina data and is therefore most relevant for this state. Also, while referencing that this level is approximately 180 percent of the federal poverty line to communicate the level more easily, it was established *independent* of the federal poverty line. Therefore, the methodological flaws in calculating the federal poverty line should not be assumed to carry over to our nonprofit poverty measure.

We calculated this line for each state and family size for thirty-seven states and the United States as a whole.[11] The line was then applied to reported census income data from 2003 to 2011 for household sizes of one to nine members. In almost all cases, the nonprofit measure of poverty is about double that of the official poverty line.

The overall conclusion from this type of analysis, as well as from the data from the nonprofits themselves, is that the population considered "needy" is much greater than the percentage of the population in poverty according to the federal definition. The population under the nonprofit poverty line is about double, in certain cases sometimes more. The federal poverty line vastly underestimates need in the country.

Conclusion

Traditional discussions of poverty have gone out of style. In open public policy discussions, poverty is not even discussed, the War on Poverty having been abandoned (Rose and Baumgartner 2013) and terms such as "economic distress" and "economic hardship" substituted for "poverty." This is not a one-to-one exchange, however. Poverty is reserved for the poorest of the poor, but a much larger portion of Americans may experience economic hardship. In the same month that the federal government reported 3.5 million people climbed above the poverty line (September 2016), the local chapter of Meals on Wheels in Chapel Hill, North Carolina, appealed to volunteers for funds because the nonprofit's client list had more than doubled in the prior five years, with most of the new additions having no ability to pay even a portion of meal cost. The number of needy children on the waiting list for weekend food backpacks at the local food pantry in Carrboro, North Carolina, went over fifty. We need a different perspective on economic condition.

Our public policy structure is based on government programs established for a societal makeup that no longer exists. Our policies are based on outdated and inaccurate measures of need. The question now becomes what to do about it, if anything. We need to move to a concept of material hardship (or alternatively, well-being) to understand social needs, and to redesign social and economic policies in line with what is a better reflection of our communities' situations. We need to recognize and partner with community organizations in how we respond. Community-level nonprofits, for the most part, serve everyone, filling gaps where government does not cover. They serve as true social safety nets of last resort, keeping people from hunger in one of the wealthiest countries in the world. At a minimum, if federal government social safety net programs no longer fit the needs of the population, by choice or external constraints, the question for public policy and administration researchers should turn to the ability—the capacity—of local and state governments and the nonprofit sector to step in (Paynter et al. 2011; Paynter 2013). Otherwise, we should accept that *as a public policy*, we tolerate hunger—poverty—hardship in our society.

NOTES

1. Some material in this chapter is also included in the article "The Disappearance of the Middle Class in America: Evidence from Overwhelmed Community Nonprofits," in *Social Work and Society Journal*, forthcoming.
2. *The Development and History of the US Poverty Thresholds—a Brief Overview*, 1992, by Gordon Fisher, US Department of Health and Human Services, found at *aspe.hhs.gov/poverty/papers/hptgssiv.htm*. See also *www.census.gov/hhes/www/poverty/about/overview/measure.html*.
3. Under the authority of 42 USC 9902 (2) (Pub. L. 97–35, title VI, § 673, as added Pub. L. 105–285, title II, § 201, October 27, 1998, 112 Stat. 2729).
4. "Lies, Damn Lies, and Poverty Statistics: The Census Bureau Is Right to Reconsider the Official Poverty Line," Jeannette Wicks-Lim, July 2010, University of Massachusetts at

Amherst Political Economy Research Institute, *www.peri.umass.edu/fileadmin/pdf/other_publication_types/magazine___journal_articles/jwl_ju110.pdf.*
5. Data on this supplemental measure are discussed in an October 2014 Census Bureau document at *www.census.gov/content/dam/Census/library/publications/2014/demo/p60–251.pdf.*
6. *www.census.gov/hhes/povmeas/methodology/supplemental/overview.html,* accessed July 3, 2015.
7. The CURS report is titled *North Carolina's Distressed Urban Tracts: A View of the State's Economically Disadvantaged Communities*; a summary and link to the report can be found at *curs.unc.edu/2014/06/08/curs-releases-north-carolinas-distressed-urban-tracts-view-states-economically-disadvantaged-communities/.*
8. For other examples of these issues, also see Callander et al. 2012; Bossert et al. 2013; Minujin et al. 2014; Mitra et al. 2013.
9. See Heflin et al. (2007), Heflin and Rafail (2009), Heflin and Butler (2013).
10. Also developed, defined, and measured by the US Department of Agriculture. See *www.ers.usda.gov/topics/food-nutrition-assistance/food-security-in-the-us/definitions-of-food-security.aspx.*
11. Data problems exist with the remaining states. Thanks to Ben Canada for providing the initial data work.

REFERENCES

Bartfeld, Judi, and R. Dunifon. 2006. "State-Level Predictors of Food Insecurity among Households with Children." *Journal of Policy Analysis and Management* 25 (4): 921–42.

Berner, M., T. Ozer, and S. Paynter. 2008. "A Portrait of Hunger, the Social Safety Net, and the Working Poor. *Policy Studies Journal* 36: 403–20.

Besharov, D., and K. Couch. 2012. *Counting the Poor: New Thinking about European Poverty Measures and Lessons for the United States.* New York: Oxford University Press.

Bossert, W., S. R. Chakravarty, and C. D'Ambrosio. 2013. "Multidimensional Poverty and Material Deprivation with Discrete Data." *Review of Income and Wealth* 59 (1): 29–43.

Callander, E., D. Schofield, and R. Shrestha. 2012. "Towards a Holistic Understanding of Poverty: A New Multidimensional Measure of Poverty for Australia." *Health Sociology Review* 21 (2): 141–55.

Chung, Y., J. B. Isaacs, and T. M. Smeeding. 2013. "Advancing Poverty Measurement and Policy: Evidence from Wisconsin during the Great Recession." *Social Service Review* 87 (3): 525–55.

Citro, Constance F., and Robert T. Michael, eds. 1995. *Measuring Poverty: A New Approach.* Washington: National Academy Press.

Collins, P. A., E. M. Power, and M. H. Little. 2014. "Municipal-Level Responses to Household Food Insecurity in Canada: A Call for Critical, Evaluative Research." *Canadian Journal of Public Health* 105 (2): E138.

Craw, M. 2010. "Deciding to Provide: Local Decisions on Providing Social Welfare." *American Journal of Political Science* 54 (4): 906–20.

Downing, E., and S. Kennedy. 2013. *Food Banks and Food Poverty.* House of Commons Library Standard Note SN06657. *researchbriefings.parliament.uk/ResearchBriefing/Summary/SN06657.*

Fiese, B. H., B. D. Koester, and E. Waxman. 2014. "Balancing Household Needs: The Non-food Needs of Food Pantry Clients and Their Implications for Program Planning." *Journal of Family and Economic Issues* 35 (3): 423–31.

Heflin, C., and J. S. Butler. 2013. "Why Do Women Enter and Exit from Material Hardship?" *Journal of Family Issues* 34 (3): 631–60.

Heflin, C., M. E. Corcoran, and Kristine Siefert. 2007. "Work Trajectories, Income Changes, and Food Insufficiency in a Michigan Welfare Population." *Social Service Review* 81 (1): 3–25.

Heflin, C., J. Sandberg, and Patrick Rafail. 2009. "The Structure of Material Hardship in US Households: An Examination of the Coherence Behind Common Measures of Well-Being." *Social Problems* 56 (4): 746–64.

Hick, R. 2013. "Poverty, Preference or Pensioners? Measuring Material Deprivation in the UK." *Fiscal Studies* 34 (1): 31–54. doi:10.1111/j.1475–5890.2013.00176.x.

Holt-Giménez, E., and R. Patel. 2012. *Food Rebellions! Crisis and the Hunger for Justice.* Oxford: Pambazuka.

Kuhls, J. P., D. L. Habash, J. E. Clutter, C. K. Spees, and K. N. Wolf. 2012. "The Ideal Food Pantry as Designed by Food Pantry Customers." *Journal of the Academy of Nutrition and Dietetics* 112 (9): A78.

McIntyre, L., A. C. Bartoo, and J. C. H. Emery. 2014. "When Working Is Not Enough: Food Insecurity in the Canadian Labour Force." *Public Health Nutrition* 17 (1): 49–57. doi:10.1017/S1368980012004053.

Meyer, B., and J. Sullivan. 2012. "Winning the War: Poverty from the Great Society to the Great Recession." *Brookings Papers on Economic Activity* 2012 (2): 133–200. doi:10.1353/eca.2012.0019.

Minujin, A., C. McCaffrey, M. Patel, and Q. Paienjton. 2014. "Redefining Poverty: Deprivation among Children in East Asia and the Pacific." *Global Social Policy* 14 (1): 3–31. doi:10.1177/1468018113504772.

Mitra, S., K. Jones, B. Vick, D. Brown, E. McGinn, and M. J. Alexander. 2013. "Implementing a Multidimensional Poverty Measure Using Mixed Methods and a Participatory Framework." *Social Indicators Research* 110 (3): 1061–81. doi:10.1007/s11205–011–9972–9.

Neter, J. E., S. C. Dijkstra, M. Visser, and I. A. Brouwer. 2014. "Food Insecurity among Dutch Food Bank Recipients: A Cross-Sectional Study." *BMJ Open* 4 (5): e004657–e004657. doi:10.1136/bmjopen-2013–004657.

Olsen, K. A. 1999. "Application of Experimental Poverty Measures to the Aged." *Social Security Bulletin* 62: 3–19. *search.proquest.com/docview/227803522?accountid=14244.*

Paynter, S. R. 2013. "Collaborative Public Management as a Hunger Prevention Strategy." *Journal of Extension* 51 (1). *www.joe.org/joe/2013february/tt4.php.*

Paynter, S., and M. Berner. 2014. "Organizational Capacity of Nonprofit Social Service Agencies." *Journal of Health and Human Services Administration* 37 (1): 111–45.

Paynter, S., M. Berner, and E. Anderson. 2011. "When Even the 'Dollar Value Meal' Costs Too Much: Food Insecurity and Long Term Dependence on Food Pantry Assistance." *Public Administration Quarterly* 35 (1): 26–58.

Ricketts, E. R., and I. V. Sawhill. 1988. "Defining and Measuring the Underclass." *Journal of Policy Analysis and Management* 7 (2): 316–25.

Rose, M., and F. R. Baumgartner. 2013. "Framing the Poor: Media Coverage and US Poverty Policy, 1960–2008." *Policy Studies Journal* 41 (1): 22–53. doi:10.1111/psj.12001.

Standard and Poor's Rating Services. 2014. *Income Inequality Weighs on State Tax Revenues.*

Van Steen, P. J. M., and P. H. Pellenbarg. 2014. "Food Banks in the Netherlands." *Tijdschrift Voor Economische En Sociale Geografie* 105 (3): 370–72. doi:10.1111/tesg.12090.

Wakefield, S., J. Fleming, C. Klassen, and A. Skinner. 2013. Sweet Charity, Revisited: Organizational Responses to Food Insecurity in Hamilton and Toronto, Canada. *Critical Social Policy* 33 (3): 427–50. doi:10.1177/0261018312458487.

3

Food, Poverty, and Lifestyle Patterns
How Diversity Matters

MICHAEL JINDRA AND NICOLAS LARCHET

In 2010, in the midst of the greatest economic crisis since the Great Depression, *Newsweek* magazine ran a cover story titled "Divided We Eat: What Food Says about Class in America and How to Bridge the Gap." The cover showed a plate broken in two halves. On its top half, a portion of quinoa and a carrot lay on a bed of kale, next to a piece of grilled salmon and a sprig of dill. The bottom half, on the other hand, offered only a wedge of pepperoni pizza. This was a portrayal of a country increasingly divided by social class over taste and healthy eating (Miller 2010).

This idea of food as a social marker is commonplace in sociology. Theories as diverse as Thorstein Veblen's "leisure class" (1899), Norbert Elias's "civilizing process" (1969), and Pierre Bourdieu's "distinction" (1984) all revolve around the notion that individual tastes and manners reflect one's position in the social structure, following a "trickle-down" model where upper-class consumption is the ideal and lower classes simply try to copy them. These influential theories, however, tend to neglect the autonomy and agency of the lower classes, as if the culture of the poor could be defined only negatively, as "backward" and lacking in diversity. Thus Bourdieu defines the "popular taste" as a "taste of necessity," which favors the most "filling" and "economical" foods, in opposition to a bourgeois "taste of liberty," which emphasizes the manners of presenting, serving, and eating food (Bourdieu 1984, 6), which unfortunately reproduces stereotypes of upper-class "culture" versus lower-class "nature" (Grignon 1985).

Social class is one aspect of a broader diversity that we argue is crucial to understanding issues of food and poverty. While much attention has been given to the structural forces of the American food system that link poverty to food insecurity and obesity, little attention has been paid to cultural issues mediating food and poverty, despite the recent growth of the field of "food and culture studies" (Counihan and Van Esterik 2013). Indeed, most social issues involve the interactions of social forces at three levels: structures, cultures, and persons, or as others put it, "macro," "meso," and "micro" (Bosi and Della Porta 2012). Any initiatives designed to address eating and health issues and why they differ across categories such as race and class cannot be just individualistic but must understand the entire sociocultural context of food habits

(Keith, Hemmerlein, and Clark 2015). Other chapters in this volume often highlight structural issues, while we focus on the diversity of how people live, including their lifestyles and the mediating role of culture. This also means understanding the major issue of the relation between individual motivations and structural constraints.

There are indeed good reasons to consider culture in a study of food and poverty, since ignoring it can lead to ineffective policies. The history of diet reform movements in the United States is replete with cultural misunderstandings between middle-class reformers and the working class and poor immigrants (Levenstein 1980). While recent nutrition interventions may be more sensitive to difference by promoting "culturally appropriate" dietary advice (Kreuter et al. 2003), some have criticized these approaches for leaving white, upper-class assumptions about nutrition largely unquestioned, and for silencing health knowledge from other cultural traditions (Kimura et al. 2014, 39).

Patterns in food consumption vary significantly across region, race/ethnicity, and social class, along with connected lifestyle behaviors. How people eat is also influenced by demographic factors such as gender, age, and the family practices of one's youth. Working back "up" the chain of influences, these family habits are influenced by regional and local patterns that vary by culture or ethnicity. Within these patterns there are also social class influences, whether one is from an upper-class, a middle-class, or a lower-class background, including factors such as income and education. These patterns may also change as groups become more wealthy and mobile and come into contact with other ways of life. There is also the strong influence of media advertising, news, popular culture, the massive growth of food industries such as fast food, and newer technologies such as the microwave, all of which have prompted major historical changes in world cuisine (Goody 2013), as for example in the transformation of pizza from a local Naples dish to an international phenomenon in the last half of the twentieth century (Helstosky 2008). The structures of the food system also limit what is available in a local area, from the presence of stores, to the choices available in those stores, which is determined by corporations gauging market demand to increase sales, and by their production system and goals of lowering costs (Nestle 2013) (see Figure 3.1).

With all these influences, we end up with particular patterns that vary internationally and nationally, and all the way down to the family level. Even individual variations in food consumption and connected factors such as self-control have an impact on overall health and life success (Mischel 2014), though these factors are in turn influenced by income, socialization, and other contexts. In other words, causal factors go in multiple ways—behavior affects our well-being, and our well-being affects behavior. For instance, people eating together regularly makes for better families and more stability, with positive impacts on well-being including wealth (Fischler 2011). Declining health creates an increased risk of poverty, owing to how it impacts work and stress and increases medical bills (Maroto 2015). What influences health? According to one study, behavioral factors contribute approximately 40 percent to health outcomes, with 30 percent due to genetics and the rest to environmental or structural factors (Schroeder 2007). These percentages can certainly be debated, and the division is too definitive, as these factors influence each other. If we want to understand why groups of people differ in their use of food, we need to understand all these influences, looking

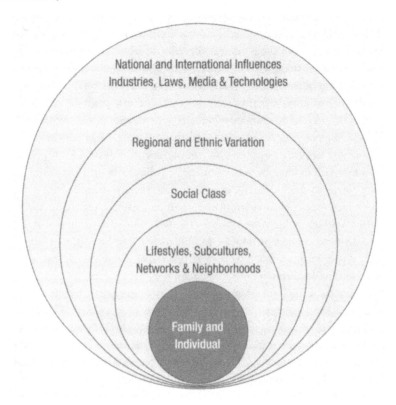

FIGURE 3.1. Life influences on food habits, from the world to the individual.

for regional, ethnic, class, gender, lifestyle, and neighborhood variation in diet that can help us understand the complex mediations between food, poverty, and health outcomes in the contemporary United States.

Regional and Ethnic Variation in Diet

Sidney Mintz once argued that there is no American cuisine, but only regional cuisines influenced by the cuisines of other nations (1996). Anthropologists see diet as a primary marker of "in-group" and "out-group" identities (Brown and Mussell 1984, 5). Even today, when one would assume that American eating habits have become homogenized by market forces, there are distinct regional trends: for instance, northeasterners spend significantly more than the average Americans on hot dogs, fresh fish, bread, and tea (Kittler, Sucher, and Nelms 2012, 459). Regional variation does not stop at the most "traditional" aspects of regional cuisines: in the 1980s geographers found that Californians had the largest number of "health" and "natural" food stores per capita in the United States and were more likely to adopt "exotic" produce in their diet, making California the "innovative center for foodways trends," while the Midwest and South were the most traditional regions in this respect (Shortridge and Shortridge 1989).

As a result of early migration and settlement patterns in the United States, regional and ethnic foodways are often intertwined (Brown and Mussell 1984). This is most apparent in the southwestern and southeastern regions of the United States, where

Case Study 1: The Invention of "Soul Food"

Calling the regional cuisine of the southeastern United States "soul food" or "southern food" is a hotly debated question (Chavis 2008). A culinary equivalent to "soul music," the term "soul food" first came into use in the 1960s to claim a distinctly African American cuisine at the peak of the civil rights movement. Brought to northern cities by rural black migrants, "soul food" developed as a response to the integrationist aspirations of an established black middle class, which labeled the "consumption habits of poor black southerners as "unsanitary." The adoption of soul food as part of black urban identity is thus a potent example of "upward percolation" (Poe 1999), reversing the familiar "trickle-down" model of consumption.

A lot of the foods thought of as typically "southern" originated in West Africa, such as okra, watermelon, black-eyed peas, and rice (Carney 2001). Other southern staples like pork, sweet potatoes, and maize were brought to Africa by European traders and were quickly adopted by West African cultures such as the Igbo and Mande before some of their people were forcibly sent to the Americas (Opie 2010). The hardships of slavery greatly influenced "soul food" as black cooks invented elaborate recipes and seasonings to make the best of leftovers from the master's table, such as turkey necks, pigs' feet, and intestines ("chitterlings").

regional cuisines have been largely shaped by Mexican and African American influences respectively. Deemed "central to the region's image, its personality, and its character" (Egerton 1987, 2), the culinary tradition known as "southern food" is an especially complex cultural phenomenon where geography, religion, class, race, and identity intersect. In the South, Protestants, those with lower levels of income and education, and black people are more likely to eat southern foods such as okra, catfish, moon pie, and boiled peanuts (Latshaw 2009). Because of its association with African roots and the labor of black cooks in plantation kitchens, southern food has become a "preserver of Black culture" (Hughes 1997, 272–73,), making African American dietary patterns especially resistant to nutrition interventions (James 2004).

Since some of the highest levels of cardiovascular disease and obesity in the nation are to be found in the so-called "Stroke Belt" of the southeastern United States (Lanska and Kuller 1995), some epidemiological studies have looked for differences in socioeconomic status to explain this disadvantage (Liao et al. 2009), while others have blamed dietary patterns, calling for the adoption of a "plant-based diet" instead of a "Southern style diet" (Judd et al. 2013). Whatever the emphasis is on—class or culture—these regional disparities in health cannot be explained by income or race alone, since low-income whites living in the northern plains region have a substantially higher life expectancy than low-income whites in Appalachia and the Mississippi valley (Murray et al. 2006). The longevity among Asian Americans (highest in the United States) appears to be partly related to their diets and lifestyles—low fat intake and high intake of vegetables and fruits—with Latinos having lower intakes of vegetables than other groups (Murray et al. 2006). The role of other factors, such as emotions, also vary among groups. Black women reported eating for positive reasons whereas white women associated eating with negative emotions (Keith, Hemmerlein, and Clark 2015). Religion is also a factor that is often intertwined with race and ethnicity in the way it categorizes different foods as "pure" or "impure" and thus influences our notions of the body (Norman 2012). All these patterns reveal strong group differences in food consumption, preferences, and associated lifestyles, varying by factors such as race/ethnicity, class, and subculture.

Accounting for Social Class: Economic versus Cultural Capital

Let's turn our attention to social class as an influence on food consumption. The classic formulation of a relationship between income and food consumption was stated by the German statistician Ernst Engel (1895): as income increases, the proportion of income spent on food decreases. Thus in 2011, the poorest quintile of Americans spent 16 percent of their income on food, compared to 11 percent for the richest quintile, though the richest quintile still spent three times more on food than the poorest quintile, and five times more on dining out (Thompson 2013).

For Pierre Bourdieu (1984), differences in food consumption depend on the different kinds of "capital" possessed by different classes and fractions of classes: industrial and commercial employers, who are relatively wealthier in "economic capital" (income, property) than in "cultural capital" (diplomas), tend to favor "rich" and "heavy" foods, which differ only in quality and cost from the foods eaten by blue- and white-collar workers. Professionals and teachers, on the other hand, who are relatively wealthier in "cultural capital," mark their distance from those groups in their appetite for "light, low-calorie products" (Bourdieu 1984, 186).

Observed in 1970s France, the trend toward health-conscious eating habits among the upper classes is common across Europe and the United States: as a general rule, so-called healthy or natural foods such as lean meats, fish, whole grains, and fresh produce are more common among groups of higher socioeconomic status, whereas fatty meats, refined grains, and added fats are associated with a lower socioeconomic status (N. Darmon and Drewnowski 2008).

Bourdieu's contribution invites us to understand food in relation with other consumption patterns, as a coherent system of "dispositions" expressing distinctive "lifestyles" and "class cultures." In his classic study of poor families in East Harlem, David Caplovitz observed that the poor were more likely to pay more for inferior products, falling prey to unscrupulous merchants and creditors. To make sense of this apparent paradox, he developed the notion of "compensatory consumption" (Caplovitz 1967): since the poor have little opportunity to base their identity on occupational or educational achievements, they may compensate for blocked mobility through their participation in mass consumption, which can hurt both pocketbook and health.

As is evident through interviewing consumers, these sociological explanations often take a backseat to more immediate explanations. Unsurprisingly, people name taste as the most important influence on food choices, followed by cost (Glanz et al. 1998). These reasons for food choices are important of course, but one must remember that they are strongly influenced by social forces and cultural contexts that operate on an unconscious level. Associated factors like attitudes toward body image, aesthetic norms,

Case Study 2: Food and Social Class

Figure 3.2 is a simplified version of the "food space" and "social space" diagrams in Pierre Bourdieu's Distinction (Bourdieu 1984, 128–29, 186). Occupational groups relatively wealthier in "cultural capital" are on the left of the "social space," while those wealthier in "economic capital" are on the right. The vertical axis, total capital volume, is "economic capital" and "cultural capital" combined (from "lower classes" at the bottom to "upper" or "dominant classes" at the top). The "food space" diagram, showing foods and cooking styles most common to each group, is based on various statistical analyses of food consumption surveys in 1960s and 1970s France. Note that a contemporary North American food space would look slightly different (Watson 2012).

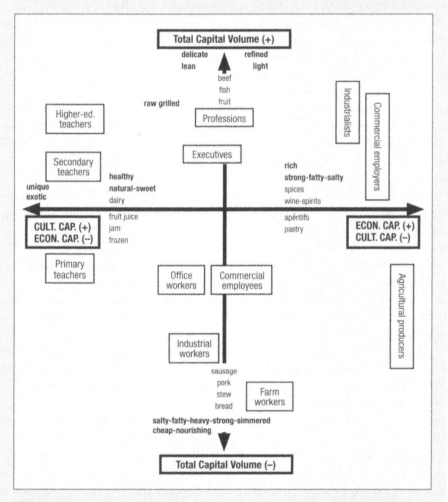

FIGURE 3.2. Correspondence between "food space" and "social space" according to Pierre Bourdieu.

and health vary substantially among people, based on class and ethnicity. The "thin" extreme of anorexia is found mainly among middle- and upper-class white women (M. Darmon 2009), while African Americans of all classes tend to accept larger body sizes (Keith, Hemmerlein, and Clark 2015). As we discuss below, opinions about nutrition interventions such as weight-loss programs also differ significantly by class and ethnicity.

Beyond Class to Lifestyles, Subcultures, Networks, and Neighborhoods

Bourdieu's model of "distinction" is better at acknowledging diversity and agency among the upper classes than among the lower classes, but there is also quite a bit of diversity among the poor. For instance, poor people living in urban, suburban, or rural areas have varied access to the same services for their basic needs (e.g., there is more food insecurity in rural areas), while the urban poor themselves differ in their orientations toward work, child rearing, education, or assistance (Holloway et al. 1997). One still finds a vast array of occupational subcultures among the poor in today's American cities, such as itinerants, street sellers, scavengers, intermittent workers, and the homeless, as well as immigrant cultures that have resisted dominant consumerist orientations (Jindra 2014). Though the opportunities of the poor and minorities can be limited by structural constraints, they still have some agency to develop distinct lifestyles and traditions, as the history of "soul food" shows.

Epidemiologists working with marketers have identified seven different "health lifestyle clusters" among the US population, from those who have high levels of concern about nutrition and weight control ("Physical Fantastics") to those who are more interested in taste or convenience ("Noninterested Nihilists") (Glanz et al. 1998). The recent growth of "foodies" is a primary example of how these subcultures relate to other factors such as class: people at higher levels of income and education have the privilege to be choosy about the foods they eat while avoiding overt snobbery and exclusion (Johnston and Baumann 2009), echoing Bourdieu's analysis of the "taste of liberty" of those groups who are wealthier in "cultural capital" (Bourdieu 1984).

There is also diversity in "household cultures" (Dake and Thompson 1993), such as practices concerning eating, cleaning, sociality, and consumption habits. Some families have scheduled communal mealtimes, prompt cleanup, and savings patterns, in contrast to those who, for instance, rely more on takeout food at irregular times. These practices are set rather early in primary socialization, as children learn the habits of their families, contributing to generational patterns and ongoing inequality. Indeed, there is a growing body of evidence that shows how family and social environments (e.g., eating together, whether mothers work) play an important role in the development of children's eating patterns, diet quality, and/or obesity (Fischler 2011). Television in particular plays an important role, as high levels of viewing are connected to high-fat convenience foods and a lack of exercise. Exposure to high levels of food advertising also plays a role. In general, greater TV means "higher intakes of energy, fat, sweet and salty snacks, and carbonated beverages and lower intakes of fruit and vegetables" with direct correlations between number of hours watched and high levels of obesity (Coon and Tucker 2002, 423). These connections are even more important given that television viewing is highest among low-income groups and particularly among African Americans (Nielsen Company 2014).

The neighborhood in which one lives also has a strong effect on one's life. The consumption of fast food, and its concentration in specific neighborhoods, is said to contribute to obesity (Powell, Chaloupka, and Bao 2007). We will explore this below when discussing "food deserts," but a key thing to remember about neighborhoods is that the social environment appears to play a more important role than the physical environment. That is, the strongest influences on people are other people and relationships, more so than the design or location of buildings and public spaces. In one study of weight-loss attitudes among urban poor black and white women, barriers to physical activity were more related to social influences such as the existence of "supporting networks of trusted peers," rather than to the physical space such as the absence of sidewalks—though these also differ markedly by race (Keith, Hemmerlein, and Clark 2015).

This takes us to the level of social networks. These, of course, are strongly influenced by our class, ethnicity, and lifestyle affiliations, as we hang around those most similar to us in our tastes, outlooks, and habits. Peers have a strong influence on eating habits, exercise, and ultimately chronic diseases like obesity: public health researchers revisiting the Framingham Heart Study findings have thus been able to follow the spread of obesity in a social network over thirty-two years (1971–2002), especially among pairs of friends and siblings of the same sex—that is, people tended to gain weight when their friends and relatives gained weight around them (Christakis and Fowler 2007). Interestingly, the weight gain of immediate neighbors did not affect one's chance of weight gain in the latter study, ruling out the influence of exposure to local environmental factors.

Then there are also "psychosocial" factors that affect our eating behavior, such how we handle stress—higher for those in poverty—and resist temptation (Thirlaway and Upton 2009, 67). In sum, we must remember all the factors that affect human action, from "macro" influences such as regional, ethnic, and class determinants, to "micro" influences such as socialization into cultures, family structure, and the effect of the social and physical environments (e.g., social networks and neighborhoods) in which one lives.

Policy Implications and Initiatives

The larger environment of a plethora of food choice, with many convenient but often unhealthy options, combined with increasingly sedentary lifestyles means that we face an ever-growing problem of inequality in health. This is exacerbated by growing income inequalities, combined with the increasing cost of fresh produce and the decreasing cost of snacks and soda that make "energy dense" foods (i.e., foods rich in fat and sugar) less expensive (Drewnowski and Specter 2004). Life expectancy in the United States is lower than in many other high-income countries, and our food habits are partly to blame for these "extremely large" geographic, racial, and class disparities in health (Krueger, Bhaloo, and Rosenau 2009).

Various initiatives have been proposed to deal with the situation. Federal food assistance programs such as WIC (for mothers with young children) and SNAP (food stamps) are large sources of food for low-income groups, and there is an ongoing debate over whether to tighten allowable categories of food to be purchased (Rosenberg 2013). In 2009 WIC changed its rules to require that milk must be reduced fat, and bread and rice must be whole grain, and participating stores must carry these. There is also a category of voucher specifically for produce. Early evidence shows that it has resulted in purchases of healthier foods (Rosenberg 2013).

The FDA (Food and Drug Administration) continually revises the food pyramid to encourage healthy eating, though it has been known to be subject to political pressure from the food industry (Nestle 2013). More recently, Michelle Obama's nationwide "Let's Move" campaign aimed at improving physical activity and healthy eating. There are also many local initiatives: at historically black Spelman College, for instance, after noticing that half of the female students had problems with obesity or diabetes, President Beverly Tatum eliminated intercollegiate sports in 2012 and diverted its funding toward health programs on campus that encouraged exercise and healthy eating.

One cannot forget the multibillion-dollar diet industry, and the increased numbers of weight-loss programs that are implemented by institutions (with some controversy) such as health care systems or corporations looking to lower employee health care costs. As we've seen above, however, these popular programs are undertaken with individuals who are influenced by many different social forces. For one, these programs are received differently based on race and class, with exercise programs and healthy eating regimens generally regarded as middle- and upper-class phenomena (Wardle and Steptoe 2003). The poor also have different contexts for making decisions than higher-income individuals, with higher overall stress leading to decisions that focus more on the short term (Banerjee and Mullainathan 2007). One recent study found significant differences in how black and white women perceived and reacted to these programs (Keith, Hemmerlein, and Clark 2015). As mentioned above, not only do black women have much less social support for healthy eating and losing weight, but they also connect eating with pleasure much more than white women (who are thus at increased risk for anorexia).

Other initiatives to improve healthy eating target the physical environment and how that limits or forces certain choices on individuals, or they focus on the overall food system. The "food desert" thesis, for instance, argues that the lack of grocery stores carrying healthy options in poorer neighborhoods contributes to high obesity and poor health. This has prompted a movement designed to counter food deserts by placing healthy eating options in these areas. A USDA (US Department of Agriculture) report, however, found that the "food desert" diagnosis was grossly exaggerated: only 2.2 percent of American households live more than one mile from a supermarket without access to a car, and 93 percent of the residents of low-income neighborhoods manage to drive to a supermarket to do their grocery shopping, either in their own car or with a parent or friend (Ver Ploeg 2009). More recently, other researchers have also found little evidence for the "food desert" thesis (Guthman 2011). Proponents of the importance of "food deserts" go against several factors, such as strong cultural and taste preferences for certain foods, and the simple fact that fruits and vegetables can cost more per calorie, making it harder for low-income groups to afford them (Drewnowski and Specter 2004). Even giving away healthy food does not mean that people will eat it, as we commonly see with the tossing of fruits and vegetables in school lunchrooms around the country (Upton, Upton, and Taylor 2012). Connected to this, the attempt to create "alternative food movements" to reach poor and minority consumers has been beset by the class and cultural distance between their organizers and the population (Alkon and McCullen 2011; Kato 2013; Larchet 2014).

Because of the role played by informal peer pressure and social controls to conform to one's group or culture, these are not easy things to change. Unspoken social norms within a group (e.g., what to consume and how to spend leisure time) are stronger than even verbal social support (Ball et al. 2010). We are strongly influenced by others, and any intervention strategies around healthy eating need to take this into consideration by helping people see this influence, and by tackling the norms behind the practice. Simple educational initiatives don't work as well (Thirlaway and Upton 2009, 79), though cities such as Oklahoma City have made progress with multipronged community-wide efforts that engage people personally (Tavernise 2012).

Unsurprisingly, there are gaps between our good intentions and our ability to change other people's behaviors, especially when it comes to potent cultural symbols like food habits, which anthropologists have long recognized as especially resistant to change (Mead 1943). Human behavior toward food is certainly influenced by biological factors, but it needs to be understood in its sociocultural context, from the long-standing influences of regional, ethnic, and class cultures down to family structures and our "psychosocial" selves. Some community programs, such as Bridges Out of Poverty, are designed to help participants understand all these factors, and then give them possible alternatives that can be adopted as "life plans." Other programs focus on the tough demographic of school kids (Thirlaway and Upton 2009, 79–81) or utilize a "stages of change" model that examines a person's readiness to change eating behaviors (Webb et al. 2014). Recognizing the entrenched inequalities of American life, the largest food bank network in the United States, Feeding America, is also beginning to encourage local agencies to help their clients long term through complex services, rather than just food handouts. This kind of "relational work" can include mentoring, coaching, or case management, what one staff member called a "revolutionary" change away from straight charity (Jindra and Jindra 2015). Overall, relational work can help people who have difficulty navigating the increasing complexity of American consumer life, including the food system, though one must watch out for issues such as the differences in power relations between clients and staff.

To grasp the complexity of food and poverty, one needs to understand the unique lives of people, including the interplay of their individual biographies and cultural histories, the structural constraints that weigh on them, and their potentialities or agency. Instead of taking only a "top-down" structural approach (e.g., the "food desert" thesis) or an individualistic approach (life as a series of choices), it is important to understand how diverse people live, paying attention to the multiple contextual factors of region, race/ethnicity, religion, class, social networks, neighborhoods, and families. These all relate to the processes of our everyday lives, such as emotions (e.g., how we feel about food and our bodies) and beliefs that create and maintain patterned lifestyles (Smith 2015).

Finally, one must not forget that these factors reflect as much as they contribute to ongoing socioeconomic inequalities, since poor health related to a poor diet—hunger and food insecurity, or diabetes and obesity—continue to disproportionately affect lower-income populations, restricting their future life chances. Though a recent analysis of the National Health and Nutrition Examination Survey data from 1999 to 2010 indicates that dietary quality has overall improved among adults in the United States, it is not happening among the poor: indeed, the "dietary gap" between those with the highest and lowest levels of socioeconomic status increased over time (D. Wang et al. 2014).

REFERENCES

Abramson, Corey. 2012. "From 'Either-Or' to 'When and How': A Context-Dependent Model of Culture in Action." *Journal for the Theory of Social Behaviour* 42 (2): 155–80.

Alkon, Alison Hope, and Christie Grace McCullen. 2011. "Whiteness and Farmers Markets: Performances, Perpetuations . . . Contestations?" *Antipode* 43 (4): 937–59.

Ball, Kylie, Robert W. Jeffery, Gavin Abbott, Sarah A. McNaughton, and David Crawford. 2010. "Is Healthy Behavior Contagious: Associations of Social Norms with Physical Activity and Healthy Eating." *International Journal of Behavioral Nutrition and Physical Activity* 7 (1): 86.

Banerjee, A., and S. Mullainathan. 2007. "Climbing Out of Poverty: Long Term Decisions under Income Stress." Working paper presented at the Eleventh BREAD Conference on Development Economics, London, October 5–6.

Bosi, Lorenzo, and Donatella Della Porta. 2012. "Micro-mobilization into Armed Groups: Ideological, Instrumental and Solidaristic Paths." *Qualitative Sociology* 35 (4): 361–83.

Bourdieu, Pierre. 1984. *Distinction: A Social Critique of the Judgement of Taste.* Cambridge, MA: Harvard University Press.

Brown, Linda Keller, and Kay Mussell. 1984. "Introduction." In *Ethnic and Regional Foodways in the United States: The Performance of Group Identity,* edited by Linda Keller Brown and Kay Mussell, 3–15. Knoxville: University of Tennessee Press.

Caplovitz, David. 1967. *The Poor Pay More: Consumer Practices of Low-Income Families.* New York: Free Press.

Carney, Judith Ann. 2001. *Black Rice: The African Origins of Rice Cultivation in the Americas.* Cambridge, MA: Harvard University Press.

Chavis, Shaun. 2008. "Is There a Difference between Southern and Soul?" In *Cornbread Nation 4: The Best of Southern Food Writing,* edited by Dale Volberg Reed, John Shelton Reed, and John T. Edge, 4: 237–44. Athens: University of Georgia Press.

Christakis, Nicholas A., and James H. Fowler. 2007. "The Spread of Obesity in a Large Social Network over 32 Years." *New England Journal of Medicine* 357 (4): 370–79.

Coon, K. A., and K. L. Tucker. 2002. "Television and Children's Consumption Patterns." *Minerva Pediatrica* 54 (5): 423–36.

Counihan, Carole, and Penny Van Esterik. 2013. *Food and Culture: A Reader.* 3rd ed. New York: Routledge.

Dake, Karl, and M. Thompson. 1993. "The Meanings of Sustainable Development: Household Strategies for Managing Needs and Resources." In *Human Ecology: Crossing Boundaries,* edited by Scott Wright, 421–36. Fort Collins, CO: Society for Human Ecology.

Darmon, Muriel. 2009. "The Fifth Element: Social Class and the Sociology of Anorexia." *Sociology* 43 (4): 717–33.

Darmon, Nicole, and Adam Drewnowski. 2008. "Does Social Class Predict Diet Quality?" *American Journal of Clinical Nutrition* 87 (5): 1107–17.

Drewnowski, Adam, and S. E. Specter. 2004. "Poverty and Obesity: The Role of Energy Density and Energy Costs." *American Journal of Clinical Nutrition* 79 (1): 6–16.

Egerton, John. 1987. *Southern Food: At Home, on the Road, in History*. Chapel Hill: University of North Carolina Press.

Elbel, Brian, Alyssa Moran, L. Beth Dixon, Kamila Kiszko, Jonathan Cantor, Courtney Abrams, and Tod Mijanovich. 2015. "Assessment of a Government-Subsidized Supermarket in a High-Need Area on Household Food Availability and Children's Dietary Intakes." *Public Health Nutrition* 18 (15): 2881–90.

Elias, Norbert. 1969. *The Civilizing Process*. Vol. 1, *The History of Manners*. Oxford: Blackwell.

Engel, E. 1895. "Die Lebenskosten Belgischer Arbeiter-Familien Früher Und Jetzt." *International Statistical Institute Bulletin* 9: 1–74.

Fischler, Claude. 2011. "Commensality, Society and Culture." *Social Science Information* 50 (3–4): 528–48.

Glanz, Karen, Michael Basil, Edward Maibach, Jeanne Goldberg, and Dan Snyder. 1998. "Why Americans Eat What They Do: Taste, Nutrition, Cost, Convenience, and Weight Control Concerns as Influences on Food Consumption." *Journal of the American Dietetic Association* 98 (10): 1118–26.

Goody, Jack. 2013. "Industrial Food: Towards the Development of a World Cuisine." In *Food and Culture: A Reader*, 3rd ed., edited by Carole Counihan and Penny Van Esterik, 72–90. New York: Routledge.

Grignon, Claude. 1985. "Sociology of Taste and the Realist Novel: Representations of Popular Eating in E. Zola." *Food and Foodways* 1 (1–2): 117–60.

Guthman, Julie. 2011. *Weighing In: Obesity, Food Justice, and the Limits of Capitalism*. Berkeley: University of California Press.

Helstosky, Carol. 2008. *Pizza: A Global History*. Reaktion Books.

Holloway, Susan, Bruce Fuller, Marylee F. Rambaud, and Costanza Eggers-Piérola. 1997. *Through My Own Eyes: Single Mothers and the Cultures of Poverty*. Cambridge, MA: Harvard University Press.

Hughes, Marvalene H. 1997. "Soul, Black Women, and Food." In *Food and Culture: A Reader*, 1st ed., edited by Carole Counihan and Penny Van Esterik, 272–80. New York: Psychology Press.

James, Delores. 2004. "Factors Influencing Food Choices, Dietary Intake, and Nutrition-Related Attitudes among African Americans: Application of a Culturally Sensitive Model." *Ethnicity and Health* 9 (4): 349–67.

Jindra, Michael. 2014. "The Dilemma of Equality and Diversity." *Current Anthropology* 55 (3): 316–34.

Jindra, Michael, and Ines W. Jindra. 2015. "The Rise of Antipoverty Relational Work." *Stanford Social Innovation Review*, March 17. *www.ssireview.org/blog/entry/the_rise_of_antipoverty_relational_work/*.

Johnston, Josée, and Shyon Baumann. 2009. *Foodies: Democracy and Distinction in the Gourmet Foodscape*. New York: Routledge.

Judd, Suzanne E., Orlando M. Gutiérrez, P. K. Newby, George Howard, Virginia J. Howard, Julie L. Locher, Brett M. Kissela, and James M. Shikany. 2013. "Dietary Patterns Are Associated with Incident Stroke and Contribute to Excess Risk of Stroke in Black Americans." *Stroke* 44 (12): 3305–11.

Kato, Yuki. 2013. "Not Just the Price of Food: Challenges of an Urban Agriculture Organization in Engaging Local Residents." *Sociological Inquiry* 83 (3): 369–91.

Keith, NiCole R., Kimberly A. Hemmerlein, and Daniel O. Clark. 2015. "Weight Loss Attitudes and Social Forces in Urban Poor Black and White Women." *American Journal of Health Behavior* 39 (1): 34–42.

Kimura, Aya H., Charlotte Biltekoff, Jessica Mudry, and Jessica Hayes-Conroy. 2014. "Nutrition as a Project." *Gastronomica: The Journal of Food and Culture* 14 (3): 34–45.

Kittler, Pamela Goyan, Kathryn Sucher, and Marcia Nelms. 2012. *Food and Culture.* 6th ed. Farmington Hills, MI: Cengage Learning.

Kreuter, Matthew W., Susan N. Lukwago, Dawn C. Bucholtz, Eddie M. Clark, and Vetta Sanders-Thompson. 2003. "Achieving Cultural Appropriateness in Health Promotion Programs: Targeted and Tailored Approaches." *Health Education and Behavior* 30 (2): 133–46.

Krueger, Patrick M., Tajudaullah Bhaloo, and Pauline V. Rosenau. 2009. "Health Lifestyles in the United States and Canada: Are We Really So Different?" *Social Science Quarterly* 90 (5): 1380–402.

Lanska, Douglas J., and Lewis H. Kuller. 1995. "The Geography of Stroke Mortality in the United States and the Concept of a Stroke Belt." *Stroke* 26 (7): 1145–49.

Larchet, Nicolas. 2014. "Learning from the Corner Store: Food Reformers and the Black Urban Poor in a Southern US City." *Food, Culture and Society* 17 (3): 395–416.

Latshaw, Beth A. 2009. "Food for Thought: Race, Region, Identity, and Foodways in the American South." *Southern Cultures* 15 (4): 106–28.

Levenstein, Harvey. 1980. "The New England Kitchen and the Origins of Modern American Eating Habits." *American Quarterly* 32 (4): 369–86.

Liao, Youlian, Kurt J. Greenlund, Janet B. Croft, Nora L. Keenan, and Wayne H. Giles. 2009. "Factors Explaining Excess Stroke Prevalence in the US Stroke Belt." *Stroke* 40 (10): 3336–41.

Maroto, Michelle Lee. 2015. "Pathways into Bankruptcy: Accumulating Disadvantage and the Consequences of Adverse Life Events." *Sociological Inquiry* 85 (2): 183–216.

Mead, Margaret. 1943. "The Problem of Changing Food Habits." *Bulletin of the National Research Council* 108 (325): 20–31.

Miller, Lisa. 2010. "Divided We Eat: What Food Says about Class in America and How to Bridge the Gap." *Newsweek*, November 22. *www.newsweek.com/what-food-says-about-class-america-69951/.*

Mintz, Sidney Wilfred. 1996. "Eating American." In *Tasting Food, Tasting Freedom: Excursions into Eating, Culture, and the Past*, edited by Sidney Mintz, 106–24. Boston: Beacon.

Mischel, Walter. 2014. *The Marshmallow Test: Understanding Self-Control and How to Master It.* New York: Random House.

Murray, C. J. L., S. C. Kulkarni, C. Michaud, N. Tomijima, M. T. Bulzacchelli, T. J. Iandiorio, and M. Ezzati. 2006. "Eight Americas: Investigating Mortality Disparities across Races, Counties, and Race-Counties in the United States." *PLoS Medicine* 3 (9): e260.

Nestle, Marion. 2013. *Food Politics: How the Food Industry Influences Nutrition and Health.* 3rd ed. Berkeley: University of California Press.

Nielsen Company. 2014. "The Total Audience Report." March 12. *www.nielsen.com/us/en/insights/reports/2014/the-total-audience-report.html/.*

Norman, Corrie E. 2012. "Food and Religion." In *The Oxford Handbook of Food History*, edited by Jeffrey M. Pilcher, 409–27. Oxford University Press.

Opie, Frederick Douglass. 2010. *Hog and Hominy: Soul Food from Africa to America.* New York: Columbia University Press.

Poe, Tracy N. 1999. "The Origins of Soul Food in Black Urban Identity: Chicago, 1915–1947." *American Studies International* 37 (1): 4–33.

Powell, Lisa M., Frank J. Chaloupka, and Yanjun Bao. 2007. "The Availability of Fast-Food and Full-Service Restaurants in the United States: Associations with Neighborhood Characteristics." *American Journal of Preventive Medicine* 33 (4, Supplement): S240–45.

Rosenberg, Tina. 2013. "To Fight Obesity, a Carrot, and a Stick." *New York Times*, November 16. *opinionator.blogs.nytimes.com/2013/11/16/to-fight-obesity-a-carrot-and-a-stick/*.

Schroeder, Steven A. 2007. "We Can Do Better—Improving the Health of the American People." *New England Journal of Medicine* 357 (12): 1221–28.

Shortridge, Barbara G., and James R. Shortridge. 1989. "Consumption of Fresh Produce in the Metropolitan United States." *Geographical Review* 79 (1): 79–98.

Smith, Christian. 2015. *To Flourish or Destruct: A Personalist Theory of Human Goods, Motivations, Failure, and Evil.* Chicago: University of Chicago Press.

Tavernise, Sabrina. 2012. "Door to Door in the Heartland, Preaching Healthy Living." *New York Times*, September 10. *www.nytimes.com/2012/09/11/health/door-to-door-in-oklahoma-city-preaching-healthy-living.html/*.

Thirlaway, Kathryn, and Dominic Upton. 2009. *The Psychology of Lifestyle: Promoting Healthy Behavior.* London: Routledge.

Thompson, Derek. 2013. "Cheap Eats: How America Spends Money on Food." *Atlantic*, March 8. *www.theatlantic.com/business/archive/2013/03/cheap-eats-how-america-spends-money-on-food/273811/*.

Upton, D., P. Upton, and C. Taylor. 2012. "Fruit and Vegetable Intake of Primary School Children: A Study of School Meals." *Journal of Human Nutrition and Dietetics* 25 (6): 557–62.

Veblen, Thorstein. 1899. *The Theory of the Leisure Class.* New York: Macmillan.

Ver Ploeg, Michele. 2009. "Access to Affordable and Nutritious Food—Measuring and Understanding Food Deserts and Their Consequences: Report to Congress." Washington, DC: USDA Economic Research Service.

Wang, Dong D., Cindy W. Leung, Yanping Li, Eric L. Ding, Stephanie E. Chiuve, Frank B. Hu, and Walter C. Willett. 2014. "Trends in Dietary Quality among Adults in the United States, 1999 through 2010." *JAMA Internal Medicine* 174 (10): 1587–95.

Wardle, J., and A. Steptoe. 2003. "Socioeconomic Differences in Attitudes and Beliefs about Healthy Lifestyles." *Journal of Epidemiology and Community Health* 57 (6): 440–43.

Watson, Molly. 2012. "Bourdieu's Food Space." *Gastronomica Web Exclusives*, June 18. *gastronomica.org/2012/06/18/bourdieus-food-space/*.

Webb, Fern J., Jagdish Khubchandani, Michelle Doldren, Joyce Balls-Berry, Shirley Blanchard, Liane Hannah, Jevetta Stanford, and Selena Webster-Bass. 2014. "African-American Women's Eating Habits and Intention to Change: A Pilot Study." *Journal of Racial and Ethnic Health Disparities* 1 (3): 199–206.

PART TWO

PROBLEMS

The structural inequalities related to food and poverty are both complex and long-standing. These inequalities have severe negative consequences including food insecurity, lack of food access, obesity, and associated health impacts. These social problems demonstrate the paradox of food and poverty; calorically dense unhealthy foods may be consumed because of a lack of food access, leading to obesity. People who are living in the same household may be obese and hungry, and even the same person may experience both. This constant struggle to not only eat but to eat healthfully highlights the vulnerability in the lives of the poor. The stress that comes from having to worry about food, say choosing between food and bills, adds to the problems and consequences of living in poverty.

Not everyone is impacted equally by these food access issues. Racial and ethnic minorities have a higher likelihood of food insecurity. Those living in rural and micropolitan areas, as well as food deserts across all geographies, have limited access to food and food assistance. The elderly are an often overlooked group that has difficulty with food insecurity and food access.

Food assistance, both through the government and community based, was designed to alleviate the previously described food insecurity. The food assistance safety net is under political attack, potentially limiting availability. There are other problems with the provision of food assistance, including barriers to access, limited funding, waiting lists, and the stigma associated with utilizing assistance.

Food deserts, the definitions of which are explored in detail in the following chapters, provide an opportunity to visualize some of these inequalities. While new programs are attempting to address these problems, this access issue remains significant. Food deserts are more prevalent in economically depressed areas as well as areas with higher percentages of minority residents.

It should be evident by now how intertwined the many facets of structural inequalities in the US food system are. Food insecurity is linked to food access; higher rates of food insecurity and lack of access to food are found among disadvantaged groups including the poor, racial and ethnic minorities, children, and the elderly. The negative health consequences of food insecurity, especially obesity, are more likely to impact those groups as well.

4

Food Spending Profiles for White, Black, and Hispanic Households Living in Poverty

RAPHAËL CHARRON-CHÉNIER

Having enough to eat can be a serious problem for households living in poverty. Buying food is just one of the many competing needs poor families must meet. Yet food is unique in that it is an absolutely essential need; its consumption cannot be indefinitely postponed. Making sure there is enough can therefore mean having to make serious sacrifices. Parents, for example, might have to skip a meal or forego health care so that their children have adequate food. To manage the financial burden that buying food represents, poor families need to turn to a variety of strategies. They can, for example, turn to income support programs and local food banks. They can rely on kin, friends, and even casual acquaintances for the financial and material help they need. Or they can try to keep costs low by opting for lower-quality alternatives or by shopping at discount grocery stores (Desmond 2012; Walker et al. 2011).

These different strategies, however, are not equally available to all low-income families. Widespread inequality in the conditions faced by white, black, and Hispanic households in the United States means that members of these groups have to rely on very different and very unequal sets of resources. Even at the lowest income levels, white Americans tend to enjoy certain key advantages over their nonwhite counterparts. The inequalities that exist between ethnic and racial groups in the United States almost certainly impact their ability to put food on the table and, importantly, the magnitude of the financial sacrifice that doing so represents.

In this chapter, I use a broad sociological perspective to shed light on food spending patterns for white, black, and Hispanic families living in poverty and provide a brief overview of the racial and ethnic inequalities that structure poor families' material circumstances and their access to resources, highlighting how these impact poor households' food spending patterns. Using household spending data from the 2006 to 2014 Consumer Expenditure Surveys, I then provide a detailed picture of food spending trends for poor white, black, and Hispanic households. Overall, I show that buying food is a considerably larger financial burden for poor black and Hispanic households than for poor white households, even though these households tend to spend less on food overall than white households do.

Determinants of Food Spending
Demand-Side Processes

To understand the impact of the broader social and economic context on poor households' food spending patterns, we can conceptualize food spending as the result of two types of processes: demand-side and supply-side.

Demand-side processes are factors that influence households' *ability* to purchase goods and services. Research on economic disparities by race and ethnicity in the United States suggests that black and Hispanic households are disadvantaged relative to whites in terms of their ability to spend money on goods and services. Here, I examine three key causes of nonwhite households' lower spending power: differences in access to employment, differences in access to wealth and credit, and differences in access to supplementary income sources.

Access to employment. A significant proportion of adults living in poverty hold part- or full-time jobs. Employment is not only a source of income but can also provide access to valuable fringe benefits, like health insurance. Access to employment and employment benefits, however, is not equal across racial and ethnic groups. Compared with whites, black and Hispanic workers tend to have lower wages (McCall 2001) and are more likely to hold more precarious jobs that offer fewer fringe benefits (Kalleberg 2011). As research has shown, one reason for this is that many employers prefer hiring whites over blacks and Hispanics for entry-level positions (Pager, Western, and Bonikowski 2009). Black job seekers are also less successful than whites in using their personal contacts for finding a job, partly because employers are less willing to accept recommendations from their black employees (Smith 2007). For Hispanics born outside the United States and living there without legal documentation, finding stable and well-paid work can be extremely difficult. Even among employed individuals, occupational segregation into lower-paying jobs remains a pervasive problem, especially for black women (Stainback and Tomaskovic-Devey 2012).

Overall, being more likely to have a job means being more likely to have a steady income source that can be used for making sure there is enough food on the table, without having to engage in as many cost-cutting sacrifices. Racial and ethnic inequality in access to jobs means that—even for households living in poverty—whites are likely to have more money to spend on food than nonwhites.

Wealth and credit. White households also benefit from greater access to savings, credit, and informal transfers. Whites have higher levels of wealth than blacks and Hispanics in the United States (Keister, Vallejo, and Borelli 2015; Shapiro 2004). Because low-income individuals often rely on their relatives for financial support, lower levels of wealth for blacks and Hispanics means that their family networks will have fewer resources to share. Even among the poor, important differences in wealth can be found. For example, a portion of low-income individuals own their homes, which is a significant tool for managing financial uncertainty. Housing values in areas with high concentrations of racial and ethnic minorities, however, tend to be lower than in majority white areas (Krivo and Kaufman 2004). Black and Hispanic families were also disproportionately likely to lose their home in the aftermath of the 2007–2009 financial crisis (Rugh and Massey 2010). In terms of access to credit and other financial services, low-income nonwhite households are also more likely to live in areas without traditional banking services, and to therefore rely on high-cost fringe services like cash checking, pawnshops, and payday lending (Barr 2012). These problems are compounded for undocumented migrants, who lack access to formal financial institutions entirely.

Overall then, lower wealth, lower home values, and lower access to mainstream financial institutions mean that poor nonwhite households have fewer accumulated resources to draw on and experience greater difficulties obtaining credit to weather hardships. This necessarily leads to greater difficulty maintaining steady access to food.

Income support. White households also tend to be advantaged in terms of access to public and charitable sources of income support. In the United States, provision of social services like welfare, job training programs, and health care is highly decentralized and often in the hands of private sector actors (Morgan and Campbell 2011). This decentralization imposes significant disadvantages on low-income and nonwhite recipients. Fewer social service providers tend to be located in majority black low-income neighborhoods than in majority white low-income neighborhoods (Allard 2009). Welfare and government cash assistance in jurisdictions where recipients are nonwhite also tend to be less generous and more punitive than in majority white jurisdictions (Fording, Schram, and Soss 2011). Overall, this means that poor nonwhite families are more likely to have to rely on their own (already lower) income and wealth to acquire goods and services. This means that acquiring food likely represents a greater burden on black and Hispanic households' resources than on white households'.

Supply-Side Processes

In addition to demand-side inequalities, low-income black and Hispanic households are also more likely than whites to live in areas where access to goods and services is difficult. I label these constraints *supply-side* factors. Difficulties with access to affordable, quality food in particular have been well documented for low-income and majority nonwhite neighborhoods. These neighborhoods tend to have lower concentrations of large grocery retailers, lower food availability, and higher food prices than average (Powell et al. 2007; Richardson et al. 2012). As a result, households in these neighborhoods must rely on lower-quality food retailers (like convenience stores) that often carry fewer fresh products and sell at a higher price.

Yet food retail is not the only type of commercial activity that is adversely affected in low-income and racially segregated neighborhoods. Raising capital for small businesses has been difficult for entrepreneurs in these neighborhoods, despite government attempts to remedy the situation—like the Community Reinvestment Act (Blanchflower, Levine, and Zimmerman 2003). These capital constraints lead to higher rates of business failures in segregated neighborhoods (Fairlie and Robb 2007). The overall result is that residents of racially segregated neighborhoods have access to fewer and lower-quality retail and service providers than residents of majority white neighborhoods (Small and McDermott 2006), making it difficult to acquire goods and services at a reasonable cost. This means that nonwhite households are likely to have to devote a greater share of their income to acquiring all basic goods and services, including food. These added financial constraints coupled with already discussed lower resources mean that black and Hispanic households are likely more financially burdened by food purchases than white households.

Empirical Trends in Food Spending

The remainder of this chapter uses data from the Consumer Expenditure Survey to examine food spending trends for white, black, and Hispanic households in light of the racial and ethnic differences in demand- and supply-side constraints outlined in the previous section.

The Consumer Expenditure Surveys

To provide estimates of food spending, I use data from the Bureau of Labor Statistics' Consumer Expenditure Survey (CE). The CE is a nationally representative quarterly survey of US households and provides detailed information on all major household expenditures. The CE is the most complete and extensive expenditure survey in the United States and plays a crucial role in monitoring the state of the American economy. Data for the CE are collected in respondents' homes by trained Census Bureau personnel over several interviews and are validated using transaction and purchase records whenever possible. Detailed economic and demographic data for each household are also collected during this process. For additional details on the CE, see the Consumer Expenditure Survey website (*www.bls.gov/cex*).

All estimates presented below come from quarterly expenditure data covering the period between April 2006 and March 2014 inclusively. This timeframe covers the foreclosure crisis and the recession that followed it, allowing me to highlight issues of food security in an economically difficult period. I use data from all white, black, and Hispanic respondents in the sample. Households reporting no food expenditures, reporting food expenditures larger than their total spending, or reporting annual spending figures greater than ten times their yearly income were excluded from the sample (less than 1.5 percent of the total sample is excluded). Unless otherwise noted, I use data from poor households only (defined as those households whose income was below the federal poverty line for households of their size for that year). The final analytic sample consists of 214,631 household quarters obtained from 74,588 unique households, with each household contributing an average of 2.9 observations.

Comparing across Race and Ethnicity

I produce estimates of food spending trends for three racial and ethnic groups: whites, blacks, and Hispanics. To capture important heterogeneity across Hispanic households, I classified this group further into language categories (English- or Spanish-speaking), based on the language in which respondents chose to conduct their CE interview. Language serves as a very rough proxy for nativity and documentation status, which are not measured directly in the CE. My analyses assume that compared to the English-speaking group, the Spanish-speaking Hispanic group is made up of a larger proportion of recent migrants, of foreign-born individuals, and of individuals without legal documentation. Ethnic self-identification questions in the CE tend to support this assumption. Approximately 70 percent of Spanish-speaking Hispanics in the sample reported being Mexican, Cuban, or Central American, compared to 26 percent identifying as Mexican American, Cuban American, Chicano, or Puerto Rican. By contrast, only 39 percent of the English-speaking Hispanics reported being Mexican, Cuban, or Central American, while 54 percent reported being Mexican American, Cuban American, Chicano, or Puerto Rican.

Food Spending in the Consumer Expenditure Survey

To examine patterns of food purchases, I use households' reported quarterly spending on food, as provided in the summary expenditure section of the CE interview survey. This measure of overall food spending can be split into two components: food consumed at home (i.e., groceries) and food consumed away from home (i.e., eating out). Food at home captures all spending on food consumed and prepared at home. Food away from home captures food purchased at restaurants, cafés, fast-food places, catered events, cafeterias, and at school. Food away from home can be conceptualized as a more discretionary type of food spending, associated with convenience or entertainment. When relevant, the figures below will distinguish between the two types of food spending.

Figures and Analyses

Characteristics of Poor Households

To understand food spending patterns among poor white, black, and Hispanic households, I first present information on these households' socioeconomic and demographic characteristics. Table 4.1 shows mean values and proportions for selected variables, by race and ethnicity. The data presented in Table 4.1 reveal considerable inequality by race and ethnicity on key indicators of social position, even among households living in poverty. As a general trend, socioeconomic measures presented in Table 4.1 suggest that poor white households are doing better than poor English-speaking Hispanic households, which are in turn doing better than poor black and poor Spanish-speaking Hispanic households.

Poor white households have the highest median income compared with other racial and ethnic groups, especially when considering that white households tend to be smaller than others. At 2.25 total members on average, this means that annual income per member for white households is slightly over $12,000. White households also report the highest quarterly spending at $9,432, which translates to an annual average spending amount of approximately $38,000—or about 138 percent of their total income. This high spending-to-income ratio indicates relatively high reliance on credit and informal transfers, although this figure is lower than for nonwhite households. Poor white households also have the lowest proportion of household heads with no high school degree (15 percent) and the highest portion of household heads with college or graduate degrees (24 percent). They also have the highest proportion of homeowners (60 percent). These trends suggest that poverty may be more transitory and less intense for this group, especially when compared with blacks and Hispanics.

TABLE 4.1. Characteristics of poor households by race and ethnicity

	White	Black	Hispanic English-speaking	Hispanic Spanish-speaking
N	37,382	11,037	4,856	4,564
Average Number in Household				
Adults	1.80	1.85	2.17	2.36
Children	0.45	0.79	1.15	1.20
Median Annual Income	$27,250	$19,362	$22,282	$20,027
Quarterly Spending				
Total Spending	$9,432	$6,660	$7,726	$6,914
Food Spending	$1,526	$1,290	$1,547	$1,591
Food at Home	$1,080	$1,029	$1,210	$1,294
Food Away	$447	$261	$337	$297
Education				
No High School	15%	26%	38%	63%
High School	28%	32%	28%	20%
Some College	33%	30%	23%	11%
College	16%	8%	8%	5%
Graduate Degree	8%	4%	3%	1%
Work Status				
Working	64%	59%	71%	72%
Out of Work	21%	15%	9%	12%
Retired	15%	26%	20%	16%
Housing Tenure				
Own Home (w/ Mortgage)	31%	21%	23%	19%
Own Home (w/o Mortgage)	31%	17%	15%	19%
Rent	34%	59%	58%	60%
City Size				
Over 4,000,000	23%	34%	42%	38%
1,200,000 to 4,000,000	21%	24%	23%	23%
330,000 to 1,200,000	6%	8%	4%	7%
125,000 to 330,000	31%	20%	23%	16%
Under 125,000	19%	14%	8%	16%
Region				
Northeast	23%	34%	42%	38%
Midwest	21%	24%	23%	23%
South	6%	8%	4%	7%
West	31%	20%	23%	16%

Weighted averages over all household-quarters, 2006–2014. Data source: Bureau of Labor Statistics, Consumer Expenditure Surveys.

Poor English-speaking Hispanics have the second-highest median income out of the four racial and ethnic groups. This income figure is somewhat misleading, however, as English-speaking Hispanics also have significantly larger households than whites. At 3.32 members on average, these households' median per member income is only slightly over half that of white households. Household spending for English-speaking Hispanics is the second-highest out of the four groups—$7,726 per quarter or about $31,000 every year. English-speaking Hispanic households' spending-to-income ratio is very close to white households' (139 percent), suggesting similar reliance on credit and informal transfers. Poor English-speaking Hispanic households' socioeconomic characteristics suggest that they might be more durably poor than whites, however. These households have the lowest proportion of out-of-work heads (9 percent) and are much more likely to be poor despite employment (71 percent have a head who is currently working). Fewer of these households own their homes (about 38 percent), and a much greater portion holds no more than a high school degree (about 66 percent).

Black households and Spanish-speaking Hispanic households living in poverty have much worse socioeconomic indicators than the other two groups. For black households, median yearly income is only slightly more than two-thirds the amount for white households. Because black households are slightly larger than white households (2.64 members on average), their income per member is low compared to whites, although it is slightly higher than for English-speaking Hispanics. Black households' total spending is the lowest of the three groups ($6,660 per quarter or about $27,000 annually). Despite low spending, black households' spending-to-income ratio is the highest of the four groups (141 percent), suggesting that black households incur greater financial risk for an overall lower spending power. Like English-speaking Hispanics, black households' poverty appears less transitory than white households'. Black households are less likely than white households to own their homes (almost 60 percent are renters), are more likely to have no more than a high school education (58 percent of black households), and are more likely to be retired (26 percent of black households, the highest proportion out of the four groups).

Spanish-speaking Hispanic households are similar to black households in term of median income and total spending. Yet because Spanish-speaking Hispanic households are much larger (3.56 members on average), their income per member is the lowest (only $5,625 per household member, less than half the figure for white households). Importantly, this group has the lowest educational attainment (more than 60 percent of Spanish-speaking Hispanic household heads do not have a high school diploma). Figures for work status and homeownership are otherwise similar to those for English-speaking Hispanics.

Comparing Household Spending across the Poverty Line

These significant socioeconomic differences among white, black, and Hispanic households living in poverty provide important context for understanding racial and ethnic differences in food spending. Another important piece of contextual information comes from examining how food spending fits in households' overall budget. Figure 4.1 shows how poor and nonpoor households allocate their yearly spending across five core

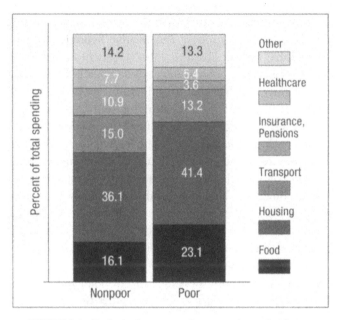

FIGURE 4.1. Budgets for poor and nonpoor households.

categories of goods and services: food, housing, transportation, personal insurance and pensions, and health care. The data used is from the last full available year of the CE (2013) and includes households from all four racial and ethnic groups examined.

The data presented in Figure 4.1 show that all households—regardless of whether they are poor or not—devote more than half of their spending to food and housing. Households spend the largest share of their resources on housing (more than a third of total spending). Food spending comes in second, making up approximately one fifth of total spending for an average income household. Of course, such broad categories mask important heterogeneity in spending across poor and nonpoor households. For instance, while housing is the largest category of spending for both poor and nonpoor households, the majority of nonpoor households' housing spending goes to owned housing, which is a form of wealth. By contrast, the majority of poor households' housing spending is devoted to rent, which does not lead to any asset accumulation.

What Figure 4.1 indicates is that poor households need to devote a greater share of their resources to basic goods and services than do nonpoor households. Housing, food, transportation, and health care made up about 83 percent of poor households' total spending in 2013, but only 75 percent of nonpoor households'. This lower relative spending on core essentials allows nonpoor households to invest in financial assets like pensions and personal insurance (almost 11 percent of spending for nonpoor households compared with only about 4 percent for poor households).

This information allows us to contextualize poor households' food spending. Poor households' higher relative spending on food is indicative of a situation with little financial leeway, where most resources need to be spent on necessities. It is important to note that poor households' greater *relative* spending on food actually hides lower *absolute* spending amounts. Poor households' total food spending totals approximately $1,191 per quarter, while nonpoor households' food spending totals approximately $1,850 per quarter. Poor households, in other words, are using more of their resources than nonpoor households for obtaining food, but are obtaining almost $2,500 less of it every year.

That devoting a large share of one's resources to buying food is a constrained choice driven in part by necessity can be seen more clearly when examining the relationship between household income and food spending. Panel 1 from Figure 4.2 shows the relationship between quarterly food spending and total household income. The vertical line shows the federal poverty threshold for a family of four in 2013 ($23,550). The solid curved line shows total food spending (groceries and eating out). To provide a comparison, the dashed curved line shows estimated spending on eating out only. Panel 2 provides similar information, but shows the *percentage* of total spending devoted to these food categories, rather than the total dollar amount.

As Panel 1 shows, the amount of money a household spends on food increases steadily as their income goes up. Most of this increase, however, is attributable to an increase in spending on food consumed at restaurants, fast-food outlets, cafés, and other out-of-home venues. By comparison, total spending on groceries (represented by the distance between the solid and the dashed lines) is relatively stable across income. What we see, in short, is that households with more money significantly increase their "convenience" food spending (eating out), but keep "utilitarian" food expenses (groceries) about constant.

These trends emerge even more clearly when we look at the portion of households' budgets devoted to different types of food spending. The most striking feature of Panel 2 is that despite the increase in total food spending shown in Panel 1, food's total share of households' budget drops precipitously with higher income. This decline is almost entirely due to a drop in the share of the household budget devoted to groceries. The share of total household spending devoted to food away from home remains roughly constant at about 5 percent of total spending across the entire income range.

Food Spending among Poor White, Black, and Hispanic Households

So far, the data have shown that social and economic disadvantage is associated with lower total food spending, with a greater proportion of food spending going to groceries (rather than eating out), and with having to devote a greater share of the household budget to food purchases. These trends can now be used to make sense of food spending patterns among white, black, and Hispanic households living in poverty.

The first panel of Figure 4.3 shows total quarterly spending on food for white, black, and Hispanic households with incomes below the federal poverty line, averaged over the entire 2006 to 2014 period. Even at such low income levels, we see considerable variation in food spending across the four racial and ethnic groups. White households, for example, spend almost a thousand dollars more than black households on food every year. In part, this is due to white households' higher spending on eating out—the highest amount out of the four groups. Black households spend the least on food overall, followed by Spanish-speaking Hispanic households. White households and English-speaking Hispanics households have comparable levels of total food spending, despite the fact that English-speaking Hispanic households are nearly one and a half times as large as white households. Compared with whites, however, more of Hispanic households' food spending is devoted to groceries.

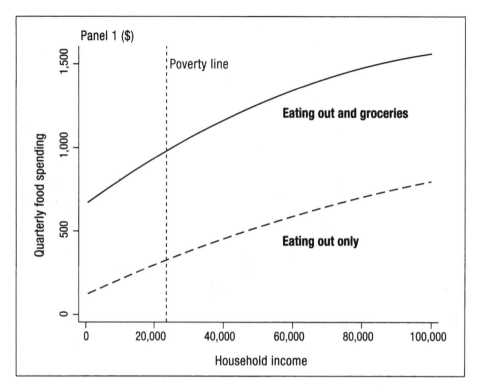

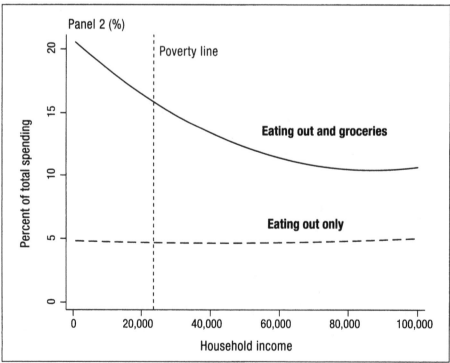

FIGURE 4.2. Food spending across income.

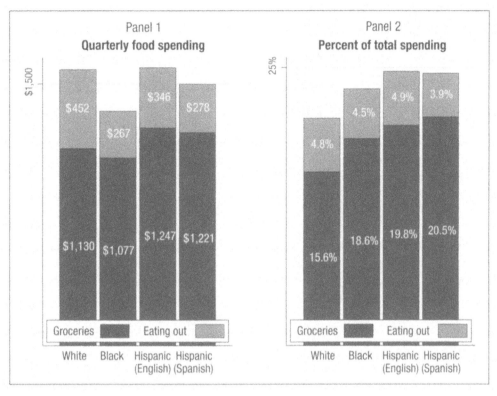

FIGURE 4.3. Food spending for households living in poverty.

The second panel of Figure 4.3 shows food spending for the four groups as a proportion of their total spending. Despite white households' relatively high food spending, food purchases actually represent a smaller portion of their total spending relative to other households. By contrast, black households' low food spending represents a relatively high portion of their total expenditures. Hispanic households devoted the highest share of their income to food. These differences are almost entirely attributable to differences in grocery purchases; the share of spending households devote to eating out is roughly constant across racial and ethnic groups. Most of the difference in budget shares for food among poor households, in other words, is likely due to differences in the constraints these households face.

Overall, these trends suggest that poor white households are comparatively advantaged in terms of the burden food spending represents for them. Black households fare much worse, with relatively low spending (which can indicate low quantity or quality of food) still representing a relatively large financial burden. Hispanic households are also relatively burdened by their food spending. For both Hispanic groups, however, this is arguably a function of larger household sizes. Among Hispanics, the data reveal considerable heterogeneity. Spanish-speaking Hispanic households spend less on and are more burdened by grocery expenditures than English-speaking Hispanic households. Variation in the amounts spent on food away from home supports this general interpretation, with white households having the highest percentage of their total food spending devoted to food away from home (about 29 percent, compared to

19 percent for Spanish-speaking Hispanics, 20 percent for blacks, and 22 percent for English-speaking Hispanics).

Overall then, white households' food consumption patterns suggest that they have the least constrained access to food out of the four groups. These households spend more on groceries and on eating out, but are less financially burdened than other groups by these expenditures. English-speaking Hispanic households are the most similar to whites on these dimensions, with similar spending levels, but greater financial burdens. Black households and Spanish-speaking Hispanic households fare poorly, both being relatively highly burdened by their food spending, but having relatively low spending amounts, especially on a per capita basis.

Food Spending over Time for Poor and Nonpoor Households

Living in poverty means having to use a large portion of your resources for meeting basic needs. As shown above, this problem is considerably worse for households of color, who must use more of their resources than whites toward buying food, even when the actual amount acquired (measured in dollars) is smaller. In this section, I briefly discuss trends in food-related financial burdens over the 2006 to 2014 period, which covers the foreclosure crisis, the financial crisis, and the economic recession that followed them. As above, the basis for this discussion is household spending data from by the Consumer Expenditure Survey.

Spending on groceries went up for both poor and nonpoor households and the rate of increase was larger for households living in poverty. Nevertheless, nonpoor households consistently spent more on groceries than poor household through the entire 2006 to 2014 period. For nonpoor households, spending increased by about 12 percent between 2007 and 2012 and has since remained stable at this increased level. Grocery spending for poor households also increased between 2007 and 2012 but at a much sharper rate, with spending reaching 19 percent higher than the 2007 level at its peak. In 2014, grocery spending for poor households remained 16 percent greater than it had been in 2007.

Examining the budget shares devoted to grocery spending across the same period reveals that poor households were consistently more burdened by food spending than were nonpoor households, despite their lower spending levels. For poor households, the proportion of spending devoted to groceries increased slightly between 2010 and 2013, but had returned to precrisis levels by 2014. For nonpoor households, data show a very slight increase in the share of spending devoted to groceries over the whole period. Overall, however, the gap between poor and nonpoor households in the proportion of their budget devoted to food stayed large and roughly constant between 2006 and 2014.

Taken together, these patterns suggest that the financial crisis was associated with a substantial initial increase in food prices. Nonpoor households were able to absorb this increase through most of the subsequent recession, likely by engaging in strategies to cut food costs, and by reducing nonfood spending and devoting more resources to food. Poor households, by contrast, were not able to control rising food prices, likely because they had already been engaging in strategies to cut down food costs and had very little superfluous consumption to cut. Food spending kept a relatively stable share of spending for poor households over the period, suggesting they were not as successful in shifting their budget around and instead saw their total spending increase significantly, putting them in financially more precarious positions.

Food Spending over Time for Poor White, Black, and Hispanic Households

With 2006 to 2014 trends in poor and nonpoor households' food spending in mind, we can turn to poor white, black, and Hispanic households' food spending across the same period. Differences in food spending across the four groups were remarkably stable across the housing crisis and the recession. Black households spent the least on groceries in every year examined, followed by white households, and then by Hispanic households. These data do reveal, however, that the previously noted similarities in English- and Spanish-speaking Hispanic households' food spending are a recent (and possibly temporary) trend. English-speaking Hispanics actually spent considerably less on groceries than Spanish-speaking Hispanics for most years between 2006 and 2014.

Examining change over time, the data suggest that spending patterns across 2006–2014 for poor white households are similar to those reported by households living above the poverty line. After an initial spike in food spending in 2007, spending levels recede slightly and stay roughly stable until 2011, at which point they begin to increase again. Black households' spending trends are somewhat similar, although the increase in spending after 2010 is faster than for white households, leaving blacks and whites with a much smaller average difference in spending in 2014 than at any previous time since 2006.

For English-speaking Hispanic households, spending patterns correspond more closely to the general pattern for households living in poverty. Food spending increases steadily until 2010, after which point spending remains high relative to pre–financial crisis levels. For Spanish-speaking Hispanics, we observe the largest increases of all four groups in 2007, followed by a slow return to precrisis spending levels. Estimates from the first quarter of 2014 suggest that spending was on the increase again at the beginning of the year.

Examining budget shares for grocery spending for the four racial and ethnic groups over the same period helps contextualize these findings. The trends show a clear differentiation among the four groups. White households are consistently less financially burdened by food expenditures than other households. This is true across the entire period, even though the share of white households' expenditures going to groceries increases slightly over the period. At between 14 percent and 16 percent, poor whites' budget share for groceries through the period is roughly comparable to that of nonpoor households. By contrast, Spanish-speaking Hispanic households are consistently more burdened than other households by their food spending. Grocery spending for Spanish-speaking Hispanics represents more than 20 percent of all expenditures over the entire period. Black households and English-speaking Hispanic households have comparable burdens over the entire period. In terms of total burden, these two groups are in an intermediary position between white and Spanish-speaking households. Given that black households have the lowest spending levels of the four groups, this intermediate burden level indicates a particularly difficult financial situation.

Overall, the trends over time indicate little movement in the relative position of the four groups but do suggest a slight increase in the total financial burden represented by food expenditures for all groups. Groups that entered the financial crisis in a position of relative advantage (whites) found themselves in the same position of relative advantage at the end of the period. The same holds true for the relatively disadvantaged groups. The relative inequality between the groups also does not appear to have changed significantly across the period, at least in terms of food spending. Inequalities in other domains, such as financial precarity or overall consumption levels, may have increased significantly, however, which could impact households' long-term food security in ways that are not captured here.

Food spending is a central part of any households' budget. For poor households in particular, putting food on the table can mean having to engage in all sorts of sacrifices. Yet, the extent to which poor households are able to make ends meet depends in important ways on their broader social context. Race and ethnicity are among the more important predictors of social situation in the United States. Understanding racial and ethnic differences in food spending, therefore, is an important means of understanding inequality in food access.

To understand racial and ethnic differences in food spending, this chapter first provided contextual information on poor and nonpoor households' food expenditures. This allowed me to make three key observations. First, the total amount spent on groceries by a given household is relatively stable across income, meaning that increases in food spending are more likely to be driven by external constraints than household preferences. Second, the proportion of money spent on eating out is a reasonable indicator of how much discretionary spending a household is able to engage in. And third, the percentage of their total spending a household devotes to food is a reasonable measure of the financial burden food represents for them. With these broad observations in hand, we can make sense of empirical trends in poor white, black, and Hispanic households' food spending.

First, poor white households appear to be in a much more favorable position in terms of food access than poor nonwhite households. White households spend more on food than nonwhite households, are less financially burdened by their food spending than nonwhite households, and are able to engage in a greater amount of discretionary food spending than nonwhite households. While poor white households' food spending profile show signs of significant worsening as a result of the financial crisis and the recession that followed it, their position relative to nonwhites has stayed the same or has even improved slightly over the 2006 to 2014 period. Overall, poor whites' food spending profile appears more similar to the food spending profile for nonpoor households than to the spending profile of nonwhite households living in poverty.

Among nonwhite households, there is considerable heterogeneity in food spending. English-speaking Hispanic households have relatively high food spending, but given their higher overall income and higher overall spending, they were also relatively less financially burdened and enjoyed a greater share of discretionary food spending when compared with black and Spanish-speaking Hispanic households. Black and Spanish-speaking Hispanic households both fare poorly when compared to the other two groups. While food spending represents a similar or slightly higher burden for black households compared with English-speaking Hispanic households over the period studied, their overall food spending and their discretionary food spending are much lower. The evidence presented here suggests that Spanish-speaking households fare the worst in terms of food spending profiles. The financial burden of food spending was highest for Spanish-speaking households through the entire period, while discretionary food spending was lowest.

Overall, the data on food spending patterns among white, black, and Hispanic households presented in this chapter strongly suggest that inequalities in households' ability to access quality food are consistent with broader social and economic inequalities in the United States. Access to food issues do not arise in a vacuum. They are powerfully shaped by the social context in which households find themselves. Efforts to alleviate food security and food access problems for poor households, in other words, need to take into account the unique forms of social and economic disadvantages that systemic racism and citizenship-based exclusion impose on blacks and Hispanics relative to whites.

REFERENCES

Allard, Scott W. 2009. *Out of Reach: Place, Poverty, and the New American Welfare State*. New Haven, CT: Yale University Press.

Barr, Michael S. 2012. *No Slack: The Financial Lives of Low-Income Americans*. Washington, DC: Brookings Institution Press.

Blanchflower, David G., Phillip B. Levine, and David J. Zimmerman. 2003. "Discrimination in the Small-Business Credit Market." *Review of Economics and Statistics* 85 (4): 930–43.

Desmond, Matthew. 2012. "Disposable Ties and the Urban Poor." *American Journal of Sociology* 117 (5): 1295–335.

Fairlie, Robert W., and Alicia M. Robb. 2007. "Why Are Black-Owned Businesses Less Successful Than White-Owned Businesses? The Role of Families, Inheritances, and Business Human Capital." *Journal of Labor Economics* 25 (2): 289–323.

Fording, Richard C., Sanford Schram, and Joe Soss. 2011. *Disciplining the Poor: Neoliberal Paternalism and the Persistent Power of Race*. Chicago: University of Chicago Press.

Kalleberg, Arne L. 2011. *Good Jobs, Bad Jobs: The Rise of Polarized and Precarious Employment Systems in the United States, 1970s to 2000s*. New York: Russell Sage Foundation.

Keister, Lisa A., Jody Agius Vallejo, and E. Paige Borelli. 2015. "Mexican American Mobility: Early Life Processes and Adult Wealth Ownership." *Social Forces* 93 (3): 1015–46.

Krivo, Lauren Joy, and Robert L. Kaufman. 2004. "Housing and Wealth Inequality: Racial-Ethnic Differences in Home Equity in the United States." *Demography* 41 (3): 585–605.

McCall, Leslie. 2001. "Sources of Racial Wage Inequality in Metropolitan Labor Markets: Racial, Ethnic, and Gender Differences." *American Sociological Review* 66 (4): 520–41.

Morgan, Kimberly J., and Andrea Louise Campbell. 2011. *The Delegated Welfare State: Medicare, Markets, and the Governance of Social Policy*. New York: Oxford University Press.

Pager, Devah, Bruce Western, and Bart Bonikowski. 2009. "Discrimination in a Low-Wage Labor Market: A Field Experiment." *American Sociological Review* 74 (5): 777–99.

Powell, Lisa M., Sandy Slater, Donka Mirtcheva, Yanjun Bao, and Frank J. Chaloupka. 2007. "Food Store Availability and Neighborhood Characteristics in the United States." *Preventive Medicine* 44 (3): 189–95.

Richardson, Andrea S., Jane Boone-Heinonen, Barry M. Popkin, and Penny Gordon-Larsen. 2012. "Are Neighbourhood Food Resources Distributed Inequitably by Income and Race in the USA? Epidemiological Findings across the Urban Spectrum." BMJ Open 2 (2): 1–9.

Rugh, Jacob S., and Douglas S. Massey. 2010. "Racial Segregation and the American Foreclosure Crisis." *American Sociological Review* 75 (5): 629–51.

Shapiro, Thomas M. 2004. *The Hidden Cost of Being African American: How Wealth Perpetuates Inequality.* New York: Oxford University Press.

Small, Mario Luis, and Monica McDermott. 2006. "The Presence of Organizational Resources in Poor Urban Neighborhoods: An Analysis of Average and Contextual Effects." *Social Forces* 84 (3): 1697–724.

Smith, Sandra Susan. 2007. *Lone Pursuit: Distrust and Defensive Individualism among the Black Poor.* New York: Russell Sage Foundation.

Stainback, Kevin, and Donald Tomaskovic-Devey. 2012. *Documenting Desegregation: Racial and Gender Segregation in Private-Sector Employment since the Civil Rights Act.* New York: Russell Sage Foundation.

Walker, Renee E., Craig S. Fryer, James Butler, Christopher R. Keane, Andrea Kriska, and Jessica G. Burke. 2011. "Factors Influencing Food Buying Practices in Residents of a Low-Income Food Desert and a Low-Income Food Oasis." *Journal of Mixed Methods Research* 5 (3): 247–67.

5

The Geography of Risk

A Case Study of Food Insecurity, Poverty, and Food Assistance between the Urban and the Rural

MICHAEL D. GILLESPIE

A growing body of research explores the relationship between geographic place and risk factors for impoverishment and hunger, especially various environmental and community conditions (Lichter and Brown 2011; Tickamyer 2006). As poverty grows in the general population and for particular demographic groups, the ability of individuals and family households to avoid food insecurity depends on the geographic distribution of resources. In result, the use of geography within sociological studies of inequality have emerged as a theme to compare where such conditions are more or less prominent (Lobao, Hooks, and Tickamyer 2007a). The increasing incidence of poverty in suburban spaces—moving from central cities—and renewed interest in sustained poverty found in remote rural America make these essential geographies on which to focus research (Kneebone and Berube 2013; Reardon and Bischoff 2011); however, for those who live unstably above the federal poverty threshold, areas that exist between central and suburban cities and remote countryside also hold insecurities and risk.

This chapter is a case study of the prevalence of poverty and food insecurity in one of fourteen counties served by the Eastern Illinois Foodbank. Through a descriptive statistical analysis using common community demographic indicators and US Census Bureau data supported by qualitative descriptions, I explore the geographic distribution of poverty, food insecurity, and food assistance within Coles County, Illinois, as well as comparatively to the region, state, and nation.

Food Insecurity Research for Micropolitan Geographies

The importance of the geographic—or "place-based"—conditions of existence that impact poverty and food insecurity have been established (Garasky, Morton, and Greder 2004; Gieryn 2000). Intensive reviews that have anchored the characteristics of individuals and families with the specific structural context of poverty and food insecurity highlight the importance of including the community or county in the sociological analysis of poverty and food insecurity (Allard 2013; Lobao, Hooks, and Tickamyer

2007b; Logan 2012; Sharkey 2013). However, poverty and food insecurity, continually assessed for metropolitan and central cities, inner-ring suburbs, and remote rural places such as Appalachia, the US South, and Native American reservations (Duncan 1996; Kneebone and Berube 2013), also exists at disproportionate levels in less-analyzed micropolitan communities.

In 2013, there were 536 designated micropolitan areas in the United States that exhibit essential geographic relations: urban clusters with dense populations surrounded by tracts of sparse rural spaces. By definition, micropolitan regions are considered an urban cluster, a geographic area based on a core population of at least twenty-five hundred persons but fewer than fifty thousand persons. Furthermore, these regions consist of one or more core counties and any adjacent counties that have a high degree of social and economic integration (as measured by commuting to work), and as such, seem to be an important focal point for research (Office of Management and Budget 2013; US Census Bureau 2011). Micropolitan areas, like Coles County, Illinois, which lack large urban centers and formal suburban metropolitan areas, but by definition are not rural, exist in the gap between the typical urban/rural duality common to poverty and food insecurity research (Lichter and Brown 2011). Coles County is an exemplar micropolitan region, serving as a central county with a densely settled core, and is an integral entity providing public and private services, employment, and other points of social and economic necessity for adjacent outlying counties.

Food Insecurity, Food Assistance, and Geography

Food security is a household condition in which all members at all times have access to enough food for an active, healthy life. Households that experience food insecurity have problems accessing food and experience a reduction in the quality of their diet; in the extreme, food insecure households have multiple indications of reduced food intake and disrupted eating patterns due to inadequate resources to acquire food (Coleman-Jensen, Gregory, and Singh 2014). Common characteristics of food insecure households include those with dependent children, especially five years of age and younger, households headed by a single parent, nonwhite households, and low-income households, specifically with annual incomes below 185 percent of the poverty threshold; these household conditions mirror those risk factors for an increased risk of poverty (Coleman-Jensen, Gregory, and Singh 2014; DeNavas-Walt and Proctor 2014).

Food insecurity, like poverty, is directly related to income. Even with annual household incomes above the federal poverty threshold, costs of living and stagnation in the growth of wages lends to family households finding it more difficult to make ends meet. Low-income family households with annual earnings above the federal poverty threshold often participate in one or more public assistance programs including Temporary Aid for Needy Families (TANF), the Supplemental Nutrition Assistance Program (SNAP; formerly food stamps), Housing Assistance, Supplemental Security Income (SSI), the Special Supplemental Nutrition Program for Women, Infants, and Children (WIC), Unemployment Insurance (UI), federal- or state-sponsored public health insurance programs (Medicaid), and, if employed, the Earned Income Tax Credit (EITC) (Halpern-Meekin et al. 2015; Seefeldt and Graham 2013). In

2013, for example, more than three in five households (62.2 percent) who are classified as food insecure and with incomes less than 185 percent of the federal poverty threshold participated in at least one federal food and nutrition assistance program (Coleman-Jensen, Gregory, and Singh 2014; Poppendieck 2014).

Food insecurity for individuals and households can be considered a condition of relative poverty complete with life experiences marked by real and perceived insecurity and with income levels less than twice the federal poverty line. The increased risk for family households with incomes below 185 percent of poverty, established by research and evaluation of federal food programs (Coleman-Jensen, Gregory, and Singh 2014), provides a distinct baseline to compare potential barriers for obtaining and utilizing a nutritionally adequate diet relative to acceptable dietary standards. All poor families, however, are not necessarily food insecure owing in part to the patchwork of social services; likewise, not all food insecure families have incomes near the poverty threshold but are limited in their access to public food assistance (Gundersen, Kreider, and Pepper 2011). Many federal nutrition programs, acknowledging the increased risk of families and households above the federal poverty threshold, have income limits—means tests—at various levels including 130 percent of poverty for SNAP, which is the only food assistance program for the general population. Other programs, such as reduced-price school meal programs and WIC, have a higher income limit of 185 percent of poverty but serve specific populations. States do have some flexibility to establish means tests for other social services, and the State of Illinois Department of Human Services allows individuals and families with incomes up to 185 percent of poverty to receive the services of nonpublic services from food pantries, soup kitchens, and homeless shelters.

Family households with incomes above, but near, the federal poverty threshold are also at an increased risk of experiencing a poverty spell: a temporary, often short-term cycle when a family household experiences a loss of income placing them at or below the federal poverty threshold (Bane and Ellwood 1986). More households experience a single or a few poverty spells than extended periods of long-term or intergenerational poverty, and these are often the result of a job loss or reduction in work hours; a change in family structure such as a divorce, separation, or death; declines in welfare or social assistance income; or some unexpected event like a change in health status and increased medical costs, or increased maintenance costs for unplanned home or automobile repairs (Blank and Barr 2009; Hays 2003).

There is some opposition to the idea that food insecurity and poverty are related, let alone that food insecurity can be a measure of relative poverty placing someone at risk of experiencing a poverty spell. Because of perceived consumption activities of the poor and near poor in the United States, for example, Rector and Sheffield (2011) argue that, globally, these households have much more access to, and ownership of, consumer goods and services compared to poor persons around the world. The presence of amenities in low-wage and poor households such as microwaves and air conditioning units, as well as entertainment conveniences like DVD players and video gaming systems, regardless of their age (older models) or how they were obtained (including secondhand, by resale, or as gifts), according to Rector and Sheffield, are evidence that poverty in the United States is an indication of affluence compared to impoverished groups in less prosperous societies. But standards of living are not the same in underdeveloped, developing, and economically advanced countries, making this attention on the consumer choices of poor and near-poor individuals and families in the United States shortsighted. Any measure of insecurity should be based on the country's own standard of living and stage of development; contrasting globally incomparable subsistence levels ignores the importance of including geography in the analysis of poverty and reinforces an enduring historical skepticism of the "undeserving poor" with inappropriate cultural behaviors (Katz 1986; Katz 2013).

In reality, despite ownership of, or access to, goods and services, these households are situated in social and geographic conditions of existence where a poverty spell may be one life circumstance away. Proponents for understanding the relationship between food insecurity and poverty, especially for those with incomes above the poverty threshold, argue that acquiring adequate and healthful food challenges households to balance their most basic human needs with the practical strains of where food assistance agencies are geographically located, as well as economic pressures with increasing transportation, housing, and health care costs (Halpern-Meekin et al. 2015). For example, according to the US Department of Agriculture (USDA), the ability to meet even the most basic healthful food diet, let alone a thrifty, minimum subsistence food plan, places the poor and near poor in stark contrast to individuals and families above the 185 percent income level. Across all households, the median weekly spending on food per person is $50.00, 16 percent higher than the cost of the minimum subsistence thrifty food plan used to determine food stamp benefit levels. However, for food insecure households with incomes lower than 185 percent of the federal poverty threshold, the median weekly food budget per person is $37.50, approximately 6 percent less than the minimal thrifty food plan (Coleman-Jensen, Gregory, and Singh 2014).

In summary, the concept of food insecurity is an adequate proxy for poverty, especially in relation to the ability to meet basic human needs and the quality, reliability, and geographic proximity of resources available to obtain food. While not all low-income family households are food insecure, income levels relative to the official poverty line can represent a risk threshold for food insecurity as well as an increased chance for an individual or family unit to fall into poverty, even for a brief period.

Measuring Poverty and Food Insecurity

Data that report the number and percentage of the population in poverty or at risk of food insecurity are based on income. For example, in 2013, the poverty threshold for an individual was $11,888; therefore if an individual's annual income is less than this value, that person is considered officially poor. By comparison, for a family household of four with two adults and two children in 2013, the poverty threshold was $23,624 (DeNavas-Walt and Proctor 2014).

The second income level, 185 percent of poverty, is 1.85 times the level of income based on the size of the family household. This food insecurity line represents the level of income where individuals and families are at increased risk of not being able to provide enough food for all family members (Coleman-Jensen, Gregory, and Singh

2014). For 2013, the food insecurity line for individuals is $21,993, and for a family of four with two adults and two children it is $43,704. Both the poverty line and the food insecurity line will be analyzed for individuals because poverty is measured and recorded at the family household level. Using the percentage of individuals ensures that all members of a family are counted, regardless of age, and whether someone lives alone or with one or more related individuals.

There are noted inconsistencies and validity issues with using Census Bureau estimates of poverty, but for statistical and reporting purposes, the thresholds are the key statistical and computation measurement of poverty and income used in official government documents. Historical and contemporary issues with the official poverty measure are well documented (Short 2013) but purposefully utilized here because they remain the official measure of impoverishment (for specific poverty definitions, see the technical document US Census Bureau 2013).

As a method for comparative data inquiry and evaluation, these descriptive data, including percentages and income ratios, are incorporated into maps in order to visualize statistical evidence. This descriptive analysis uses the census tract as the unit of analysis; a census tract is the smallest geographic unit, based on population size, within each county that guarantees intraregion and intracounty comparisons can be reliably estimated. Census tracts represent small, relatively permanent subdivisions of a county and generally have a population size between twelve hundred and eight thousand people, with an ideal size of four thousand people. Census tracts are not as direct a representation of neighborhoods as the block-group level—areas commonly available for dense urban populations—rather, census tracts are adequate measures of subcounty level comparisons (Logan 2012).

Data available through the American Community Survey (ACS) produced by the US Census Bureau allows for poverty and the risk of food insecurity to be analyzed across geographic areas, including between census tracts within Coles County and between the counties included in the Eastern Illinois Foodbank service area. Because many of these areas are rural with small populations, these data are available in five-year averages, which produce more consistent and reliable estimates (US Census Bureau 2006).

Coles County and the East-Central Illinois Region

This chapter provides a case study of one county to describe inequalities in micropolitan geographies and argues that we should also consider these places, which often bridge the urban and the rural. The target county for this case study, Coles County, Illinois, is ideal for analysis as it has recently been designated as "at-risk" by both the regional food bank and by the Social IMPACT Research Center (2013), a statewide research think tank.

Coles County is located in east-central Illinois in a fourteen-county region served by the Eastern Illinois Foodbank (EIF).[1] The food bank is based in Urbana, Illinois, in Champaign County, the largest county in the region. The fourteen counties served by the EIF in 2013 are diverse in their population size and levels of poverty; Champaign County, home to the University of Illinois, is the most populous, with 187,274 persons, and Jasper County is remote and rural, with only 9,526 in population. Piatt

County, although classified as metropolitan, has the lowest poverty level, 6.23 percent, close to rural Jasper County (6.63 percent). The highest percentage of the population in poverty for the region is found in Champaign County (22.26 percent) and micropolitan Coles County (21.99 percent).

Coles County, like most micropolitan regions, has characteristics in common with both urban and rural spaces. For example, it has a midrange population of 53,732 persons but does retain an urban cluster that is interdependent with rural areas inside and outside of the county's borders. Like larger metropolitan areas, there are small, centralized, population-dense census tracts, but like rural counties, there are large, outlying tracts where populations are less concentrated. Geographically, Coles County has a higher proportion of the population who reside in rural areas compared to the state and country, but fewer than the region as a whole.

As shown in Table 5.1, Coles County is demographically racially homogeneous, with nearly 95 percent of the population identifying as white, non-Hispanic; there is a slight majority of females (52.07 percent), the median age of thirty-two years is lower given the presence of a regional state university, but over 80 percent of the population is eighteen years of age or older.

Further, like urban areas, employment opportunities, entertainment, and personal services are also centralized in Coles County, providing "metropolitan functions" for county and area residents (Brown, Cromartie, and Kulcsar 2004). All the major employers in the county are based in one of the two principal cities, Charleston or Mattoon. The largest employer in the county, in Mattoon, is a regional hospital system, which has less than two-thousand employees ranging from highly skilled physicians to hourly support and service positions. The second largest employer in the county, located in Charleston, is a midsize regional public university with approximately sixteen hundred full-time and two hundred part-time employees in a wide range of skill- and credential-based positions as well as hourly and temporary workers. The two remaining employers with substantial positions are both in Mattoon; the first is a private printing and production company with approximately one thousand positions, and the second is a small community college maintained by roughly one thousand educators, professionals, and support staff. The remainder of the county's industry relies heavily on the manufacturing, production, and utility sectors, as well as municipal offices, and commercial and private farms.

This local micropolitan economy generates a wide disparity in median household and family incomes; by comparison, Coles County is a low-wage micropolitan area with a median income of only $37,400, contrasted with nearly $47,000 for the region, and $57,000 for the state; the level of unemployment, however, is comparable to the region and the state. Given the nature of employers and available positions in the county—a characteristically micropolitan transitioning economy (Cortes, Davidson, and McKinnis 2015)—the contrast of low unemployment with the concentration of low-wages means that people are able to find some level of work, but at wages that produce lagging median household and family incomes.

This brief demographic and economic snapshot of Coles County provides justification for micropolitan statistical areas to be better incorporated in food insecurity and poverty research if we are to fully comprehend the depth and breadth of insecurity in all regions of the country.

TABLE 5.1. Demographics

	U.S.	Illinois	Region	Coles Co.
Total Population	311,536,594	12,848,554	520,904	53,732
Percent of the Population Living in Rural Areas	19.27%	11.51%	35.17%	24.29%
Male	49.19%	49.06%	49.50%	47.93%
Female	50.81%	50.94%	50.50%	52.07%
Median Age	37.3 years	36.8 years	40.3 years	32 years
18 years and older	76.29%	75.98%	78.68%	81.79%
White	76.40%	74.32%	87.39%	94.73%
African-American	13.64%	15.33%	8.50%	4.64%
American Indian / Alaska Native	1.65%	0.66%	0.62%	0.65%
Asian	5.73%	5.35%	4.46%	1.31%
Native Hawaiian / Pacific Islander	0.38%	0.09%	0.05%	0.10%
Other Race	5.26%	6.45%	0.92%	0.60%
Hispanic/Latino (of any race)	16.62%	16.04%	3.90%	2.21%
Median Income - All Households	$53,046	$56,797	$46,843	$37,040
Median Income - Family Households	$64,719	$70,344	$58,682	$53,465
Annual Average Unemployment Rate, 2013	7.4%	9.1%	8.4%	8.8%
Poor Individuals	15.37%	14.13%	18.27%	21.99%
Poor Families (All)	11.30%	10.30%	10.53%	13.00%
Poor Families with Children	17.83%	16.43%	18.56%	22.50%
Food Insecure Individuals	31.58%	29.09%	35.38%	42.48%
Food Insecure Families (All)	25.09%	22.86%	24.92%	31.10%
Food Insecure Families with Children	35.64%	33.11%	38.42%	46.54%
Percent of All Households Receiving Cash Assistance and/or SNAP	13.15%	12.57%	11.90%	15.05%

Sources: U.S. Census Bureau ACS 2009–2013 5-Year Estimates; U.S. Census Bureau Urban and Rural Classification Data; Bureau of Labor Statistics Local Area Unemployment Estimates

Demographic Comparison

As previously discussed, Table 5.1 compares the United States, the state of Illinois, the eastern Illinois region, and Coles County along traditional demographic measures including sex, age, race and ethnicity, and income; further included are common indicators of economic status including unemployment and poverty rates, as are the percentage of the population at risk of food insecurity for individuals, families, and families with children.

Given that Coles County is a micropolitan geographic area, it shares characteristics with both centralized, dense urban areas as well as large rural areas with small populations. Of the fourteen counties that composed the east-central Illinois region in 2013, which include urban metropolitan areas as well as rural spaces, individuals, families, and families with children in Coles County are also more likely to be poor and at risk of food insecurity compared to the region, state, and nation. More than one in five individuals (21.99 percent), one in seven families (13.00 percent), and one in five families with children (22.50 percent) have annual incomes below the federal poverty threshold. Moreover, more than two in five individuals (42.48 percent), nearly one-third of all families (31.10 percent) and one-half of families with children (46.54 percent) are at risk of food insecurity, with annual incomes below 185 percent of poverty. Especially for families with children, the difference in this level of risk between Coles County and the region (8.12 percentage points), the state (13.43 percentage points), and the nation (10.90 percentage points) mirrors the disparity in median family and household incomes. As discussed above, persons are as likely to be employed in Coles County as throughout the region and the state, but the typical household and family income reinforce the lower wages of, and increased risk for, county residents. This relationship has been found in other micropolitan areas because, commonly, they exhibit a regional economy that is restrained by the nature of employment available with little growth, diversification, or expansion (Cortes, Davidson, and McKinnis 2015).

Figure 5.1 shows the percentage of the population in poverty and those at risk of food insecurity across the fourteen counties of the eastern Illinois region. The level of poverty for Coles County in comparison to the other counties in the region is elevated but near the level of Champaign and Vermillion Counties (the two largest counties by population and classified as metropolitan statistical areas). Coles County, the only micropolitan statistical area in the region, is the sole county with a level of risk for food insecurity above 40 percent; the remaining eleven counties are designated rural areas and have similar poverty rates.

Given these levels of poverty and food insecurity, it would be expected that public social and food assistance programs would be utilized. However, referring to Table 5.1, only 15 percent of Coles County households receive any form of public assistance, a one to three percentage point difference compared to the region, state, and country. Furthermore, only 37.46 percent of poor households in Coles County receive SNAP, a figure equal to the regional level, but nearly nine percentage points behind the state and country. These statistics for the level of utilization of publicly available social welfare programs in Coles County is clearly lower than the heightened level of poverty and food insecurity found in the county.

Juxtaposed to public assistance, the latest analysis of data collected in 2013 for the national, state, and regional network of food banks (Feeding America 2014a; Feeding America 2014b; Feeding America 2014c) shows that 72 percent of food bank clients nationwide, 70 percent in Illinois, and 72.3 percent in the eastern Illinois region have

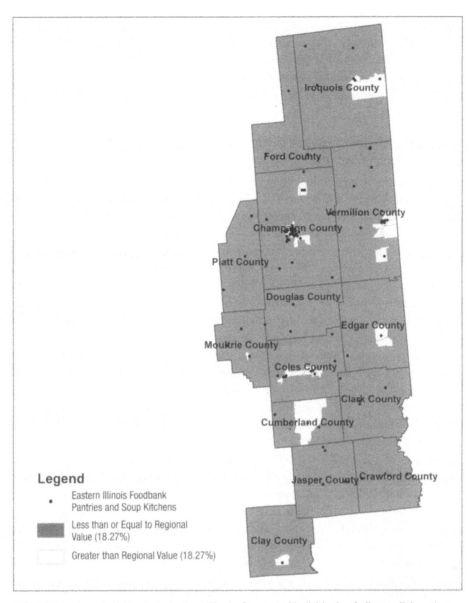

FIGURE 5.1. Poor individuals in eastern Illinois. Percent of individuals of all ages living at or below 100% of poverty eastern Illinois counties by census tract. Census tracts above and below the percentage for the Eastern Illinois Foodbank service area (18.27%). Data from US Census Bureau, American FactFinder database, 2009–2013, 5-Year Estimates. *factfinder. census.gov*

household incomes below the poverty threshold. Further, only 55 percent of clients nationwide, 58.2 percent in Illinois, and 63.2 percent in the region receive SNAP benefits. Finally, across the nation, 28 percent of food bank clients have incomes above the eligibility level to receive SNAP benefits, compared to 37 percent in Illinois and 43.4 percent in the region. While county-level food bank data is not available, based on these comparisons and the poverty and food insecurity indicators for Coles County, it is expected that each of these measures would be higher for food bank clients that receive assistance from food pantries and soup kitchens in Coles County. With higher numbers of persons seeking assistance within their community rather than through governmental programs, it is important to consider how insecure households access these resources.

Regional and County-Based Comparisons of Poverty and Food Insecurity

In this context, the geographic distribution of poverty and food insecurity can be analyzed across the region and within Coles County. Because the percentage of individuals who are poor are included in the percentage of individuals at risk of food insecurity, the following description focuses on the later—the food insecure population.

Figure 5.2 illustrates the percentage of the population by census tract that have incomes below 185 percent of poverty compared to the percentage of the population at risk across the entire region, 35.38 percent. The risk of food insecurity at the county level, as explored in Figure 5.2, is more unevenly distributed than poverty across the region; but at the census tract level only four of the fourteen counties do not have at least one census tract above the 35.38 percent regional value of food insecurity risk. The most prominent counties remain the metropolitan Champaign and Vermillion Counties, and again the micropolitan Coles County mirrors the increased risk found in these larger counties. Only four rural counties have one or two tracts with elevated food insecurity risk, but an outlier rural county, Edgar County, has nearly 40 percent of its population at risk while the percentage in poverty is similar to the other rural counties in the region (see Figure 5.1).

To assess the proximity of food assistance agencies with food insecure populations, Figure 5.2 also includes as a marker for each food bank partner in the region, whether there is a food pantry or soup kitchen. Overlaying the location of these services with areas that have populations with an increased risk of food insecurity highlights the geography of food assistance and need. Regionally, food pantries and soup kitchens are located in tracts with both elevated and nonelevated risk but are more prominent in metropolitan Champaign (thirty-six agencies) and Vermillion (fourteen agencies) Counties. Only one county, Clay, has a single agency, whereas the remaining rural counties have at least three food pantries and/or soup kitchens. Coles County, being micropolitan, but with the highest level of risk, has only ten agencies, eight of which are located in areas with the densest populations.

Another consideration for the availability of food relief through pantries and soup kitchens is the number of individuals at risk of food insecurity compared to the number of food bank partner agencies in the county. For example, in Coles County there are ten agencies but 20,922 individuals at risk, which means the ratio of potential insecure individuals for each community pantry or soup kitchen is approximately 2,092 individuals. This ratio, weighed against that for the other counties in the region, is the third highest and one of only three with ratios over two thousand persons per agency; the two counties with larger ratios are Clay County, which only has one pantry, and Edgar County, which has three agencies and the second-highest percentage of the population at risk of food insecurity behind Coles County.

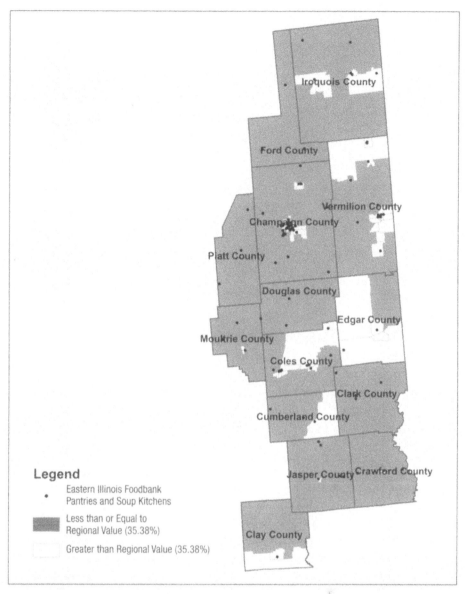

FIGURE 5.2. Food insecure individuals in eastern Illinois. Percent of individuals of all ages living at or below 185% of poverty eastern Illinois counties by census tract. Census tracts above and below the percentage for the Eastern Illinois Foodbank service area (35.38%). Data from US Census Bureau, American FactFinder database, 2009–2013, 5-Year Estimates. *factfinder.census.gov*

Coles County Census Tracts

Coles County, with the highest percentage of individuals at risk of food insecurity within the region, and with risk levels higher than the state and national values, has a demonstrated level of need for food assistance programs. Figure 5.3 focuses in on the county and shows each census tract with the percentage of the tracts' population who

FIGURE 5.3. Food insecure individuals in Coles County, Illinois. Individuals of all ages living at or below 185% of poverty as a percent of all individuals. Data from US Census Bureau, American FactFinder database, 2009–2013, 5-Year Estimates. *factfinder.census.gov*

have incomes below 185 percent of poverty and at risk of food insecurity; each tract is also numbered and labeled with its per capita income. Within Coles County's twelve census tracts, which vary widely in size owing to population density, there are disparities in the level of risk for food insecurity.

Tract 9 has the lowest food insecurity risk, with less than 25 percent of the population at or below 185 percent of poverty; the remainder of the county, however, exhibits higher values. Seven tracts have 25 to 50 percent of their population at risk, and four tracts have 50 to 75 percent of their population potentially food insecure. The tracts with the highest levels of risk are present in both principal cities of Charleston and Mattoon.

From Figure 5.3, it is clear that there are certain census tracts where the concentration of risk for food insecurity in the county's population is disproportionately high. Poverty and food insecurity are directly related to, and measured through, income, and therefore it is not alarming that the four tracts with the lowest per capita incomes have the highest percentage of their population at risk of food insecurity. What is noteworthy, however, and again what simulates larger, metropolitan areas, is a concentration of the highest incomes into one or a few tracts. For Coles County, tract 9 has the highest per capita income ($40,627) in the county—nearly $10,000 higher than the next highest tract. Moreover, this tract shares a border with three of the four tracts with the lowest per capita income and highest rates of risk.

Considering the qualitative character of these places reflects common segregated and inequitable characteristics of micropolitan areas (Brown, Cromartie, and Kulcsar 2004). For example, tract 8 in Charleston, which includes some family residences, primarily covers the campus of the regional four-year state university—a relationship common in multiple metropolitan and micropolitan areas—and reflects, in part, the low per capita income expected of most college students. Tract 7 holds the county seat as well as student and family housing, but tract 5 is characterized by mostly "older" and historical neighborhoods, which is locally regarded as the most impoverished portion of Charleston. Finally, tract 4 includes a corridor of shuttered manufacturing firms and farms, but also newly renovated centers for health and human services including the regional hospital. Tract 9, which stands in stark contrast to the remainder of the county, is mostly residential, with a younger housing stock of newly built houses and residential subdivisions with little to no farms, businesses, and services.

Like the distribution of food insecurity for the entire region as shown in Figure 5.2, focusing on Coles County confirms the inequitable distribution of food insecurity and sufficiently identifies where the need for assistance is elevated. The center of the county, geographically, is covered in part by tracts 4, 6, 7, and 8, where risk is highest; while there is need throughout the county, the highest levels are where the most-dense populations reside.

In terms of the availability of food relief agencies six of the ten programs in Coles County are located in tracts with 50 to 75 percent of the population living at risk; however, of these six programs, some may be more or less accessible to all persons. For example, the program in tract 7 is a high school food pantry and primarily serves the needs of the students and their families. In tract 5, the two agencies are traditional community food pantries open to qualifying residents. Of the three providers in tract 4, two are large, traditional community pantries, and the third is based out of a church. The remaining two programs in Mattoon include a regional homeless shelter (in tract 12) and a second small church-based pantry in tract 3. There are two outlying food pantries as well, one in Ashmore in tract 6 and one in Oakland in tract 1; both of these areas are relatively smaller in population than the center of the county and encompass part of the rural portion of this micropolitan area. In total, only five of the ten agencies in Coles County are located in areas with the highest risk and, as food bank partners, open to the general population with incomes at or below 185 percent of poverty.

Coles County, Illinois, a distinct micropolitan statistical area in the Eastern Illinois Foodbank service region, provides a case in which an often neglected geographic area can be explored to understand the breadth and depth of poverty and food insecurity, as well as the availability of food assistance. As discussed above, micropolitan areas are often left out of analyses of the geography of poverty and food insecurity, overshadowed by the traditional focus on metropolitan, suburban, and rural areas. However, as Coles County demonstrates, the risk of food insecurity and the incidence of poverty can be escalated in these midsized counties and regions in the United States. If there is continued concern with poverty in central cities, inner-ring suburban areas, and rural spaces, the fact that geographies like Coles County have heightened levels of poverty and increased risk for food insecurity should spark interest in further developing our knowledge of the geographic distribution of poverty and food insecurity between the urban and the rural.

Linked to household income, food insecurity may be a reality for low-income households with enough income to place them above the official poverty threshold; yet, the threat of a poverty spell or extended period of the compromised acquisition of food for all household members is a daily concern. This emphasizes the important consideration that food insecurity is a measure of relative poverty. Well-studied for urban metropolitan and rural areas, this poverty/food insecurity relationship holds for micropolitan statistical areas as well; as demonstrated, Coles County has a higher level of risk of food insecurity than the metropolitan and rural areas within the eastern Illinois region.

As a case study of one micropolitan region in the United States, the quantitative evidence may correlate with other micropolitan areas across the country, but the qualitative description of Coles County, as well as the county as a single case, is not meant to be generalizable. What is important to recall is that geographic areas are distinct in their own conditions of existence, and to truly understand the nature of poverty and food insecurity in one area is a focused project. Just like urban areas and rural areas may share statistical indicators of impoverishment (Lobao, Hooks, and Tickamyer 2007a), the conditions in New York City differ from that in Chicago or Los Angeles, and rural poverty in the southern United States is decidedly different than on First Nations reservations or in Appalachia. Micropolitan areas across the country should be treated as such—statistical commonalities with important qualitative distinctions. Most crucial is to remember that, possessing a mix of characteristics from urban and rural areas, micropolitan spaces reflect a unique character that expands the understanding of poverty, food insecurity, and inequality in the United States; this case study argues for their incorporation.

To address this risk, the eligibility, application, and use of private food assistance agencies are also geographically distributed and contribute to understanding or assessment of need or accessibility. Across the eastern Illinois region, more or less of the population at risk of food insecurity may qualify for public food assistance, such as SNAP, but as discussed, this is underutilized. Rather, larger proportions of food insecure individuals and families may access food pantries and soup kitchens in order to meet their needs, and the number and geographic distribution of food assistance programs sponsored by the regional food bank brings more relief to hungry persons than public provisions. For the eastern Illinois region, the largest counties by population have the most food agencies generating a lower ratio of households at risk of food insecurity to food bank partner agencies; however, in rural counties with few resources, and the higher level of risk in Coles County, the ratio of the food insecure population to these resources are high. Moreover, as Coles County acts as an anchor to adjacent rural counties, the level of actual need within this micropolitan statistical area may transcend county-based indicators.

Despite the higher number of individuals at risk per food assistance agency within Coles County, the programs partnered with the regional food bank are geographically located, over all, in proximity to the greatest level of need. Of the ten sponsored programs in the county, five pantries are within census tracts where the risk of food insecurity is highest. The five remaining programs appear to serve a particular population: two food pantries serve outlying rural townships, and one within each principal city serves a specific set of clients (a high school pantry and a homeless shelter).

Each of these relationships—the incidence of poverty, the risk of food insecurity, and the ability of the food insecure population to access food assistance from food pantries and soup kitchens—establishes micropolitan areas as a concerted focus of future research on poverty and food insecurity.

NOTE

1. In 2015, the Eastern Illinois Foodbank expanded to cover a seventeen-county region, assuming the administrative oversight of Dewitt, Livingston, and McLean Counties.

REFERENCES

Allard, Scott W. 2013. "Placing Food Security in a Spatial Context." Workshop on Research Gaps and Opportunities on the Causes and Consequences of Child Hunger. National Academy of Sciences, Committee on National Statistics, Washington, DC.

Bane, Mary J., and David T. Ellwood. 1986. "Slipping into and Out of Poverty: The Dynamics of Spells." *Journal of Human Resources* 21: 1–23.

Blank, Rebecca M., and Michael S. Barr, eds. 2009. *Insufficient Funds: Savings, Assets, Credit, and Banking among Low-Income Households.* New York: Russell Sage Foundation.

Brown, David L., John B. Cromartie, and Laszlo J. Kulcsar. 2004. "Micropolitan Areas and the Measurement of American Urbanization." *Population Research and Policy Review* 23: 399–418.

Coleman-Jensen, Alisha, Christian Gregory, and Anita Singh. 2014. "Household Food Security in the United States in 2013." Report Number: ERR-173. US Department of Agriculture, Economic Research Service, Washington, DC.

Cortes, Bienvenido S., Michael Davidson, and Michael McKinnis. 2015. "Growth and Volatility of Micropolitan Statistical Areas in the US." *Global Conference on Business and Finance Proceedings* 10: 77–86.

DeNavas-Walt, Carmen, and Bernadette D. Proctor. 2014. "Income and Poverty in the United States: 2013." Report Number: P60–249. US Census Bureau, Washington, DC.

Duncan, Cynthia M. 1996. "Understanding Persistent Poverty: Social Class Context in Rural Communities." *Rural Sociology* 61 (1): 103–24.

Feeding America. 2014a. "Hunger in America 2014: Agency Report for the Eastern Illinois Foodbank." Feeding America, Chicago.

———. 2014b. "Hunger in America 2014: National Report." Feeding America, Chicago.

———. 2014c. "Hunger in America 2014: State Report for Illinois." Feeding America, Chicago.

Garasky, Steven, Lois W. Morton, and Kimberly Greder. 2004. "The Food Environment and Food Security: Perceptions of Rural, Suburban, and Urban Food Pantry Clients in Iowa." *Family Economics and Nutrition Review* 16 (2): 41–48.

Gieryn, Thomas F. 2000. "A Space for Place in Sociology." *Annual Review of Sociology* 26: 463–96.

Gundersen, Craig, Brent Kreider, and John Pepper. 2011. "The Economics of Food Insecurity in the United States." *Applied Economic Perspectives and Policy* 33: 281–303.

Halpern-Meekin, Sarah, Kathryn Edin, Laura Tach, and Jennifer Sykes. 2015. *It's Not Like I'm Poor: How Working Families Make Ends Meet in a Post-welfare World.* Oakland: University of California Press.

Hays, Sharon. 2003. *Flat Broke with Children: Women in the Age of Welfare Reform.* New York: Oxford University Press.

Katz, Michael B. 1986. *In the Shadow of the Poor House: A Social History of Welfare in America.* New York: Basic Books.

———. 2013. *The Undeserving Poor: America's Enduring Confrontation with Poverty.* 2nd ed. New York: Oxford University Press.

Kneebone, Elizabeth, and Alan Berube. 2013. *Confronting Suburban Poverty in America.* Washington, DC: Brookings Institution Press.

Lichter, Daniel T., and David L. Brown. 2011. "Rural America in an Urban Society: Changing Spatial and Social Boundaries." *Annual Review of Sociology* 37: 565–92.

Lobao, Linda M., Gregory Hooks, and Ann R. Tickamyer. 2007a. "Introduction: Advancing the Sociology of Spatial Inequality." *The Sociology of Spatial Inequality*, edited by L. M. Lobao, G. Hooks, and A. R. Tickamyer, 1–25. Albany: State University of New York Press.

———. 2007b. *The Sociology of Spatial Inequality.* Albany: State University of New York Press.

Logan, John R. 2012. "Making a Place for Space: Spatial Thinking in Social Science." *Annual Review of Sociology* 38: 507–24.

Office of Management and Budget. 2013. "Revised Delineations of Metropolitan Statistical Areas, Micropolitan Statistical Areas, and Combined Statistical Areas, and Guidance on Uses of the Delineations of These Areas." Report Number: OMB Bulletin No. 13–01. Executive Office of the President, Office of Management and Budget, Washington, DC.

Poppendieck, Janet. 2014. "Food Assistance, Hunger and the End of Welfare in the USA." In *First World Hunger Revisited: Food Charity or the Right to Food?*, 2nd ed., edited by G. Riches and T. Silvasti, 176–90. London: Palgrave Macmillan.

Reardon, Sean F., and Kendra Bischoff. 2011. "Income Inequality and Income Segregation." *American Journal of Sociology* 116: 1092–153.

Rector, Robert, and Rachel Sheffield. 2011. "Executive Summary: Air Conditioning, Cable TV, and an Xbox: What Is Poverty in the United States Today?" Report Number: 2575. Heritage Foundation, Washington, DC.

Seefeldt, Kristin S., and John D. Graham. 2013. *America's Poor and the Great Recession.* Bloomington: Indiana University Press.

Sharkey, Patrick. 2013. *Stuck in Place: Urban Neighborhoods and the End of Progress toward Racial Equality.* Chicago: University of Chicago Press.

Short, Kathleen. 2013. "The Research Supplemental Poverty Measure: 2012." Report Number: P60–247. US Census Bureau, Washington, DC.

Social IMPACT Research Center. 2013. "Illinois 33%: Report on Illinois Poverty." Social IMPACT Research Center, Chicago.

Tickamyer, Ann R. 2006. "Rural Poverty." In *Handbook of Rural Studies*, edited by P. Cloke, T. Marsden, and P. Mooney, 411–26. London: Sage.

US Census Bureau. 2006. "Design and Methodology: American Community Survey." Report Number: TP67. US Government Printing Office, Washington, DC.

———. 2011. "2010 Census Redistricting Data (Public Law 94–171) Summary File: 2010 Census of Population and Housing, Technical Documentation." Report Number: PL/10–2 (RV). US Government Printing Office, Washington, DC.

———. 2013. "American Community Survey and Puerto Rico Community Survey 2012 Subject Definitions." US Census Bureau, Washington, DC.

6

Poverty, Food Insecurity, and Health among Youth

DON WILLIS AND KEVIN M. FITZPATRICK

Health is intimate. It is a matter of life and death, as well as quality of life. Not only does it impact how we navigate our daily lives, but it can dramatically affect relationships, jobs, and sense of self. Simply put, we experience health on a deeply personal level. And while there is an extant body of literature that documents this connection, we also know that, good or bad, health is not evenly distributed (Wilkinson 2005; Marmot 2004). Some people are more likely to experience healthy lives than others and, in turn, have significant social and cultural advantages contingent on that good health. Moreover, these health inequities do not happen by chance; they are achieved through a particular way of relating to one another and the places we both inhabit and construct. The result: unequal lives in the most literal sense.

Thus, health is not just intimate and personal; rather, it epitomizes the intersection of biography and history. Health is an alchemy of unique personal factors and social forces operating beyond the individual. Therefore, understanding health requires what C. Wright Mills called a "sociological imagination," that is, a capacity to trace the "ways in which personal troubles are connected to public issues" (Mills 2000, 185). With this connection in mind, the goal of this chapter is to spark the sociological imagination in a way that might complicate the common understanding of health as the result of individual choices and behaviors by clarifying its linkages to poverty, and, a particular indicator of poverty, food insecurity.

Who Is at Risk?

Poor health closely follows patterns of socioeconomic disparity and concentrated poverty (Fitzpatrick and LaGory 2011). Families with lower incomes and limited education can expect shorter, less healthy lives than those higher up the socioeconomic ladder. Unequal health is related to unequal exposure to risks for poor health, and socioeconomic status can be considered a fundamental cause of disease because it determines who becomes "at risk of risk" (Link and Phelan 1995, 85). For example, fewer than 10 percent of households above 185 percent of the poverty line were food insecure in 2014. That is in stark contrast to the nearly 40 percent of households below the poverty line who experienced food insecurity the same year (Coleman-Jensen et al. 2015). Food insecurity, for children especially, is a serious health risk. The seriousness of diet-related diseases such as obesity, diabetes, and cardiovascular diseases is clear as they continue to be leading causes of premature death in the US population as a whole (Mokdad et al. 2004; US Burden of Disease Collaborators 2013). These patterns of unequal health and risk exposure cannot be explained by differences in choices and behavior; rather, they require an understanding of the context that encompasses everyday lives.

Poverty, like health, is also unevenly distributed. Some are more likely to experience poverty than others, namely children, and especially minority children. Since the mid-1970s up to 2010, poverty rates for children (under age eighteen) have been higher than any other age group (DeNavas-Walt and Proctor 2015). This disproportionate burden of poverty on youth makes them a particularly vulnerable population when it comes to health and well-being. For young people experiencing poverty, it is not just general life chances (e.g., learning basic skills, getting a degree, getting a job, etc.) that are at stake, but life itself. Indeed, the odds of an infant dying before his or her first birthday are heightened for those born into lower socio-economic status. Moreover, childhood is an especially crucial period in the overall development of health and well-being across the life course. Experiences of poverty and insecurity in childhood can have lasting effects on health and well-being well into adulthood.

Linking Poverty, Food, and Health

Context matters. Everyday choices and behaviors impact our health, but those everyday choices and behaviors do not occur in a vacuum—they happen within, and are shaped by, a complicated, multidimensional environment. Part of what makes up that environment are other human beings, that is, the social context. Social contexts can either constrain or enable healthy living. Constraints may operate indirectly through their influences on choices and behaviors or directly through effects on the body (i.e., air or water pollution). As we have already described, poverty is a particularly constraining context to live and (sometimes literally) breathe in.

Among the many constraints of living in poverty are the strains placed on household food budgets. Moreover, housing costs limit the types of neighborhoods where low-income families can afford to live in relation to healthy foods. If access to food is primarily limited to the convenience store where there is no fresh produce or vegetables, place matters with profound effects on nutrition and health. There is a material reality of poverty that puts its inhabitants at a higher risk of bad health, in part owing to less nutritious diets. However, to paint a complete picture of poverty and how it impacts health we must also acknowledge the psychosocial dimensions of food insecurity. Of course, separating out the material from the psychosocial can be a difficult and, at times, pointless endeavor. But in the case of food insecurity the point is crucial to understanding the depth at which it, and poverty in general, operate when they impact health and well-being. The sections below provide some insight into how material as well as the psychosocial dimensions of food insecurity as a form of poverty act to stunt what might otherwise be healthy lives.

Material Dimensions of Food Insecurity

The most obvious and direct impact of food on health is through its nutritional value, or lack thereof. Meals for the food insecure might decrease in size, frequency, or quality. Food insecure children tend to experience diets higher in sugar, fiber, and fat, and lower in vegetable consumption; moreover, they report more perceived barriers to physical activity and, subsequently, less actual physical activity (Fram, Ritchie, et al. 2015). While some conflate food insecurity and hunger with a lack of calories, it is the deficiency in basic nutrients that is most harmful to health and even more difficult to see. Globally, nearly two in three deaths of children are attributed to nutritional deficiencies (Caballero 2002). Carolan refers to micronutrient malnutrition as "hidden hunger" (2011, 63), because it does not necessarily look like the sunken-in bodies of starving children that many associate with hunger. Children in the United States with calorie-rich diets and low vegetable consumption remain food insecure, and worse, their bodies remain hungry for proper nutrition regardless of weight status.

Given the insight that food insecure children have worse diets and more barriers to physical activity than their food secure counterparts, we have one logical explanation for the relationship between food insecurity and obesity. This suggests that food insecurity poses a serious nutritional/material risk for children's physical health. But the impact of food insecurity on physical health goes far beyond obesity. Research has shown relationships between household food insecurity and children's physical function (Casey et al. 2005), hospitalization (Cook et al. 2006), asthma (Kirkpatrick, McIntyre, and Potestio 2010), oral health (Chi et al. 2014), and cardiovascular health such as hypertension, hyperlipidemia, and diabetes (Seligman, Laraia, and Kushel 2010). Clearly there are significant nutritional/material pathways through which food insecurity directly impacts physical health.

In addition to the *consequences* of material conditions of food insecurity, there are also certain physical realities, such as geographic location, that might be considered part of what *causes* food insecurity. This claim, however, is contentious—as highlighted near the end of the following section.

Insecure Spaces

A privilege uncommon to the poor is the ability to choose where to live. Both economic position and life-course position play significant roles in determining the spaces we inhabit. Being both a child and poor, therefore, significantly constrains people's ability to choose where they live and the spaces they may occupy on a daily basis. Not only are the poor priced out of certain neighborhoods, but the act of moving is itself an expensive endeavor. This limited mobility of poor and youth populations has serious implications for their health. While poverty and age constrain the spaces we inhabit, the spaces we inhabit subsequently constrain a number of other daily activities (e.g., diet and exercise) that shape health over time. Thus, while space impacts everyone's health, low-income youth are at a heightened vulnerability to experience this "spatial disadvantage."

The spaces we occupy are important predictors of health outcomes. Simply put, "space imposes bounds on both our access to resources and knowledge of the resources available" (Fitzpatrick and LaGory 2011, 69). As noted earlier, some spaces have limited access to grocers carrying fruits and vegetables. Food insecure households tend to be farther from supermarkets, but closer to convenience stores (Thomas 2010). Supermarkets tend to be located in or near white, wealthy neighborhoods as opposed to poor, black neighborhoods, which are home to a disproportionate number of convenience and liquor stores (Morland et al. 2002). Adolescents whose school neighborhoods are characterized by higher availability of convenience stores tend to have a higher BMI (Body Mass Index), while neighborhoods with more supermarkets are associated with lower BMI among adolescents (Powell et al. 2007). The spaces we occupy when we are at home, school, or work can expose us to either healthy or unhealthy foods, and this exposure can make a significant difference in our nutritional health.

Spaces with limited access to healthy foods are often referred to as "food deserts." One might reasonably suspect that food deserts represent a breakdown in the US industrial food system, or a failure of the free market. This view of the problem misses the point; that is, these spaces are void of healthy food precisely *because* of the existing US food system, which treats food as primarily a commodity. When controlling for the purchasing power of zip codes within the Chicago area, Alwitt and Donley (1997) found that there was no difference in the number of supermarkets between high-income and low-income areas. Supermarket owners are responding rationally given the profit-driven logic of capitalism. This reveals one of the major reasons why market-based solutions are limited in their capacity to feed the poor in a way that would support their health and well-being. Treating food as a commodity in a free market (that is, primarily based on its exchange value from which profit is to be extracted) rather than as a substance intended for human health (its use value) is part of what drives healthy food away from those who need it the most. As economist Amartya Sen pointed out over thirty years ago, "there is nothing extraordinary in the market mechanism taking food away from famine-stricken areas to elsewhere. Market demands are not reflections of biological needs or psychological desires, but choices based on exchange entitlement relations" (1981, 161). From this view, spaces such as food deserts are seen as *achievements* of market mechanisms, rather than a failure or accidental outcome.

Moreover, the distance between a family and the nearest supermarket matters little if they lack the money to purchase food. Scarcity is simply not the fundamental *cause* of hunger or food insecurity (Sen 1981; Lappé and Lappé 2002; Scanlan, Jenkins, and Peterson 2010). A poor family surrounded by a cornucopia of food remains food insecure. A wealthy family living at the center of a food desert remains capable of accessing most any food they please. The barrier between the poor and healthy food is partly geographical, but it is absolutely social—even the geographic barriers are deeply related to the social structuring of residence by class and race. When we treat a vital source of health and well-being like food as a commodity, we have put in place an economic structure that inherently favors the health of the wealthy over that of the poor.

Psychosocial Dimensions of Food Insecurity

Food insecurity is partially a material condition—an empty refrigerator, a neighborhood with nothing but gas station food and liquor stores, the physical pangs of hunger or stunting of development—but it also has deeper, less obvious, consequences. Food is not just a material thing with solely nutritional purposes—food carries social meaning. For example, sharing a meal can signify to those involved that, at that time and place, no competition exists for vital resources such as food. Another example is the act of feeding, which is linked to traditional gender roles for women in the United States (DeVault 1994). Because of this linkage between feeding and gender roles, mothers in food insecure households may experience more than economic and nutritional strain, but also social strain related to the gendered expectation for women to be caretakers (e.g., food shoppers and preparers, and increasingly family nutritionists). This added social strain may in part be why food insecurity is so consistently related to obesity for women as opposed to men, for whom there is rarely any connection (Franklin et al. 2012).

Food can also signify social status. As Pierre Bourdieu (1984) has argued, feeding and eating practices are a key part of how distinctive social classes are reproduced in everyday acts, and how class ultimately inhabits our bodies. Lifestyle differences in food and eating may be one way that people become aware of, or actively distinguish, their social status from others. This is important for health because perceptions of disparity can impact health through psychosocial factors such as stress, self-esteem, stigma, and depression (Wilkinson 2005; Marmot 2004), and perceived differences in eating and food access may also signal those distinctions. Complicating this link between status and health even further is that social class is not experienced in the same way across all social contexts; moreover, it may not be experienced the same way across various stages of the life course. Children rarely, if ever, balance a checkbook or know the dollar amounts of their parents' bank accounts; they are, however, often aware of the food to which they do, or do not, have access (Fram, Frongillo, Jones, et al. 2011). Food may be one of the primary materials through which children experience social status, which would make inconsistent access or limited access to healthy food a particularly salient stressor.

In sum, there are at least two possible ways in which food insecurity may expose youth to stressors: (1) through its indication of lower social status and the stress that follows, and (2) through the worry and anxiety related directly to the inconsistency, limited quantity, or poor quality of meals. A psychosocial framework can help us better understand how these stressors impact children's health.

A Psychosocial Framework

The psychosocial approach to health disparities focuses on disproportionate exposure to both risk and protective factors within our environment. Psychosocial factors impact health through the physiological responses to stress, which is why the major risk factors—depression, anxiety, isolation, and insecurity—tend to be either sources or symptoms of chronic stress or major life events (Wilkinson 2005). Central to the psychosocial approach is an understanding of how stress develops in the body. First, this means identifying various sources of stress. Food insecurity, for example, is a source of stress for both caretakers and children (Fram, Frongillo, Jones, et al. 2011). Second, we must understand what other factors might mediate or moderate the influence of these stressors on the body, such as social support or social capital. Friends and family members might act as buffers, somehow softening the blow of stressful events like running out of money for food. Finally, attention is given to the manifestations of stress in physical and mental health (e.g., obesity). "Allostatic load" is a term referring to the physiological changes in the body after long periods of exposure to chronic stress (McEwen 1998). Most importantly, the concept illustrates that the impact of stress is cumulative over time—stress leaves lasting marks on our minds and bodies. Taken together, these three conceptual domains—sources, mediators, and manifestations of stress—make up what is referred to as the "stress process" (Pearlin et al. 1981), which provides a general framework for understanding and talking about the influence of stress on health.

Research has drawn clear lines between food insecurity and stress or anxiety among youth (Fram, Frongillo, Jones, et al. 2011), as well as between obesity and a host of psychosocial factors (Fitzpatrick, Willis, and O'Connor 2014). We might deduce from these studies that food insecurity is likely to be impacting weight status, in part, through the psychosocial stressors that accompany it; however, few studies have yet to draw this more complete picture of the stress process as it relates to food insecurity and weight status. Some research has found an interaction between maternal stress and food insecurity with childhood obesity (Lohman et al. 2009). This would suggest that a mother's experience of stress could moderate the impact of food insecurity on children's weight status, but it cannot tell us how the child's own experiences of food insecurity and stress are impacting their weight status.

Insecure Places

We have discussed how stress impacts health, but we have not yet examined the role that environmental factors play in determining exposure to stressful stimuli. There is a temptation to characterize stress as naturally occurring in some places more than others. While in some instances this may be true, stress is also closely related to social context. How humans interact with one another and the social structure, culture, and history that provides the context for those interactions all play a major role in shaping our exposure to stress. For example, perceived threats or even exposure to disrespect have real consequences for population health. Kennedy and colleagues (1996) provide evidence that exposure to disrespect based on race is an environmental risk associated with significant increases in state-level mortality rates for both black and white populations, though more severely for black populations. In this example, stress is not a natural phenomenon at all, but related to the contextual impact of racism.

In the section on material dimensions of food insecurity, we discussed the unequal distribution of health foods across space. But spaces, like food, are not purely material. Spaces have meaning and are more than just physical/material—they are places, they have stories, they are interpreted and felt in ways beyond their physical/material characteristics. Spaces are filtered through human interpretation, leaving them rife with symbolic nuance. While food deserts are typically defined by some degree of physical distance to healthy food, they might also be characterized by the *feelings* someone has when moving through, interacting with, and inhabiting such a space. Thinking about food deserts as places rather than just spaces provides a framework for examining the psychosocial impacts of living in these environments rather than just their nutritional risks.

On a smaller scale than a food desert, the household is also a social environment, and a food insecure household is one that elicits an overwhelming wave of mixed feelings and emotion. Qualitative evidence from Canada suggests that adults in food insecure households tend to feel a sense of alienation as well as a lack of control over their daily life (Hamelin, Beaudry, and Habicht 2002). These are indicators of stress that are associated with a number of health risks. Moreover, this sense of a lack of control was paired with an acute sense of inequity among adults and their children. For example, one parent noted the disappointment expressed by the parent's own kids when served a breakfast that was different than their friends. Parents, feeling ashamed of their difficulty in accessing food, often worked hard to hide this struggle so as to soften their children's sense of alienation. Ultimately, the context of food insecurity in the household was leading to physical pangs of hunger and illness, modified eating habits, but also deep psychological suffering marked by feelings of a loss of dignity (Hamelin, Beaudry, and Habicht 2002). The act of entertaining guests over a meal—often done to signify social status among friends and neighbors, and to build supportive social networks, was not an option for these families, and they felt that deeply. These are stories of inequality felt in ways that social epidemiologists have shown to have profound impacts on health (Wilkinson 2005; Marmot 2004).

An Intersection of the Material and Psychosocial

While there are some important theoretical and conceptual distinctions between the material and the psychosocial, it must also be recognized that phenomena we describe as fitting into one category often feed off of, and into, phenomena in the other category. Food insecurity is a particularly unique phenomenon in the sense that it does not fit neatly into either category; rather, food insecurity exemplifies one of the many instances where the material and the psychosocial conditions of poverty seem to intersect. This intersection is highlighted by one health outcome in particular that is often associated with food insecurity: obesity.

Food Insecurity and Obesity

In 1995, Dr. William H. Dietz proposed a causal relationship between two seemingly incompatible phenomena, hunger and obesity. His argument was based on an observation he had made concerning a family of obese patients who, counterintuitively, repeatedly experienced a lack of money for food near the end of each month. In response to this strain on their food budget, the family tended to rely on foods high in fat to prevent hunger. This initial observation incited a wave of research examining the association of food insecurity/hunger with weight status/obesity. From this body of research, we have learned a lot about the nuances of food insecurity and hunger, and that these phenomena do often result in unexpected consequences (i.e., overweight or obesity). But we have also learned that the association is inconsistent across groups. For example, women who experience food insecurity are especially likely to be overweight or obese while the same relationship rarely exists among men. Moreover, results for youth populations remain mixed (Dinour et al. 2007; Franklin et al. 2012; Larson and Story 2011).

What makes the food insecurity–obesity relationship seem paradoxical is a general focus on the material reality of food insecurity as a condition where access to food is inconsistent. To think of it as a paradox, however, misses the fact that part of the material reality is lack of access to *healthy* foods, as well as the psychosocial elements of food insecurity. There is evidence to suggest, for example, that while food insecure children do not have access to healthy food, they do have access to calorie-rich foods that may leave their bodies hungry for better nutrition (Fram, Ritchie, et al. 2015). Other explanations include a focus on the adapted eating habits of those who experience periodic insecurity (Franklin et al. 2012), as well as an argument that food insecure children are buffered from the lack of access to food but still experience some of the anxiety that can exacerbate weight status (Hamelin, Beaudry, and Habicht 2002). This is consistent with psychosocial theories of health as well as a body of research that links both obesity and food insecurity to various indicators of psychological and social well-being (Lohman et al. 2009). The buffering hypothesis, however, gives the impression that parents are the only actors in the story of food insecurity and child health. Moreover, it maintains parents as the unit of analysis, acting as spokespersons on behalf of youth experiences. An improved line of research would be to maintain the focus on psychosocial mechanisms linking food insecurity to obesity, but to survey children directly. While some research suggests that there is indeed a relationship between food insecurity and obesity among children, other researchers have found no association between the two. All these studies to date, however, rely on the reports from parents on their children's food insecurity despite evidence that youth experience food insecurity differently than adults (Fram, Frongillo, Jones, et al. 2011) and respond differently to questions about food insecurity status (Fram, Frongillo, Draper, and Fishbein 2013).

This methodological limitation leaves a considerable gap in the literature and our understanding of the association between food insecurity and weight status. However, new cross-sectional survey data collected from middle school students (fifth through seventh grade) in Northwest Arkansas allows us to fill this gap by utilizing a food insecurity survey instrument developed by Connell and colleagues (2004), who used cognitive interview methods to modify the US Department of Agriculture adult instrument for use by children. For the most part, the questions remain the same with only slight changes that make the survey accessible to youth. For example, the phrase "low-cost" is replaced by the word "cheap."

Case Study: Evidence from Northwest Arkansas Middle School Students

To answer the question of whether food insecurity and obesity are associated among youth populations, individual-level data with reports from children themselves was required. In 2011, we collected such data from students, including their own reports of food insecurity, self-reported height and weight from which BMI and weight status can be determined, basic demographic information (i.e., age, sex, race, class), and other social and psychological information (i.e., social relationships, self-esteem, depression); no personal identifiers were collected. From a sampling frame that included 361 eligible fifth- through seventh-grade students attending a single middle school, 334 students completed the survey, leaving us with a completion rate of 92 percent.

Preliminary analyses of descriptive statistics suggest that, like the rest of the country, this middle school is an environment where both obesity and food insecurity coexist. Over half (57 percent) of the students reported experiencing at least one of the five indicators of food insecurity within the past year. At the same time, nearly one in three (29.6 percent) reported a combined height and weight that would place them within the category of overweight or obese according to the Centers for Disease Control guidelines. But are any of these students experiencing food insecurity while also overweight or obese? The answer is yes. Nearly 40 percent of food insecure students are also overweight or obese (37.7 percent). While this shows that the majority of food insecure students are still in the healthy weight category, the prevalence of overweight and obesity among food secure students was comparatively much lower (23.5 percent). Further statistical testing reveals that this difference is significant at the $p < .01$ level. Given that result, we feel confident that these numbers represent real differences in weight status between food insecure and food secure students.

This data, therefore, suggests that a relationship between food insecurity and overweight/obesity among youth does exist. The data also provides some hints at what might explain this relationship. A more detailed multivariate analysis shows a positive association between food insecurity and weight status: as the severity of food insecurity increases, so does weight status. However, when psychosocial factors such as depression, perceived social status, self-esteem, and a measure of social capital are introduced into the model, the relationship between food insecurity and weight status disappears. This implies that psychosocial factors may be playing some mediating role in the relationship between food insecurity and weight status; that is, food insecurity might be operating through psychosocial factors to influence weight status among children. This could have significant policy implications for organizations aimed at alleviating the negative health effects of food insecurity. For example, if food insecurity increases weight status partly because of lower perceived social status, increased depressive symptoms, low self-esteem, or reduced social capital, then food pantries might be an important location for outreach by mental health professionals or mentorship programs.

While this evidence is compelling, the analyses are preliminary. Further statistical testing is needed to confirm that psychosocial factors are indeed mediating the relationship. Regardless, there appears to be a clear relationship between food insecurity and obesity among these middle school students. Results of our preliminary testing run counter to conclusions made by Gundersen, Garasky, and colleagues (2009) and Gundersen, Lohman, and colleagues (2008) for similar age groups; however, this may be due to the use of responses from children themselves in our own study. As these authors themselves point out in their own work, the use of parents as spokespersons for children's experiences is a serious limitation. Some of our previous work also confirms that this relationship exists but notes that parent responses to the food insecurity measure are not predictive of students' weight status (Fitzpatrick and Willis 2015). Had we not asked children to give their own reports of food insecurity, we may have been led to similar conclusions as Gundersen and colleagues.

Food insecurity is a particularly risky condition because it involves the combinative effects of material/nutritional risks of poverty and the psychosocial risk factors related to perceived distinctions in social status. Moreover, when material conditions do not lead to the expected outcomes, psychosocial factors may provide some insights for explaining what appear to be contradictions. Additionally, it is likely that psychosocial and material dimensions interact with one another to create a multiplicative effect on health outcomes.

"Poor choices" has become the default explanation for social problems. The poor are poor, we are told, because they make bad choices. Similar arguments are made when it comes to health and well-being. Not only is this myopic, but it is inherently flawed because it assumes everyone has the same choices/options to begin with, that we all *started* climbing the socioeconomic ladder from the same rung. Kids, and low-income kids especially, are afforded very few choices when it comes to residence, where they will go to school, what ends up in the refrigerator, or how often they will get to go outside (in unsafe neighborhoods it may not be an option). When we see disparities in health at very young ages we must think harder about what might be at the root of the problem. Kids offer an opportunity to get ahead of what can be a cyclical relationship between poverty and poor health. Because early life experiences can have a significant impact on health in later life, the lives of youth are crucial to the effort of breaking that cycle.

While we know that youth typically have limited opportunities to make important decisions (e.g., where to live, what to eat, etc.), we acknowledge youth as actors within the environments they inhabit—limited choices do not equate to zero choices, and it certainly does not equate to a lack of awareness about those limited choices. Youth experiences are simply different from adult experiences. To obtain a direct source of information about youth experiences, we must ask youth directly. Because of this, we feel it is crucial for researchers to, within reason, allow youth to speak for themselves when it comes to issues of poverty and inconsistent access to food. As demonstrated in this chapter, allowing youth to respond to surveys themselves can provide crucial insights into the impact of food insecurity and our understanding of health disparities in general.

Although the focus of this chapter has been on the experience of poverty and food insecurity, its psychosocial and material elements, and the consequences of those conditions for human health, we also recognize that these experiences are shaped by factors further "upstream" in the causal chain, and that the existence of poverty and food insecurity are not natural but achieved through a particular political and economic structuring of society. While tackling the immediate symptoms of poverty (i.e., hunger, homelessness, etc.) is necessary, it is also important to address the underlying cause. To do this we can look to examples from other places that have redefined what it means to be a citizen. Frances Moore Lappé and Anna Lappé describe in their book *Hope's Edge* (2002) a city in Brazil known as Belo Horizonte, which decided that citizenship entails a right to food. The programs implemented by the city are credited with lowering the very high mortality rate (35.3 per thousand births) for children by 72 percent in less than a decade (FAO 2015).

To determine that citizenship comes with a right to food, as the city of Belo Horizonte has done, is a fundamentally different approach to distributing food than the consumer-commodity relationship that characterizes food distribution in the United States. Questions of how to solve hunger and food insecurity inherently involve questions about how the state views and treats both food and its citizens. In other words, political leaders must ask themselves if their citizenry is to be viewed first as consumers and second as humans with vital needs or vice versa. Moreover, they must ask themselves whether food is primarily a commodity or a resource of vital nutritional and social importance. Hopefully, the view of citizens as humans with a right to vital nutritional and social resources such as food will begin to take hold in places beyond Belo Horizonte.

REFERENCES

Alwitt, Linda. F., and Thomas D. Donley. 1997. "Retail Stores in Poor Urban Neighborhoods." *Journal of Consumer Affairs* 31 (1): 139–64. doi:org/10.1111/j.1745–6606.1997.tb00830.x.

Bourdieu, Pierre. 1984. *Distinction: A Social Critique of the Judgement of Taste.* Cambridge, MA: Harvard University Press.

Caballero, Benjamin. 2002. "Global Patterns of Child Health: The Role of Nutrition." *Annals of Nutrition and Metabolism* 46 (Supplement 1): 3–7. doi:10.1159/000066400.

Carolan, Michael. 2011. *The Real Cost of Cheap Food.* New York: Earthscan.

Casey, Patrick H., Kitty L. Szeto, James M. Robbins, Janice E. Stuff, Carol Connell, Jeffery M. Gossett, and Pippa M. Simpson. 2005. "Child Health-Related Quality of Life and Household Food Security." *Archives of Pediatrics and Adolescent Medicine* 159 (1): 51–56.

Chi, Donald L., Erin E. Masterson, Adam C. Carle, Lloyd A. Mancl, and Susan E. Coldwell. 2014. "Socioeconomic Status, Food Security, and Dental Caries in US Children: Mediation Analyses of Data from the National Health and Nutrition Examination Survey, 2007–2008." *American Journal of Public Health* 104 (5): 860–64. doi:10.2105/AJPH.2013.301699.

Coleman-Jensen, Alisha, Matthew P. Rabbitt, Christian Gregory, and Anita Singh. 2015. "Household Food Security in the United States in 2014," ERR-194, US Department of Agriculture, Economic Research Service, September.

Connell, Carol L., Mark Nord, Kristi L. Lofton, and Kathy Yadrick. 2004. "Food Security of Older Children Can Be Assessed Using a Standardized Survey Instrument." *Journal of Nutrition* 134 (10): 2566–72.

Cook, John T., Deborah A. Frank, Suzette M. Levenson, Nicole B. Neault, Tim C. Heeren, Maurine M. Black, et al. 2006. "Child Food Insecurity Increases Risks Posed by Household Food Insecurity to Young Children's Health." *Journal of Nutrition* 136 (4): 1073–76.

DeNavas-Walt, Carmen, and Bernadette D. Proctor. 2015. US Census Bureau, Current Population Reports, P60–252, "Income and Poverty in the United States: 2014," Washington, DC: US Government Printing Office.

DeVault, Marjorie L. 1994. *Feeding the Family: The Social Organization of Caring as Gendered Work.* Chicago: University of Chicago Press.

Dietz, William H. 1995. "Does Hunger Cause Obesity?" *Pediatrics* 95 (5): 766–67.

Dinour, Lauren M., Dara Bergen, and Ming-Chin Yeh. 2007. "The Food Insecurity–Obesity Paradox: A Review of the Literature and the Role Food Stamps May Play." *Journal of the American Dietetic Association* 107 (11): 1952–61. doi:10.1016/j.jada.2007.08.006.

FAO (Food and Agriculture Organization of the United Nations). 2015. "Belo Horizonte: Growing Greener Cities in Latin America and the Caribbean." *www.fao.org/ag/agp/ greenercities/en/ggclac/belo_horizonte.html.*

Fitzpatrick, Kevin M., and Mark LaGory. 2011. *Unhealthy Cities: Poverty, Race, and Place in America.* New York: Routledge.

Fitzpatrick, Kevin M., and Don Willis. 2015. "Parent/Student Risk and Protective Factors in Understanding Early Adolescent's Body Mass Index." *Journal of Early Adolescence*, February, 0272431615570058. doi:10.1177/0272431615570058.

Fitzpatrick, Kevin M., Don Willis, and Gail O'Connor. 2014. "Circumstances, Resources, and Weight Status Outcomes among Middle School Students." *Journal of Early Adolescence* 34 (8): 1058–74.

Fram, Maryah Stella, Edward A. Frongillo, Carrie L. Draper, and Eliza M. Fishbein. 2013. "Development and Validation of a Child Report Assessment of Child Food Insecurity and Comparison to Parent Report Assessment." *Journal of Hunger and Environmental Nutrition* 8 (2): 128–45. doi:10.1080/19320248.2013.790775.

Fram, Maryah Stella, Edward A. Frongillo, Sonya J. Jones, Roger C. Williams, Michael P. Burke, Kendra P. DeLoach, and Christine E. Blake. 2011. "Children Are Aware of Food Insecurity and Take Responsibility for Managing Food Resources." *Journal of Nutrition* 141 (6): 1114–19.

Fram, Maryah Stella, Lorrene D. Ritchie, Nila Rosen, and Edward A. Frongillo. 2015. "Child Experience of Food Insecurity Is Associated with Child Diet and Physical Activity." *Journal of Nutrition* 145 (3): 499–504. doi:org/10.3945/jn.114.194365.

Franklin, Brandi, Ashley Jones, Dejuan Love, Stephane Puckett, Justin Macklin, and Shelley White-Means. 2012. "Exploring Mediators of Food Insecurity and Obesity: A Review of Recent Literature." *Journal of Community Health* 37 (1): 253–64.

Gundersen, Craig, Steven Garasky, and Brenda J. Lohman. 2009. "Food Insecurity Is Not Associated with Childhood Obesity as Assessed Using Multiple Measures of Obesity." *Journal of Nutrition* 139 (6): 1173–78.

Gundersen, Craig, Brenda J. Lohman, Joey C. Eisenmann, Steven Garasky, and Susan D. Stewart. 2008. "Child-Specific Food Insecurity and Overweight Are Not Associated in a Sample of 10- to 15-Year-Old Low-Income Youth." *Journal of Nutrition* 138 (2): 371–78.

Gundersen, Craig, Brenda J. Lohman, Steven Garasky, Susan Stewart, and Joey Eisenmann. 2008. "Food Security, Maternal Stressors, and Overweight among Low-Income US Children: Results from the National Health and Nutrition Examination Survey (1999– 2002)." *Pediatrics* 122 (3): e529–40.

Hamelin, Anne-Marie, Micheline Beaudry, and Jean-Pierre Habicht. 2002. "Characterization of Household Food Insecurity in Québec: Food and Feelings." *Social Science and Medicine* 54 (1): 119–32. doi:10.1016/S0277–9536(01)00013–2.

Kennedy, B. P., I. Kawachi, K. Lochner, C. Jones, and D. Prothrow-Stith. 1996. "(Dis) Respect and Black Mortality." *Ethnicity and Disease* 7: 207–14.

Kirkpatrick Sharon I., Lynn McIntyre, Melissa L. Potestio. 2010. "Child Hunger and Long-Term Adverse Consequences for Health." *Arch. Pediatr. Adolesc. Med.* 164 (8): 754–62. doi:10.1001/archpediatrics.2010.117.

Lappé, Francis M., and Anna Lappé. 2002. *Hope's Edge: The Next Diet for a Small Planet.* New York: Jeremy P. Tarcher/Putnam.

Larson, Nicole I., and Mary T. Story. 2011. "Food Insecurity and Weight Status among US Children and Families: A Review of the Literature." *American Journal of Preventive Medicine* 40 (2): 166–73.

Link, Bruce G., and Jo Phelan. 1995. "Social Conditions as Fundamental Causes of Disease." *Journal of Health and Social Behavior* 35: 80–94. doi:10.2307/2626958.

Lohman, Brenda J., Susan Stewart, Craig Gundersen, Steven Garasky, and Joey C. Eisenmann. 2009. "Adolescent Overweight and Obesity: Links to Food Insecurity and Individual, Maternal, and Family Stressors." *Journal of Adolescent Health: Official Publication of the Society for Adolescent Medicine* 45 (3): 230–37.

Marmot, Michael. 2004. *The Status Syndrome: How Social Status Affects Our Health and Longevity.* New York: Henry Holt.

McEwen, Bruce S. 1998. "Stress, Adaptation, and Disease: Allostasis and Allostatic Load." *Annals of the New York Academy of Sciences* 840 (1): 33–44. doi:10.1111/j.1749–6632.1998. tb09546.x.

Mills, C. Wright. 2000. *The Sociological Imagination.* New York: Oxford University Press.

Mokdad, Ali H., James S. Marks, Donna F. Stroup, and Julie L. Gerberding. 2004. "Actual Causes of Death in the United States, 2000." *Journal of the American Medical Association* 291 (10): 1238–45.

Morland, Kimberly, Steve Wing, Ana Diez Roux, and Charles Poole. 2002. "Neighborhood Characteristics Associated with the Location of Food Stores and Food Service Places." *American Journal of Preventive Medicine* 22 (1): 23–29. doi:10.1016/ S0749–3797(01)00403–2.

Pearlin, Leonard I., Elizabeth G. Menaghan, Morton A. Lieberman, and Joseph T. Mullan. 1981. "The Stress Process." *Journal of Health and Social Behavior* 22 (4): 337–56. doi:org/10.2307/2136676.

Powell, Lisa M., M. Christopher Auld, Frank J. Chaloupka, Patrick M. O'Malley, and Lloyd D. Johnston. 2007. "Associations between Access to Food Stores and Adolescent Body Mass Index." *American Journal of Preventive Medicine: Bridging the Gap Research Informing Practice and Policy for Healthy Youth Behavior* 33 (4, Supplement): S301–7. doi:10.1016/j. amepre.2007.07.007.

Seligman, Hilary K., Barbara A. Laraia, and Margot B. Kushel. 2010. "Food Insecurity Is Associated with Chronic Disease among Low-Income NHANES Participants." *Journal of Nutrition* 140 (2): 304–10.

Scanlan, Stephen J., J. Craig Jenkins, Lindsey Peterson. 2010. "The Scarcity Fallacy." *Contexts.* contexts.org/articles/the-scarcity-fallacy/.

Sen, Amartya. 1981. *Poverty and Famines: An Essay on Entitlement and Deprivation.* Oxford: Clarendon.

Thomas, Brian J. 2010. "Food Deserts and the Sociology of Space: Distance to Food Retailers and Food Insecurity in an Urban American Neighborhood." *International Journal of Human Social Science* 5 (6): 400–409.

US Burden of Disease Collaborators. 2013. "The State of US Health, 1990–2010: Burden of Diseases, Injuries, and Risk Factors." *Journal of the American Medical Association* 310 (6): 591–606. doi:10.1001/jama.2013.13805.

Wilkinson, Richard. 2005. *The Impact of Inequality: How to Make Sick Societies Healthier.* New York: New Press.

7

The Role of Coupons in Exacerbating Food Insecurity and Obesity

KAITLAND M. BYRD, W. CARSON BYRD,
AND SAMUEL R. COOK

Food insecurity is closely linked to social inequality and negative health outcomes. In recent years these issues are more problematic and increasing in both public and scholarly discussions. One heralded solution to food insecurity is finding a way for families with limited incomes to stretch their money for food expenditures. Governmental programs like Supplemental Nutrition Assistance Programs (SNAP), free and reduced-price lunches, and Women Infants and Children (WIC) are all widely accepted, although politically contentious, programs aimed at reducing hunger and food insecurity for members of the lower class (Fox et al. 2004). Community-based programs including soup kitchens and food pantries are another alternative to improve food access to people at the community level. At the individual level, people are free to choose what food products they spend their limited money on. However, these choices are often made with narrow perspectives of how negative (and positive) health consequences can result from strictly financial decisions about food (French 2003).

The choices of food purchasing are shaped by many considerations, one of which is how filling certain foods are in relation to the number of people in a household to be fed. This consideration places people with limited financial resources in a difficult position. Even with federal or community assistance, healthy food is often expensive and considered a "bad deal" as these foods may not be considered as filling for the cost (Phipps, Kumanyika, et al. 2014). Within this social context newspapers, reality television shows, and grocery stores advertise coupons and "[extreme] couponing" as a way to stretch financial resources by buying specific products that are on sale at a given time (Grose 2013). Although coupons are a way of saving money, there is little attention paid to what products are on sale and the possible health consequences of couponing to battle food insecurity. That is, relying on the "bottom dollar" may assist with purchasing food, but this approach does not adequately contextualize the position of food choices, a person's health, or how to effectively combat food insecurity and reduce health disparities. With this in mind, we ask the following: What types of food and food products are often on sale in store ads and coupons? Additionally, we ask: What health consequences could result from relying on store ads and coupons for food purchases?

The constant balancing act between ways to save money on food and unhealthy food choices reinforces the link between social inequality, food insecurity, and obesity. In order to possibly reduce such inequality and health disparities, we explore alternative solutions to the reliance on coupons and store ads. One of these solutions we examine is the implementation of a program utilizing farmers' markets in the rural community included in our study. Specifically, the recently enacted policy by the local farmers' market doubles SNAP money people spend at the market. For example, a person can spend $10 in SNAP on food at the market and purchase $20 worth of food each day the market is open. Thus, this program maximizes the worth of a dollar for individuals and families dealing with food insecurity making it more feasible for them to spend money on healthy food options (Baronberg et al. 2013).

Our study provides a unique look at how saving money through couponing and relying on sale ads influences not only the food options available for people, but also how such approaches to food insecurity may negate any possible savings by directly impacting a person's health. Through this examination, we attempt to pinpoint alternative community-oriented approaches to increasing food, health, and well-being.

Couponing and Food Insecurity

Food insecurity is defined as the lack of access to adequate nutritional food or the lack of ability to acquire nutritional food (Andrews and Bickel 1998). Food insecurity is common in low-income areas, which often have limited access to grocery stores; instead residents have to rely on convenience stores. However, food insecurity can exist anywhere if a household does not possess adequate funds to cover food expenditures (Townsend et al. 2001).

There has been a significant amount of research addressing the link between poverty, food insecurity, and nutritional outcomes. Since poverty and food insecurity determine how much and what types of food are available, a person's health is shaped by restricting conditions, leading to negative health consequences, often those associated with obesity (Bhattacharya et al. 2004). Obesity has become a global problem and is associated with numerous leading causes of death. By 2008, over one-third of children were overweight or obese in the United States. Obesity increases the risk for numerous health problems including diabetes and heart disease. The increase in rates of diabetes parallels the increase in rates of obesity among children and adults (CDC 2017).

People with a low income face numerous challenges to maintaining a healthy diet. Healthy eating is linked to higher food expenditures and is often unobtainable for people living with a low income. The location also impacts the availability of a variety of foods. Urban areas often have high concentrations of poverty and lack supermarkets. Instead residents have to rely on convenience markets and fast-food outlets, both of which are characterized by empty calorie food (Walker et al. 2014). Low-income areas have very few stores selling fresh produce compared to an overwhelming number of fast-food chains and stores selling processed foods (Morland et al. 2008).

Mhurchu and colleagues (2013) identify two types of environments shaping dietary behaviors and subsequent health. A food environment is based on the type and availability of food outlets including grocery stores and fast-food chains. The consumer environment focuses on the availability, price, promotion, and nutrition of available products (Mhurchu et al. 2013). The type of food environment present in an area also includes the quality of products available. Block and Kouba (2006) found dramatic differences between the quality and price of products available at grocery stores compared to larger supermarkets. Smaller grocery stores were more likely to have suboptimal produce, but the prices were cheaper compared to supermarkets. While all these factors significantly impact the food security of a household, one way people can stretch their grocery budget is through the use of coupons and store sale ads. However, these cost-saving devices are not equally applied to healthy and processed foods.

Marketing also plays an important role in shaping the food choices people make. While increasing the access to healthy food has little impact on healthy food consumption, product placement consistently impacts food choices. The more shelf space dedicated to energy-dense food is correlated with a higher body mass index (BMI), but the same relationship does not exist for fruit and vegetable shelf space. Increasing the amount of available fruits and vegetables is not enough to change behavior, without also decreasing the amount of available energy-dense foods (Glanz et al. 2012). The shelf positioning of products also impacts how people perceive those foods. Specifically, low-fat versions of junk food were seen as less healthy but better tasting when positioned closely to other healthy foods, compared to when they were positioned with similar foods that were not low fat (Glanz et al. 2012).

Consumers decide what foods to consume based on perceived quality, taste, price, and nutrition. However, nutrition is seldom reflected in the actual purchases they make (French 2003; Glanz et al. 2012). Price is frequently mentioned as one of the most important factors in deciding what types of food to purchase (Phipps, Kumanyika, et al. 2014). Coupons and store sales are the most common ways to save money on groceries. Although coupons have existed for over a century, their use was minimal until the recession (Berning 2014). During the aftermath of the recession, in 2011, 2.9 billion coupons were redeemed in one fiscal year. There was little difference between the demographics of households using coupons and those that did not, although households who used coupons were more likely to be unemployed. However, household purchases using coupons were higher in fat, sodium, and sugar compared to household purchases that did not use coupons (Berning 2014).

Coupons shape consumers' choices by acting as a source of information, advertisement, and price discount (Dong and Leibtag 2010). Grocery stores also help shape consumer choices by promoting unhealthy food. Unhealthy foods are identified as foods that are high in fat, sodium, and added sugars (Lopez and Seligman 2014). Stores offer a majority of sales on products other than fresh produce. Lopez and Seligman (2014) found less than 5 percent of store sales were for fresh fruits and vegetables, while 25 percent were for processed foods, and 12 percent were for sugar-sweetened beverages. One reason why grocery stores avoid placing fruits and vegetables on sale is because their goal is to make a profit. The USDA estimates grocery stores lose $15 billion annually on unsold fruits and vegetable because of how volatile the market is for fresh produce (Lopez and Seligman 2014).

Even when fresh produce is on sale shoppers still tend to buy processed foods. Among low-income shoppers the odds of buying food on sale was highest for grain-based snacks, sweet snacks, and sweetened beverages. Lopez and Seligman (2014) found that when women would buy fruits and vegetables, they were only able to do so if the products were on sale; otherwise they were unable to afford fresh produce (Phipps, Kumanyika, et al. 2014). Cereal coupons also led to a higher rate of purchasing cereals high in sugar and salt compared to purchasing not involving coupons (Berning 2014).

When coupons or vouchers were given for fresh fruits and vegetables sales increased, compared to when no coupons were available. However the impact coupons have on fresh fruit and vegetable purchases is based on how much fresh produce a household already consumes before the discount and how often a household uses coupons (Dong and Leibtag 2010). Coupons and price reductions significantly impacted the sale of low-fat foods. The higher the price reduction, the higher the rate of consumption (French 2003; Phipps, Braitman, et al. 2013).

Although coupons offer a way for people to save money, the use of coupons is not without problems. Society emphasizes consumerism; purchasing high-priced products is a marker of status. This leads to people wanting to avoid any stigma associated with saving money through coupon usage (Argo and Main 2008). Bonnici and colleagues (2011) explored reasons why consumers avoided using coupons: coupons were associated with low-quality products, the coupons were left at home or had expired, and the size and quantity restrictions made them a hassle to use (Bonnici et al. 2011; Phipps, Braitman, et al. 2013). Even when produce coupons were available, only fruit consumption was impacted. Vegetable consumption was not impacted because people were less familiar with the taste and appearance of vegetables. Vegetables also require knowledge and time to prepare, making people less likely to purchase vegetables that were more complicated than salad or potatoes (Phipps, Braitman, et al. 2013). This suggests price alone is not enough to encourage vegetable consumption because of the amount of time and knowledge required to prepare a dish that uses vegetables other than potatoes and salad.

Affording healthy foods is not a result of low-income family choices, or how much money they have in their pockets, but goes much deeper to the stark economic inequality that has swallowed families across the United States following deindustrialization beginning in the 1970s and the switch to a service economy in the late 1980s. To afford healthy foods that often cost more than processed foods relates to obtaining a secure job with a high enough income to pay bills and expenses outside of purchasing groceries. The declining wages and longer hours that accompany the increasing service jobs results in family members working longer hours to earn as much as many industrial jobs of the past paid that required fewer hours of employees. Thus, regardless of who is cooking in the kitchen, they are likely to spend less time than is needed given the financial realities they are experiencing.

We use coupons and store sale ads collected in two different locales in a southeastern state during a three-month period in 2013. One locale is part of a major metropolitan area (larger than one million residents), while the other is a small-to-midsize town in a more rural community (less than forty-five thousand residents). These coupons and sale ads were collected from major newspapers in each area, which represented multiple grocery chains spanning varying socioeconomic communities. Although it could be argued that it is advantageous to limit our data collection to particular stores available in neighborhoods that are likely to serve one socioeconomic community or another, these stores have multiple locations in varying communities, and the coupons can be used at the multiple grocery chains. Thus, it would be difficult to parse out the actual availability of products by grocery chain by socioeconomic community. Also, the grocery chains included in our data collection are large regional and national chains and do not include chains that target more affluent customers such as Earthfare, Trader Joe's, and Whole Foods. Although these stores were present in the large metropolitan area, they did not advertise in the major newspapers examined in our study. All the grocery stores in the smaller, rural community advertised in the newspaper included in our study.

In our analyses, we examine (1) what products are on sale; (2) how much is being saved by using a coupon or sale ad; and (3) how comparable healthy products are to nonhealthy products in terms of price and availability. Additionally, we contextualize our analyses by describing the efforts of the grocery stores to possibly increase healthy food options and combat food insecurity. This information provides important nuance to understanding why certain foods are sold at lower prices and/or are more available to consumers in comparison to other types of foods and products. Moreover, this indicates how grocery stores can influence the efforts of farmers' markets and community organizations to increase healthy food options and the availability of such options for those with fewer socioeconomic resources. We hypothesize that although coupons and store sales offer a way to stretch the financial expenditures on food, this option actually limits healthy food options.

Although the media and researchers often focus on couponing among families, the reliance on sale advertisements can also have important effects on families' health and finances. Table 7.1 displays the comparison between the average number of items for each of eleven food groupings across the two locales' sale advertisements collected in this study. These numbers represent averages across multiple grocery store chains in these locales and are not dependent on one store or another. The first two columns present the averages in each locale, while the third column provides a statistical test for whether these average numbers of items for each group significantly differed across these two locales.

The four groups of items that received the most products in sale advertisements across both locales were the following: processed foods, other household products, meat, and alcohol. Following these four groups, the remaining groups of items varied for each locale. Importantly, processed food sales are the overwhelming filler of sale advertisement pages for actual food in both locales. With the exception of meat, the remaining staples of family meals are rarely given discounts for families in either the large metropolitan area or the rural town to take advantage of when shopping for their food. Our examination of the differences in the number of items offered in sale advertisements across the two locales found four significant differences. The sale advertisements in the large metro area contained more sales on household products, meat, alcohol, and fruits than were offered to families living in the rural town.

Table 7.2 presents a comparison between sale advertisements and coupons across both locales. In this comparison the mean, or average, represents the proportion of

TABLE 7.1. Comparison of number of various foods and products offered in store advertisements by locale

Type of Food	Locale		Means Test
	Large Metro	**Rural Town**	
Vegetables	7.32	8.66	-1.34
Fruits	7.40	4.11	3.29*
Meat	18.36	9.71	8.65*
Dairy	4.96	6.40	-1.44
Beans and grains	5.40	3.97	1.43
Processed	44.12	37.20	6.92
Sugary drinks	8.24	6.09	2.15
Store bakery	3.60	3.20	.40
Store deli	5.36	4.54	.82
Alcohol	10.68	6.31	4.37*
Other household products	36.44	14.66	21.78*
N	25	35	

* Significant difference between amount of foods and products offered in each area ($p < .05$).

TABLE 7.2. Average mentions of various food items in sale advertisements and coupons

Type of Food	Paper Insert		Means Test
	Sale Advertisement	**Coupon**	
Vegetables	.98	.01	.97*
Fruits	1.00	.02	.98*
Meat	1.00	.05	.95*
Dairy	.95	.06	.89*
Beans and grains	.98	.08	.91*
Processed	1.00	.15	.85*
Sugary drinks	.98	.02	.96*
Alcohol	.98	.01	.97*
Other household products	1.00	.49	.51*
N	60	644	

* Significant difference between mention of food type between sale advertisement and coupon ($p < .05$).

sale advertisements and coupons that mentioned at least one item across nine different groupings. The means range from "0" (no mention of an item) to "1.0," which indicates that 100 percent of sale advertisements or coupons mentioned an item under a particular type of food. The same groupings were used as in Table 7.1 with two exceptions. As coupons are not store specific, bakery and deli items that are readily found in grocery store sale advertisements are not available for coupons and are not included in the comparisons.

Although the first table found food staples such as fruits, vegetables, dairy, and beans and grains lagging far behind processed foods in sale advertisements, when we compare whether an item for each group is mentioned in sale advertisements compared to coupons, another story arises. The first pattern that is readily apparent in this comparison is the sheer number of food items mentioned in sale advertisements compared to coupons. Sale advertisements readily advertised an item for each group almost 100 percent of the time. This is not surprising as sale advertisements for grocery stores are based on a much more intimate knowledge of the marketing and advertising units within grocery store corporations. These units have plentiful information on stock and inventories across stores, scheduled deliveries of incoming products such as seasonal fruits and vegetables, and other information that makes crafting sale advertisements that are more "holistic" in the food items they offer possible. The second pattern that emerges from this analysis is the paltry number of coupons for actual food items. Fully 49 percent of all coupons collected in this study were for household products such as cleaning supplies, baby supplies including diapers, and pet supplies. The next largest group of coupons was for processed foods (15 percent of all coupons). Following these types of food were coupons for beans and grains (8 percent), dairy products (6 percent), meat products (2 percent), fruits (2 percent), and vegetables (1 percent). Sugary drinks such as soft drinks accounted for 2 percent of coupons, and alcohol accounted for 1 percent of coupons. However, a more nuanced examination of coupons regarding how much is saved using a coupon points out how different foods are discounted, baiting low-income consumers with deals on less healthy options for their families.

Table 7.3 contains an analysis of the average savings, number of units of a food item required to use a coupon, the average savings per unit calculation for each type of food, and the distribution of coupons across the types of food. Two additional groupings were delineated from the examination of coupons: health foods and products, and restaurants. The first new grouping, health foods and products, contained such items as meal replacements (e.g., Cliff Bars, Powerbars), vitamins, and water. The second additional grouping, restaurants, indicates coupons that were inserted in papers along with grocery coupons. Although not often seen as related to couponing, the ability to get a discount at a restaurant can influence the consumption patterns of families, which can also influence their health.

Table 7.3 indicates a variety of interesting findings. In relation to the savings a person can expect from a coupon, the overall savings using coupons was slightly more than a dollar and a half ($1.59). The largest savings among each grouping was found for restaurant coupons ($3.11), followed by health foods and products ($2.05), other household products ($1.87), alcohol ($1.50), and sugary drinks such as soft drinks ($1.15). Out of these top five saving groups only two (restaurants and sugary drinks) are daily suppliers of food for families. Although many of the items included in health foods and products are consumed on a daily basis, arguably these food items are rarely consumed for every meal during a day. What is important to note is the food that families save the least on: vegetables ($1.00), fruits ($0.96), processed foods ($0.91), beans and grains ($0.89), and dairy ($0.88). That is, the least savings coupons offer families are for the most consumed foods.

TABLE 7.3. Average savings per item and number of units required for savings across coupons

Type of Food	Savings (in dollars)	Required units	Savings per unit	Group Totals N	Group Totals %
Vegetables	1.00	1.57	.71	7	1.10
Fruits	.96	1.69	.69	13	2.04
Meat	1.06	1.28	.90	29	4.56
Dairy	.88	2.19	.64	36	5.66
Beans and grains	.89	1.65	.63	49	7.70
Processed	.91	1.58	.69	99	15.57
Sugary drinks	1.15	1.75	.81	12	1.89
Alcohol	1.50	2.75	.75	4	.63
Health foods and products	2.05	1.46	1.78	35	5.50
Restaurants	3.11	1.83	1.81	36	5.66
Other household products	1.87	1.30	1.62	317	49.84
All coupons	1.59	1.48	1.28	636	100.00

Turning to the savings per unit across each grouping, the top three items families save on using coupons remain the same: restaurants ($1.81), health foods and products ($1.78), and other household products ($1.62). Following these groups, the remaining types of food are fairly condensed together with averages between 63¢ per unit and 90¢ per unit savings on each coupon. Although most of these items offer similar amounts of savings per unit, how regularly these coupons are offered to families is not similar, which influences what food discounts are accessible to families. For example, although processed foods and fruits offer savings of 69 cents per unit for families, processed food coupons account for over 15 percent of all coupons collected during this study, while coupons for fruit accounted for only 2 percent of all coupons. Thus, even though processed foods are not discounted more than fruits, they are more prevalent among all coupons, which can influence what families, particularly low-income families that rely on coupons, choose to buy. Moreover, the fruits that were offered discounts with coupons were frequently found in cans, as juice cocktails, or in packaging with syrups high in sugar, which can reduce the overall nutritional value of the fruit. Although fruits were not overwhelmingly found in these forms, low-income families with children navigate the difficulty of increasing the number of foods their children try as they develop but must do so with the constraints of both their financial budgets and their child's tastes and preferences, which could lead them to purchase more fruits in the forms of juice cocktails and processed foods given these contexts.

Coupons are products of a profit-driven economy rather than philanthropic design. Food security is not part of that equation, and if coupons happen to help alleviate hunger at any point it is sheer coincidence. If that equation is to be modified to promote food security in a substantive way—one that ensures that healthy food choices are available to low- or fixed-income families and individuals—nothing less than a complete overhaul of the value system grounding a coupon economy seems necessary. In a society emphasizing profit over health there are few alternatives promoting the consumption of healthy food while making that food available to low-income households.

The evidence from the coupons and store sale ads in our study corresponds with the findings of previous research, highlighting the frequency of processed products over fresh produce (Lopez and Seligman 2014). There are few differences across locations in the types of products available at decreased prices. The lack of variance across geographical locations suggests the underlying problems facing low-income families' food choices are similar, so a solution to increase accessibility to healthier food options could easily be applied across geographical regions as well.

One example of an alternative solution is the approach taken to the SNAP program, which has been implemented at local farmers' markets around the United States. While the acceptance of SNAP by local producers often requires vendors to compromise profits, there are tax incentives. Moreover, an increasing number of farmers' markets have subsidized vendors to allow SNAP points to count double in an effort to ensure that low-income households have access to healthy food. In the smaller, rural town where the coupons and sale ads were collected, the local farmers' market subsidizes SNAP. The number of low-income households taking advantage of the double-SNAP program at the farmers' market went from only three customers in 2012, when it was first implemented, to approximately 150 customers in 2015. This particular market has spent approximately $9,700 in support of double-SNAP points, although some of those funds are contingent on additional fundraising activities. The point is the double-SNAP program has been effective in confronting the nutritional security of low-income households in the area. Doubling points effectively works on the same principle of coupons, the difference being that profit is not the pivotal objective.

From a practical standpoint, retailers might consider implementing a similar strategy for select items, such as fresh produce or nonprocessed foods, as a means of controlling surplus. If an additional incentive is necessary to temper concerns over lost profits, state and federal governments might consider tax incentives for those retailers offering double-SNAP. At the very least, these would provide a more direct assurance that charitable contributions are going to a tangible and worthy cause.

This study supports previous research findings regarding the emphasis placed on profit instead of healthy food. However, there are potential alternatives to increasing the availability of healthy food and thus decreasing the negative health consequences. The sale of fresh produce increases when price reductions are made available, whether in a grocery store setting (Phipps, Braitman, et al. 2013) or a farmers' market.

Coupons and store sale ads offer households a way to reduce their expenditures on groceries, however these money savings come at an increased risk for the negative health consequences associated with an unhealthy diet. Grocery stores, as well as farmers' markets, need to continue to seek alternatives to coupons and sale ads to increase the likelihood low-income households will buy fresh produce. For this to occur, the emphasis needs to be placed on health and healthy foods instead of on the profit margins of these stores. In the case of farmers' markets, these programs are undertaken when the main focus is placed on helping people have increased access to healthy produce, not increased profit margins.

This study faces a few limitations worth noting that can limit our understanding of how people shop for food in different venues. First, there is little information about the population using coupons. This makes it difficult to conduct a comparison of the coupon-using population, and what coupons they frequently use, to devise possible changes for stores to implement and increase health food purchases. Second, there are limited real-world examples of people using coupons or other available healthy food discounts, aside from the aforementioned SNAP program at farmers' markets. Further research is needed to identify effective strategies of not only implementing such alternatives for purchasing healthy food, but also increasing the knowledge and use of these strategies to combat food insecurity among low-income families.

Regardless of whether or how such possible alternative systems are established for low-income families to gain more access to healthy food items, the current study suggests further consideration of an often overlooked aspect of food security: kitchen knowledge. Coupons are most frequently available for processed foods that require little time, equipment, or knowledge to prepare. These products and their ensuing popularity flourished with the technological advances that accompanied the post–World War II expansion of the US economy. Processed foods were heralded as a time-saving device for women working outside of the home (Kamp 2006). This need for quicker food options for families working longer hours is the dividing line in which middle- and upper-middle-class families are able to take advantage of healthy food options beyond simply affording them. That is, even if low-income families are able to afford healthy food options, they (1) must have jobs that allow them to work less for a sustainable living wage to take more time to cook these foods given the generally longer prep time needed for such meals, and (2) must have some of the needed kitchen equipment and knowledge of how to cook such foods that have been pushed to the higher socioeconomic sectors of society.

Simply reducing food insecurity to the presence or absence of food grossly ignores the consequences of unhealthy diets that are perpetuated by processed foods and the money-saving attempts supported by couponing. In all, these two considerations indicate how narrow food insecurity can be applied to society. If we limit our understanding of coupons as a choice among families of limited means, this can lead to "victim blaming" (Ryan 1976), which obscures the structural inequality that can make such choices seem simple to families with more secure, well-paying jobs. Couponing and the use of sale ads, when situated in the proper context, unveil the depth of food insecurity as an integral part of durable inequalities (Tilly 1998). That is, the broader socioeconomic context that impacts families positions coupons as a stable option for putting food on the table with the limited amount of time it takes to cook more processed foods as people work longer hours for less money, and cooking with little knowledge beyond the instructions on a box and how to use a microwave or an (operational) oven. Instead a more complete picture needs to be developed to understand how families and individuals can not only save money on food, but spend their money in healthier ways. Despite their manifest purpose, coupons are not a solution to this increasing problem, and alternative strategies for increasing healthy food options is an imperative avenue for scholars, policy makers, and community members as a whole to invest in to decrease food insecurity.

REFERENCES

Andrews, Margaret, and Gary Bickel. 1998. "Household Food Security in the United States 1995: Results from the Food Security Measurements Project." *Family Economics and Nutrition Review* 11 (1/2): 17–28.

Argo, Jennifer J., and Kelley J. Main. 2008. "Stigma by Association in Coupon Redemption: Looking Cheap Because of Others." *Journal of Consumer Research* 35 (4): 559–52.

Baronberg, Sabrina, Lilian Dunn, Cathy Nonas, Rachel Dannefer, and Rachel Sacks. 2013. "The Impact of New York City's Health Bucks Program on Electronic Benefit Transfer Spending at Farmers Markets, 2006–2009." *Preventing Chronic Disease* 10 (13): 1–13.

Berning, Joshua P. 2014. "The Effect of Breakfast Cereal Coupons on the Nutritional Quality of Household Purchases." *International Food and Agribusiness Management Review* 17 (A): 41–60.

Bhattacharya, Jayanta, Janet Currie, and Steven Haider. 2004. "Poverty, Food Insecurity, and Nutritional Outcomes in Children and Adults." *Journal of Health Economics* 23 (4): 839–62.

Block, Daniel, and Joanne Kouba. 2006. "A Comparison of the Availability and Affordability of a Market Basket in Two Communities in the Chicago Area." *Public Health Nutrition* 9 (7): 837–45.

Bonnici, Joseph, David P. Campbell, William B. Fredenberger, and Kathryn H. Hunnicutt. 2011. "Consumer Issues in Coupon Usage: An Exploratory Analysis." *Journal of Applied Business Research* 13 (1): 31–40.

CDC (Centers for Disease Control and Prevention), National Center for Health Statistics. 2017. "National Diabetes Statistics Report, 2017: Estimates of Diabetes and Its Burden in the United States." *www.cdc.gov/diabetes/pdfs/data/statistics/national-diabetes-statistics-report.pdf.*

Dong, Diansheng, and Ephraim Leibtag. 2010. "Promoting Fruit and Vegetable Consumption: Are Coupons More Effective Than Pure Price Discounts?" USDA Economic Research Report No. 96. *www.ers.usda.gov/webdocs/publications/46387/7041_err96_1_.pdf?v=41056.*

Fox, Mary Kay, William Hamilton, and Biing-Hwan Lin. 2004. "Effects of Food Assistance and Nutrition Programs on Nutrition and Health: Vol. 4, Executive Summary on the Literature Review." USDA Economic Research Report No. 19–4. *www.ers.usda.gov/webdocs/publications/46575/30216_fanrr19–4_002.pdf?v=41479.*

French, Simone A. "Pricing Effects on Food Choices." 2003. *Journal of* Nutrition 133: 841–43.

Glanz, Karen, Michael D. M. Bader, and Shally Iyer. 2012. "Retail Grocery Store Marketing Strategies and Obesity: An Integrative Review." *American Journal of Preventative Medicine* 42 (5): 503–12.

Grose, Jessica. 2013. "The All-Consuming Pleasures of 'Extreme Couponing.'" Bloomberg. February 28. *www.bloomberg.com/news/articles/2013–02–28/the-all-consuming-pleasures-of-extreme-couponing.*

Kamp, David. 2006. *The United States of Arugula: How We Became a Gourmet Nation.* New York: Broadway Books.

Lopez, Andrea, and Hilary K. Seligman. 2014. "Online Grocery Store Coupons and Unhealthy Foods, United States." *Preventing Chronic Disease* 11 (13): 2–11.

Mhurchu, C. Ni, S. Vandevijvere, W. Waterlander. L. E. Thornton, B. Kelly, A. J. Cameron, W. Snowdon, and B. Swinburn. 2013. "Monitoring the Availability of Healthy and

Unhealthy Foods and Non-alcoholic Beverages in Community and Consumer Retail Food Environments Globally." *Obesity* 14 (1): 108–19.

Morland, Kimberly, Steve Wing, Ana Diez Roux, and Charles Poole. 2008. "Neighborhood Characteristics Associated with the Location of Food Stores and Food Service Places." In *Race, Ethnicity, and Health*, edited by T. A. LaVeist, 448–62. San Francisco: Jossey-Bass.

Phipps, Etienne J., Leonard E. Braitman, Shana D. Stites, Samantha L. Wallace, S. Brook Singletary, and Lacy H. Hunt. 2013. "The Use of Financial Incentives to Increase Fresh Fruit and Vegetable Purchases in Lower-Income Households: Results of a Pilot Study." *Journal of Health Care for the Poor and Underserved* 24 (2): 864–74.

Phipps, Etienne J., Shiriki K. Kumanyika, Shana D. Stites, S. Brook Singletary, Clarissa Cooblall, and Katherine Isselmann DiSantis. 2014. "Buying Food on Sale: A Mixed Methods Study with Shoppers at an Urban Supermarket, Philadelphia, Pennsylvania, 2010–2012." *Preventing Chronic Disease* 11 (1511): 1–12.

Ryan, William. 1976. *Blaming the Victim*. New York: Vintage.

Tilly, Charles. 1998. *Durable Inequality*. Berkeley: University of California Press.

Townsend, Marilyn S., Janet Peerson, Bradley Love, Cheryl Achterberg, and Suzanne P. Murphy. 2001. "Food Insecurity Is Positively Related to Overweight in Women." *Journal of Nutrition* 131 (6): 1738–45.

Walker, Renee E., Christopher R. Keane, and Jessica G. Burke. 2014. "Disparities and Access to Healthy Food in the United States: A Review of Food Deserts literature." *Health and Place* 16 (5): 876–84.

8

The Rise and Falter of Emergency Food Assistance

JENNIFER W. BOUEK

On the morning of February 11, 1982, hundreds of people lined up outside of the People's United Methodist Church in Long Island City, Queens (Gaiter 1982). They were waiting for the five-pound blocks of government cheese being distributed for free. By 8 a.m. the line was a block long, an hour and a half before the church was scheduled to open, and by 1:30 p.m. the cheese was gone. Despite the thirty-nine hundred pounds of cheese that the church had ordered, some people still went home without any, hopeful that more would soon be on its way. Suffering from an economic downturn, high unemployment, and the threat of hunger, many individuals were relieved to be receiving any sort of aid. Others, including antihunger and social justice advocates, argued that surplus cheese was not an adequate solution to widespread hunger.

A few weeks prior to February 11, the federal government had released millions of pounds of surplus cheese from government storage in response to public outcry over rising rates of poverty and hunger (Reagan 1981). This cheese was transferred to churches, community centers, and other nonprofit outlets all over the country with instructions to distribute it to those in need. With the Reagan administration's emphasis on fiscal austerity, doling out the millions of pounds of surplus cheese solved two problems for the government: it addressed hunger but also saved on storing and warehousing expenses. In the months following, the Reagan administration released subsequent surpluses in rapid succession, and in 1983, the program was expanded and formalized by Congress. In 1990, this system of surplus food distribution as an antihunger program became permanent with the formation of the Emergency Food Assistance Program (TEFAP).

These events mark the establishment of our current emergency food assistance network, a network made up of food banks and food pantries operating out of churches and community centers. The present-day emergency food assistance network, in many ways, remains similar to that of 1981. Much of the food distributed to beneficiaries is still considered government surplus, although food banks now work to acquire food from a number of other sources as well. Emergency food continues to be distributed through community nonprofit outlets, many religiously based. And people continue to line church fences and walls early in the morning, sometimes lining up an hour or more before the food pantry is scheduled to open. The following scene from my field notes could easily be mistaken for one of the initial emergency food distributions in the 1980s:

> Fifteen to twenty people are lined up along a wrought-iron fence surrounding an old stone church, the South Street Baptist. The line, consisting of mostly middle-aged women, begins at a pair of heavy doors, winds down a few stone steps, and along the sidewalk. It is sunny but cold, a mid-February morning in the northeastern United States, hovering just above freezing. The people are waiting for the food pantry inside the church to open. It is already 9:10 a.m., and the pantry was supposed to open at 9:00 a.m. They shuffle and chat, keeping their minds off the cold and the passing time. At 9:15 a.m. one of the three volunteers opens the doors, and the waiting women file inside the chilly church foyer and down a set of stairs.

The process of obtaining emergency food has changed very little since the inception of the network decades ago. The uncertainty, too, has changed little. Beneficiaries still remain uneasy about whether they will get enough groceries or the groceries that they really need, like meat and bread.

Behind these scenes, however, the infrastructure supporting the emergency food network has changed dramatically. The network has grown tremendously in size and sophistication over the past thirty-six years. The majority of the two hundred or so food banks across the country are now interconnected, sharing food and resources, and have developed into a complex hub-and-spoke system that efficiently distributes food around the country. Each food bank operates within a delineated catchment area, providing the food and resources to its local food pantries, which eventually distribute the food to individual beneficiaries. One centralized, national, nonprofit body, Feeding America, works to channel national corporate donations toward regional food banks. Now, food banks source food not only from the federal government's TEFAP initiative but also from national and regional corporate donors, wholesalers and farmers, and community-level food drives, in addition to their growing purchasing budgets. Yet, despite this increase in sophistication, resource scarcity remains a problem for the network, and uncertainty pervades the present and the future.

To learn about the emergency food assistance network, I began by interviewing key staff members of one northeastern food bank, which I refer to here as the State Food Bank.[1] I then undertook archival analysis of the State Food Bank's financial reports, operations reports, and annual reports to understand the environment in which the food bank was working. Following, I observed the food distribution process, often stepping in to help volunteers at ten food pantries over a period of eleven months. I additionally interviewed the managers at each of these pantries and informally interviewed other volunteers during my observation periods.

In this chapter, I draw on this research to discuss the unpredictable nature of the network, recent trends in resource scarcity, and how one food bank is working to reconcile supply and demand. Although the emergency food assistance network operates independently from federal food assistance programs, such as the Supplemental

Nutrition Assistance Program (SNAP), the emergency food assistance network is now fully institutionalized within the American welfare state. Millions of families rely on its services. While estimates vary, ranging from seventeen million people to forty-seven million people, all sources report a dramatic increase in the number of beneficiaries from 2007 to 2013 (Coleman-Jensen, Gregory, and Singh 2014; Feeding America 2014). Yet, these services are often unpredictable, and, increasingly, they are threatened by declines in donations, especially in the context of rising need.

An Unpredictable System

If you talk with the volunteers and staff running food pantries, they will likely tell you that the emergency food assistance network is intended to provide only sporadic and temporary relief for families in need. As one volunteer pantry manager explained to me while discussing her attendance policies: "This is what you do when you're in a tight spot." Increasingly, though, families may remain in "tight spots" for long periods of time, and many families rely regularly on emergency food as part of their monthly grocery budget (Feeding America 2014). In my case study, the number of families using food pantries affiliated with the State Food Bank increased by 91 percent between 2007 and 2014. Similar influxes were witnessed in other food banks across the country.

A primary obstacle in accessing emergency food assistance is that the services must be obtained in person and on the pantry's schedule according to the pantry's process. This often means standing in lines outside for upward of an hour, occasionally in inclement weather. The times that food pantries are open are not always convenient, especially for working families, and are not always followed closely. During my fieldwork, pantries were frequently relaxed about their operating hours, opening late or closing early. Because of this, people often lined up early. Pantries also occasionally changed the process for distributing food without notifying beneficiaries. At one pantry, a change in the process temporarily halted food distribution to at least half of the people still waiting, and anxiety quickly traveled up and down the line. From my field notes:

> There was general confusion in the line. The pantry had started giving numbers out to the first and then second wave of people, about twenty to thirty people in each wave. Your number indicated when you would be called in to get food. Rather than giving everyone a number and then proceeding to food like they usually did, they had stopped giving out numbers and had started giving the first two waves food. Now there was chaos around the front entrance.

Because of tension between the need for emergency food and the general lack of communication and transparency over how the food is distributed, beneficiaries often adjust to the anxiety-producing unpredictability of food pantries by lining up early and asserting their place in line as best they can. But because emergency food is considered charity rather than entitlement, beneficiaries have no claim over their right to receive food.

Eligibility to receive emergency food also varies among food pantries. Some food pantries require little to no documentation, distributing food to anyone who asks. Other food pantries may require proof of income, proof of residence, or proof of household composition, including birth certificates for young children. Some pantries refuse to serve the homeless, sending them to shelters or kitchens instead. Because nearly all emergency food providers are nonprofit organizations and operate with little oversight, providers are able to distribute food according to how they see fit, as long as the food is distributed for free and stored according to regulated health standards, the providers are open to the eligible public, and recipients have no obligation to attend religious services. Providers typically choose to serve a limited geographic area, which they define as their community. This practice restricts the number of families that a pantry will need to serve but simultaneously restricts the number of pantries families are able to access. If a family's community has no food pantry, they are not guaranteed to be fed elsewhere. For example, one of the food pantries I visited was experiencing an influx of beneficiaries from a neighboring area where the only food pantry had recently closed, but, as the pantry manager explained, they were unable or unwilling to help. Again, from my field notes: "Recently, a food pantry in West Rainbury closed. I asked why, and the [manager] didn't know. People from West Rainbury, she said, have been coming to the Dade food pantry looking for help, but the Dade food pantry only helps people in Dade and have been turning these people away. [The manager] says: that is our mission, to help the people of Dade."

While other pantries I visited often provided unqualified beneficiaries with something, it was not uncommon for pantries to attempt to define their target audience and channel unqualified need elsewhere.

Once you have made it into the food pantry and have demonstrated your eligibility, you can begin the process of collecting your food. Unlike means-tested benefit programs, like SNAP, what you receive from food pantries can be highly variable since the emergency food network is fueled largely by donations. The amount and type of foods that clients receive can and do differ regularly. Most food pantries aim to provide families with several days' worth of food, although the amount of food distributed does not always vary according to family size so that a family of three might receive as much as a family of five. Recipients typically receive a variety of goods, including rice or pasta, canned vegetables or fruits, canned beans, juice, and occasionally fresh items such as produce, most commonly onions, carrots, and potatoes, and sometimes even meat or ice cream or gourmet cheeses, depending on the food pantry's resources. Rarely do pantries have enough of everything, though, to supply each recipient with a uniform set of groceries, so supplies often vary from visit to visit and from client to client. This variability, in large part, stems from the sources of food. TEFAP foods, for example, function as a type of agricultural market mechanism. So if one year there is a glut of blueberries, the USDA will buy some of those blueberries to be distributed through TEFAP to keep the market price of blueberries high. The next year it might be chicken or cranberries.

Because emergency food is distributed by mostly unregulated private citizens, there can be significant variation in the delivery of services across space and time, depending on the dedication and skills of those individuals involved. The same variation has been found in the past at other nonprofit social services (Smith and Lipsky 1993). This means that two similarly situated people, each receiving emergency food through a food pantry, may have completely different experiences and receive a different quantity and quality of food depending on the pantry to which they have access.

Rising Demand, Declining Supply

Beyond the daily uncertainty of emergency food, the infrastructure supporting the network is also facing vulnerability. The women and men who I observed waiting against the stone walls of old churches and stuccoed walls of community centers, and alongside chain-link fences waiting for entry into food pantries are among the many who have recently looked to the emergency food assistance network for help. For example, at the time of my visit, one of the churches housing a large food pantry was serving a historically high number of clients. Their list of beneficiaries was in the thousands and had increased tenfold over the past several years. This urgent rise in demand is relatively consistent across the State Food Bank pantries. When considering all its member pantries, the State Food Bank is facing an unprecedented increase in the number of beneficiaries it supports, reporting a 91 percent increase from 2007 to 2014.

Indeed, the increase in need is consistent with national reports as well. Data from the Current Population Survey presented in Figures 8.1 and 8.2 suggests a uniform rise in pantry use across various household compositions, within and outside of cities, and across the country. This rise is driven both by the general state of the US economic environment and by cuts to public benefit programs. Unemployment and underemployment rates rose substantially following the Great Recession, although they have declined significantly since (US Bureau of Labor Statistics 2015). Similar to the early 1980s when the emergency food assistance network first emerged, a weak economy has been met with declines in public assistance. For example, cash welfare benefits and government spending on Temporary Assistance for Needy Families have declined precipitously since 1996 (Moffitt 2013) and saw no increase with the onset of the Great Recession. The value of SNAP benefits, or food stamps, has also continued to decline owing to inflation, and new work requirements and time limits have been instituted in a number of states making access more cumbersome (Nord 2013). As a result, many of those unable to access public benefits or those who fail to qualify turn to the emergency food assistance network.

Despite the rising number of beneficiaries, the State Food Bank and its member pantries are struggling with historically low levels of funding and food donations. Although government grants have always made up a small portion of the State Food Bank's budget, even this small amount has diminished as government grants declined from 2003 to 2013 by 23 percent. Temporary supplemental funding from the American Recovery and Reinvestment Act (ARRA), which supplied states with additional administrative funding to store and distribute TEFAP foods, ended in 2010, and from 2010 to 2014, pounds of TEFAP-sourced food in the State Food Bank network declined by 26 percent. These declines are not isolated to emergency food providers but are in line with current funding trends for most nonprofit social service providers who have seen continual diminishment in funding and increased threat, if not realization, of budget cuts over recent decades (Grønbjerg and Salamon 2012).

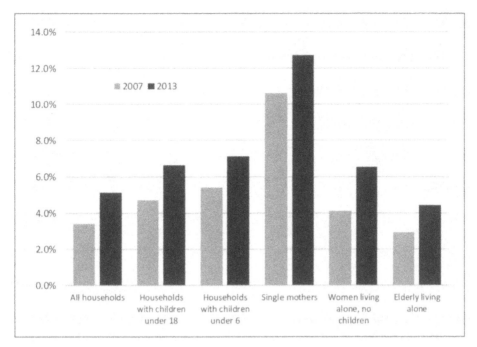

FIGURE 8.1. Changes in food pantry use by household composition, Current Population Survey 2007 and 2013. Sources: Nord, Andrews, and Carlson 2008; Coleman-Jensen, Gregory, and Singh 2014.

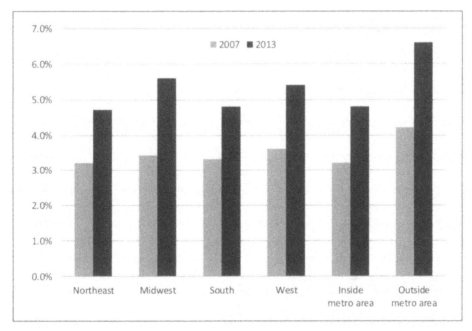

FIGURE 8.2. Changes in food pantry use by region and urbanicity, Current Population Survey 2007 and 2013. Sources: Nord, Andrews, and Carlson 2008; Coleman-Jensen, Gregory, and Singh 2014.

The decline and stagnation in government support has been exacerbated by drops in corporate food donations. Pounds of food donated to the State Food Bank network from corporate retailers and distributors declined by 20 percent between 2006 and 2014. Compounding the dilemma, State Food Bank's number of corporate food donors has also declined by 39 percent between 2000 and 2013 from 155 to 95. To make up the difference, the State Food Bank has begun purchasing more and more food. Pounds of purchased food were up 230 percent from 2006 to 2015. But purchasing is expensive, and funds are equally as scarce as food donations.

In the face of these challenges, the State Food Bank and its member pantries have adopted several strategies to save costs and monitor resources. For example, food pantries often closely control the amount and types of food that a beneficiary is given. Several of the pantries I visited placed restrictions around the type of packaging beneficiaries were allowed to use to take food home, a rule intended to establish consistency between beneficiaries. One pantry in my study, for example, gave clients one designated bag upon registration. The client was allowed to collect food from the pantry using only this bag. If the bag was lost, the client had to purchase another for five dollars. The pantry manager explained that they had had the bags custom designed to accommodate three to five meals for the week. In another pantry, the manager deemed clients' bags, brought from home, either appropriate or not, based on size. Bags he perceived as too big were deemed inappropriate. If the bag was inappropriate, the client was not allowed to receive food. This excerpt from my field notes illustrates the scene: "Peter [the pantry manager] allowed one person to approach his desk at a time. He asked to see their bag and to see their ID. If the person was not a Saturday person, he turned them away. If the person's bag was deemed too big he did not allow them to use it. This happened to one girl, Julie. She had two bags, but they were both too big."

All the food pantries additionally had volunteers guiding beneficiaries through the pantry, letting them know what they could have and how much. By limiting beneficiaries' packaging or overseeing the beneficiaries shopping, the food pantry is better able to control the amount of food distributed to clients, ensuring equality between clients but also monitoring the pantry's total distribution.

The State Food Bank has also taken several steps to minimize costs and operate with less donated food. While these steps keep the broader network sustainable, they also place equitable beneficiary access in question. For example, one of the ways that the State Food Bank has minimized costs is by concentrating their resources on the largest pantries that serve the most people. As explained to me by a State Food Bank executive, because they "can't get more food into the building," they focus their efforts on the food pantries that "serve the highest need population." These largest agencies are more likely to have relationships with local grocery stores through which they can access incremental food donations and are more likely to receive small grants from the State Food Bank that offset the fees that all pantries pay to receive food from the State Food Bank, typically around ten cents per pound. By concentrating resources among the highest-need populations and supporting the pantries that serve the most clients, the State Food Bank is maximizing its cost-benefit ratio. The network is able to serve the greatest number of people in the most cost-effective way. However, this strategy simultaneously limits the breadth of the network and the population that can be adequately served. For those not living within close proximity to the largest food pantries or in high-need areas, access to emergency food is potentially compromised.

The State Food Bank has also begun externalizing costs to pantry volunteers to limit labor and transportation expenses related to picking up local retail grocery donations. The State Food Bank procurement department has, over the past couple of years, initiated relationships between the local grocery stores who want to donate and the pantries located near the grocery store. The grocery stores and pantries then work directly with one another so that pantry volunteers can pick up food. Prior to initiating these relationships, the State Food Bank sent trucks to pick up all grocery donations, which would be taken to the State Food Bank warehouse and placed on the online ordering system. However, a State Food Bank executive told me that these trips were perceived as inefficient because there were often not enough groceries to necessitate an entire truck. To cut costs on labor and gas, the food bank removed itself as the middleman and connected food pantries directly to grocery stores. Efficient for the food bank and beneficial for select pantries, this program displaces costs, both time and money, onto individual volunteers and employees. It also prioritizes pantries with well-resourced volunteers. The pantry must have volunteers who have the money, time, and vehicles necessary to complete this operation on a consistent basis. A State Food Bank executive explained how the matchmaking works between pantry and grocery store: "Some of the stores will only be able to do this Wednesday at nine. It's not that they're rigid, they have their staff . . . they're doing a nice thing, and so it really depends on their availability to make the donation, and so if the [pantry] can't get somebody there at that moment when it's available, then they can't get it. To a certain extent, it's up to us to try to be the matchmaker and to make sure that the folks are matched up."

Although beneficial to the overall network because costs are reduced and clients fed, this strategy places the burden on individuals within the network. Additionally, many pantries have not been offered a relationship with a local grocery store nor even know about this opportunity and, therefore, are not able to access the food donations that were at one point posted on the online ordering platform available to all pantries.

A final strategy that the State Food Bank has begun to consider is an evolution of the organization's mission. As retail donations, the historic lifeblood of the network, decline, the food bank has had to consider how else and how better it can help those in need. One consideration is working as an informational and resource gateway organization. In an effort to transform, the State Food Bank has begun to offer job training programs, nutritional and healthy lifestyle education and information, and enrollment assistance in government programs like SNAP and Medicaid. Said one State Food Bank executive about his vision for the future of the network: "Now, when there isn't that sort of surplus food out there, I think the focus has to shift from pounds [of food] to the people in need. . . . The folks that we're serving don't have access to the information that you need to be able to access some of these resources, and if we can help them do that, that's major."

As the network loses its resources to provide material goods, the State Food Bank is transforming into more of an information resource and training center, connecting people to other existing sources of aid. But, as one State Food Bank executive expressed, the question still lingers: "If we shut down because there's not surplus food, where are those people going to get food?"

Concluding Thoughts

In this chapter, I have introduced the emergency food assistance network, a vital yet understudied system of social service providers in the United States. Since the early 1980s, the emergency food network has grown into a large national bureaucracy that operates complementarily to federal food assistance programs. The emergency food assistance network provides important aid to families who either do not qualify for federal programs or for whom federal programs do not provide sufficient aid. However, the network has recently encountered a challenging environment that threatens its continued existence: a significant increase in demand coupled with a decline in resources. The network thus far has been able to manage this challenge by adopting strategies that permit network actors to maximize efficiencies while still serving a growing number of clients. These strategies, however, have potential implications for clients, including the inequitable distribution of food and the uncertain future of emergency food assistance.

This chapter is not intended to be critical of the emergency food assistance network nor of the State Food Bank nor the food pantries I visited. My intention here, rather, is to think critically about the implications of the strategies adopted in the name of fiscal austerity and, more broadly, about the way that the poor are treated in the United States in general. When public assistance is administered by a variable consortium of volunteer and paid nonprofit staff who are provided few resources and presented with incredible demands, inconsistencies should be expected. From my understanding the State Food Bank and its partners are doing incredibly well and have been wonderfully creative in their tactics considering the dire context. The State Food Bank is supporting more beneficiaries than ever. That work should be applauded. More than anything, my research suggests not an evaluation of emergency food assistance but a critical evaluation of the broader American welfare system that necessitates such a network.

As more families turn to the emergency food assistance network for help, the significance of the network becomes increasingly clear. An improved and up-to-date understanding of the emergency food network is vital if public policy is to improve the conditions of American families in need. However, the focus perhaps should not be on the emergency food network, but rather on the factors driving a growing number of families to emergency food. As Poppendieck (1998) and others have pointed out, emergency food assistance is not the best nor the most respectful form of assistance. Rather, emergency food assistance arose out of convenience. The government was able to offload the expensive storage of surplus cheese and call it a public benefit; today, the government is able to support agricultural markets and call it food assistance. Although the days of five-pound cheese blocks seem to have passed, we should still consider the social mechanisms, such as an inequitable education system, a punitive welfare state, and widespread unemployment and underemployment, that lead families to the food pantries in the first place. Once they are there, we might also consider how their needs might best be addressed with respect and dignity.

NOTE

1. I have changed the names of all organizations to protect the individuals with whom I worked.

REFERENCES

Coleman-Jensen, Alisha, Christian Gregory, and Anita Singh. 2014. *Household Food Security in the United States in 2013*. ERR-173. US Department of Agriculture, Economic Research Service, September.

Feeding America. *Hunger in America*. 2010. By James Mabli, Rhoda Cohen, Frank Potter, and Zhanyun Zhao. National Report Prepared for Feeding America. Chicago.

———. 2014. *Hunger in America*. By Nancy Weinfield, Gregory Mills, Christine Borger, Maeve Gearing, Theodore Macaluso, Jill Montaquila, and Sheila Zedlewski. National Report Prepared for Feeding America. Chicago.

Gaiter, Dorothy J. 1982. "First of Surplus Cheese Is Given to City's Needy." *New York Times*, February 11. *www.nytimes.com/1982/02/11/nyregion/first-of-surplus-cheese-is-given-to-city-s-needy.html*.

Grønbjerg, Kirsten A., and Lester M. Salamon. 2012. "Devolution, Privatization and the Changing Shape of Government-Nonprofit Relations." In *The State of the Nonprofit Sector*, edited by Lester M. Salamon, 2nd ed., 447–70. Washington, DC: Brookings Institution Press.

Moffitt, Robert A. 2013. "The Great Recession and the Social Safety Net." *Annals of the American Academy of Political and Social Science* 650 (1): 143–66.

Nord, Mark. 2013. *Effects of the Decline in the Real Value of SNAP Benefits from 2009 to 2011*. ERR-151. US Department of Agriculture, Economic Research Service, August.

Nord, Mark, Margaret Andrews, and Steven Carlson. 2008. *Household Food Security in the United States, 2007*. ERR-66. US Department of Agriculture, Economic Research Service, November.

Poppendieck, Janet. 1998. *Sweet Charity? Emergency Food and the End of Entitlement*. New York: Penguin Books.

Reagan, Ronald. 1981. Presidential statement, "Cheese Inventory of the Commodity Credit Corporation." *Weekly Compilation of Presidential Documents* 17 (52): 1398–99.

Smith, Steven Rathgeb, and Michael Lipsky. 1993. *Nonprofits for Hire: The Welfare State in the Age of Contracting*. Cambridge, MA: Harvard University Press.

US Bureau of Labor Statistics. 2015. *Labor Force Statistics from the Current Population Survey*. Washington, DC.

9

The Complex Challenges to Participation in Federal Nutrition Programs

RACHEL WILKERSON, KATHY KREY, AND LINDA ENGLISH

In Lubbock, Texas, an unassuming woman operates gospel radio services. At a summer meals kickoff event, a one-day celebration to mark the beginning of summer and let area residents know about free food at summer meals sites in their neighborhood, she explains that she buys food out of pocket to feed children in her neighborhood during the summer months. The YMCA a block from her house serves free summer meals, but she is unfamiliar with the program and consequently has never directed the children to the free food.

In Anton, Texas, a small town in the Texas panhandle, the last grocery store closed in 2014. The senior citizen center has one computer accessible by the manager. Gathered around tables playing dominoes, everyone is eating government-subsidized mashed potatoes and gravy. They are eligible for the Supplemental Nutrition Assistance Program (SNAP), but few are enrolled. It is too little, they say; it is just not worth the hassle to fill out the application.

Underresourced communities called *colonias*, from the Spanish for "neighborhood," stitch a community together across the Texas Rio Grande valley. Many families there do not apply for SNAP because they know others are worse off, and they do not want to take something that is allotted for them. "We can always make rice and beans," they say. "That is not for us."

Federal nutrition assistance, including SNAP, and child nutrition programs form the first line of defense against hunger in America. SNAP provides funds to food insecure individuals as determined by a series of eligibility requirements. As a benchmark, a joint study by Feeding Texas and the Texas Hunger Initiative (THI), called Blueprint to End Hunger ("Blueprint to End Hunger" 2011), estimates that Texas residents leave $5.5 billion in SNAP benefits on the table each year. That amount reflects the high number of eligible participants who did not take advantage of nutrition assistance. This chapter aims to uncover the complex reasons why citizens may not access benefits.

SNAP participation is widespread and involves a diverse population: the majority of Americans will enroll in or have already benefited from SNAP. More than half of all Americans between the ages of twenty and sixty-five will receive food stamps at some point in their lifetimes. Individuals tend to be enrolled in SNAP over short periods of time, but their enrollment may by recurring. Only one in ten use SNAP for five consecutive years (Rank and Hirschl 2005). This contradicts the perception that SNAP usage is primarily a long-term income addition for a certain demographic. On the contrary, SNAP usage constitutes a temporary safety net for all types of households. As SNAP is such a critical feature of the safety net provided to the American population, the barriers complicating program participation vary along with the diverse circumstances of the participants. Although SNAP participation rates vary widely by location, a substantial portion of the eligible population never enrolls.

Another nationwide method of food assistance, child nutrition programs, provide meals to children through initiatives like the School Breakfast Program, the National School Lunch Program (NSLP), the Summer Food Service Program (SFSP), and the Child and Adult Care Food Program (CACFP). These programs play a critical role in the infrastructure of public schools, as evidenced by a 2015 Southern Education Foundation study showing that, for the first time in the history of the program, the majority of public school children are eligible for free and reduced-price lunch ("New Majority" 2015). Another component of the safety net, the Special Supplemental Nutrition Program for Women, Infants, and Children (WIC) offers funds for groceries to growing families. Over half of all infants and one quarter of children ages one through four in the United States now participate in the WIC program (Oliveira et al. 2002).

Child nutrition programs are often integral to the community and subject to less political dialogue than SNAP. However, while the school lunch program has high participation rates, school breakfast programs and summer and afterschool meals programs often have participation rates that are a fraction of the participation in school lunches. According to the Food and Research Action Center, in Texas only 12 percent of children who receive free and reduced-price lunches during the school year participate in the summer meals program. Additionally, 25 percent of schools that offer NSLP do not offer the School Breakfast Program (SBP) (Currie 2003). Take-up rates for WIC are typically high for pregnant women and infants, but lower for children. Barriers that keep food insecure individuals from obtaining benefits also riddle these nutrition programs.

Hidden within aggregate numbers are the stories of citizens who either deliberately or unintentionally decided against government benefits. These stories include elderly individuals who do not want to take the funds when someone else needs them more, the woman feeding children out of her house because she did not know there was a summer meals site right around the corner, and the immigrant who thought that signing his children up for SNAP put his immigration status in jeopardy. That number hides a dozen misconceptions—economic, sociological, and cultural reasons why a person in need of food could not or did not access the available government benefits to meet his or her nutrition needs.

To better understand why people do not access benefits requires asking two questions. First, why are eligible populations unable to access benefits? Awareness and logistical challenges are two of the primary reasons that people cannot access the benefits they need. Secondly, we must also ask why people choose not to access benefits—a question of human choice. People may choose not to apply for SNAP because of misconceptions, socioeconomic expectations, or cultural pressures. The step between deciding to apply for benefits and actually procuring them is rife with challenges.

In order to accurately represent the complex challenge of access to and participation in nutrition programs, we categorize barriers as challenges that (a) limit access, (b) impose programmatic restrictions, and (c) stymie program participation. Building a barriers framework allows us to consider the varied and nuanced obstacles that arise as food insecure citizens navigate federal nutrition programs. We will consider barriers facing SNAP, WIC, and child nutrition programs. Access barriers consist of factors that hinder individuals from obtaining nutrition resources, whether by completing a SNAP application or attending a meal site for a child nutrition program. Programmatic barriers consist of systemic rules, regulations, and restrictions that may create artificial constructs blocking food insecure persons from obtaining food assistance. Finally, participation barriers encompass the various reasons why children, families, and individuals may elect not to seek federal food assistance. Examining the economic cost of the program reveals the ancillary factors that affect the decision-making processes of food insecure persons. We also address the formidable challenges of stigma and cultural expectations. In total, this framework for defining the barriers to participation provides a multifaceted look at the many points at which barriers confront those seeking food assistance.

Access Barriers

Food insecure individuals may refrain from accessing benefits because they are unaware of them, they may not have transportation to the location of assistance, or they may be prohibited from completing applications owing to failures of communication or excessive documentation. These barriers describe the obstacles restricting seekers' access simply to initiate the process of obtaining meals or resources to supplement their nutrition. For example, a family may be too daunted by the SNAP application, or a child may not have transportation to a summer meal site.

A critical problem for all nutrition programs is a lack of awareness—food insecure individuals cannot obtain available food if they are unaware of programs. For example, a survey by the Dallas Coalition for Hunger Solutions (Johnson 2015) noted that seniors in particular might not be aware that they are eligible for SNAP benefits. Individuals who may have been turned down for SNAP previously may not realize that they have become eligible as they have grown older. Elderly populations are often unaware of programmatic changes that offer more assistance. Awareness is also a critical challenge for summer meals sites. In spite of marketing efforts by state agencies and nonprofits, families are often unaware that free meals are available in their neighborhoods. Simply put, people cannot obtain benefits if they are unaware of their availability.

Accessing benefits like SNAP or summer meals requires travel to where the benefits are available, perhaps an eligibility office or a summer meal site. Transportation to application assistance prohibits citizens from applying for SNAP. A lack of transportation also represents a challenge for out-of-school meals programs. A survey conducted by THI ("National Summer Meals Sponsor Survey: Texas Results" 2014) noted that summer meals sponsors, both schools and nonprofits, report transportation as a major obstacle (20 percent and 18 percent, respectively), especially in rural areas. Sponsors report that churches and other organizations are often willing to volunteer vans for transportation, but additional funds would be needed for fuel. Additionally, some site locations require children to walk further than their parents are comfortable with or require them to walk across busy intersections.

Across the nation, school officials seek innovative solutions to the challenge of transportation. "Texas City is such a vast area, and the city has camps or daycares at certain locations," said a school nutrition official for Texas City ISD. "But when we looked at the map, there were a lot of areas, like apartments, [where residents] couldn't walk to those locations. So we came up with the idea to try to go out to those areas and reach out to them" (Texas City school nutrition official 2015). Roblyer and his colleagues fashioned a school bus with a cooler that delivers meals to children in the summer. The bus is equipped with music and water misters, emphasizing summer fun and consequently minimizing the stigma associated with free meals.

Site location heavily determines a community's access to the summer meals program. Research shows that a site must be less than one mile away for children to feel safe walking to it. In a 2014 study of children's summer food needs and experiences ("Texas Out of School Meals: A Study of Summer and Afterschool Meal Programs in Texas" 2014), parents expressed that they did not have access to cars during the day and could not afford the bus fare to travel to the nearest summer meal sites. "There are going to be areas where in order to reach a school, the children would have to cross a major thoroughfare," said the transportation director for McAllen ISD. "We also understand that during the school year, [the children's] main mode of transportation to and from the school is the school bus" (McAllen ISD transportation director 2015). The importance of public transportation to communities cannot be separated from the challenge of food insecurity.

Beyond the issue of transportation, absenteeism also impedes access to meals. This particularly affects school meals issues. Children are unable to access meals at school if they are late or absent from school. Late buses or unstable family situations may be at the root of tardiness, which especially limits access to school breakfast.

Programmatic Barriers

Turning our attention now to programmatic barriers, we examine rules and regulations that prohibit seekers from accessing federal nutrition programs. First, we examine eligibility barriers for families and individuals in the process of applying for SNAP, and then we examine programmatic barriers to determining eligibility for child nutrition programs. The challenges to eligibility are twofold—first, not all food insecure populations are eligible for programs, and, second, proving eligibility is a complicated process where many food insecure individuals fall through the cracks.

Eligibility for SNAP is determined primarily by a maze of income and asset tests that vary by state. For all SNAP households, federal eligibility is limited to those with gross incomes up to 130 percent of the federal poverty line. Participants must also show a net income of less than or equal to 100 percent of the poverty line and are subject to asset tests. SNAP is administered by states, which have discretion to adapt the program to best meet the needs of their residents.

Net income is gross income minus certain deductions. The gross income limit for a family of four is $2,628 per month, and the net income limit for a family of four is $2,021. For households without elderly or disabled family members, income must fall at or below 130 percent of the federal poverty line, and they are allowed countable assets of no more than $2,250. Households with any elderly or disabled members are exempt from the gross income limit and may have up to $3,250 in assets ("Supplemental Nutrition Assistance Program [SNAP]" 2014).

For SNAP households that face asset tests, all but four states (Delaware, Minnesota, North Dakota, and Washington) have aligned their vehicle rules with those for other federal assistance programs; twenty-nine states and Washington, DC, have aligned their vehicle rules with programs that exclude all vehicles from the resource test. Fourteen states retained gross income limits for households without elderly or disabled. Twenty-eight states raised the gross income limit to 160–200 percent of the federal poverty line for households without elderly or the disabled. A Mathematica policy report (Leftin et al. 2013) notes that New Hampshire raised gross income limits for households with children aged twenty-one or younger. In some states, people in noncash TANF programs are categorically eligible. Depending on the case, applicants may be asked for pay stubs or utility bills and be asked to complete asset tests (Rosen, Hoey, and Steed 2001). Asset tests confound an already complicated process, and there is a motion to prohibit them in an effort to move toward more transparent government policies. While thirty-four states have done away with the asset tests, they remain a part of the application process in Alaska, Arkansas, Idaho, Indiana, Louisiana, Kansas, Maine, Michigan, Missouri, Nebraska, South Dakota, Tennessee, Texas, Utah, Virginia, and Wyoming (CFED Assets and Opportunity Scorecard Policy Map 2017).

The complex process of determining eligibility begins with highly detailed income and asset tests that are subject not only to income levels but also to asset testing, job requirements, number of people in a household, and other benefits received. A caseworker may advise an applicant incorrectly simply because he or she has an incomplete picture of the applicant's financial situation. Eligibility may be particularly difficult to determine for special populations. For example, a caseworker may incorrectly discourage ineligible immigrants from applying on behalf of eligible family members (Kaye, Lee, and Chen 2013) or incorrectly advise a family with mixed immigration status of their eligibility. Furthermore, limited access to phone or e-mail inhibits notification of changes to eligibility. The eligibility of elderly and disabled individuals is often calculated incorrectly because their medical bills are not taken into account. For instance, the Medicaid spend-down may not be counted for an elderly applicant, thus rendering his or her application falsely ineligible.

The fact that the federal SNAP program is administered at the state level adds an additional element of complexity to the process of determining eligibility. State-specific program implementation and administration (with the flexibility provided by the federal government) makes it more likely that income-eligible residents of some states participate and keep their benefits while in other states, residents are less likely to enroll and more likely to lose their benefits. In Florida for example, a six-month recertification period makes more participants vulnerable to being disqualified or accidentally dropped from the program owing to unintentional missteps. Recertification requires that clients take action once they receive a notice in the mail. Many times the notification letter is not received, if a client failed to update a new address, for example, and benefits automatically expire regardless of receipt of recertification notification. Oregon, however, has removed barriers to participation including adopting a standard certification period of twelve months, which helps increase duration of SNAP participation. Varying political climates mean that states often interpret the goals and intent of the SNAP program differently, resulting in very different experiences for potential applicants (Edwards et al. 2012).

Some states work to ameliorate administrative barriers. SNAP participation plummeted over 40 percent from 1993 to 2000 along with the take-up rate (the fraction of eligible persons participating). The fall in take-up rate was a concern for many advocates, and states responded with a variety of policy adjustments. These adjustments included expanding categorical eligibility, reducing required paperwork, increasing the dollar amount of vehicles excluded from asset calculations, or implementing more generous asset tests (Ziliak 2013).

The years after the 1996 comprehensive welfare reform titled the Personal Responsibility and Work Opportunity Reconciliation Act of 1996 saw SNAP participation and costs plummet, largely owing to the decrease in the share of eligible families receiving benefits. Welfare laws were intended to encourage work, but, because of problems in the state administration systems in the first years of the new law, many were cut off from SNAP when they secured jobs, even though they remained eligible for the program. In 1994, 75 percent of eligible households received SNAP, compared to 54 percent in 2002, and 83 percent in 2014 (Rosenbaum and Keith-Jennings 2015). Aside from the difficulties of the application, some food insecure are prohibited from applying at all. Certain populations are ineligible for SNAP regardless of their income, including some who have committed a felony, those who are on strike, undocumented immigrants, and certain legal immigrants. For example, in 1996 most states banned drug felons from SNAP for life; however, many states are now reversing course. In September 2015, Texas became the forty-fifth state to allow people with felony drug convictions (who have completed their sentences) to be eligible to for SNAP benefits. If recipients violate terms of their parole they are disqualified for two years, and if they reoffend on drug charges, they face a lifetime ban. Currently, seven states do not allow those with felony drug records to receive SNAP benefits.

These legislative rules can limit the food assistance available to ineligible individuals and their families. A one-time successful application to SNAP is insufficient to ensure food security. SNAP participants are subject to a cycle of renewals and continued scrutiny, a problem commonly known as churn. Examining the patterns of entering and exiting SNAP offers a snapshot of these programmatic barriers. While changes in employment and income were the most common factors associated with entering and exiting SNAP, 30 percent of households did not show an event related to improved financial circumstances or reduced need that would stimulate an exit from SNAP. It is possible that the administrative or bureaucratic barriers outlined above contributed to this gap in benefits (Mills et al. 2014).

Further analysis of the problem of households entering and exiting SNAP reveals the problem of churn—when a household exits the program and then reenters within four months. Recipients are most likely to exit the program during the time of recertification—the period of time at the end of the certification period when households must renew or recertify their benefits to prevent interruption. Possible reasons for unexpected lapses in resources can be stimulated by changes in household circumstances, such as a move. Other barriers include challenges and stressors like mental and physical health, literacy, and language proficiency. Additionally, state agencies may fail to send clear, timely messages to participants whose benefits are about to lapse. While most participants are off the program for one month or less, this lapse in food security may further destabilize families and individuals. Clients experience a great deal of stress when off the program—sometimes learning that their benefits have lapsed only when they attempt to purchase groceries. Loss of benefits leads to broader financial insecurity during an already vulnerable time (Mills et al. 2014).

After food insecure individuals have obtained access and determined eligibility, they must clear the logistic hurdles associated with obtaining the actual benefits themselves. Benefit barriers encompass anything that prohibit individuals from tangibly obtaining benefits (in the case of SNAP, money; for child nutrition programs, the meal). A key challenge for SNAP recipients stems from the electronic benefits transfer (EBT) system. Electronic snafus may lead to transaction errors at stores. Sometimes benefits may not transfer over to the next month (Kaye, Lee, and Chen 2013). While state agencies have mechanisms in place to address these gaps in coverage, such as issuing temporary EBT cards, recipients may be unaware, or staff time may be limited. Additionally, documentation errors may prohibit families from being able to purchase food. The *Boston Globe* covered a story of a woman who was denied at the cash register because her husband's photo, rather than her own, was on the SNAP identification card (Woolhouse 2014). Processing applications for federal programs takes staff time and a sufficient number of caseworkers. Budget cuts may limit states' ability to process applications in a timely manner. Food and nutrition services tracks the application processing timeliness rate via a quality-control system. While states are required to process applications within thirty days, too many families do not receive their benefits within the statutory time frames (Oliviera et al. 2002).

Child nutrition programs are also subject to bureaucratic and administrative barriers, though many of these fall on the contracting entity—that is, the school or the sponsor providing the meal; however, this chapter is limited to discussing barriers that directly face food insecure families and individuals. Eligibility for child nutrition programs centers primarily on paperwork for free and reduced-price lunch obtained from each family in a school. The primary barrier is simply not receiving the paperwork back from the parents. Even though many families in a community qualify for free or reduced-price school meals, they may not be receiving the financial benefits. Many parents may not receive an application, fill it out, or turn it back in. Additionally, parents may not realize that even if they do not wish to have their child participate in the free or reduced-price meals program, by completing and submitting an application their school district can benefit from at-risk funding. Additionally, families may not realize that if their income changes, at any time, they can reapply for free or reduced-price meals.

Some schools have adopted universally free service models that provide free breakfast, lunch, or both to all students in a school regardless of their individual eligibility status. This is an option on campuses where high numbers of those enrolled are eligible for free or reduced-price lunch. This benchmark—the level of free and reduced-price lunch eligibility—also determines which locations may seek reimbursement through the summer meals program. This creates an artificial cliff: schools that may be one percentage point below the cut off for a given state are not eligible for the summer food service program benefit and may be left without a way to meet the needs of their school. With the summer meals program, sponsors may operate either open or closed meal sites. For organizations that have enrolled attendees, such as a summer day camp, they may operate the summer meals program as a "closed site" where only pre-enrolled children are offered meals, while open sites are located at organizations where they are accessible to any child in the neighborhood who wants to attend the meal site. Having closed sites increases the types of organizations that may participate in the summer meals program, day camps for example. However, it is necessary to have open sites available as well so that neighborhood children, who may not be enrolled in the summer day camp, have a meal site option.

Lastly, the WIC program carries its own unique eligibility determinations. WIC recipients have to be deemed nutritionally at risk, which states have substantial leeway in determining. The definition requires anthropometric standards such as body-mass index, weight for age, height for age, or hemoglobin or hematocrit values. For example, in New Hampshire, infants below the twenty-fifth percentile in height for their age are "at risk," while in Massachusetts, infants must be below the eleventh percentile to be considered at risk (Currie 2003). Programmatically, WIC faces benefits barriers, namely that participants can use their benefits to purchase foods only at WIC-approved stores and farmers' markets. Furthermore, vouchers are valid only for specified time periods and to purchase very specific items or brands, which makes using the benefits difficult.

Participation Barriers

With accessibility challenges and programmatic barriers addressed, we turn our attention to the problem of participation barriers to address the problem of why food insecure individuals may refrain from participating in government programs. Here we examine how some of the factors outlined above interact to form a decision to not pursue federal food assistance, primarily the effect of cultural expectations, stigma, and economic cost.

Immigrant populations may choose not to access government programs; even eligible individuals in families of mixed immigration status may refrain from applying out of a misguided fear of endangering the immigration status of their family members (Kersey, Geppert, and Cutts 2006). The fact of the matter is that Immigration and Naturalization Services do not consider noncash benefits such as SNAP in determining if an individual is inadmissible to the United States because of their dependence on the government for subsistence. Latino families in particular may not have valid immigration documents, further complicating their case for SNAP eligibility (Quandt et al. 2006). Additionally, immigrant populations face language barriers and past experience with government officials that contribute to a fear of government programs.

Even though immigrants' US-born children are citizens, Latino families are much less likely than non-Latino families to receive SNAP (Kersey et al. 2006). Latino immigrants see themselves as part of a binational community and are concerned that the shame of their inability to feed their families in the United States will spread to their communities of origin in Latin America (Quandt et al. 2006). Further complicating the shame factor is the fear that applying for food assistance programs may trigger investigation of a family for child neglect (Rivera-Ottenberger and Werby 2007). Interestingly, this belief does not extend to child nutrition programs, partly because such programs can be framed as educational. One survey found that 90 percent of Latino participants reported that their children receive school breakfast and lunch, while only 30 percent participated in SNAP (Chavez, Telleen, and Kim 2007). Similarly, another study found that almost 30 percent of eligible households in a *colonia* did not access WIC resources (Sharkey, Dean, and Nalty 2013).

Furthermore, language barriers are often overwhelming for new populations who may not know English. Isolated Spanish-speaking households have access rates 13 percent lower than those of nonisolated Spanish-speaking households (per census classification of linguistic isolation among Spanish speakers) (Newman and Scherpf 2013). Language barriers extend to less common languages as well. For example, residents in Houston's Vietnamese neighborhoods (home to the third most common language in Texas, after English and Spanish) are often left without available resource languages. Even when translation resources are available, the additional effort required to search them out often culminates in a perception of the SNAP application as unnecessarily arduous.

The stigma associated with government programs is another crucial programmatic barrier to access. While research suggests that food stamp recipients may be better off than undernourished nonrecipients in terms of emotional distress, SNAP participation may be associated with the propensity to generate negative mental and emotional health effects. In locations where SNAP participants may be subject to public censure, potential participants may refrain from enrolling in SNAP (Heflin and Ziliak 2008). Stigma affects participation in child nutrition programs. Some teen participants mention the stigma attached to the free summer meal programs. Even though advertising states that the meals are free and available to everyone, there is still a perception that the programs exist only for children who are unable to find more socially acceptable alternatives. Many are hesitant to participate in free summer meals programs if the friends accompanying them do not participate in the program.

Elderly populations constitute another demographic that may be less likely to access SNAP. In general, access rates decline with age. Specifically, elderly persons who live alone or with only one other elderly person are less likely to access SNAP. Seniors who live with at least one nonelderly family member have rates similar to the statewide average. This suggests the importance of family structure to SNAP access (Newman and Scherpf 2013). Family members may view their parents' enrollment in benefits as a negative reflection on their care of their own parents, further compounding to the unnecessary shame and the stigma sometimes associated with benefits.

Participation barriers stem not only from the challenges unique to disadvantaged groups, but also from the real economic costs that program participation requires. The SNAP application process enacts a substantial economic cost that rarely figures into policy negotiations: these economic factors include the time and out-of-pocket costs required to maintain eligibility as well as the time costs associated with utilizing the benefits. In addition to being income poor, most food stamp–eligible populations are also relatively time poor since they are unable to take advantage of time-saving products and strategies that many middle- and upper-income households utilize on a daily basis (see, e.g., Vickery 1977). For example, a household without a dishwasher spends extra time in cleanup activities following a meal, a family without a washing machine or dryer must make extended trips to a Laundromat, and households that are unable to stock up on necessities make multiple trips to the store for needed items. The absence of a parent in the household or the lack of dependable transportation greatly exacerbates the time poverty experienced by low-income families. Compared to their two-parent counterparts, single-parent households have half of the time available to split between work and managing household activities (e.g., shopping, cooking, cleaning). Without vehicles for personal use, households may be forced to rely on a series of bus exchanges (each entailing a significant wait time) to travel relatively short distances to reach Laundromats, grocery stores, health care providers, and social support service offices.

In light of these economic considerations, it is understandable that 27 percent of eligible nonparticipants surveyed in 2000 would not apply for food assistance even if they were certain they would be eligible, and 4 percent said they were uncertain whether they would apply. The majority of these individuals (64 percent) cited the "perceived costs of applying—including the paperwork required, the necessity of taking time away from work or dependent care responsibilities, and the difficulty of getting to the food stamp office"—as reasons for not applying for benefits (Bartlett et al. 2004). Similar economic costs were also cited as sources of significant dissatisfaction with SNAP among applicants who completed the application process. On average, applicants each spent 6.1 hours at the SNAP office (and traveling between it and their home), often making several phone calls to the office and making several trips to the office and other locations to acquire the necessary documents. In addition to the time spent and hassle involved in completing the application process, 39 percent of working applicants had to miss work in order to complete this process, and 9 percent incurred expenses for child care or care for elderly household members (Bartlett et al. 2004, 4.9).

While these out-of-pocket expenses and lost wages may be small relative to the size of the food assistance benefits (6–13 percent of the average monthly benefit, according to Ponza et al. 1999), they still represent a cost that income-poor households must bear immediately, only in anticipation of an uncertain amount of future benefits. When considering that participation in WIC requires education classes and visits to the doctor, in addition to the application and recertification visits required for other social support services, the time costs and out-of-pocket costs of participating in WIC are potentially even more cumbersome. Requiring clients to visit a WIC office more often or imposing more stringent requirements for documentation of eligibility both involve substantial time costs and monetary costs, thus discouraging participation in the WIC program (Bitler, Currie, and Scholz 2003).

In addition to the time and monetary costs of applying for (and maintaining eligibility to receive) assistance, recipients incur substantial costs utilizing the benefits received. Specifically, meals eaten at home require not only the ingredients purchased but also the time spent shopping, preparing meals, and cleaning up afterward. As compared to nonrecipients, these costs are especially high for SNAP recipients, who are less likely to have access to private transportation and other time-saving devices, more likely to live beyond walking distance to a supermarket, and prohibited from using benefits to purchase ready-to-eat meals (or meals eaten on store premises). Purchasing food that requires substantial preparation time (e.g., avoiding ready-to-cook foods, purchasing dried beans instead of canned, or purchasing a whole chicken instead of precut pieces) is one way that income-poor individuals can stretch their food budget, but the consequence is that SNAP recipients tend to spend more time (on average) preparing food than nonrecipients do (Raschke 2012).

A tremendous amount of evidence supports the idea that households eligible to receive food assistance compare the economic costs of participating in SNAP and WIC with the size of benefits that they are eligible to receive (e.g., Bitler, Currie, and Scholz 2003; Blank and Ruggles 1996; Brien and Swann 2001; Currie and Grogger 2001). When food stamp offices require less frequent recertification, thus lowering the cost of participating in the program, single parents (who are most likely to experience child care difficulties during the application and recertification process) and rural households (which tend to incur the greatest transportation costs during the process) are more likely to participate in the program. Families are also more likely to utilize SNAP, WIC, and school nutrition programs when their households are eligible to receive increased benefits, when they are assisted in navigating the complex application process, and when documenting eligibility is less burdensome. The decision to apply for benefits is complicated by economic realities, disadvantages of different demographic groups, and an enduring stigma associated with government benefits.

At a surface level, the process for connecting citizens with benefits seems straightforward: connect a family in need with SNAP funds, connect a child to a meal site. However, the reality is that food insecure individuals confront a maze of restrictions that reduce take-up rates for federal programs. In his book *Aid on the Edge of Chaos*, Ben Ramalingam (2014, 80) quotes a senior United States Agency for International Development (USAID) colleague who notes that "the whole system disguises rather than navigates complexity, and it does so at various levels. . . . This maintains a series of collective illusions and overly simplistic assumptions about the nature of systems, about the nature of change, and about the nature of human actors." Examining the complex system of obtaining benefits from the viewpoint of different actors in the system pulls back the curtain on the simplistic rhetoric that surrounds the food access debate.

Our framework for examining why people do not participate in nutrition programs consists of barriers to access, navigating the program requirements, and participation. In other words, we investigate the reasons why people do not instigate the process of acquiring benefits in the first place, why they may choose not to fight their way through the program requirements, and why they may choose not to participate. Barriers to access include lack of awareness about the program and limited transportation. Navigating the program requirements create a maze for families looking to access benefits through SNAP. Food insecure populations may elect not to participate in programs that they would benefit from because they are time poor, or because the stigma and other social costs to using benefits are too high.

Often, the realities of barriers facing the food insecure are lost in the polemic against government nutrition programs. The food insecure population in America does not necessarily have access to government benefits. A number of barriers along the way may hinder vulnerable populations from accessing food via public benefits. Barriers to access, eligibility, and benefits are some of the reasons that people do not participate in nutrition programs. This careful look at the rationale behind how citizens choose to access benefits prompts a real consideration about how we think about benefits. Acquiring benefits is not as simple as a straight transaction; rather benefits exist in a wider web of time and transportation constraints, complicated by bureaucracy and transaction errors.

A holistic look at the challenges of accessing government benefits considers the family dynamics, household composition, time poverty, immigration status, stigma, and transportation challenges. Food insecurity, the basic need of obtaining and maintaining a regular household food supply, is often symptomatic of other underlying issues. A thorough look at the challenges of food insecurity must necessarily take into account the insights of poverty advocates beyond the food insecurity space. By identifying and understanding the barriers facing each of the government programs, we can work together to dismantle them.

REFERENCES

Bartlett, Susan, Nancy R. Burstein, William Hamilton, and Ryan Kling. 2004. "Food Stamp Program Access Study: Final Report." Washington, DC: US Department of Agriculture, Economic Research Service. E-FAN-03–013–3.

Bitler, Marianne. P., Janet Currie, and John K. Scholz. 2003. "WIC Eligibility and Participation." *Journal of Human Resources* 38: 1139–79.

Blank, Rebecca, and Patricia Ruggles. 1996. "When Do Women Use AFDC and Food Stamps? The Dynamics of Eligibility vs. Participation." *Journal of Human Resources* 31 (1): 57–89.

"Blueprint to End Hunger." 2011. Texas Hunger Initiative. *baylor.app.box.com/s/iv5fvus98q65dr3sueinevzszjsjk4tl.*

Brien, Michael J., and Christopher A. Swann. 2001. "Prenatal WIC Participation and Infant Health: Selection and Maternal Fixed Effects." University of Virginia Department of Economics, unpublished manuscript.

CFED Assets and Opportunity Scorecard Policy Map. 2017. *scorecard.assetsandopportunity.org/latest/report/policy-map.*

Chavez, N., S. Telleen, and Y. O. Kim. 2007. "Food Insufficiency in Urban Latino Families." *Journal of Immigrant Minority Health* 9 (3): 197–204.

Currie, Janet. 2003. "U.S. Food and Nutrition Programs." In *Means Tested Transfer Programs in the United States*, edited by Robert A. Moffitt, 199–289. Chicago: University of Chicago Press.

Currie, Janet, Jeffrey Grogger, Gary Burtless, and Robert F. Schoeni. 2001. "Explaining Recent Declines in Food Stamp Program Participation." In *Brookings-Wharton Papers on Urban Affairs*, 203–44. Washington, DC: Brookings Institution Press.

Edwards, M., C. Heflin, P. Mueser, S. Porter, and B. Weber. 2012. "The Great Recession and SNAP Caseloads: A Tale of Two States." Rural Studies Program Working Paper Series. Corvallis: Oregon State University. *ruralstudies.oregonstate.edu/sites/default/files/snaptaleof2states_rspworkingpaper1401.pdf*.

Heflin, C. M., and J. P. Ziliak. 2008. "Food Insufficiency, Food Stamp Participation, and Mental Health." *Social Science Quarterly* 89 (3): 706–27.

Johnson, Charlotte. 2015. "Senior Hunger Action Team Comprehensive Report." Dallas Coalition for Hunger Solutions. *dallashungersolutions.org/wp-content/uploads/SeniorHungerActionTeamReport.pdf*.

Kaye, L., E. Lee, and Y. Chen. 2013. "Barriers to Food Stamps in New York State: A Perspective from the Field." *Journal of Poverty* 17 (1): 13–28.

Kersey, M., J. Geppert, and D. B. Cutts. 2006. "Hunger in Young Children of Mexican Immigrant Families." *Public Health Nutrition* 10 (4): 390–95.

Leftin, J., A. Dodd, K. Filion, R. Wang, A. Gothro, and K. Cunnyngham. 2013. "Analysis of Proposed Changes to SNAP Eligibility and Benefit Determination in the 2013 Farm Bill and Comparison of Cardiometabolic Health Status for SNAP Participants and Low Income Nonparticipants." Washington, DC: Mathematica Policy Research. *www.mathematica-mpr.com/~/media/publications/PDFs/nutrition/SNAP_Analysis_Health_Impact.pdf*.

McAllen ISD transportation director. 2015. Discussion with the author, September 22.

Mills, G. B., T. Vericker, K. Lippold, L. Wheaton, and S. Elkin. 2014. "Understanding the Rates, Causes and Costs of Churning in the Supplemental Nutrition Assistance Program." Washington, DC: Urban Institute. *www.urban.org/research/publication/understanding-rates-causes-and-costs-churning-supplemental-nutrition-assistance-program-snap*.

"National Summer Meals Sponsor Survey: Texas Results." 2014. Texas Hunger Initiative. *www.baylor.edu/texashunger/doc.php/226927.pdf*.

"A New Majority: Low Income Students Now a Majority In the Nation's Public Schools." 2015. Southern Education Foundation. Atlanta. *www.southerneducation.org/getattachment/4ac62e27–5260–47a5–9d02–14896ec3a531/A-New-Majority-2015-Update-Low-Income-Students-Now.aspx*.

Newman, C., and E. Scherpf. 2013. "Supplemental Nutrition Assistance Program (SNAP) Access at the State and County Levels: Evidence from Texas SNAP Administrative Records and the American Community Survey." ERR-156, US Department of Agriculture, Economic Research Service.

Oliveira, V., E. Racine, J. Olmsted, and L. M. Ghelfi. 2002. "The WIC Program: Background, Trends and Issues." USDA ERS Food Assistance and Nutrition Research Report No. 27. Washington, DC: USDA.

Ponza, M., J. Ohls, L. Moreno, A. Zambrowski, and R. Cohen. 1999. "Customer Service in the Food Stamp Program." Contract no. 53–3198–40–025. Washington, DC: Food and Nutrition Service, US Department of Agriculture, July.

Quandt, S. A., J. I. Shoaf, J. Tapia, M. Hernández-Pelletier, H. M. Clark, T. A. Arcury. 2006. "Experiences of Latino Immigrant Families in North Carolina Help Explain Levels of Food Insecurity and Hunger." *Journal of Nutrition* 136 (10): 2638–44.

Ramalingam, B. 2014. *Aid on the Edge of Chaos: Rethinking International Cooperation in a Complex World*. Oxford: Oxford University Press.

Rank, M. R., and T. A. Hirschl. 2005. "Likelihood of Using Food Stamps during the Adulthood Years." *Journal of Nutrition Education and Behavior* 37 (3): 137–46.

Raschke, C. 2012. "Food Stamps and the Time Cost of Food Preparation." *Review of Economics of the Household* 10 (2): 259–75. doi:10.1007/s11150–011–9128–3.

Rivera-Ottenberger, A., and E. Werby. 2007. "Latino Participation in Food Assistance Programs: A Study Conducted for Project Bread." Last modified March 1. *scholarworks.umb.edu/csp_pubs/13*.

Rosen, J., R. Hoey, and T. Steed. 2001. "Removing Access Barriers to Food Stamp and SSI Benefits for Homeless People." *Clearinghouse Review Journal of Poverty Law and Policy* 34 (11): 679–96.

Rosenbaum, D., and B. Keith-Jennings. 2015. "SNAP Costs Declining, Expected to Fall Much Further." Center on Budget Policy and Priorities. *www.cbpp.org/research/snap-costs-declining-expected-to-fall-much-further*.

Sharkey, J., W. Dean, and C. Nalty. 2013. "Child Hunger and the Protective Effects of Supplemental Nutrition Assistance Program (SNAP) and Alternate Food Sources among Mexican-Origin Families in Texas Border Colonias." *BMC Pediatrics* 13: 143. doi:10.1186/1471-2431-13-143.

"Supplemental Nutrition Assistance Program (SNAP)." 2014. United States Department of Agriculture. *www.fns.usda.gov/snap/eligibility*.

Texas City school nutrition official. 2015. Discussion with the author, September 11.

"Texas Out of School Meals: A Study of Summer and Afterschool Meal Programs in Texas." 2014. Texas Hunger Initiative. *baylor.app.box.com/files/0/f/3523908821/1/f_25883032579*.

Woolhouse, Megan. 2014. "US Orders Mass. to Fix Food Stamp Procedures." 2014. *Boston Globe*, December 8. *www.bostonglobe.com/business/2014/12/08/usda-says-photos-food-stamp-cards-blocking-some-families-from-benefits/W0JbAUE6J0rODLX7UboMMK/story.html*.

Vickery, C. 1977. "The Time-Poor: A New Look at Poverty." *Journal of Human Resources* 12 (1): 27.

Ziliak, J. 2013. "Why Are So Many Americans on Food Stamps? The Role of Economy, Policy, and Demographics." University of Kentucky Center for Poverty Research Discussion Paper Series, DP2013–01.

10

Access to Food Assistance for Food Insecure Seniors

MARIE C. GUALTIERI

As Anna, an older woman in her mid-eighties, sat in her armchair wearing a white robe, she looked up at me. Her eyes filled with tears as she said, "Thank you for this food. I haven't been able to get to the store like I used to after my knee replacement surgery a few months ago." Access to food assistance—defined here as programs and organized initiatives designed to help people of lesser means get food—presents issues for myriad people, but seniors face unique and specific challenges that make food assistance especially difficult to obtain. Compared to the general population, food insecure seniors are more likely to have declining physical health and mental capacity, as well as problems related to a lack of transportation and limited geographic mobility, even in their own neighborhoods. It is crucial for service providers to understand these barriers faced by the food insecure senior population so they can better serve those in need. This chapter focuses on these challenges as they relate to seniors accessing food assistance programs and the importance of quality assessment tools in determining the needs of food insecure seniors. This subject is increasingly timely with the concurrent forces of the oncoming wave of the aging baby boomer population, social impacts of the recent economic crisis and recession, and recent political targeting of the budgets of federal- and state-level food assistance programs.

Currently in the United States, there are approximately 10 million individuals over the age of sixty who face the threat of food insecurity, which is approximately 16 percent of the older adult population (Meals on Wheels America 2017). This number has continued to increase over the years and is projected to continue to increase as the baby boomer population ages, and medical advancements allow us to live longer (National Foundation to End Senior Hunger 2014; Ziliak and Gundersen 2015). But before we discuss barriers of accessibility to food assistance programs, we need to first become acquainted with who is food insecure. National research has examined the demographics of seniors who experience food insecurity, which is important because service providers need to take into account who is experiencing food insecurity to make their programs accessible to these individuals. However, the demographic data from these reports are not analyzed on a multivariate level, meaning that the data are typically reported in terms of singular characteristics (Ziliak et al. 2008; Ziliak and Gundersen 2009; 2011; 2013; 2015; National Foundation to End Senior Hunger 2014). Therefore, we have the knowledge that older females face food insecurity more than their male counterparts, but we do not know about interactions with variables like race or if the persons in question are caring for a grandchild. Thus, we are left without really knowing why specific populations of seniors face food insecurity while others do not.

This chapter focuses on the experiences of food insecurity among seniors in the United States by drawing on relevant literature and original research conducted by the author. More specifically, the research conducted included semistructured, face-to-face interviews with twenty-one seniors (fifteen unmarried individuals and three married couples) on the waiting list for a home-delivered meals service to examine how the participants obtained and prepared food, and their usage of other resources, with social support being one of them. These participants were found with assistance from the community agency that runs the local home-delivered meals program, which gave the author access to their waiting list. After consent was given, the interviews, from which the quotes below are taken, took about an hour to complete.

Demographics

Previous research has determined several important patterns regarding seniors and food insecurity. First, seniors with a physical disability are more likely to experience food insecurity (Ziliak and Gundersen 2013). Research has also shown a connection to both mental and physical disabilities among seniors experiencing food insecurity (Wallace et al. 2007; Auslander and White 2009; Brewer et al. 2010). More specifically, previous research has found that physical disabilities make it difficult for seniors to prepare meals for themselves (Wallace et al. 2007; Gualtieri and Donley 2016). Additionally, seniors who were once mobile and healthy place themselves at higher risk for illness, disease, and physical disability when they *become* food insecure; this is because they are experiencing aging and nutritional deficiency simultaneously (Wallace et al. 2007). Seniors typically take medication to assist with physical and cognitive impairments, but food insecure seniors face unique barriers in this regard. Findings from previous research suggest that the medications typically prescribed to seniors cannot be taken on an empty stomach. However, if food insecure seniors then buy food, they are less likely to purchase their medication because of the lack of funds (Wallace et al. 2007). Therefore, these seniors are not able to take their medicine either way, and their health situation is at risk for escalating.

However, it is difficult to pinpoint what occurs first for much of this population—food insecurity or disability. For instance, when examining the food insecurity–obesity paradox among individuals fifty and older (meaning when individuals develop unhealthy diets because less nutritious foods are easier to afford), scholars found that individuals who were food insecure (according to a household food insecurity survey) were more likely to experience health issues, specifically weight-related disability, arthritis, and joint pain (Brewer et al. 2010). Similarly difficult, medical professionals have issues in medicating seniors whose symptoms mimic serious diseases, such as Alzheimer's.

Some researchers argue that owing to the combined factors of the natural aging process and food insecurity, seniors experience psychosocial effects from malnutrition that are similar to the symptoms of Alzheimer's and other illnesses (Auslander and White 2009). Therefore, doctors can misdiagnose patients with diseases and medicate them when what they really need is proper nourishment. This is not only problematic for reasons of misdiagnosis, but also because this leaves some of these individuals paying money for prescribed medications that they may not need, while still trying to afford the rest of their living expenses, including food (Jordan 2007).

National research also indicates that older females are experiencing higher rates of food insecurity than males (Ziliak et al. 2008; Ziliak and Gundersen 2009; 2011; 2013; National Foundation to End Senior Hunger 2014). Little is known about why exactly this is the case, but hypotheses include women's longer life expectancy than men, and the fact that women are generally living with more limited funds. Typically, if they are retired from work, women are living off of lower lifetime earnings due to the wage gap between women and men. But women who never had a career are living solely off of social security benefits. Additionally, most senior women are widows, which means that they do not have a dual income coming into the household.

Although food insecurity had increased among all age demographics in 2007 (Coleman-Jensen et al. 2014), researchers have found that seniors below the age of sixty nine—or the "young old"—are those who face the most problems with it ("Learn about Hunger" 2013; Wallace et al. 2007; Ziliak and Gundersen 2011; 2013; National Foundation to End Senior Hunger 2014). A reason for this is because the baby boomers are getting older, so the "young old" population is bigger than the one before it. Moreover, as seniors age, the severity of food insecurity experienced actually decreases (AbuSabha et al. 2011; Ziliak and Gundersen 2013), but no study addresses why this age disparity exists. However, it is important to note that this rate might change as the baby boomers cohort does age.

Cause of Food Insecurity

Income

Currently, food insecurity is associated mainly with income. Food prices saw rapid increases beginning in 2006 and continuing to this day (Wenzlau 2013). Regardless of the financial crisis and recession occurring in the United States in 2008, food prices still increased while people were being laid off from their jobs or having their salaries and benefits cut. Additionally, the recession caused cost of living raises to be frozen for programs serving the elderly, such as social security from years 2009 to 2011 (Sedensky 2010). Social security is vital to many seniors; without it, the number of seniors living in poverty would quintuple (DeNavas-Walt et al. 2012). Owing to the freeze of social security payments, seniors had to adjust to a stagnant monthly income while expenditures on such things as food, rent, taxes, prescribed medications, and medical care rose.

In a recent qualitative study examining seniors' experiences with food insecurity while on the waiting list for a federally funded, home-delivered meal service, my co-author and I found that income was the major reason why they were food insecure

(Gualtieri and Donley 2016). In interviews, a majority of these twenty-one seniors (ages sixty-two to ninety-three) stated that they do not use other food services (such as food banks) because they are unaware of the resources in their communities, meaning that they did not know of resources that were available to them, which leaves grocery stores as the only viable resource for these individuals to use to obtain food. Seniors discussed how the cost of food is an issue of primary concern and explained the strategies they use to make sure they get the best deal when purchasing food. For example, they mainly shop in the buy-one-get-one area of the stores and clip coupons if they can. Unfortunately, most of the seniors interviewed stated that they would like to use coupons to save money on food, but they cannot because they have failing eyesight, have had numerous eye surgeries, or have arthritis in their hands making it painful to use scissors. Even using these strategies, *all* the seniors felt that they do not get enough food when going to the grocery store and even sometimes have cut back in the amount of the food they get at the end of the month while they wait for their next social security or benefit check to arrive.

In addition to social security, some of the seniors interviewed received food stamps or SNAP benefits. Nationally, over four million low-income individuals over the age of sixty receive SNAP benefits (Barber 2012). However, it has been documented that seniors have the lowest participation rate in the program owing to multiple factors, such as barriers of mobility, transportation, use of technology, and stigma (Barber 2012). The benefits of those interviewed in the study ranged from $15 to $150, averaging approximately $101 a month, or a little more than $3 a day for food. Moreover, all the seniors who received food stamps mentioned that the amount given to them keeps getting cut. In addition to the benefits mentioned above, a few seniors also received a small amount of retirement pay or earned income from temporary side jobs. One participant received a small amount of money ($10) from Veteran's Affairs (VA).

Many of those interviewed independently brought up the idea of "making it stretch." As I was talking with Barbara, a sweet ninety-one-year-old white woman with silver curls who uses a walker, she explained: "You run out of things. You don't like to, but you do. I grew up during the Great Depression, and I have four sisters. We never went hungry; my mother made a lot of casseroles, but they were very frugal and meticulous with money. So I grew up in a thrifty environment. You just make it stretch." This "stretch" is also associated with other monetary obligations of these seniors. For example, Robert, a tall, frail sixty-four-year-old man who mentioned that he was embarrassed by his situation, faced a battle between the costs of medication and food: "Most of my medications are expensive, and I have to choose between food and getting my medications. And I find out I choose medication over food. And I need to take food with my medication. I try to balance, but I'm in between a hammer and a hard place. I would love to have food, and I would love to have my medication. But I have to make a decision." This supports previous literature (Wallace et al. 2007) that some seniors must choose between the two.

Moreover, the study consisted of both couples and individuals on the home-delivered meals waiting list. Because of this, we were able to compare the monthly household incomes of both groups. The average monthly income for couples was

$1,576, while the average monthly income for individuals was $1,146. Therefore, couples do not necessarily have an average monthly income that is twice the amount that individuals receive, even though they are trying to cover expenses for two people. Thus, being married does not necessarily mean that you are better off in old age.

Mobility and Transportation

Beyond financial resources, other factors associated with food insecurity among seniors are functional impairments, health problems, and lack of social support. In their study of persons aged sixty to ninety-six years old, Lee and Frongillo (2001) examined two different data sets—the 1988–1994 National Health and Nutrition Examination Survey (NHANES III) and the 1994 Nutrition Survey of the Elderly in New York (NSENY), which was provided by the Elderly Nutrition Program in New York. The NHANES III (N=6558) asked questions related to food insecurity, health issues, physical functioning, sociodemographic information, and economic factors. The NSENY (N=406) had information relating to food insecurity, nutritional risk, and eligibility for a home-delivered meal program of the senior population in New York (Lee and Frongillo 2001). Findings suggest that in addition to functional impairments, elders living in poverty, of minority status, with less education, and who were socially isolated were associated most with food insecurity (Lee and Frongillo 2001).

The findings of Lee and Frongillo's (2001) quantitative study using survey data are consistent with the interviews I conducted with seniors on a home-delivered meals program's waiting list (Gualtieri and Donley 2016). In the latter, transportation was an issue for the seniors owing to lessened physical and cognitive abilities. Among the seniors interviewed who own a car, all had issues driving. Two had had extensive eye surgeries, but they still had trouble seeing and thus would call on neighbors or their children to drive them to the stores. Some of the participants used to use public transportation services such as the local bus system, but they had to stop using it as they aged. Anna used to take the bus every week to purchase groceries, but after she had a knee replacement surgery she was not even physically able to wash herself, let alone go out and buy groceries. Cognitive impairments also played a role. Adeline, a ninety-three-year-old woman in her pajamas and bathrobe, spoke about her experiences in the grocery store. As she sat and slowly sipped her cold tea, she recalled the times she would get confused walking up and down the aisles, not knowing where she was. The last time she went to the grocery store was years ago, and she had to solicit help from her daughter, who ultimately had to move in with Adeline to make sure she was safe. Her daughter then was put in charge of going grocery shopping, but this proved difficult for her daughter since she was unemployed and also experiencing food insecurity.

It is obvious that seniors face unique challenges in regards to food access, as exhibited in the descriptions above. However, we must ask ourselves the following questions beyond basic access: Once seniors do have food, how do they prepare it? What kind of food are they eating, and what sort of eating habits do they have? Do they get help from others? The following is the study's (Gualtieri and Donley 2016) account of seniors' experiences in preparing meals, navigating nutrition demands, and using their social support networks. It is important to examine these factors, because to best respond to potential clients' needs, coordinators of agencies that host food assistance programs need to consider and understand how these seniors also navigate the issues of food preparation and nutrition.

Preparing Meals

Preparing meals proved challenging for the majority of the individuals, mainly owing to health and mobility issues. Most have issues with standing for long periods of time. In order to prepare and cook meals, these individuals try to cook a little bit at a time, alternating with sitting down to rest. One of these individuals, Barbara, uses a walker, so it is hard for her to move around and reach for pots and pans. As a result, she would heat up microwaveable meals instead of cooking. Even though this was still difficult for her, she explained that it was more feasible than trying to boil water and work with multiple ingredients at the same time. Darla, who suffered from a stroke nine years earlier, could not move the left side of her upper body. Similar to Barbara, this made it difficult for her to cook meals on the stove, which is why she too mainly ate microwavable dinners.

Owing to knee replacement surgeries, Anna and Rhonda are unable to move around easily. Anna had given up on cooking fresh meals altogether. Instead, she would eat vegetables from a can or cold cereal. After Rhonda had had a similar diet to Anna's, her son gave her the idea to use a slow cooker to prepare meals, which she found helpful, although, because of a lack of access to food, Rhonda just makes meals from a hodgepodge of ingredients that she can find in her cabinets or refrigerator, rather than following recipes.

Marcy and Adeline both shared horror stories of times when they recently tried to cook with their gas stovetops. Marcy has terrible arthritis that makes it difficult for her to hold objects, such as pots and pans. Often, she would drop a pot of boiling water all over the kitchen floor when trying to transfer it from the stove to the sink to drain the water out. She also wears oxygen and does not like to cook by fire with it on; there were times when her oxygen cord would get stuck to cabinet handles and would yank her back when she was trying to cook. Therefore, she takes her oxygen cords off when she cooks and has difficulty breathing when using the stove. Adeline has tried to cook several times in her older age, but during the interview she showed the burn marks that were all over her arms from her attempts at cooking. Now, her daughter cooks for her. But this is the same daughter mentioned earlier that was unemployed and experiencing food insecurity, as well. Therefore, the meals mainly consisted of ramen noodles and mashed potatoes, which could be purchased in bulk at a low price.

Because these individuals have such difficulty in preparing meals, some may wonder why these seniors do not live in assisted-living facilities. In Florida, the state with the highest population of seniors, the average cost of private nursing facilities is $93,440 annually according to 2013 estimates (Florida Health Care Association 2014). However, the costs for a senior to have three home-delivered meals a day would be approximately $7,117.50 annually,[1] which is provided for by agencies that are subsidized through federal funds. There is also an independence aspect to why seniors do not live in assisted-living facilities. Using this type of resource marks a time in the seniors' lives where they are no longer independent (Roe et al. 2001). While the participants in the study did feel guilty using resources such as family or friends to help them, they were still in their own space—in homes that they have lived in for almost fifty years in some cases.

Nutrition

A majority of the seniors interviewed did not skip meals. However, what they consider a "meal" is more variable than we might think. In fact, a majority of those who said that they "do not skip meals" said that while they might not have a meal, they will eat something to "fill the emptiness" throughout the day or eat less to make their food go further. Therefore, they are still not getting three square meals a day. The remainder of individuals skips meals—ranging from a few times a month to nearly every day. When asked if they feel that they eat nutritious, balanced meals, 60 percent of the seniors said that they sometimes do, while 20 percent said that they never do, and the remaining 20 percent said that they often do.[2] However, there were some discrepancies between answers to this question and the actual foods they had been eating. Additionally, cost was the main reason why interviewees stated they ate these specific foods.

For example, Marcy said she believed that she always eats balanced, nutritious meals. However, her typical day of meals is oatmeal for breakfast, toast for lunch, and a baked potato for dinner. Sometimes she will have a can of vegetables or pick from a ham that has been in her freezer since Christmas, which was a few months prior to her interview. She also claimed that she eats these foods every day because it is what she can afford, and therefore, she has no variety. Robert discussed similar issues as he explained his typical day of meals; a smoothie made with food (meaning whatever food was in his fridge at the time, and mixing it in a blender), milk, and oatmeal for breakfast, something that he can have as leftovers for the whole week for lunch, and crackers and cheese for dinner. As much as Robert said that he would like variety because he does not enjoy eating the same foods every day, he explained that he does not have a choice. Robert went on to say:

> I'm in a stage where I'm cornered. By cornered I mean I have no choice. It's just where I am, and I do what I do because I have no better choice. I think this country has forgotten the elders. We gave so much because there was a time I was very productive, and I didn't have to depend on anyone for anything. I didn't think I would get to that stage, but it happened to me to the point where I need help, and help is not available. I don't think it's right, I don't think it's fair, and I'm pretty sure I'm not the only one under these circumstances. This is not right.

Adeline also spoke about foods that she wishes she could have but cannot afford, such as lamb. Adeline would spend her days eating cereal, mashed potatoes and gravy, and chicken if she is "lucky." When asked if she eats these foods because of choice, how much they cost, or because of access, she said, "To live—just to live." Barbara was similar, in that she is supposed to watch her salt and sugar intake, but can afford only certain foods so she eats food that she is technically not supposed to have just so she can survive.

Social Support

Many seniors in the study had some sort of social support, whether it was a neighbor, friends, or family members. However, even then, not all of them were always able to rely on their sources for extra help. More specifically, these individuals have a strong dependence on their sources for support and find themselves in a bind if their neighbors, friends, or relatives are unavailable. This is problematic because there is a huge difference between saying that you have social support and having unreliable social support. But, often, when seniors report that they have social support, care managers at agencies automatically assume that they are taken care of, which is not necessarily the case.

Barbara, for example, often relied on her neighbor to drive her to the grocery store to get food. She also talked about a friend from church that would come to her house and drop off cooked meals from time to time. And although she had family in the area, her sisters would be very busy and were unable to help her, and sometimes, her neighbor and friend were not able to help out because of their own obligations. Barbara mentioned:

> My neighbor is reliable but has commitments himself. He's retired, and we've been neighbors for over fifty years, and he has appointments, and he and his wife visits their son for a couple a weeks at a time. Sometimes my sister will help, but her husband is an invalid, so she has her hands full. She can't leave him alone. So I cannot rely on her. My other sister is a crossing guard and is not available because of her work schedule. She's also not able to drive at night, so she cannot really help. My other sister lives kind of far away and is not available.

Ron has a similar issue. He had no transportation to get food and had trouble standing for long periods of time, so his neighbor offered to go to the local church to get him food from the church food pantry. Ron said, "He's hard to do without." Because the neighbor played such a crucial role in acquiring food, at the time of our interview, Ron and his partner feared that the next few months would be very difficult for them because their neighbor had to go out of town to help his daughter with some medical issues. They also did not know when or if the neighbor would be back. Because of this change, Ron and Henry had to figure out how to cope without one of their major food resources. Moreover, they now were not able to supplement the food that they had purchased at Walmart with food from the food pantry and therefore had to readjust their grocery list when they were able to shop.

Marcy talked about receiving social support from far away. She explained that she had a friend who lived in the Midwest, and they have been friends for years. Because Marcy did not have any family members alive to help her, her friend would call the local grocery store chain to send Marcy a gift card from time to time. Her friend also had a ham delivered to her over the holidays. The ham lasted Marcy a long time, as she had picked at it every day for three months and still had more left in her freezer. James, who was sixty-nine years old and immobile, had a neighbor that he lovingly called "his babysitter" who would come over every day to check up on him. The neighbor did not give him any food but would watch basketball games on the TV with him. James's living situation was different from others that were interviewed; he lived in a room that he had rented out in a house. The owner did not live there, but she would come over every Sunday with food for James and the other people who lived there. While he paid for the food, James was limited in what food he had because the owner of the house did not necessarily take requests in what he wanted to eat. The foods she brought were typically nonperishable.

Relatives did play an important role in some of these individuals' lives. Rhonda, who cannot drive, was grateful to have her son living with her because aside from her sixth recent knee replacement, she was also caring for her blind and schizophrenic brother. Her son was able to go to the store every once in a while, and her daughter would visit to take Rhonda to the grocery store. But getting around was still difficult for Rhonda, and having another person living there, who has specific and challenging medical needs, means there are more mouths to feed and prescriptions to fill. They often "sacrifice and make sure to pick out things that will last." Adeline is also thankful that her daughter lives with her because she cannot drive and is unable to cook. She also cannot go shopping because, as mentioned above, she often "gets lost" in the grocery store. Her daughter occasionally visits three local food pantries to add to their food supply. Even though it is still not enough food to last, it would be difficult to obtain and prepare meals without her daughter. Coretta's relatives did not live with her, but had always made it a point to "check up" on her weekly after she had her heart attack. She also would have passing-out spells that was a major concern to her children. Because she lived alone with no transportation, and it was difficult for her to stand, her children would come by weekly with food for her and would sometimes help her cook meals.

Only one individual interviewed did not have any social support. But that was just for this specific sample of individuals and does not translate to how many people on the waiting list have no social support. Robert had no children and had siblings that live four hours away or out of the country. While he had transportation, he lacked finances to be able to pay for all his expenses and food. Not only does he not know of any other resources other than the home-delivered meal service to assist him, but also he believed that the paperwork for most services was cumbersome and that the people who worked there overly scrutinize clients. He said, "Whatever is left of my dignity, I want to keep."

Barriers to Food Access Programs

There are many barriers associated with food access that are specific to the senior population. These barriers are often related to the procedures an individual must follow in order to receive services by food assistance programs. First, the eligibility requirements for age-centered food programs usually limit participation to people aged sixty or sixty-five and older. They also typically include the need for an individual to be below the official poverty line. However, this can be problematic for the new "young old" population experiencing food insecurity (Ziliak and Gundersen 2013), and for the large population of seniors facing hunger that live just above the poverty line (Ziliak and Gundersen 2013). Because many seniors live technically above but close to the poverty line, they are ineligible for certain assistance programs and therefore are left without enough to eat.

There are also challenges and constraints in obtaining both food and benefits for food supplementation. Both typically require mobility, which proves to be difficult for seniors who have a physical disability and/or no driver's license or car (Wolfe et al. 2003). Moreover, a participant in programs like food pantries not only must be present to receive the food, but he or she typically must go to a particular location to file paperwork to even start receiving the benefits. One may presume that if seniors cannot get to these locations by themselves, they can ask others in their social support system to get the food for them, or to give them a ride. However, if seniors are fortunate to have any form of social support, it is not always reliable, and for that reason, problematic (Gualtieri and Donley 2016). Additionally, coordinators of these programs tend to assume that these seniors can then prepare these foods at home easily in a safe way, which is also not always the case (Gualtieri and Donley 2016).

Previous research discusses another barrier facing the senior population: filling out paperwork and the demanding process of obtaining certain benefits if they are eligible (AbuSabha at al. 2011). Typically, in order to receive benefits, one must go to a distribution site or office to fill out paperwork or to register. Physical mobility issues, as mentioned above, negatively influence the likelihood of travel to access these benefits. Furthermore, even when the amount of paperwork required to apply for benefits is not an issue, the font size and amount of writing needed to fill out forms proves difficult for some portion of seniors. Additionally, if a senior is a member of a household and wants to receive benefits such as SNAP, then not only would a member of the household have to go to the office to fill out paperwork and answer income and resource questions, but site visits and interviews must take place before that senior receives an EBT card. The rigor of this process alone could deter families from completing the first step for eligibility.

Programs that do exist might not fully consider the abilities and needs of the various populations they serve. Jordan (2007) argues that some food assistance programs, such as the Thrifty Food Plan (TFP) in Seattle, have additional participant requirements upon enrollment that could constrain seniors' access. This specific program not only involves a copious amount of enrollment paperwork but also requires that participants spend an average of 3.5 hours per day preparing food (Jordan 2007). However, as discussed, some seniors find it hard to stand for long periods of time and are thus unable to complete this task even if they do not have a documented physical disability (Gualtieri and Donley 2016; Wolfe et al. 2003).

Finally, a barrier that cannot be controlled by those in need is a waiting list. Because there is not enough funding for food assistance programs, potential clients are often placed on a waiting list ranked by priority. This priority to receive assistance is determined by how each individual, in this case a senior, "scores" on a needs assessment. In the study discussed in this chapter, the time that the seniors we interviewed had spent on the waiting list ranged from two months to two years and nine months. Also, because some seniors face cognitive issues as they age, they might not understand the questions on the assessment to be enrolled in the program, and therefore, their need could be underestimated.

Measurement Issues

There are multiple issues related to the assessment tools used to determine the needs of seniors for food assistance programs. The first issue is that the responses to eligibility questionnaires are all self-reported. This is concerning because we see from the interviews that there are discrepancies between what the seniors self-reported regarding nutrition and their actual food consumption. Also, while the agency gave us the names and contact information for seniors who were willing to participate in our study, they also made sure that they gave us potential participants that they knew would understand our questions. Self-reporting bias also lends itself as an issue if the seniors are not capable of understanding the questions being asked, and, therefore, may not report the severity of their situation.

Similarly imperative, the federal assessment questions themselves have been constructed in a way that has led to such discrepancies. All the questions ask about food insecurity solely in relation to income. Yet, from the studies covered in this chapter, we know that finances are not the only reason why these seniors are food insecure. When running out of food, it is the lack of transportation and the lack of mobility that hinders them from obtaining more food. The problems these seniors face are underestimated by the assessment tool, and they are not placed properly on the waiting list or in these programs at all.

According to a research report by Ziliak and Gundersen (2013), marriage protects seniors from becoming food insecure. Overall, married seniors are 20 percent less likely to be at risk for hunger than their single counterparts, given the higher income distributions among couples (Ziliak and Gundersen 2013). Popular wisdom suggests that couples make more money than individuals, and as a result are "better off" in a food insecure situation than individuals. The sample data confirm otherwise. We found the issue of food insecurity experienced by individuals and couples is similar. Therefore, we suggest that questions strictly for couples should be added to the questionnaire so that their situation can be accurately measured as well.

Also problematic is the fact that *all* programs that are federally funded to assist food insecure seniors use the questionnaire as a part of their required assessment tools. Yet, having a waiting list for programs in general suggests that there is a clear unmet need for food assistance, specifically ones that provide home delivery. The bottom line is that these questions clearly do not get to the issue that the providers at agencies seek to understand. If these questions do not change to address other factors besides income contributing to an individual's food insecurity, such as those that have been found in our study, agencies and the nation as a whole will never be able to fully grasp and accommodate the needs of the senior population, which has been predicted to increase over the next fifty years.

Food insecurity is unfortunately not a new phenomenon experienced by seniors living in the United States. Yet, owing to medical advancements making longer lives feasible, and because the baby boomer generation is aging, the number of seniors experiencing food insecurity is expected to increase in the coming years. However, budget cuts and lack of federal funds have food assistance programs establishing and expanding waiting lists as the demand for such services far surpasses the supply. Because this issue is projected to worsen, food access needs to become a more pertinent topic of conversation among policy makers at local, state, and federal levels.

Ultimately, there needs to be more funding given to food assistance programs, specifically home-delivered meal programs, which have been found to be beneficial to seniors who lack transportation and mobility. Previous studies have revealed that older seniors living alone often eat less and are at higher risk for poor nutritional health (Darnton-Hill 1992; Mion, McDowell, and Heaney 1994; Ramic et al. 2011). A lack of good nutrition puts seniors at higher risk for "cardiac problems, infections, deep venous thrombosis and pressure ulcers, perioperative mortality and multiorgan failure" (Brownie 2006, 110–11). In 2011, Tufts University researchers modified the USDA's (US Department of Agriculture) Food Guide Pyramid for Older Adults to match the new food pyramid, known as MyPlate.

Under this food guide, it is recommended that older adults consume fewer calories but the same or more nutrients (i.e., fortified grains, whole wheat bread, bright-colored vegetables, and deep-colored fruit) to fulfill their unique dietary needs (Tufts University 2011). MyPlate also recommends that seniors drink plenty of water, and engage in light physical activity throughout the day to stay healthy. According to Millward (2008, 1188), "the key to health and active longevity may be sufficient appropriate exercise and healthy eating to ensure adequate intakes of protein and most other key nutrients to maintain muscle and bone strength and mobility." It would benefit these seniors to receive home-delivered meals because the foods included in these meals are approved by the Food and Drug Administration (FDA) and follow nutritional guidelines specific to aging seniors.

Moreover, for many seniors, receiving home-delivered meals is more than just a convenience but, rather, is survival. Betty, a seventy-five-year-old mother of two and a widow of a former military officer, said: "I just feel bad because I know that in order to get the [food assistance program] you must be in dire need. And that's not right because we've put in a lot for years, and years, and years—you should be able to get a little bit out of the system. I don't think they owe me that, but it would be the generous thing to do. They spend so much money on other things that are stupid to me, but I'm not the government."

Marcy had similar sentiments, in the sense that home-delivered meals are an actual need. Knowing that the waiting list was not the food assistance program's fault, but rather the lack of government funding, she mentioned, "We don't ask for it because you want to, but because you need to. I told someone the other day that I'll be dead before I get [into the food assistance program]." With more funding given to home-delivered meal programs, seniors can get the nutrition that they need, which will help them lead longer, more productive lives.

NOTES

1. This number is derived from a single meal cost of $6.50. This number multiplied by three meals a day, then by 365, equals $7,117.50.
2. The three answer choices were: often, sometimes, or never.

REFERENCES

AbuSabha, Rayane, Gene Shackman, Barbara Bonk, and Steven J. Samuels. 2011. "Food Security and Senior Participation in the Commodity Supplemental Food Program." *Journal of Hunger and Environmental Nutrition* 6 (1): 1–9.

Auslander, Judith, and Diana White. 2009. "The Psycho-social Aspect of Malnutrition and Seniors." *oregonhunger.org/files/Psyco%20Social%20paper.pdf.*

Barber, Lura. 2012. "SNAP and Older Adults." National Center for Benefits Outreach and Enrollment. Report for the National Council on Aging. *www.nasuad.org/documentation/ I_R/call_notes/4–5-12%20SNAP%20Presentation%20-%20NCOA.pdf.*

Brewer, Dawn, Christina S. Catlett, Katie N. Porter, Jung Sun Lee, Dorothy B. Hausman, Sudha Reddy, and Mary Ann Johnson. 2010. "Physical Limitations Contribute to Food Insecurity and the Food Insecurity–Obesity Paradox in Older Adults at Senior Centers in Georgia." *Journal of Nutrition for the Elderly* 29 (2): 150–69.

Brownie, Sonya. 2006. "Why Are Elderly Individuals at Risk of Nutritional Deficiency?" *International Journal of Nursing Practice* 12: 110–18.

Coleman-Jensen, Alisha, Christian Gregory, and Anita Singh. 2014. "Household Food Security in the United States, 2013." USDA-ERS Economic Research Report No. 173. *www.ers.usda.gov/media/1565415/err173.pdf.*

Darnton-Hill, Ian. 1992. "Psychosocial Aspects of Nutrition and Aging." *Nutrition Reviews* 50: 476–79.

DeNavas-Walt, Carmen, Bernadette D. Proctor, and Jessica C. Smith. 2012. "Income, Poverty, and Health Insurance Coverage in the United States: 2011." Current Population Reports. September. *www.census.gov/prod/2012pubs/p60–243.pdf.*

Florida Health Care Association. 2014. "Facts about Long Term Care in Florida." *www.fhca. org/media_center/long_term_health_care_facts.*

Gualtieri, Marie C., and Amy M. Donley. 2016. "Senior Hunger: The Importance of Quality Assessment Tools in Determining Need." *Journal of Applied Social Science* 10 (1): 8–21.

Jordan, Jamillah. 2007. "Grocery Gap Project: Race, Hunger, and Food Access." Congressional Hunger Center. *www.hungercenter.org/publications/the-grocery-gap-project-race-hunger-and-food-access.*

"Learn about Hunger." 2013. AARP Foundation. *www.aarp.org/aarp-foundation/our-work/ hunger/learn-about-hunger.*

Lee, Jung Sun, and Edward A. Frongillo Jr. 2001. "Factors Associated with Food Insecurity among US Elderly Persons: Importance of Functional Impairments." *Journal of Gerontology* 56B: 594–99.

Meals on Wheels America. 2017. "Hunger in Older Adults: Challenges and Opportunities for the Aging Services Network." Washington, DC: AARP Foundation. *www. mealsonwheelsamerica.org/docs/default-source/research/hungerinolderadults-fullreport-feb2017.pdf?sfvrsn=2.*

Millward, D. Joe. 2008. "Sufficient Protein for Our Elders?" *American Journal of Clinical Nutrition* 88: 1187–88.

Mion L. C., J. A. McDowell, and L. K. Heaney. 1994. "Nutritional Assessment of the Elderly in the Ambulatory Care Setting." *Nurse Practitioner Forum* 5: 46–51.

National Foundation to End Senior Hunger. 2014. "Spotlight on Senior Health: Adverse Health Outcomes of Food Insecure Older Americans." National Foundation to End

Senior Hunger (NFESH) Report. *www.hungernwnc.org/about-hunger/Spotlight%200n% 20Senior%20Health.pdf.*

Ramic, Enisa, Nurka Pranjic, Olivera Batic-Mujanovic, Enisa Karic, Alic Alibasic, and Alma Esad. 2011. "The Effect of Loneliness on Malnutrition in Elderly Population." *Medical Archives.* 65: 92–95.

Roe, Brenda, Maxine Whattam, Heather Young, and Margaret Dimond. 2001. "Elders' Perceptions of Formal and Informal Care: Aspects of Getting and Receiving Help for Their Activities of Daily Living." *Journal of Clinical Nursing* 10: 398–405.

Sedensky, Matt. 2010. "Seniors Brace for Social Security Freeze." *Huffington Post. www. huffingtonpost.com/2010/10/11/seniors-brace-for-social-security-freeze_n_758887.html.*

Tufts University. 2011. "My Plate for Older Adults." *www.nutrition.tufts.edu/research/ myplate-older-adults.*

Wallace, Steven P., Cricel Molina, and Mona Jhawar. 2007. "Falls, Disability and Food Insecurity Present Challenges to Healthy Aging." UCLA Center for Health Policy Research Brief. *healthpolicy.ucla.edu/publications/Documents/PDF/Healthy_Aging_ PB_051507.pdf.*

Wenzlau, Sophie. 2013. "Global Food Prices Continue to Rise." Worldwatch Institute. *www. worldwatch.org/global-food-prices-continue-rise-0.*

Wolfe, Wendy S., Edward A. Frongillo, and Pascale Valois. 2003. "Understanding the Experience of Food Insecurity by Elders Suggests Ways to Improve Its Measurement." *Journal of Nutrition* 133: 2762–69.

Ziliak, James P., and Craig C. Gundersen. 2009. "Senior Hunger in the United States: Differences across States and Rural and Urban Areas." National Foundation to End Senior Hunger (NFESH) Report. *www.mowaa.org/document.doc?id=193.*

———. 2011. "Food Insecurity among Older Adults." Technical Report Submitted to the AARP Foundation. *www.aarp.org/content/dam/aarp/aarp_foundation/pdf_2011/ AARPFoundation_HungerReport_2011.pdf.*

———. 2013. "Spotlight on Food Insecurity among Senior Americans: 2011." National Foundation to End Senior Hunger (NFESH) Report. *nfesh.org/wp-content/uploads/state- of-senior-hunger-2011-full-report.pdf.*

———. 2015. "The State of Senior Hunger in America 2013: An Annual Report." National Foundation to End Senior Hunger (NFESH) Report. *nfesh.org/wp-content/uploads/state- of-senior-hunger-2013-full-report.pdf.*

Ziliak, James P., Craig C. Gundersen, and Margaret Haist. 2008. "The Causes, Consequences, and Future of Senior Hunger in America." University of Kentucky Center for Poverty Research Special Reports. *www.mowaa.org/document.doc?id=13.*

11

Food Deserts and Injustice
Poverty, Food Insecurity, and Food Sovereignty in Three Rust Belt Cities

STEPHEN J. SCANLAN AND SAM REGAS

Food Deserts and the Rust Belt

"If a parent wants to pack a piece of fruit in a child's lunch . . . they shouldn't have to take three city buses [to acquire it]." These words from First Lady Michelle Obama (cited in Aubrey 2011) are at the heart of the challenges food deserts present for food security in rural and urban settings throughout the country and their impact on nutrition and health. As a component of her "Let's Move" campaign to eliminate childhood obesity, food deserts are important to food justice and the inequality that gets in the way of it.

In this chapter we analyze food deserts and food insecurity in three Rust Belt cities: Cleveland, Detroit, and Milwaukee. We examine the intersection of deindustrialization's legacy and the Great Recession with poverty and inequality and how access to nutritious food is problematic for the poor in urban environments, particularly food deserts. Utilizing a food justice perspective and emphasizing the limited food sovereignty poor citizens have, we connect this to food politics, health, and social movements to empower individuals and neighborhoods seeking food security.

We extend the study of food deserts from their roots in geography to sociology. Borrowing from subfields such as environmental sociology, food studies, social movements, stratification, and urban ecology, we emphasize food justice for understanding and alleviating inner-city hunger. Findings reveal multiple layers of injustice associated with food deserts, connecting not only with poverty and health but also ecology, education, work, and broader inequalities. Taken together these indicate important spatial inequality dimensions of food sovereignty and food justice and the challenge to what we call the "food opportunity structures" in meeting the needs of inner-city residents.

The concept of "food desert" has arisen from policy efforts seeking to understand and alleviate hunger and improve nutrition. Geographers in the United Kingdom Department of Health's Nutrition Task Force defined food deserts as "areas of relative exclusion where people experience physical and economic barriers to accessing healthy food" (as cited in Reisig and Hobbis 2000, 138). In parallel efforts the US Department of Agriculture (USDA) has collaborated with the Health and Human Services and Treasury Departments to define a food desert as "a census tract with a substantial share of residents who live in low-income areas that have low levels of access to a grocery store or healthy, affordable food retail outlet" (US Department of Agriculture 2014). Food deserts are dependent on "fringe stores" that provide few healthy options (Garry 2010), such as convenience stores, dollar stores, gas stations, liquor stores, or pharmacies. Full-service grocery stores on the other hand feature fresh and packaged food, including produce and full dairy and meat options alongside greater refrigerated offerings (Hurst 2010). Variations on these definitions exist, with discussion refining the meaning of food deserts and how to account for them (Shaw 2006). Diet and nutritional impacts from limited access to healthy food among low-income and discriminated-against groups is central to the food deserts discussion (Gordon et al. 2011; LeDoux and Vojnovic 2012)

Demographic, health, racial/ethnic, socioeconomic, and urban versus rural factors emerge for consideration within food deserts (J. Block, Scribner, and DeSalvo 2004; Budzynska et al. 2013; Chung and Myers 1999; Freeman 2007; Gordon et al. 2011; Moore and Diez Roux 2006; Morton et al. 2005; Roche 2013; Whitley 2013). Ultimately food deserts are about poverty and inequality and how the "most disadvantaged of the disadvantaged" (LeDoux and Vojnovic 2012, 3) are affected. Spatial inequality is highly relevant here, the core idea being that place and space can determine the distribution and attainment of societal opportunities, resources, and rewards, reflecting altered life chances associated with a context of advantage or disadvantage (Lobao, Hooks, and Tickamyer 2007). Carter, Dubois, and Tremblay (2013) and LeDoux and Vojnovic (2012) connect this specifically to food deserts in that where one lives determines access to healthy food. Food deserts reflect patterns of privilege and exclusion that perpetuate inequality—not only race, class, and gender but also education, employment, health care, and housing, among others.

Food justice (Alkon and Agyeman 2011) is interwoven in these considerations, emphasizing food access and the "food gap" problem in impoverished communities (Winne 2008) and how the industrial food system has failed to ensure food security (Cockrall-King 2012). This and various "food activism" approaches (D. Block et al. 2012) focus on food sovereignty and how grassroots empowerment can overcome the negative consequences of living in food deserts.

Food security, food deserts, and food justice in Cuyahoga, Milwaukee, and Wayne Counties connect with deindustrialization and the creation of the Rust Belt that defined the experiences of Cleveland, Milwaukee, and Detroit respectively. After the struggle and efforts of people in adapting to the evolving service-based, technology-driven, global economy, the Great Recession brought new challenges (Donald 2013; Oberg 2011), particularly high unemployment and the foreclosure crisis. Ironically, however, closed factories, out-migration, and foreclosed houses can potentially create opportunity in the blight created by deindustrialization.

The creation of the Rust Belt impacted dozens of cities in the Great Lakes and industrial Midwest (see Feyrer, Sacerdote and Stern 2007; High 2003; Hobor 2012;

D. Wilson and Wouters 2003). The documentary *Roger and Me*—filmmaker and social critic Michael Moore's homage to the decline of his hometown of Flint, Michigan—provided one of the most meaningful snapshots of the struggles confronting communities where factories close and unemployment and poverty rates increase. Marked by the loss of tens of thousands of jobs in the automotive and steel industries in particular, deindustrialization has been devastating, forcing economic transformation in some of America's greatest cities to maintain survival.

Food insecurity, food deserts, and the rise of charitable giving networks reflect the many years of struggle experienced by citizens in the Rust Belt to meet their basic needs. Shackman and colleagues (2015), for example, documented the spike in food pantry use alongside unemployment and economic collapse in the Great Recession. The decline of inner-city communities specifically has also been documented by William Julius Wilson (1987; 1996), who examined the opportunity structures of the urban poor in light of changes in the American economy, the creation of "jobless ghettoes," shifting family dynamics, public perceptions of poverty and welfare, policy reform, and race. Although critiqued for assumptions regarding the limited significance he attached to racial inequality as a source of inner-cities' plight (Willie 1989), William Julius Wilson brought widespread attention to the impacts of deindustrialization. Out of such debates came a new discussion of the black experience in America (West 1993) and research on issues defining the lives of the urban poor such as education (Kozol 1991), the family (Edin 1993), segregation (Massey and Denton 1993), and work (Waldinger 1996). The legacies of these studies matter greatly for spatial dimensions of inequality and crises tied to food deserts, poverty, and food insecurity.

Race thus intersects with the deindustrialization patterns of the Rust Belt. In the early twentieth century, emerging manufacturing opportunities in the North coupled with racial unrest and the decline of tenant farming in the South led many African Americans to cities like Cleveland, Detroit, and Milwaukee (Colten and Buckley 2014). This "great migration" was often met with resistance and segregation patterns that limited opportunities (Massey and Denton 1993). Throughout the twentieth century, white flight from the inner city and eventual economic downturns in the once-thriving industrial sector left African Americans even more economically impoverished and isolated—both geographically and socioeconomically—from whites in the suburbs (Haines 2010, 2). This legacy remains and is quite important in that Cleveland, Detroit, and Milwaukee all are typically among the most highly segregated cities in the United States. Without this segregation the disastrous social and economic outcomes observed in inner cities would not have occurred (Charles 2003, 169).

Food deserts and their connection to poverty and food insecurity are just one among many such disastrous inner-city outcomes. For example, LeDoux and Vojnovic (2012) highlight the consequences of decades of change, in which

> technological advances, organizational restructuring, and consolidation in the
> supermarket industry combined with commercial blight in the central business
> district, residential suburbanization, increased personal mobility, and racial and
> economic segregation led to the formation of decentralized superstores and the

concentration of supermarket chains on the urban fringes where land prices, insurance premiums, and utility costs were lower and customer purchasing power was higher than in the urban centers.

This pattern parallels deindustrialization, leaving the inner city not only without industry and employment but without access to essential services and in a context of disadvantage.

Divestment and urban decline in the Rust Belt have resulted in limited economic opportunity and development, challenges for education, health issues, housing decline, and growth in crime among other concerns. This is tied closely to poverty and race issues captured in spatial inequality that continue to segregate and negatively affect the life chances of those living in the inner city. Reinforcing LeDoux and Vojnovic (2012), we examine how food deserts and food insecurity shaped by the concern of the absence of a meaningful place to shop for food has been caught in this spiral of urban change and as a consequence created a pattern of limited food opportunity structures for millions.

Food insecurity is lacking access to enough food needed to live an active, healthy life (Reutlinger 1986). Feeding America, the nation's largest nonprofit hunger organization, notes that food insecurity can be thought of simply as not knowing where one's next meal is coming from (Feeding America 2014a; see also Feeding America 2014b). The US Department of Agriculture (2014) further reinforces this, emphasizing how households alter diets regarding what or how much food can be consumed. Coleman-Jensen, Gregory, and Singh (2016) provide a recent snapshot of the more than forty-two million Americans living in food insecure households.

Offering further conceptualization, DeRose, Messer, and Millman (1998) argue that food insecurity entails three elements: food shortage, poverty, and deprivation. Food shortage concerns "how much food is available," a fundamental starting point in examining hunger in food deserts. Secondly, food poverty considers the economic, physical, or social access to existing food, another key aspect of food deserts where poverty or lack of transportation inhibit access. Finally, food deprivation incorporates whether the available and accessible food serves nutritional needs, this question too being essential for understanding food deserts where it is not food that is inaccessible but *healthy food*. Food deserts may have plenty of fast-food restaurants or carry-outs offering very little variety or few fresh fruits and vegetables. Each of these components reflects important considerations individually but at the same time overlap to exacerbate hunger in food deserts.

Central to the links between food deserts and food insecurity are food sovereignty and food justice (Alkon and Agyeman 2011; Gottlieb and Joshi 2010; Holt-Giménez and Patel 2012). McMichael (2004, 347) defines food sovereignty as "the social right of a community or country to determine its own policies regarding food security and the cultural, social, and ecological conditions under which it is sustained." Although typically associated with food sovereignty connected to globalization processes (also see Menezes 2001), as Daniel Block and colleagues (2012) argue, the concept applies to food deserts in the United States with equal significance, using language reflecting the idea of "community food security" (Myers and Sbicca 2015). Demands for food sovereignty drive food activism and empowerment efforts of communities.

Food deserts and food insecurity are questions of food justice, which Gottlieb and Joshi describe as "ensuring that the benefits and risks of where, what, and how food is grown and produced, transported and distributed, and accessed and eaten are shared fairly" (2010, 6). This too is a far-reaching concept encompassing many challenges associated with the political economy of the world food system, including the environment and poverty. Food deserts reflect problems of distribution and access that result in limited food opportunity structures, reflecting the inequities and spatial inequality defining hunger. Food deserts are part of a larger system of injustice, and coupled with the call for food sovereignty, demands for ending food injustice define food movements. With food insecurity in the United States becoming more problematic since the Great Recession, the issue has commanded attention, particularly among groups most vulnerable to hunger and food deserts.

To examine our cases, we use data from the USDA Economic Research Service *Food Access Research Atlas* (US Department of Agriculture 2013), supplemented with the five-year (2009–2013) averages from the US Bureau of the Census American FactFinder Database of the *American Community Survey* (2015). In addition, we use materials from the *Cleveland Plain Dealer*, *Detroit Free Press*, and *Milwaukee Journal Sentinel* to provide context, as well as websites from community organizations addressing food security to examine social change considerations.

As noted, food deserts are low-income census tracts where people have limited access to healthy food. The US Department of Agriculture (2015) considers a census tract low income if it meets *any* of the following criteria:

1. The tract has a poverty rate of 20 percent or more; *or*
2. The tract has a median family income less than or equal to 80 percent of the state in which it resides; *or*
3. The tract is in a metropolitan area and has a median family income less than or equal to 80 percent of the metropolitan area's median family income. (US Department of Agriculture 2015)

According to the US Department of Agriculture (2015) "low access to healthy food is defined as being far from a supermarket, supercenter, or large grocery store ("supermarket" for short). A census tract is considered to have low access if a significant number or share of individuals in the tract is far from a supermarket." The USDA develops multiple constructs for determining access based on distance, originally using one mile and ten miles for urban and rural census tracts respectively. Subsequent measures use half-mile/ten-mile and one-mile/twenty-mile demarcations.

We use a more specific construct that incorporates transportation into the concept, "delineating low-income tracts in which a significant number of households are located far from a supermarket and do not have access to a vehicle" (US Department of Agriculture 2015). Vehicle access connects with the ability to acquire healthy food and also is important to poverty and spatial inequality. Although the counties examined offer multiple forms of public transportation, this cannot always be relied on because service is not convenient to all neighborhoods and because using it can be time-consuming. Our measure starts with low-income, low-food-access census tracts and considers them to have lack of vehicle access if one of the following is true:

1. At least one hundred households are more than half a mile from the nearest supermarket and have no access to a vehicle; *or*
2. At least five hundred people or 33 percent of the population live more than twenty miles from the nearest supermarket, regardless of vehicle access. (US Department of Agriculture 2015)

Because Cuyahoga, Milwaukee, and Wayne Counties are metropolitan areas, we use the first of these constructs.

With census tracts as the unit of analysis we compare food deserts and non–food deserts using multiple indicators from the US Census American FactFinder Database (US Bureau of the Census 2015) categorized as:

1. *Income and poverty measures*: Median household income, poverty rate, child poverty rate, percentage of households receiving Supplemental Nutrition Assistance Program (SNAP) benefits, and percentage of households without health care coverage.
2. *Demographic considerations*: Census tract population; racial composition including percentage black, Hispanic, non-Hispanic white; percentage foreign born; and educational attainment.
3. *Work and the economy*: Percentage employed in construction, percentage employed in manufacturing, percentage employed in service occupations, the unemployment rate, and mean commuting time to work.

Poverty/low income and vehicle access considerations are included in the definition of food deserts, but incorporating these here reveals the disparity between the census tracts and thus more specific details. On the whole, the indicators provide a thorough snapshot of the key demographic and socioeconomic considerations important to assessing food insecurity.

We use descriptive statistics and independent sample T-tests for the difference of means to compare food deserts to non–food deserts in our cases in 2010 (the most recent data available). To provide context we compare the descriptive statistics for the aggregate of food deserts in each county to the United States as a whole, also enabling comparison across the counties of interest. The T-tests enable comparison in a way that determines where significant differences occur between census tracts.

Food Deserts: Patterns and Implications

With people already struggling to recover from deindustrialization, the Great Recession exacerbated poverty and food insecurity in the postindustrial Midwest, making food deserts more prevalent (e.g., Oberg 2011; Shackman et al. 2015). Table 11.1 presents demographic, economic, and social characteristics of the population living in the

TABLE 11.1. Selected demographic, economic, and social characteristics of the population living in food deserts: Cuyahoga, Milwaukee, and Wayne Counties versus the United States as a whole

Indicator	Cuyahoga County	Milwaukee County	Wayne County	United States as a Whole
Food Deserts				
Total census tracts that are food deserts	67	89	103	10,455
Percent of census tracts that are food deserts	19.9%	22.6%	16.9%	14.3%
Population living in food deserts	235,193	221,059	290,590	44,802,246
Demographics				
Mean population	2,643	3,299	2,821	4,277
Percent white, non-Hispanic	32.0%	27.8%	13.4%	74.0%
Percent black	56.3%	55.3%d	79.1%	12.6%
Percent Hispanic	8.7%	9.9%	4.5%	16.6%
Percent foreign-born	4.8%	6.5%	4.5%	12.9%
Percent college graduates	13.9%	13.0%	10.1%	18.0%
Work and the Economy				
Percent employed in construction	3.7%	2.7%	3.2%	6.2%
Percent employed in manufacturing	11.9%	14.0%	6.3%	10.5%
Percent employed in service occupations	29.3%	29.1%	31.9%	18.1%
Unemployment rate	11.5%	10.8%	15.2%	6.2%
Mean commuting time to work (minutes)	24.7	23.1	26.6	25.5
Income and Poverty				
Median household income	$26,192	$29,103	$24,526	$53,046
Poverty rate	35.8%	34.5%	42.2%	15.4%
Child poverty rate	50.3%	45.2%	59.4%	21.6%
Percent receiving SNAP benefits	34.5%	35.8%	43.4%	12.4%
Percent without healthcare coverage	16.6%	14.1%	19.7%	14.9%
Percent without vehicle access	27.0%	25.0%	27.1%	4.4%

food deserts of Cuyahoga, Milwaukee, and Wayne Counties compared to the United States as a whole, and Figures 11.1, 11.2, and 11.3 map the prevalence of food deserts in these counties using the US Department of Agriculture food desert mapping tool (2017). Reinforcing Moore and Diez Roux (2006), food deserts reveal concentrated poverty, racial segregation, and multiple challenges pertaining to mobility and work reflecting spatial inequality.

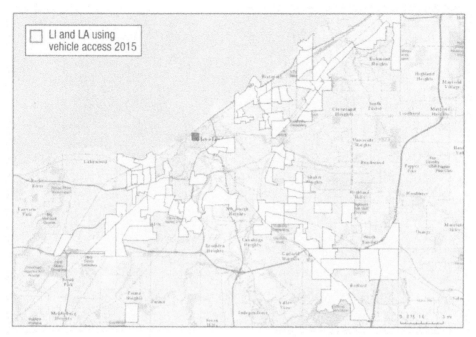

FIGURE 11.1. Cleveland, Ohio, food deserts, June 30, 2017. LI refers to low-income census tracts; LA refers to low-access census tracts (meaning limited access to food and transportation opportunities). The small dark square is the "center point" used by the USDA mapping tool for the city. Source: USDA Economic Research Service, ESRI. For more information see *www.ers.usda.gov/data-products/food-access-research-atlas/ documentation.*

There are 259 food deserts in the counties examined, with Cuyahoga, Milwaukee, and Wayne Counties home to 89, 67, and 103 respectively. Although Detroit/Wayne County has the greatest number of food deserts and the largest population living in them at 290,590, Milwaukee County has the highest percentage of census tracts (22.6 percent) that are food deserts, followed by Cuyahoga County (19.9 percent) and then Wayne (16.6 percent). These figures indicate greater concentration of food access problems than for the 14.3 percent of census tracts in the United States as a whole that are food deserts. Considering population specifically, nearly three-quarters of a million people reside in the food deserts of these three counties.

This is tied closely to inequality and a context of disadvantage in food deserts. Given the type of food desert examined that includes vehicle access, residents are greatly disadvantaged—in upward of 25 percent of the population in the three counties compared to only 4.4 percent for the United States as a whole. Furthermore, in considering income and poverty, findings reveal that taken together (see Table 11.2 for combined means), the food deserts in Cuyahoga, Milwaukee, and Wayne Counties have median household incomes *less than 50 percent* of that for the United States as a whole and poverty rates *232 percent greater* than the rest of the country. The child poverty rate specifically is *244 percent greater!* Food and health care needs are quite evident, with the food deserts indicating much greater demand for SNAP benefits combined with a higher proportion without access to health care. Such detrimental impacts (Freeman

FIGURE 11.2. Milwaukee, Wisconsin, food deserts, June 30, 2017. LI refers to low-income census tracts; LA refers to low-access census tracts (meaning limited access to food and transportation opportunities). The small dark square is the "center point" used by the USDA mapping tool for the city. Source: USDA Economic Research Service, ESRI. For more information see *www.ers.usda.gov/data-products/food-access-research-atlas/ documentation.*

2007) and health care disparity are highly problematic given that people living in food deserts are more likely to suffer from diabetes, heart disease, and obesity associated with poor nutrition.

The disparities are not just about income and poverty, however. There is clearly a race/ethnicity dimension also, reinforcing Gordon and colleagues (2011). The food deserts are disproportionately black, with 79.1 percent in Wayne County in particular, far greater than the US percentage of 12.6 percent. The concentration of African Americans in the Rust Belt's inner cities reflects the historical consequences of migration, deindustrialization, and segregation. Examining food deserts amplifies this, with food opportunity structures taking on a racial dimension alongside poverty.

Finally, other elements examined here reveal additional barriers to mobility, opportunity, and the workplace. The proportion of the population in food deserts who are college graduates is well below the national average while unemployment rates are far

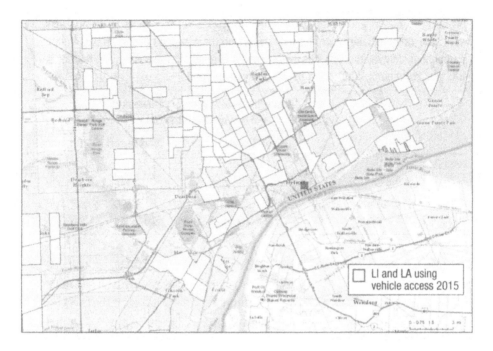

FIGURE 11.3. Detroit, Michigan, food deserts, June 30, 2017. LI refers to low-income census tracts; LA refers to low-access census tracts (meaning limited access to food and transportation opportunities). The small dark square is the "center point" used by the USDA mapping tool for the city. Source: USDA Economic Research Service, ESRI. For more information see *www.ers.usda.gov/data-products/food-access-research-atlas/ documentation.*

greater, with each having double-digit rates and Wayne County (15.2 percent) being the highest. There is a much greater dependency on employment in service occupations than the United States as a whole and less opportunity in construction trades, revealing a limited income opportunity and stymied growth. Employment in manufacturing reveals a different story, with only Wayne County having a percentage employed in this sector below the national average of 10.5 percent. However, given the historical significance of manufacturing in these places, the numbers reflect the relative decline of opportunity associated with deindustrialization and the loss of tens of thousands of jobs. Although numbers remain "above average," this is not up to the standard that made these manufacturing centers great.

Table 11.2 reinforces these findings, revealing the means and standard deviations for various income, poverty, demographic, work, and economic indicators for food desert versus non–food desert census tracts. With a couple of exceptions, the food deserts differ significantly from non–food deserts, indicating a context of disadvantage and greater hardship.

As with comparisons to the United States as a whole, food deserts in our cases are characterized by households with lower income, higher poverty and child poverty rates, greater reliance on SNAP benefits, lower levels of health care coverage, and less access to vehicles. In addition, there is lower educational attainment, higher unemployment,

TABLE 11.2. Means and standard deviations for various income, poverty, demographic, work, and economic indicators for food desert versus non–food desert census tracts in Cuyahoga, Milwaukee, and Wayne Counties and results for one-sample t-test for the difference of means, 2009–2013 (N = 1,354 census tracts)

	Census Tracts in Cuyahoga, Milwaukee, and Wayne Counties (S.D.)		One-Sample T-Test for Difference
	Food Desert	**Non–Food Desert**	
Food Deserts			
Total	259	1,095	N.A.
Percent of census tracts	19.1%	80.9%	N.A.
Population	746,842	3,280,725	N.A.
Income and Poverty			
Median household income	$26,282 (8,499)	$47,709 (25,732)	22.7***
Poverty rate	38.0% (14.8)	22.0% (17.6)	-15.1***
Child poverty rate	52.6% (21.7)	29.3% (25.0)	-15.0***
Percent receiving SNAP benefits	38.3% (14.1)	21.8% (18.0)	-16.1***
Percent without healthcare coverage	17.2% (5.8)	13.5% (7.7)	-8.4***
Percent without vehicle access	26.5% (12.7)	13.7% (12.6)	-14.5***
Demographics			
Mean population	2,884 (1181)	2,996 (1.405)	1.3
Percent white, non-Hispanic	23.5% (26.1)	53.8% (35.9)	15.5***
Percent black	65.1% (33.3)	34.6% (37.9)	-12.9***
Percent Hispanic	7.3% (13.1)	6.9% (13.6)	-0.485
Percent foreign-born	5.1% (6.7)	7.4% (8.6)	4.631***
Percent college graduates	13.0% (10.0)	25.2% (19.0)	14.4***
Work and the Economy			
Percent employed in construction	3.3% (3.5)	3.7% (3.0)	1.7*
Percent employed in manufacturing	12.9% (6.3)	13.8% (6.1)	2.2**
Percent employed in service occupations	30.3% (9.4)	21.6% (10.4)	-13.1***
Unemployment rate	12.8% (5.6)	9.4% (5.8)	-8.8***
Mean commuting time to work (minutes)	25.1 (4.8)	24.1 (3.9)	-3.0***

*Significant at p = .10, 2-tailed test
**Significant at p = .05, 2-tailed test
***Significant at p = .01 or greater, 2-tailed test

and greater dependence on the service sector for jobs, with less employment in construction and manufacturing. Recalling from Table 11.1, manufacturing opportunities in Cuyahoga and Milwaukee Counties are actually above average when compared to the United States as a whole—however, further scrutinizing this finding, results show that this employment is actually significantly lower in food deserts, meaning its impact is less beneficial. Opportunity structures are therefore limited for residents in neighborhoods where the need is greatest. Finally, although there is no significant difference with regard to Hispanics, the food desert counties on the whole are predominantly black, with African Americans making up nearly two-thirds of the population. Furthermore, food deserts are seemingly not enclaves of concentrated immigrant populations either, with the percentage of foreign-born population significantly greater outside of food deserts. Extending discussions by William Julius Wilson (1987; 1996) and the decline of the American inner city to food security, findings reveal a great need for considering the racial composition of food deserts. This demands greater attention regarding connections to poverty and its many forms and consequences alongside high levels of segregation. Spatial inequality is reinforced in comparing food deserts to non–food deserts, with the gulf between these communities greatly limiting the life chances and food opportunity structures.

On the whole, food deserts and their connection to poverty and food insecurity encapsulate larger problems of inequality in the United States and cities in particular. Ongoing issues of education, fair wages, health and access to health care, race relations, and unemployment can be overlaid with food deserts, revealing the complex intersection of multiple challenges. Reflective of spatial inequality and a context of disadvantage, these concerns point to a great injustice that demands awareness and action.

For this reason, food deserts are at the core of food justice. Inequitable access to and distribution of food needed to achieve a healthy and active lifestyle in a nation and world of plenty represents a great tragedy of the times. The growing gulf between the country's wealthy and poor has reached its highest level in decades. Injustice on the food insecurity front is exacerbated by tough economic times, and findings show that. The injustice reflected in the prevalence of food deserts and the demographic, economic, race, and spatial dimensions examined here demand that human needs be put first in the food system.

Examining famine on a global scale, Sen (1981) developed what is known as the "entitlement approach" to food security, emphasizing the distributional problems associated with food as a form of deprivation in human capabilities linked to poverty. Much can be learned from this perspective and its application to food deserts in the United States. It is in demands for economic opportunity and food sovereignty that change must happen.

Food insecurity and poverty are in many ways inseparable, reflecting a cycle of misfortune ensnaring a large segment of the population. These problems reflect concentrated disadvantage closely associated with the historical legacies of deindustrialization, segregation, and spatial inequality that make policy change difficult. However, social change and the transformation of America's urban environments and food systems are not without hope. Exciting innovations and a growing alternative food movement are taking place not only in Cuyahoga, Milwaukee, and Wayne Counties but across the country. Cleveland, Milwaukee, and Detroit reveal some of the starkest challenges related to deindustrialization and the formation of the Rust Belt. At the same time, however, these cities have shown great resilience. All is not lost with regard to a brighter future and addressing the poverty and food security needs of these communities through the transformation of local food systems. The cases here exemplify rebound from struggle though with challenges far from over.

Movements for Food Sovereignty and Food Justice

Addressing food deserts and food insecurity is closely tied to alternative food movements (Delind 2013; Fernandez et al. 2013; Follett 2009; Friedland 2010; Myers and Sbicca 2015) and urban renewal associated with sustainability and the green economy (Masi et al. 2014; Mersol-Barg 2014; Schilling and Logan 2008). Community organizations and concerned citizens have taken the lead in empowering themselves, using the local food system as their medium, while at the same time local governments and community organizations have increased efforts in addressing food deserts and food insecurity.

The alternative food movement encompasses multiple perspectives and approaches with nuances too numerous to address here (see Follett 2009; Myers and Sbicca 2015). Suffice it to say that this approach challenges the neoliberal, corporate dominance of the globalized, industrial food system with an emphasis on local foodways that increase food opportunity structures. In the cases here and in other metropolitan areas across the country there is an emergent and growing interest in urban agriculture as a way to address food deserts and poverty (Cockrall-King 2012). Importantly, as Masi and colleagues note (2014), this shift has durability on cultural, economic, environmental, and political fronts, meaning that successful urban agriculture is not simply a passing effort to fill the void until something more productive emerges. It genuinely improves food security and health, provides economic opportunity, and increases the resilience and self-sufficiency of cities. Alternatives include community-supported agriculture (CSA), cooperatives, farmers' markets and farm stands, home gardening, locavore practices, seed saving, and "slow food" ideals. Food sovereignty and food justice are interwoven among these approaches, with the ultimate goal being empowerment and equity that provides vulnerable communities with much-needed food security.

Calls for food justice and embracing food security emphasize empowerment, food as a human right, and self-determination. Food insecurity has resulted from decisions being made *for* instead of *by* those most affected by hunger. This reinforces Daniel Block and colleagues, who note that "food desert communities . . . recognize the disparities in food access and are not content to let others continue to decide their food access future" (2012, 209). If food deserts are to be eliminated, then change must come from the bottom up, with a citizenry empowered to affect that change. This is happening in Cleveland, Detroit, and Milwaukee—reflecting nicely what Cockrall-King (2012) has referred to as the "new food revolution."

Not only are there many options with regard to the alternative food system practices noted above (as Exner [2015] reports, for example, greater Cleveland has forty-three CSA options), but Cuyahoga, Milwaukee, and Wayne Counties reveal some of the most innovative and effective examples of community building and food sovereignty in the country. Table 11.3 presents a sample of the many programs addressing food deserts. As seen in the brief mission statements and purposes and with greater exploration of their websites, important themes of economic opportunity, education, empowerment, equity, justice, and sustainability emerge, shaping the actions taken to address food deserts and food insecurity. Transforming the urban landscape and the blight that has defined the Rust Belt to be home to community kitchens, gardens, orchards, urban farms, and food education, production, marketing, and distribution centers ultimately can improve access to healthy, nutritious food to the poor and disenfranchised to thus create food oases that flourish with economic opportunity.

Of course, such work is not without controversy or challenges, and actions must address not only food but also politics and power, economics, race, sustainability, urban development, and other concerns (see D. Block et al. 2012). On the policy front, local governments in the cases examined here are each included in the top ten of Seedstock's list of US cities leading the way in urban agriculture ordinances (Popovitch 2014), with Detroit, Cleveland, and Milwaukee ranked first, fifth, and ninth respectively. This reveals local government efforts in making the food revolution possible, assisting with land acquisition, infrastructural needs, or zoning changes, for example. In addition, behind First Lady Michelle Obama and the "Let's Move" campaign there was a federal effort as well to address food deserts through the provision of grants, loans, and tax credits, which alongside other opportunities have assisted communities in addressing food insecurity (Koff 2015).

However, at the same time the interests of "the state" in terms of economic development most likely reflect the neoliberal, corporate interests of the food system. One particularly important consideration is responding to the conceptualization of food deserts themselves and the focus on access to a large grocery store as the core of the problem. By definition, opening a grocery store in these communities would eliminate the access problem and therefore the food desert status. However, from a food sovereignty and alternative food movements perspective, corporate dominance and "Walmartization" of the food system is something communities struggle with greatly (D. Block et al. 2012; Donald 2013). Just because the store opens does not mean that individuals will be able to shop there given food poverty and barriers to food access. Although opening a large chain store may tout the benefits of economic development and jobs, critics argue that much more is needed to address the structural inequalities that create food deserts and the poverty and segregation defining it. Reinforcing work by Daniel Block and colleagues (2012) in Chicago, we argue that food deserts reflect larger patterns of the wealth and poverty divide in the United States, emphasizing the importance of a bottom-up approach and true transformation and empowerment of these communities and their citizens. Myers and Sbicca (2015, 18) argue that a more critical approach should be taken that combats "the economic inequality and poverty that creates food insecurity and food deserts in the first place." Food sovereignty and food justice pursuits are about justice. Citizens must have options that reflect their food preferences, food needs, and abilities to satisfy them.

To conclude, America's Rust Belt communities experienced great prosperity and harsh decline. Periods of progress have been followed by collapse and new struggles.

TABLE 11.3. Examples of alternative food movement initiatives and the pursuit of food sovereignty and food justice in Cleveland, Detroit, and Milwaukee

City	Mission	Website
Cleveland		
Fair Food Network's Cleveland Urban Agriculture Project	"realizing the vision of a more sustainable and just food system . . . [by focusing on] improving healthy food access, informing public policy, strengthening funding strategies, and expanding networks and sharing knowledge."	www.fairfoodnetwork. org/what-we-do/projects/ cleveland-urban- agriculture-project
The Foundry Project	"to form an economically productive, environmentally sustainable community that creates healthy foods, profitable growth, jobs and art."	www.thefoundryproject. com
Ohio City Farm	"to provide fresh, local and healthy food to Cleveland's underserved residents, boost the local food economy, and educate the community about the importance of a complete food system."	www.ohiocity.org/ ohio-city-farm
Rid-All Green Partnership	"to transform communities, starting with 3 acres in Cleveland's Kinsman Neighborhood . . . [by reclaiming] the land for growing fruits and vegetables, farming fish, creating soil from what others throw away and more."	www.greennghetto.org
Sustainable Cleveland	"to design and develop a thriving and resilient Cleveland region that leverages its wealth of assets to build economic, social and environmental well-being for all."	www.sustainablecleveland. org/celebration-topics/ local-foods
Detroit		
Detroit Black Community Food Security Network	"to address food insecurity in Detroit's Black community, and to organize members of that community to play a more active leadership role in the local food security movement."	detroitblackfoodsecurity.org
Fair Food Network's Fair Food Detroit	"realizing the vision of a more sustainable and just food system . . . [by focusing on] improving healthy food access, informing public policy, strengthening funding strategies, and expanding networks and sharing knowledge."	www.fairfoodnetwork. org/what-we-do/projects/ fair-food-detroit

TABLE 11.3. (cont.)

City	Mission	Website
Keep Growing Detroit	"to promote a food sovereign city where the majority of fruits and vegetables Detroiters consume are grown by residents within the city's limits."	detroitagriculture.net
Michigan Urban Farming Initiative	"to engage members of the Michigan community in sustainable agriculture . . . using agriculture as a platform to promote education, sustainability, and community—while simultaneously reducing socioeconomic disparity—[and] to empower urban communities."	www.miufi.org
SEED Wayne	"dedicated to building sustainable food systems on the campus of Wayne State University and in Detroit area communities . . . to promote access to healthy foods, urban agriculture, farm-to-institution, healthy eating, and food planning and policy development."	clas.wayne.edu/seedwayne
Milwaukee		
Growing Power	"helping to provide equal access to healthy, high-quality, safe and affordable food for people in all communities."	www.growingpower.org
HOME GR/OWN Milwaukee	"empowers residents to transform neighborhoods by re-purposing City-owned vacant lots into community assets that spark new economic opportunities around local, healthy food production and distribution, and new, green community spaces."	city.milwaukee.gov/ homegrownmilwaukee. com#.VVzngVLBKpQ
Milwaukee Apple Project	"bringing antique apples back to our tables by promoting their work, and adopting the Milwaukee Apple as one of several place-based varietals we'd like to save."	www.slowfoodwise.org/ projects/regional-foods/ milwaukee-apple-project
Urban Ecology Center	"fosters ecological understanding as inspiration for change, neighborhood by neighborhood."	urbanecologycenter. org/what-we-do/ sustainable-food.html
Victory Garden Initiative	"builds communities that grow their own food, creating a community-based, socially just, environmentally sustainable, nutritious food system for all"	victorygardeninitiative.org/ mission

Deindustrialization and the Great Recession have generated far-reaching urban challenges that from a spatial inequality perspective create a context of disadvantage and limited opportunities for food desert residents not only in health and nutrition but concerning broader poverty and economic concerns.

With a food sovereignty framework for guidance and food justice as the goal, communities and organizations are taking positive steps to reverse the negative impacts of food deserts, deindustrialization, and poverty. Cleveland, Detroit, and Milwaukee are experiencing positive change, but much more progress is needed, and only time will tell how the effectiveness of urban agriculture and alternative food movements will play out. Centering the change on transformation of urban food systems can be empowering when challenges can be met in the most difficult of circumstance as these communities reveal; there is hope that resilience will take hold.

REFERENCES

Alkon, Alison Hope, and Julian Agyeman. 2011. *Cultivating Food Justice: Race, Class, and Sustainability*. Cambridge, MA: MIT Press.

Aubrey, Allison. 2011. "First Lady: Let's Move Fruits and Veggies to 'Food Deserts.'" *Shots: Health News from NPR*. *www.npr.org/sections/health-shots/2011/07/20/138544907/first-lady-lets-move-fruits-and-veggies-to-food-deserts*.

Block, Daniel R., Noel Chávez, Erika Allen, and Dinah Ramirez. 2012. "Food Sovereignty, Urban Food Access, and Food Activism: Contemplating the Connections through Examples from Chicago." *Agriculture and Human Values* 29 (2): 203–15.

Block, Jason P., Richard A. Scribner, and Karen B. DeSalvo. 2004. "Fast Food, Race/Ethnicity, and Income: A Geographic Analysis." *American Journal of Preventative Medicine* 27 (3): 211–17.

Budzynska, Katarzyna, Patricia West, Ruth T. Savoy-Moore, Darlene Lindsey, Michael Winter, and P. K. Newby. 2013. "A Food Desert in Detroit: Associations with Food Shopping and Eating Behaviors, Dietary Intakes, and Obesity." *Public Health and Nutrition* 16 (12): 2114–23.

Carter, Megan Ann, Lise Dubois, and Mark S. Tremblay. 2013. "Place and Food Insecurity: A Critical Review and Synthesis of the Literature." *Public Health and Nutrition* 17 (1): 94–112.

Charles, Camille Zubrinsky. 2003. "The Dynamics of Racial Residential Segregation." *Annual Review of Sociology* 29: 167–207.

Chung, Chanjin, and Samuel L. Myers Jr. 1999. "Do the Poor Pay More for Food? An Analysis of Grocery Store Availability and Food Price Disparities." *Journal of Consumer Affairs* 33 (2): 276–96.

Cockrall-King, Jennifer. 2012. *Food and the City: Urban Agriculture and the New Food Revolution*. Amherst, NY: Prometheus Books.

Coleman-Jensen, Alisha, Matthew P. Rabbitt, Christian Gregory, and Anita Singh. 2016. *Household Food Security in the United States in 2015*. ERR-213. Washington, DC: USDA Economic Research Service. *www.ers.usda.gov/webdocs/publications/err215/err-215.pdf*.

Colten, Craig E., and Geoffrey L. Buckley, eds. 2014. *North American Odyssey: Historical Geographies for the Twenty-First Century*. Lanham, MD: Rowman and Littlefield.

Delind, Laura B. 2013. "Critical Reflection and Civic Discourse within and across the Alternative Food Movement." *International Journal of Sociology of Agriculture and Food* 20 (3): 391–96.

DeRose, Laurie, Ellen Messer, and Sara Millman, eds. 1998. *Who's Hungry? And How Do We Know?* New York: United Nations University.

Donald, Betsy. 2013. "Food Retail and Access after the Crash: Rethinking the Food Desert Problem." *Journal of Economic Geography* 13 (2): 231–37.

Edin, Kathryn. 1993. *There's a Lot of Month Left at the End of the Money: How Welfare Recipients Make Ends Meet in Chicago.* New York: Garland.

Exner, Rich. 2015. "2015 CSA Farm Directory for Greater Cleveland and Northeast Ohio." *www.cleveland.com/datacentral/index.ssf/2015/03/2015_csa_farm_directory_for_gr.html.*

Feeding America. 2014a. "Hunger in America 2014: Executive Summary." *www.feedingamerica.org/hunger-in-america/our-research/hunger-in-america/hia-2014-executive-summary.pdf.*

———. 2014b. "Hunger in America 2014." *help.feedingamerica.org/HungerInAmerica/hunger-in-america-2014-full-report.pdf?s_src=Y15XP2B1X&s_keyword=sitelink-About-Us-feeding-america&s_referrer=google&s_subsrc=sitelink-About-Us-feeding-america&_ga=1.20699643.2119479087.1429188419.*

———. 2015. "About Us." *www.feedingamerica.org/our-response/about-us/.*

Fernandez, Margarta, Katherine Goodall, Meryl Olson, and V. Ernesto Méndez. 2013. "Agroecology and Alternative Agri-food Movements in the United States: Toward a Sustainable Agri-food System." *Agroecology and Sustainable Food Systems* 37: 115–26.

Feyrer, James, Bruce Sacerdote, and Ariel Dora Stern. 2007. "Did the Rust Belt Become Shiny? A Study of Cities and Counties That Lost Steel and Auto Jobs in the 1980s." *Brookings-Wharton Papers on Urban Affairs* 8: 41–102

Follett, Jeffrey R. 2009 "Choosing a Food Future: Differentiating among Alternative Food Options." *Journal of Agriculture and Environmental Ethics* 22: 31–51.

Freeman, Andrea. 2007. "Fast Food: Oppression through Poor Nutrition." *California Law Review* 95 (6): 2221–59.

Friedland, William H. 2010. "New Ways of Working and Organization: Alternative Agrifood Movements and Agrifood Researchers." *Rural Sociology* 75 (4): 601–27.

Garry, Michael. 2010. "New Program Addresses Food Deserts in Detroit." *Supermarket News* 58 (23): 25–26.

Gordon, Cynthia, Marnie Purciel-Hill, Nirupa R. Ghai, Leslie Kaufman, Regina Graham, and Gretchen Van Wye. 2011. "Measuring Food Security in New York's Low-Income Neighborhoods." *Health and Place* 17L 696–700.

Gottlieb, Robert, and Anupama Joshi. 2010. *Food Justice.* Cambridge, MA: MIT Press.

Haines, Lindsey. 2010. "White Flight and Urban Decay in Suburban Chicago." *Digital Commons @ Illinois Wesleyan University. digitalcommons.iwu.edu/econ_honproj/112/.*

High, Steven C. 2003. *Industrial Sunset: The Making of North America's Rust Belt, 1969–1984.* Toronto: University of Toronto Press.

Hobor, George. 2012. "Surviving the Era of Deindustrialization: The New Economic Geography of the Urban Rust Belt." *Journal of Urban Affairs* 35 (4): 417–34.

Holt-Giménez, Eric, and Raj Patel. 2012. *Food Rebellions! Crisis and the Hunger for Justice.* Oakland, CA: Food First Books.

Hurst, Nathan. 2010. "Filling the Fresh Food Void." *Detroit News*, May 17, A12.

Koff, Stephen. 2015. "Healthy Food Coalition Wants Lawmakers to Tackle Issue." *Cleveland Plain Dealer*, February 16, A5.

Kozol, Jonathan. 1991. *Savage Inequalities: Children in America's Schools.* New York: Crown.

LeDoux, Timothy F., and Igor Vojnovic. 2012. "Going Outside the Neighborhood: The Shopping Patterns and Adaptations of Disadvantaged Consumers Living in the Lower Eastside Neighborhoods of Detroit, Michigan." *Health and Place* 19: 1–14.

Lobao, Linda M., Gregory Hooks, and Ann R. Tickamyer, eds. 2007. *The Sociology of Spatial Inequality.* Albany: State University of New York Press.

Masi, Brad, Janet Fiskio, and Rumi Shammin. 2014. "Urban Agriculture in Rust Belt Cities." *Solutions Journal* 5 (1): 44–53.

Massey, Douglas S., and Nancy A. Denton. 1993. *American Apartheid: Segregation and the Making of the Underclass*. Cambridge, MA: Harvard University Press.

McMichael, Philip. 2004. *Development and Social Change*. 3rd ed. Newbury Park, CA: Sage.

Menezes, Francisco. 2001. "Food Sovereignty: A Vital Requirement for Food Security in the Context of Globalization." *Development* 44: 29–33.

Mersol-Barg, Amy E. 2014. "Urban Agriculture and the Modern Farm Bill: Cultivating Prosperity in America's Rust Belt." *Duke Environmental Law and Policy Forum* 24: 279–314.

Moore, Latetia V., and Ana V. Diez Roux. 2006. "Associations of Neighborhood Characteristics with the Location and Type of Food Stores." *American Journal of Public Health* 96 (2): 325–31.

Morton, Lois Wright, Ella Annette Bitto, Mary Jane Oakland, and Mary Sand. 2005. "Solving the Problems of Iowa Food Deserts: Food Insecurity and Civic Structure." *Rural Sociology* 70 (1): 94–112.

Myers, Justin Sean, and Joshua Sbicca. 2015. "Bridging Good Food and Good Jobs: From Secession to Confrontation within Alternative Food Movement Politics." *Geoforum* 61: 17–26.

Oberg, Charles N. 2011. "The Great Recession's Impact on Children." *Maternal and Child Health Journal* 15 (5): 553–54.

Popovitch, Trish. 2014. "10 American Cities Lead the Way with Urban Agriculture Ordinances." Seedstock. *seedstock.com/2014/05/27/10-american-cities-lead-the-way-with-urban-agriculture-ordinances/*.

Reisig V., and A. Hobbis. 2000. "Food Deserts and How to Tackle Them: A Study of One City's Approach." *Health Education Journal* 59: 137–49.

Reutlinger, Schlomo. 1986. *Poverty and Hunger: Issues and Options for Food Security in Developing Countries*. Washington, DC: World Bank.

Roche, Juste, ed. 2013. *Food Deserts and Access to Food in the United States*. Hauppauge, NY: Nova Scientific.

Schilling, Joseph, and Jonathan Logan. 2008. "Greening the Rust Belt: A Green Infrastructure Model for Right Sizing America's Shrinking Cities." *Journal of the American Planning Association* 74 (4): 451–56.

Sen, Amartya. 1981. *Poverty and Famines: An Essay on Entitlement and Deprivation*. New York: Oxford University Press.

Shackman, Gene, Chengxuan Yu, Lynn S. Edmunds, Lewis Clarke, and Jackson P. Sekhobo. 2015. "Relation between Annual Trends in Food Pantry Use and Long-Term Unemployment in New York State, 2002–2012." *American Journal of Public Health* 105 (3): e63–e65.

Shaw, Hillary J. 2006. "Food Deserts: Towards the Development of a Classification." *Geografiska Annaler Series B: Human Geography* 88B (2): 231–47.

US Bureau of the Census. 2015. *American Community Survey 5-Year Estimates, 2009–2013*. US Department of Commerce: Washington, DC. *factfinder.census.gov*.

US Department of Agriculture. 2013. *Food Access Research Atlas*. USDA Economic Research Service: Washington, DC. *www.ers.usda.gov/data-products/food-access-research-atlas.aspx#. VDw161eGfZg*.

———. 2014. "Food Deserts." USDA Economic Research Service: Washington, DC. *apps. ams.usda.gov/fooddeserts/fooddeserts.aspx*.

———. 2015. "Food Access Research Atlas Documentation." USDA Economic Research Service: Washington, DC. *www.ers.usda.gov/data-products/food-access-research-atlas/ documentation.aspx*.

————. 2017. *Food Desert Locator.* USDA Economic Research Service. Washington, DC. *www.ers.usda.gov/data-products/food-access-research-atlas/go-to-the-atlas.aspx.*

Waldinger, Roger David. 1996. *Still the Promised City? African-Americans and New Immigrants in Postindustrial New York.* Cambridge, MA: Harvard University Press.

West, Cornel. 1993. *Race Matters.* Boston: Beacon.

Whitley, Sarah. 2013. "Changing Times in Rural America: Food Assistance and Food Insecurity in Food Deserts." *Journal of Family Social Work* 16: 36–52.

Willie, Charles W. 1989. *The Caste and Class Controversy on Race and Poverty: Round Two of the Willie/Wilson Debate.* Dix Hills, NY: General Hall.

Wilson, David, and Jared Wouters. 2003. "Spatiality and Growth Discourse: The Restructuring of America's Rust Belt Cities." *Journal of Urban Affairs* 25 (2): 123–38.

Wilson, William Julius. 1987. *The Truly Disadvantaged: The Inner City, the Underclass, and Public Policy.* Chicago: University of Chicago Press.

————. 1996. *When Work Disappears: The World of the New Urban Poor.* New York: Knopf.

Winne, Mark. 2008. *Closing the Food Gap: Resetting the Table in the Land of Plenty.* Boston: Beacon.

12

Shifting Access to Food
Food Deserts in Atlanta, 1980–2010

GLORIA ROSS AND BILL WINDERS

In Atlanta, Georgia, some communities have very limited access to grocery stores that sell fresh fruits and vegetables. This is especially true for communities that include primarily low-income and black residents. People living in these neighborhoods may have to travel miles outside their neighborhood to find a grocery store. By contrast, residents of other neighborhoods in Atlanta have relatively easy access to grocery stores stocked with fresh fruits and vegetables and most other amenities that shoppers may seek. As in most other US cities, these neighborhoods are more likely to be white and middle or upper class. Nevertheless, some poorer communities and black communities do have access to healthy, affordable food. Over the past thirty years, adequate access to healthy, affordable food has shifted in Atlanta, and some communities that were food secure are now categorized as food deserts. Why do communities lack access to healthy, affordable food? And why do the locations of food deserts shift over time?

Inequality is central to defining which neighborhoods are food deserts, as the concept centers on income and poverty. Yet in this southern city, poverty and race are inextricably linked, and the impact of historically rooted racial segregation is clearly evident in the present day. Despite the civil rights movement of the 1950s and 1960s, the prominent role of African Americans in city politics for the past forty years, and the historical strength of the black middle class in Atlanta, this city has seen important elements of racial inequality increase over the past thirty years. Food deserts are set against the backdrop of this uneven landscape and, between 1980 and 2010, have shifted in ways that disproportionately impact poor black neighborhoods.

How can we explain these shifts? We argue that three factors are particularly important to consider. First, as with many cities in the United States during the 1980s and 1990s, Atlanta experienced a population shift as people—especially middle-class whites and blacks—left the city for the suburbs. Second, when the population shifted, poverty became more concentrated in south and southwest Atlanta. Third, a "supermarket war" occurred in the 1990s as a new chain—Publix—entered the Atlanta market and built many of its stores outside of the central city. These three factors resulted in the persistence and expansion of food deserts in predominantly African American neighborhoods. In short, this chapter explores the patterns of food vulnerability in Atlanta from 1980 to 2010 by situating food deserts in the context of market shifts, racial segregation, and poverty.

We focus on three factors that have influenced the development of food deserts in Atlanta: population and demographic shifts, the concentration of poverty, and the retail market. Before we turn our attention to these three important factors, we first provide historical context and background for understanding the spatial patterning of race and inequality in Atlanta. We then link this context to its relationship with poverty and describe why this particular relationship is central to understanding the vulnerabilities that food deserts create. Then, we discuss the sources for our data, which come from the US Census and retail business directories. Here, we also offer a brief discussion of the Geographic Information Systems (GIS) and geospatial methods that we use to trace and analyze food deserts in Atlanta. Finally, we show how Atlanta food deserts have shifted, and we discuss the role that the market, population shifts, and racial inequality and the concentration of poverty have played in shaping access to food in the city.

Race and Poverty in Atlanta's History

Atlanta has historically been residentially segregated by race, and it remains so today. The city's segregation is the product of decisions made by groups and individuals that shaped the physical and political landscape. The city's spatial patterning of racial segregation and the concentration of the poor is the result of systemic and structural racism that has largely guided the city's development (Bayor 1996; Stone 1989). For example, in the mid-1900s, the city government and the downtown business elite formed the dominant partnership in an urban regime that was focused on remaking the city's built landscape during a period of racial segregation (Bayor 1996). The location of Atlanta's highway is one example of this coalition's success. The business elite, "having long been concerned about the proximity of blighted residential areas to the business district . . . [advocated for a] north-south expressway (Interstates 75 and 85) [that] was to curve around the edge of downtown, forming a buffer between the business district and the black neighborhoods to the east" (Stone 1989, 32). In addition, the black neighborhoods of Buttermilk Bottom and Summerhill were cleared under the Federal Housing Act of 1949 in order to develop public-use facilities like the Atlanta–Fulton County Stadium and the Boisfeuillet Jones Atlanta Civic Center (Stone 1989, 38). Such development decisions were based on racial inequality and resulted in black neighborhoods being sacrificed to white priorities. By and large, black communities could offer little political resistance when business interests trumped local concerns.

More recently, the city's political regime has continued to bolster Atlanta's development in ways that have left poor blacks behind. The political coalition governing Atlanta is held together by a shared commitment to economic growth but has done very little, if anything, to "bring the city's resources together to meet the problems of poverty, ineffective schools, and an underdeveloped workforce" (Vale 2013, 143). As a result, this has created a tale of two cities—an Atlanta that boasts a bourgeoning

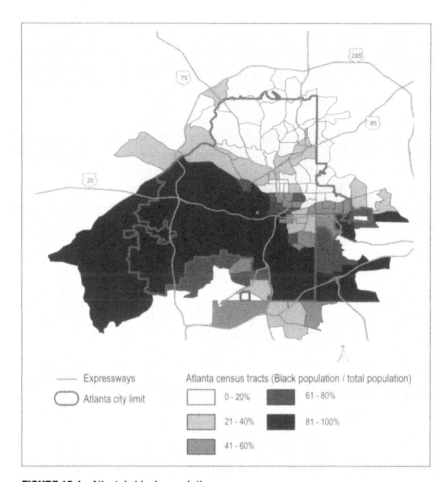

FIGURE 12.1. Atlanta's black population.

economic sector spurred by technology, finance, and the service sector, and an Atlanta that leads the nation in income inequality. Consequently, Atlanta's development—especially since 1980—has frequently neglected poor black residents.

Population shifts have also been notable in Atlanta's recent history. Although population density grew in the northern census tracts of the city from 1980 to 2010, Atlanta's black residents have remained spatially concentrated to the south and southwest areas of the city—below Interstate 20 and to the west of I-75 and I-85 (see Figure 12.1). This spatial patterning of the concentration of black residents in Atlanta has persisted and increased between 1980 and 2010. Two shifts are worth noting. First, downtown neighborhoods immediately east of where I-20 and I-75/85 intersect were 45–89 percent black (non-Hispanic) in 1980. However, in 2010, this changed, and many of the same neighborhoods lost black residents, becoming approximately 19–45 percent black. Second, neighborhoods in the far southwest corner of the city boundary had approximately 72–90 percent black residents in 1980. This racial segregation intensified in these neighborhoods throughout the proceeding thirty years, and those same neighborhoods were 89–99 percent black in 2010. This illustrates a distinct

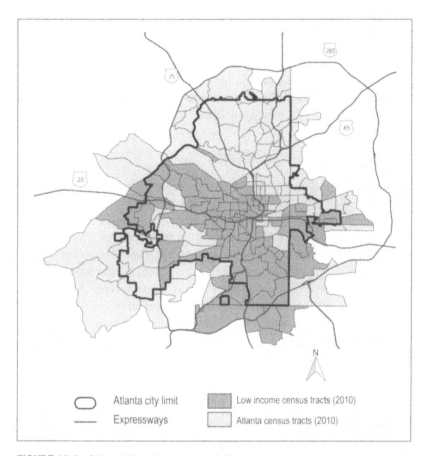

FIGURE 12.2. Atlanta's low-income population.

spatial patterning of race in Atlanta, where the majority of black residents have been concentrated to the west, south, and southwest areas of the city.

When we consider the spatial patterning of poverty of Atlanta, it maps much the same way that race does (see Figure 12.2).[1] In mapping the criteria for low-income tracts that categorize food deserts, three key points are worth highlighting. First, in 1980 and in 2010, black neighborhoods to the far west near the city boundary largely remained below a poverty rate of 20 percent and/or earned 80 percent or more of the metropolitan area's median household income. These census tracts include the middle-class black neighborhoods of Cascade Heights and South Fulton and are, by virtue of their economic status, less likely to be in a food desert. Second, the decrease in black residents east of I-75/85 in downtown corresponds to a shift in those neighborhoods' low-income status. In 1980, these downtown neighborhoods were considered low income, yet by 2010 these same neighborhoods were not low income. The decrease of black residents in these areas overlaps with the decrease in poverty and increase in median household income. Finally, poverty further intensified in areas immediately south of downtown Atlanta between 1980 and 2010. More census tracts met the criteria for low income in southwest Atlanta in 2010 than did thirty years previously. This concentration of low-income tracts corresponds to the increase of black residents in those same tracts.

This historical legacy of development politics, racial segregation, and the concentration of poverty laid the foundation for the food deserts that exist in Atlanta today. Understanding the connections between race, poverty, politics, and food deserts is important to discerning the underlying processes shaping access to food in Atlanta.

Race, Poverty, and Food Deserts

What does racial segregation and poverty have to do with Atlanta's food deserts? Put simply, most food deserts in the city of Atlanta are in census tracts that have a high proportion of African Americans living in poverty. As we explain below, poor neighborhoods that are black have a more difficult time getting out of poverty. Additionally, when more blacks move into that neighborhood, the area's chances for getting out of poverty decrease. In Atlanta, this has meant that a poor or low-income food desert with a greater concentration of black residents will likely remain a food desert.

Massey (1990, 329) demonstrates that racial segregation ensures that poor black neighborhoods will experience a greater concentration of poverty that poor white or racially mixed neighborhoods do not. According to Massey (1990), the residential segregation patterns that lead to the accumulation of poor blacks in specific parts of the city make those communities pockets of extreme concentrated poverty. This has been facilitated, in part, by a steady rise in income inequality since the 1970s that was accompanied by a decline in family income overall and a shift away from manufacturing to service industries in urban areas across the country. Racial segregation and the concentration of poverty are positively correlated because "the imposition of racial segregation on a residential structure that is also segregated by class works to the detriment of poor blacks and to the benefit of poor whites" (Massey 1990, 336). In other words, racial residential segregation acts to concentrate poverty. And because the poverty rate for blacks is greater than it is for whites, poor black neighborhoods disproportionately experience the persistence of extreme poverty.

The concentration of poverty in poor black neighborhoods in south and southwest Atlanta is significant in determining access to fresh, healthy, and affordable food in three ways. First, this concentration of poverty takes on a specific geographic and spatial characteristic (Massey 1990). Changes in the economic status of a minority group that come about from exogenous forces (deindustrialization, suburbanization of employment, rise in low-wage service sector work, etc.) will not only increase the poverty rate for that group as a whole but it will also result in the *geographic concentration of poverty*. As Massey (1990, 337) points out, "this geographic intensification of poverty occurs because the additional poverty created by the exogenous shock is spread unevenly over the metropolitan area." Therefore, under the clearly defined spatial patterns of racial and class residential segregation that have developed in Atlanta (as seen in Figures 12.1 and 12.2), poor black neighborhoods—such as those in south and southwest Atlanta—are more susceptible and vulnerable to widespread economic shocks such as increased unemployment, major market downturns, lack of capital, and changes in the overall economic vitality of the city.

Second, the concentration of poverty in black neighborhoods not only increases vulnerability to economic crises, but it also intensifies the other social and economic conditions that accompany poverty. These conditions include, for example, "reduced buying power, increased welfare dependence, high rates of family disruption, elevated crime rates, housing deterioration, elevated infant mortality rates, and decreased educational quality" (Massey 1990, 342). Therefore, the concentration of poverty that occurs when the poverty rate for blacks increases in the city also facilitates a whole set of other changing conditions that directly impact the well-being and health of those who live in the neighborhood. For example, public services that rely on local taxes are cut or severely limited, housing stock deteriorates because homeowners do not have the expendable income to maintain and rehabilitate property, and mortality rates rise because people are less able to pay for medical services. In sum, the intensification of poverty in racially segregated poor neighborhoods in Atlanta goes beyond income and unemployment; people's lives, health, and personal ability to cope and survive are adversely affected.

Third, the concentration of poverty in racially segregated neighborhoods, coupled with its associated intensification of other social and economic conditions that accompany poverty, directly affects people's ability to access fresh, healthy, and affordable food. Economic shocks, including unemployment and loss of income, directly hamper the buying power of a neighborhood. In the absence of racial or class segregation, this loss of buying power would be distributed evenly throughout the city. However, in the context of entrenched racial and class segregation in poor black neighborhoods, key economic drivers like retail profits, tax revenues, and service revenues decline, and related businesses and service organizations close. Therefore, "racial segregation takes the overall loss in black income, concentrates it spatially, and focuses it on fragile neighborhoods that are the least able to absorb" economic shocks and hardship (Massey 1990, 345). As a result, supermarkets and grocery stores—where access to fresh, healthy, and affordable food is most likely—are more likely to close. In sum, increased poverty in conditions of racial and class segregation decreases the buying power of poor black neighborhoods and through a constellation of other deteriorating social and economic conditions makes it increasingly challenging for a retail business to operate successfully in those very same neighborhoods. Therefore, racial segregation and the associated concentration of poverty are vital components to Atlanta's food desert story.

With this focus on race and poverty, our understanding of food deserts sharpens because we are able to see food access as part of larger processes. Food, although necessary for our survival, is not distributed based on need but rather on one's ability to purchase it. Consumers use their economic position to purchase this commodity—food—that will keep them alive. While there are certainly exceptions to this description (emergency food systems and food pantries, for example), the vast majority of people in the United States purchase food from supermarkets (see Economic Research Service 2016). Consequently, supermarkets have tended toward a pattern of spatial distribution that concentrates in middle- and high-income neighborhoods while largely deserting low-income communities.

Dooling and Simon (2012) demonstrate how racism and capitalism interact to produce food deserts by exploring the question of risk and vulnerability and examining the city (and its interrelated biophysical, economic, political, and cultural systems) through the lens of vulnerability. They understand vulnerability as a set of conditions that include, among other things, being impoverished, residing in a city that has lost its industrial base, "and lacking access to affordable, organic food that reflects culturally specific ingredients and produce" (Dooling and Simon 2012, 8). Importantly, this lens focuses on how conditions of being vulnerable (residing in a food desert, for example) are created and perpetuated by uneven levels of access to economic resources and political power. For Agyeman and Simons (2012, 86), communities who negotiate food access through political and economic asymmetries are not only vulnerable, but their vulnerability is consistently exacerbated with each interaction in the system. From this perspective, food deserts are the result of "a history of disinvestment in and neglect of mostly low-income urban and rural areas, which have not been recognized as profitable sites for supermarket and grocery store location and have therefore been left with limited and often less healthy, more expensive options for food access, such as corner stores and fast food establishments" (Agyeman and Simons 2012, 87). This understanding emphasizes where this vulnerability is concentrated: in low-income and poor neighborhoods that are also products of racial segregation. Food vulnerability and food deserts, then, are a result of capitalism and institutional racism.

These theoretical perspectives, when used to understand Atlanta's historical development and the shaping of food vulnerabilities, demonstrate that food access is tied to entrenched histories of racism and capitalism—systems that have concentrated poverty and entrenched racial segregation. This approach moves past food desert maps as static snapshots of food access and adds a temporal dimension by tracing their development over the past thirty years. In doing so, this analysis takes into account social structures and historical legacies of disinvestment and racial oppression throughout Atlanta. We explain the persistence and expansion of food deserts in Atlanta from 1980 to 2010 through the use of geographic information analysis (GIS).

Tracking Food Deserts

Using access to supermarkets as the central measure of a food desert, we analyze how the patterns of food deserts in Atlanta overlap with racial segregation and the concentration of poverty. We use GIS and spatial analysis to analyze demographic and economic factors that have developed and shaped food access in Atlanta over a thirty-year period from 1980 to 2010.

To explain the spatial patterning of food deserts in Atlanta, we draw on data about 2010 supermarket location from the Mergent Million Dollar Database on business and industries using the standard industry code for supermarkets. We also obtained supermarket addresses from the City of Atlanta Directory and the Atlanta Yellow Pages for the years 1981, 1990, and 2000. We then geocoded the addresses using GIS software and spatially joined this data to demographic data from a longitudinal census database compiled by Logan, Xu, and Stults (2014, 412). Drawn from the US Census, the demographic data is organized by 2010 census tract boundaries and includes a variety of variables: median household income (constant 2010 dollars), percentage of housing units vacant, percentage of population that is racial or ethnic minority, percentage unemployed, percentage below the federal poverty line, and population density (per square acre). Using this data, we produced a series of choropleth maps to illustrate the distribution of percentage black (non-Hispanic), low-income tracts, and urban food desert maps using the criteria from USDA (US Department of Agriculture) for 1980, 1990, 2000, and 2010. A "significant" share of residents was defined as at least one-third of the tract population residing more than one mile from a supermarket. A census tract was defined as low-income if it had a poverty rate of 20 percent or higher, or a median family income at or below 80 percent of the metropolitan area's median family income. We used a buffer analysis to identify a one-mile Euclidian distance from the center of low-income census tracts to supermarket locations. We employed cluster analysis to identify statistically significant high and low concentrations of supermarkets across Atlanta in 1981, 1990, 2000, and 2010.[2]

Shifting Food Deserts in Atlanta

From 1980 to 2010, Atlanta's food deserts shifted in important ways. Over this period, food desert tracts increased in the south and southwest areas of Atlanta, where the majority of the population is black and low income, from 1980 and 2010. Figure 12.3 shows that food desert tracts in 1980 were located on the northwest, southwest, and southeast tracts on the outer edge of the city. In 1980, there were thirty-three supermarkets identified. These supermarkets were located along the I-85 and I-20 highway corridors and were also distributed near downtown where the highways intersect. Consequently, neighborhoods immediately south of downtown Atlanta had access to a nearby supermarket and were not categorized as food deserts. Likewise, there were relatively few neighborhoods in southwest Atlanta with food accessibility low enough to qualify as food deserts. Finally, Atlanta food deserts in 1980 tended to be some distance from interstates and were spread throughout the city, though there was a concentration of food deserts in the northwest portion of the city.

In 1990, food desert tracts still persisted in neighborhoods near downtown Atlanta, but they also expanded to the neighborhoods immediately south, southeast, and west of downtown. Comparing 1980 and 1990, food deserts expanded along the southwest border of the city, as well as east of the city, along the I-20 corridor. Notably tracts to the north did not meet the food desert criteria, because these neighborhoods were not designated low-income or had a poverty rate of less than 20 percent and because these northern neighborhoods had a greater share of Atlanta's supermarket locations. In 1990, there were twenty-three supermarket locations within Atlanta's city boundaries, a decrease of about 30 percent from 1980. The locations where supermarkets closed help to account for the expansion in food deserts in certain parts of Atlanta.

By 2000, another important shift occurred: the neighborhoods immediately surrounding downtown had lost their food desert status (see Figure 12.3). Publix and Kroger, the dominant grocery chains in Atlanta, had located in neighborhoods close to downtown during the 1990s, as we discuss in more detail later. Additionally, areas that were once food deserts near the western city limits of Atlanta no longer met the criteria for food desert designation. However, food access declined in the neighborhoods west of downtown. In 2000, there were thirty-five supermarkets within the

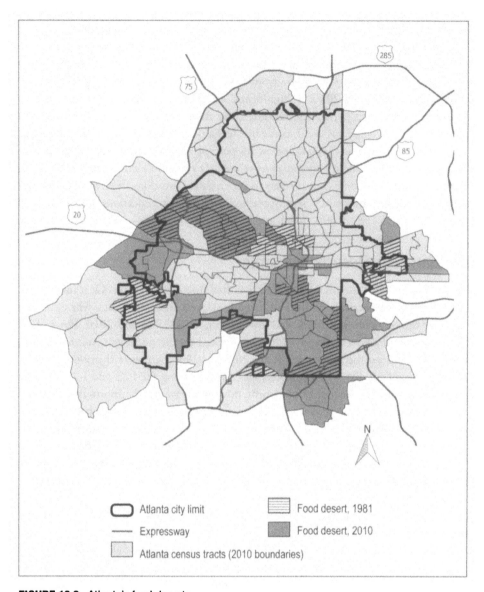

FIGURE 12.3. Atlanta's food deserts.

boundaries of the city. Thus, the number of supermarkets increased back to the level seen in 1980. Again, the placement of supermarkets shaped the city's landscape in terms of food deserts.

As Figure 12.3 shows, food deserts spread to neighborhoods south of downtown and intensified in the west and southwest neighborhoods of the city by 2010. Additionally, supermarkets that were once located south of downtown along the north-south I-75/85 highway were gone by 2010. This also led to an expansion of food deserts in southeast Atlanta. Despite the closing of grocery stores south of downtown, the density of supermarket locations to the north remained stable. In 2010 there were thirty-eight supermarkets within Atlanta, but the placement of these supermarkets demonstrate a northeastward push relative to previous years. Notably, some

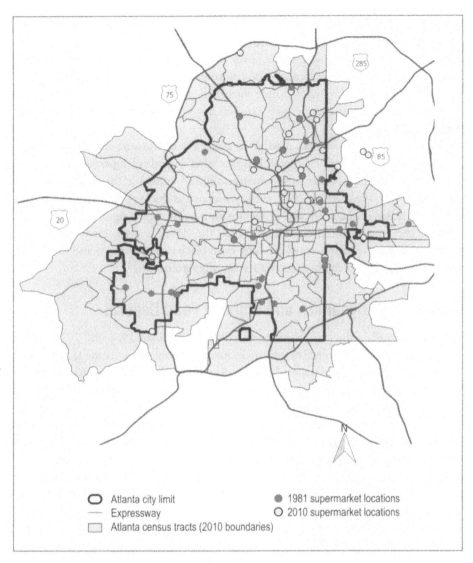

FIGURE 12.4. Supermarkets in Atlanta.

neighborhoods that experienced a decline in black residents lost their food desert status by 2010. For example, the neighborhood of the Old Fourth Ward east of downtown Atlanta, which was predominantly black in 1980, lost black residents by 2010. The poverty rate in the Old Fourth Ward had also decreased, and its median household income earnings increased by 2010 so that it was no longer designated as low-income, thus shifting its status from food desert to non–food desert.

Finally, the loss of supermarkets in south Atlanta is more clearly important. As Figure 12.4 shows, many of the supermarket locations changed between 1980 and 2010. The new supermarket locations resulted in a shift to the north of Atlanta. Between 1980 and 2010, grocery store locations were quite fluid. Furthermore, the spatial distribution of supermarkets skewed to predominantly white and higher-earning neighborhoods to the north between 1980 and 2010. Taking I-20 as a dividing line between north and south Atlanta, fifteen supermarkets were located in south Atlanta in 1980, compared to eighteen in the north. In 1990, eight supermarkets were located in south Atlanta, and fifteen were in the north. Ten years later in 2000 the gap widened as twelve supermarkets were located in south Atlanta, while north Atlanta had twenty-three. In 2010, south Atlanta had nine supermarkets, and twenty-six were located in north Atlanta. The supermarket gap between north and south Atlanta widened between 1980 and 2010.

To bolster this analysis, we used geospatial tools to measure statistically significant high and low counts of supermarkets. A cluster analysis of supermarket locations demonstrates that high counts of supermarkets already existed in the northern areas of the city by 1980. However, by 2010, the gap widened as the high count of supermarket clusters increased in the north and brought with it a statistically significant decrease in supermarkets in the central-city area. Overall, the cluster analysis demonstrates that the northward move of supermarkets away from black neighborhoods and toward the predominantly white neighborhoods is statistically significant.

Supermarket Dynamics and Shifts in Food Deserts

How can we explain the shift in Atlanta food deserts between 1980 and 2010? Racial segregation and the persistence of poverty in Atlanta are only some of the factors giving rise to the pattern of the city's food deserts. A closer look at the supermarkets themselves reveals how market shifts within the supermarket industry are important factors contributing to the development of food deserts in Atlanta. Atlanta's grocery market increased from $4 billion in the 1990s to $7 billion in the mid-2000s, and supermarkets tried several strategies over the years to increase their share of it.[3] Competition in the market was relatively stable throughout the 1980s, with Kroger in place as the number one grocer in the metropolitan area. However, there were notable disruptions in this stability in the 1990s and in the 2000s, including an increase in supermarket stores across Atlanta in what was referred to as the "supermarket wars" beginning in the early 1990s. Importantly, these shifts demonstrate how supermarkets used a location strategy based on considerations of class and income to build their stores, a strategy that ultimately left poor and black neighborhoods without supermarket access.

Throughout the 1980s, Atlanta's primary supermarket chains were stable and predictable, and not many new stores were built throughout the decade. At that time, the big three supermarkets in Atlanta were Kroger, A&P, and Winn-Dixie. Piggly-Wiggly was also a local favorite. By a large margin, Kroger was the dominant supermarket chain in Atlanta, boasting a total of sixty-five stores throughout metropolitan Atlanta during the 1980s.[4] This landscape changed drastically in the early 1990s when Publix—a privately owned supermarket chain based in Lakeland, Florida—announced that it was planning on entering the Atlanta market (*Atlanta Journal and Constitution* 1992). The arrival of Publix meant that some smaller chains would likely be pushed out and that the competition for customers would intensify. This was the start of Atlanta's supermarket war that led to major losses for smaller grocers in the metropolitan area.

With the arrival of Publix, we can clearly see how supermarket companies used a geographical location strategy for their new stores that consistently bypassed low-income, poor, and black neighborhoods in south Atlanta. As Figure 12.4

illustrates, Atlanta's supermarkets in 2010 were disproportionately located in the northern areas of the city. From the outset, Publix's strategy to overtake Kroger was to locate its stores in the high-income and majority white suburbs of northern Atlanta. When the company released its first planned sites, the pattern of the stores formed a ring north of the city, "skipping the slower growth and higher real estate costs of the central city" (Holsendolph 1992, R-3). In particular, Publix planned its first four sites in the northern, predominantly white, counties of Cobb and Gwinnett (Burritt 1991a, H-1). The Publix strategy for developing its stores was unmistakably clear: build in the northern suburbs. The area's top supermarket chains were waging a war strategy that relied on bypassing black and poor neighborhoods.[5]

One important implication of this supermarket location strategy for low-income and minority neighborhoods was the closure of independent grocers and smaller chains that could no longer compete with Publix or Kroger.[6] Four years after Publix's entered the Atlanta market, the supermarket war began to take a toll on the region's smaller supermarket chains and independent grocers. In 1995, Kroger remained the number one grocer in Atlanta with 32 percent (seventy-six stores) of the market, but Publix had jumped to number two with 15 percent of the market share (thirty-three stores) (Roush 1995, F-1). Winn-Dixie was third in Atlanta's grocery market with 13 percent, Cub Foods was fourth with about 8 percent, and A&P was fifth with 6 percent of the market (Roush 1995, F-1). The smaller chains were the very ones who operated stores in the working-class neighborhoods of Atlanta, including stores near downtown and in the southern parts of the city in areas that new Kroger and Publix development neglected. For example, the predominantly black neighborhood of Pittsburgh in south Atlanta lost all their local grocery stores, including Winn-Dixie, A&P, and Big Star Foods. Pittsburgh and similar neighborhoods in south Atlanta were hurt by population shifts between 1980 and 2010. During this period, such neighborhoods became poorer, racially segregated, and less dense in terms of population. As poverty became more concentrated, these neighborhoods were less able to financially sustain grocery stores and thus became less attractive to supermarket chains, which located new stores elsewhere.

In sum, while new supermarket chain stores opened up in Atlanta's northern suburbs, many neighborhoods in south Atlanta suffered on two fronts. First, these neighborhoods were bypassed by new supermarket development. Second, these neighborhoods saw many of the supermarkets that did exist in their neighborhoods close up shop, defeated by the supermarket wars that benefitted whiter and wealthier neighborhoods.

Why do some communities lack access to healthy affordable food, and why do the location of food deserts shift over time? In particular, racial segregation, the concentration of poverty, and market processes that influenced supermarket locations all worked to create food vulnerable neighborhoods in Atlanta between 1980 and 2010. This analysis has highlighted these three key findings.

First, racial segregation and the concentration of poverty spatially overlap with shifts in Atlanta's supermarket locations. Atlanta has a clear racial and income dividing line that splits the city into higher-income and majority white neighborhoods to the north and low-income, poor, and predominantly black neighborhoods to the south. For the most part, this dividing line has persisted and, in some areas, intensified between 1980 and 2010. From 1980 to 2010, the concentration of blacks to the southern parts of the city increased, alongside a corresponding increase in the concentration of whites to the north. The concentration of poverty and extent of racial segregation reinforces the vulnerability experienced by low-income neighborhoods, including food vulnerability.

Second, the market shift that redistributed supermarkets to the north had two important consequences for vulnerable communities. First, throughout the 1980s and early 1990s, Atlanta's poor communities disproportionately experienced the combination of population loss and supermarket flight and were less able to absorb the shocks brought on by these changes. Poor black neighborhoods were less able to sustain what little economic vitality they did have and consequently suffered the loss of supermarkets that served as access to fresh fruits and vegetables.

Third, these demographic shifts are correlated with changes in supermarket locations. This is especially evident in the early 1990s when Publix entered Atlanta's grocery market and began to build new stores in the northern suburbs. The strategy of Publix Supermarkets, according to industry analysts, was to maximize the buying power of high-earning majority white residents. Other stores followed suit, making the same demographic and economic calculations as Publix and locating their stores in the predominantly white suburbs. This market competition persisted across metropolitan Atlanta and resulted in neighborhoods to the north of the city acquiring greater access to food.

At the same time, however, changes in the market interacted with demographic shifts in racially segregated neighborhoods in south and west Atlanta and ultimately created unfavorable market conditions for supermarkets. From 1980 to 2010, black neighborhoods in south and southwest Atlanta experienced an increase in poverty and black residents. Additionally, these neighborhoods lost population density overall. These conditions made it difficult for smaller chains and independent stores, many of which were located near downtown neighborhoods, to remain competitive, and eventually they closed their stores. As a result, by 2010 the supermarket landscape looked drastically different than the one witnessed in 1980. Whereas stores like Piggly-Wiggly, Winn-Dixie, Big Star, and A&P had populated neighborhoods in south Atlanta in 1980, by 2010 the majority of tracts in south Atlanta were food deserts. Alternatively, many of the supermarket locations in 2010 were spatially skewed to the north. The extent of racial segregation in predominantly black neighborhoods further concentrated poverty and made it difficult for neighborhood retail—along with other services—to thrive.

Of course, supermarkets are not the only means of providing access to healthy, affordable food. In Atlanta, a number of alternatives to supermarkets have emerged over the past fifteen years. First, urban agriculture has expanded in the city. For example, Truly Living Well (TLW) farms are located in the predominantly black communities of East Point and Old Fourth Ward. TLW has urban farms, community outreach, and farmers' markets that provide access to fresh fruits and vegetables. Second, a number of farmers' markets have emerged throughout the city. While most of these farmers' markets are located in middle-class and white communities, some are found within short distance of poorer, black neighborhoods. And importantly, some of these markets have been accepting food stamps and WIC for a number of years. Nonetheless, even with such important alternatives, it is difficult to make up for the loss of supermarkets in poorer communities around the city.

NOTES

1. Low income is defined as a census tract with a poverty rate greater than or equal to 20 percent, or median family income less than 80 percent of the metropolitan area. For 2010 data, the median family income per census tract was $43,671. For 1980 data, the median family income per census tract was $12,483.91. If a census tract had less than 80 percent of 2010 median family income ($34,936.8) or less than 80 percent of 1980 median family income ($9,987.12), it was designated as low income.

2. Cluster analysis measures statistically significant clusters of high and low counts of supermarkets by census tracts using Z-scores to evaluate the presence of clusters and p-values to assess statistical significance.

3. Not all supermarkets that have vied for Atlanta's food dollar are competing in the same market segment. For example, Harris Teeter and Bruno's have filled Atlanta's high-end specialty grocer sector, supercenters like the once-prominent Big Star and Walmart have occupied the wholesale deep-discount grocery sector, and the now-defunct A&P, Kroger, and Publix have all historically carved out their stake in residential supermarket formats often supported by a network of regional distribution centers.

4. Nationally, Kroger Company was also capturing a large share of the grocery market. In 1989, Kroger Company had a total of 2,187 stores making nearly $19 billion a year (Burritt 1991b, A-1). By comparison, the Great Atlantic and Pacific Tea Company had 1,208 stores nationwide with $11 billion in sales a year, and Winn-Dixie had 1,236 stores with approximately $9 billion in sales (Burritt 1991b, A-1).

5. Some developers tried to entice supermarkets elsewhere, however. For example, John R. Perlman, an Atlanta retail developer, secured options to buy land in southeast Atlanta in the Grant Park neighborhood, an area "long bypassed by major retailers . . . who preferred the demographics of Atlanta suburbs." Previously, retailers and developers would study Grant Park's census tracts and see a mix of people living in $175,000 homes with those who lived in the nearby housing project. This "skewed median-income level turned off major retailers" and prevented major grocery chains from locating in the area. Perlman's reframing of the area's retail potential came at the same time that Kroger was slated to open up a store near downtown. Brad Wood, Kroger's assistant real estate manager at that time, explained the company's position: "obviously, we're a public company that answers to shareholders, so we're not going to open a store that loses money." However, as Wood noted, "we're trying to go beyond the formulas and be creative to make these in town stores work." See Murray (1992, C-1).

6. Cascade, a predominantly black middle-class neighborhood in southwest Atlanta, also experienced a "drought of grocery stores" throughout the 1980s and early 1990s. This changed in 1994 when not one, but three grocery stores—Bruno's, Publix, and Kroger—announced sites for the area that were all set to open in 1994. "After years of being ignored," wrote Parker, "residents of the predominantly African-American area generally welcome the shower of sudden attention." See Parker (1993, N-4).

REFERENCES

Agyeman, Julian, and Benjamin Simons. 2012. "Re-imagining the Local: Scale, Race, Culture and the Production of Urban Food Vulnerabilities." In *Cities, Nature and Development: The Politics and Production of Urban Vulnerabilities*, edited by S. Dooling and G. Simon, 85–100. Burlington, VT: Ashgate.

Atlanta Journal and Constitution. 1992. "$4 Billion at Stake in Metro Atlanta Grocery Market." January 26, G-1.

Bayor, Ronald. 1996. *Race and the Shaping of Twentieth-Century Atlanta*. Chapel Hill: University of North Carolina Press.

Burritt, Chris. 1991a. "Attention, Customers: Food War; Publix Grocery Chain Puts Kroger on Notice for Share of Atlanta." *Atlanta Journal and Constitution*. December 22, H-1.

———. 1991b. "Publix May Enter Metro Grocery Market; Fla.-Based Chain Talking with Developers." *Atlanta Journal and Constitution*. July 31, A-1.

Dooling, Sarah, and Gregory Simon. 2012. *Cities, Nature and Development: The Politics and Production of Urban Vulnerabilities*. Burlington, VT: Ashgate.

Economic Research Service (ERS). 2016. "Table 14. Sales of Food at Home by Type of Outlet." August 13, 2008, ERS Food Expenditure Series, US Department of Agriculture. *www.ers. usda.gov/data-products/food-expenditures*.

Holsendolph, Ernest. 1992. "Publix Super Markets Set Stage for Assault." *Atlanta Journal and Constitution*, April 21, R-3.

Logan, John, Zengwang Xu, and Brian Stults. 2014. "Interpolating US Decennial Census Tract Data from as Early as 1970 to 2010: A Longitudinal Tract Database." *Professional Geographer* 66 (3): 412–20.

Massey, Douglas. 1990. "American Apartheid: Segregation and the Making of the Underclass." *American Journal of Sociology* 96 (2): 329–57.

Murray, Sonia. 1992. "Minority Groups Criticize Publix's Hiring Practices: Supermarket Chain Has Few Minority Managers, Locations, Groups Allege." *Atlanta Journal and Constitution*, June 23, C-1.

Parker, Jennifer. 1993. "Suddenly Supermarkets Pour into Southwest Atlanta." *Atlanta Journal and Constitution*, December 30, N-4.

Roush, Chris. 1995. "Kroger Plans Mini-store Near City Hall, but Techwood Area Site Still Up in the Air; 12 New Outlets in Outlook for '96." *Atlanta Journal and Constitution*, October 12, F-1.

Stone, Clarence. 1989. *Regime Politics: Governing Atlanta 1946–1988*. Lawrence: University Press of Kansas.

Vale, Lawrence. 2013. *Purging the Poorest: Public Housing and the Design Politics of Twice-Cleared Communities*. Chicago: University of Chicago Press.

PART THREE

SOLUTIONS

How do we attempt to untangle the paradoxes of food and poverty addressed throughout this volume? What are possible solutions to the problems of food insecurity in the midst of a bounty of not always healthy food? How do we move toward greater food sovereignty for those most vulnerable in our current food system? Examining how the production and distribution of food has changed allows us to see that there are multiple possibilities for how to organize a food system. Though not an easy task, it is possible to change the way food is subsidized to prioritize healthier foods and smaller-scale agricultural production.

Previous chapters also highlight possible policy solutions. Changing the way we measure poverty could broaden the social safety net, which includes resources to address the need for food among those most vulnerable. Increasing the minimum wage could also improve food security for those working on the margins.

Federal nutrition assistance programs—such as SNAP (Supplemental Nutrition Assistance Program, commonly known as food stamps); WIC (Women Infants Children); and free and reduced-price school lunch and breakfast programs—provide crucial food sources for those near the poverty line. Yet, those who rely on these programs experience gaps in coverage. Additional programs, such as summer food service programs and backpack programs, serve to bridge the gap in need during summer months and weekends for children who rely on free and reduced-price lunch as a source of food during school. Efforts to increase access to such programs and raise awareness about their existence should be supported and expanded, since these programs are highly underutilized. Strengthening and expanding current federal nutrition assistance programs could further safeguard against food insecurity and take some of the pressure off the ever-increasing numbers who rely on food pantries and soup kitchens.

All these policy solutions could help address food insecurity, but many will likely face barriers. In the current political climate, federal support for expanding safety net programs, raising the minimum wage, or alterations to poverty measures appear unlikely. The future of the farm bill remains to be seen. Anti-immigrant initiatives leave many vulnerable, particularly those who labor at harvesting and processing food in the United States. Such policies could ultimately lead to labor shortages in agriculture and further exacerbate yet another paradox: that those who harvest food often experience food insecurity themselves.

Though change is needed at the federal level and efforts to initiate such change are worthy causes, it is noteworthy that changes, such as school lunch and nutrition programs, are also the result of local efforts and initiatives. Change is needed at many levels through multiple collaborative efforts. In a time when traction on policies at the national level will likely be met with resistance, it is heartening to note that much of the most promising work being done to address the social problems outlined in previous chapters is taking place at the community level. Smaller coalitions are tackling food insecurity and seeking food sovereignty in their own neighborhoods. Local initiatives, such as community food systems and community gardens chip away at systemic problems of food and poverty. Though many of these initiatives were created by and empower those most vulnerable and most affected by poverty and food insecurity, such initiatives face challenges related to the complex ways inequalities are connected to food systems. Nonetheless, such smaller-scale solutions are what hold promise to slowly erode larger structural inequalities related to race, class, and where one lives.

In this last section of the book, we provide some examples of this sort of pioneering work happening in communities across the United States. These accounts serve as inspiration to others for ways to tackle paradoxes of food and poverty in their own communities and regions.

13

Together at the Table

The Power of Public-Private Partnerships to Alleviate Hunger

ERIN NOLEN, JEREMY EVERETT,
DOUG MCDURHAM, AND KATHY KREY

Several years ago, an organized group of citizens from a large urban area in Texas actively opposed the proposed construction of a golf course in a wealthy neighborhood over the city's aquifer. These citizens were predominantly from low-income households in one of the city's poorest neighborhoods. The group was primarily concerned with city funds and tax incentives being spent on a recreational facility that few in the city would ever see, let alone utilize. They were also concerned that building a golf course over the water supply would contaminate drinking water for the residents of the community. Their process, like many twentieth-century organizing strategies, was to confront the city's "elite" with the sheer quantity of opposed citizens in order to publicly shame those proposing the golf course. The group of organized community members won—at least for the time being. The city council backed off the golf course proposal. It seemed as though the people garnered power by operating as an organized mass, just as Saul Alinsky (1971), the founder of modern community organizing, had promised decades prior.

Unfortunately, power was not actually redistributed in the process. Figuratively speaking, the group won the initial battle but lost the war. Five years later, the city's elites ultimately constructed their golf course because they had considerably more money and more power than the temporarily organized bloc of citizens. The group thought confrontation was the way to justice, as it tends to be in many cases. But the confrontational approach alone seems to have limits and potentially negative consequences. With that approach, people who are not already on board are rarely converted to the cause of justice. Confrontation, in essence, implies that it has already been decided who is for and who is against, which can set up a self-righteous—and self-defeating—paradigm. And confrontation often creates enemies, which can be problematic when organizers take on new causes later on.

The same city later tried a different tactic to reduce homelessness. The business community, elected officials, community advocates, and faith leaders all convened to develop a plan together. The result was one of the most progressive, comprehensive approaches to addressing homelessness in the nation. The powerful and the righteous were not pitted against each other but were asked to work together for the benefit of the city's most neglected population. Everyone won with this approach, rather than with the typical winner-take-all paradigm. This city's story of contrasts demonstrates the power of consensus building where citizens act on common ground. This social change project developed a centralized infrastructure and redistributed power through shared accountability and community ownership. This is how scalable solutions take shape.

This applies to the national problem of hunger too. The prevalence of hunger is too large and complex to be addressed by sectors working independently from one another. The way we can comprehensively address hunger is with an integrated, multisectoral response with input from both the public and private sectors. Thus, this chapter provides the reader with a snapshot of the art of developing public-private partnerships at and across the federal, state, and local levels. While this work is predicated on aspects of the collective impact model (Kania and Kramer 2011), our work also focuses on inclusivity, engaging in the social justice core of poverty work, and promoting policy change as an outcome (Wolff 2016). Three types of collaboration are outlined: statewide organizing for increasing access to federal nutrition programs, organizing for policy change at the state and federal levels, and organizing in local communities through coalition building. Each type is illustrated by examples that demonstrate potential impact.

Organizing for Statewide Public-Private Partnerships

Developing strategies that inform and drive antihunger work in local communities might be arranged by three guiding principles: *build the right team, share responsibility, and share accountability*. Building the right team starts with recognizing that no organization, no matter how holistic, is equipped to fully address the multilayered components of any given problem. By identifying all facets of the challenge at hand, the team is able to ensure that a partner is equipped, in skill or scope, to address each one. It is our experience that it is better to err on the side of inclusivity, which gives the team opportunity for creative and unexpected energy.

While it would be convenient if each collaborative partner had a completely unique mission and skill set, the real world seldom plays out this way. So organizations working together typically find that they stumble over each other and occasionally step on each other's toes. As a result, it might be tempting to exclude potential partners or rigidly enforce each organization's roles and responsibilities in the joint effort. Rather, it is advantageous to define organizational roles and embrace the multilayered strengths that each partner brings. This creates great challenges, of course, but frequent and direct communication ensures that each partner organization's creativity and human capital is maximized.

If responsibility is to be shared, then so must accountability, and this, too, depends on a strong communication infrastructure. Typically, shared accountability means that each partner is expected to fully report activities, challenges, and successes to the rest of the team, but, increasingly, shared accountability takes the form of specific performance measures and outcomes. Shared technology provides dispersed and disparate partners the ability to find common ground and can increase collective accountability.

Domestic food assistance is often provided through federal nutrition programs; therefore, we often work on increasing participation in the Supplemental Nutrition Assistance Program (SNAP) and federal child nutrition programs. Following is an example of how public-private statewide collaborations strengthened the capacity of these programs.

Case Example: Increasing Summer Meals Participation

A school social worker once shared an alarming but all too common story of a high school student whose academic performance took a nosedive near the end of his junior year. Despite numerous challenges, this student had worked hard and enjoyed an academically successful year. When the social worker pressed him for an explanation for his sudden and unexpected poor behavior and academic negligence, the student finally admitted, "If I fail two core courses, I will get to go to summer school, where lunch is served. That way, I'll at least have one good meal each day." When a student is willing to trade his education for food, the need for the Summer Food Service Program (SFSP) is evident. This dilemma was particularly discouraging given the significant resources that the federal and state administering agencies make available for the program in Texas.

Building the Right Team

Texas state agency officials were aware of low participation rates and interested in expansion efforts that are done with integrity. Prior efforts were often done casually, with little respect for regulations, food quality, or the needs of low-income families. While the federal agency gravitated toward an interest in expansion, their hesitation was well deserved, as there was much to learn. The goal of feeding more children paired with a willingness to learn from the state agency, long-term SFSP sponsors, and other stakeholders across the country provided a more sophisticated and nuanced perspective.

As this core team identified the biggest challenges to a robust execution of the Summer Meals Program, the need to include additional partners emerged. A primary barrier to participation was the isolation of rural children, so the team made a concerted effort to recruit partners whose expertise and resources could address the specific challenges of transportation and rural communities. New partners brought into the collaboration included various state agency officials, and the other statewide organizations with food system expertise. A regional dairy council brought expertise from its experience increasing access to the School Breakfast Program (SBP), and Texas AmeriCorps VISTA brought much-needed human resources. Equally important was the inclusion of a few large, multisite summer meals sponsors that had extensive experience with the many challenges of program implementation at the local level.

Shared Responsibility: State to Local

The core group began a routine of biweekly calls and occasional face-to-face meetings. The additional partners were included in frequent e-mail dialogues, as well as a multiday planning meeting in the spring and a review and evaluation meeting in the fall. This system allowed for maximum interaction for the core partners while keeping secondary partners engaged at their levels of interest and capacity.

In 2014, the team developed the first Texas summer meals expansion plan. Lofty goals were established, and each partner committed to a variety of strategies and tactics toward those goals. While a statewide plan was necessary to lay out the vision, it took regional collaborations to ensure implementation. Led by twelve THI child hunger outreach specialists in communities across the state, the regional staff members of the partners were joined by leaders from municipalities, congregations, food banks, schools, and educational service centers to replicate the planning work done on the state level. Each local, multisector coalition developed a plan that included an assessment of local strengths and needs that drove the development of goals, as well as action plans for meeting those goals. Motivated by the strong desire to reduce child food insecurity, partners eagerly and actively owned their responsibilities in the locally designed plans, thus contributing to the goals of the state plan. Like the state team, local coalitions held debriefing meetings to discern their best practices and kickoff planning for the following year.

Shared Accountability

So that their best practices could benefit the work of other coalitions across the state, regional staff took advantage of ample opportunities to disseminate and share procedural information. They consistently reported the work of their local coalitions so that documentation of their efforts could be compiled into a more comprehensive state picture. This process ensured that the federal agency and the state agency were steadily supplied with details of program barriers and stories of success that highlighted innovative, unique examples of out-of-the-box partnerships. The partnership also created an accountability structure for on-the-ground staff to make recommendations for effective outreach, implementation, and program administration to the state and federal staff who had the power to change policies. Furthermore, the USDA (US Department of Agriculture) received valuable information and data that could be incorporated into their existing reporting process. Not only were the partners able to be accountable to each other; a concrete result of the collaboration was that each partner group could also be more accountable to their own funders and stakeholders.

Building a network of stakeholders across the state to improve access to federal nutrition programs requires strategic planning that brings the right players to the table who are invested in creating and meeting mutual goals and that develops systems of accountability to measure progress and remain on track. However, the efficiency and reach of these programs is also contingent on effective policy. Next, we discuss collaborative methods to inform federal nutrition program policies and political dialogue.

Organizing Public-Private Partnerships for Policy Change

"It's refreshing to sit down with you today. Thanks for not treating us like we're the devil. We *don't* hate the poor. We're just budget conscious," said a legislative aide of the House Agriculture Committee during our visit to Capitol Hill in 2014 in Washington, DC. This meeting came on the heels of the committee's consultations with other antihunger advocates, who aggressively and adamantly prescribed a series of policy changes to keep nutrition programs intact. The topic of the Hill visit was the full SNAP review that the committee would undertake in the coming months during session. For productive conversation to take place, where trust might take shape, it was essential that antihunger organizations establish themselves as colleagues and serve as a resource—a resource with influence. In order to meaningfully influence policy, it is helpful to build consensus, so we presented a series of policy and program options for legislators and their aides to inform decision making.

When guiding policy improvements for food insecure families, a consensus-building approach is crucial to ensure an informed approach to policy recommendations.

Convening Policy Makers

Impacting policy requires a multisectoral approach organizing on the federal, state, and local levels simultaneously. This approach involves coordinating government, corporate, health, and nonprofit sectors to promote an infrastructure for public-private collaboration to maximize program administration and outreach. Texas administers fourteen federally funded programs that contribute to reducing food insecurity through state agencies. The child nutrition programs include National School Lunch Program (NSLP), School Breakfast Program (SBP), and the Summer Food Service Program (SFSP), also known as the Summer Meals Program (SMP). Other public benefit programs include SNAP, Medicaid, and the Women, Infants, and Children (WIC) program. From the outset, it was necessary to create a space where government agencies could dialogue and strategize around program delivery and maximizing efficiency with federal dollars. Prior to new collaborative policy efforts, the three commissioners whose state agencies administer these programs had not met regularly to discuss strategic program implementation. The support and buy-in of a key federal agency official launched a series of meetings, proposals, and ongoing conversations to maximize program efficiency and reach, which includes reducing bureaucratic red tape, streamlining services, and addressing gaps in program administration. These preliminary collaborative conversations led to the development of a state operations team, which was composed of government officials. While the state operations team was not needed for long-term organizing strategy, it provided a conceptual framework for cross-agency collaboration. For example, one state agency now advertises SMP, and two other agencies paid for SNAP- and WIC-accessible terminals to be put in approved farmers' markets to support local produce in low-income communities.

Convening disparate groups and coalitions is key in identifying and operating plans to address gaps in program administration, at the federal, state, and local levels. Food insecurity is a systemic problem that cannot be addressed by government or by local individuals and groups alone, and platforms for these groups to communicate with one another proved crucial. While local communities are more likely to identify solutions because they are close to the problem, a coordinated approach that involves reciprocal information sharing among all levels of influence is essential for policy change. These avenues take shape through a variety of formats, including local antihunger coalitions; organized policy groups such as the Texas Food Policy Roundtable; and participation in informing federal policy, such as through the National Commission on Hunger. It is here we are able to identify solutions that are scalable and effective beyond any specific context. The following are examples of convening groups to impact policy at both the state and federal levels—one an administrative example, the other legislative—which illustrate the complexity of the network of policy players.

Impacting Policy: Case Examples

Administrative Policy Administrative policy is distinct from legislative policy in that it shapes how programs, including antihunger programs that form the first line of defense against hunger in America, are administered by state agencies in accordance with existing law. It therefore requires an insider approach to organizing for policy change. For example, current federal provisions for the administration of the federal SMP require that sites implement a congregate feeding policy whereby children must eat their meals on site. This can be problematic for sites that host their SMP outside during hot summer months, for example. Because the federal agency grants waivers submitted by state agencies, the participation by federal officials at local summer meals sites was important so that they understood both the capacity of the program as well as the challenge of administering the program. At one Dallas site, an apartment complex arranged around a central concrete foundation where the children ate their meals provided a prime example of heat conditions. Field visits by federal officials, coupled with the strategic advocacy of program sponsors and state advocates, ushered in waiver language crafted alongside the state agency. The federal agency granted several states heat waiver privileges, allowing children to take food home from summer meal sites on days when there are heat advisories. To achieve this, advocates identified the appropriate federal agency, organized stakeholders, and requested a reasonable alternative to the existing law—thus, the appeal was a success. While consensus building is not an easy process, and occasionally changing law necessitates drastic measures, it nonetheless represents a means for effective change.

Legislative Policy Convening advocates to impact both state and federal policy often requires innovative and unexpected relationships. The Texas Food Policy Roundtable (TFPR) is such an initiative. Coming together strengthens the impetus for legislative policy action for low-income families; therefore, a core group of advocacy organizations, congregations, and industry groups came together to improve the quality of life for food insecure Texans.

One result of this coordinated effort was the passage of a bill that proposed that schools with 80 percent or more of their students qualifying for free and reduced-price lunch would offer breakfast free of charge to all interested students. The bill faced some initial pressure and scrutiny primarily by the conservative representation in the state legislature. As a result, TFPR decided it was crucial not only to bring on board those who could testify to the importance of breakfast, or even explain how the universal breakfast program has become fiscally sustainable in school districts, but to get creative in discussing the economic benefits of the program. These unlikely heroes came by a group of dairy farmers who testified to the importance of selling milk in schools to benefit dairy farmers, the agriculture industry, and, therefore, the larger economy. Staying true to the value of consensus building, bringing in a variety of stakeholders proved crucial. The day the bill was voted on by the senate, a group of elementary students from a number of schools around the central Texas area calling themselves the Hunger Warriors were present on the capitol steps to rally around the importance of breakfast and to talk about their desire for every child to have an opportunity to eat breakfast. With tears in his eyes, one particularly articulate student gave a speech in front of his peers, parents, school administrators, and advocates, expressing his hope that no student in Texas would experience hunger as he had throughout elementary school.

On a federal level, national organizations rallied around the Healthy, Hunger-Free Kids Act (HHFK) in 2010 and the US Farm Bill in 2014. And in 2014 Congress instated the National Commission on Hunger. The commission comprises antihunger champions from academia, business, health care, and nonprofit sectors, and they were tasked with reviewing the state of food insecurity in America and providing Congress with recommendations for addressing the problem. In fact, the last time we as a country reviewed our antihunger programs in a bipartisan fashion was the advent of the War on Poverty during the Lyndon B. Johnson administration in 1964. The commissioners participated in a series of field visits in nine cities to understand what organizations, schools, churches, and others are doing to address hunger. In seven cities, the commission hosted public hearings from community members. In total, the commission received both oral and written testimony from nearly two hundred people. The commission synthesized this information and made bipartisan recommendations to Congress to strengthen domestic food security through federal legislation and public and private partnerships (National Commission on Hunger 2015).

Organizing for policy change requires the continuous building of relationships, bridges of communication, and linkages among government agencies and across sectors all in an effort to build on common ground. The consensus-building policy organizing approach is unique in that it brings this constituency of policy makers, government officials, school administrators, congregants, and community members together across lines of experience and power to enhance the ability of each group to address food insecurity in the policy space.

We discussed examples of public-private collaboration through both statewide organizing to increase access to federal nutrition programs as well as through organizing around policy change to improve program efficiency and to participate in the national political dialogue on hunger. Until this point, we viewed these types of collaborations from a macro perspective. However, the nexus of antihunger efforts is happening at the community level where nonprofits, congregations, schools, and other organizations are working creatively to improve access to benefits and programs. In the next section, we discuss examples of local efforts to address hunger in communities that draw on coalition building and community-organizing strategies.

Local Public-Private Partnerships: Coalition Building

Building public-private partnerships and coalitions increases communities' capacity to alleviate hunger and poverty. In fact, collaborations and coalitions are increasingly common avenues for tackling complex social issues "by pooling abilities, expertise and resources of numerous stakeholders to positively affect community health" (Granner and Sharpe 2004, 514). Coalitions facilitate and enhance capacity through a variety of community-organizing and development strategies.

Hunger Free Communities (HFCs) are an example of this kind of coalition-led, multisector collaboration. HFCs are community-based coalitions that serve as a mechanism for local communities to operate strategically by assessing the structure and procedures of food-delivery systems, identifying resources and gaps, making decisions for change, and implementing action plans in order to provide healthy and nutritious food to an increased number of people. HFCs comprise government and civic leaders, food security stakeholders, corporate representatives, people experiencing food insecurity, and volunteers from the community. HFCs function as formal or informal collaborations, coalitions, committees, or task groups, or even some combination thereof. They are unique entities in that each HFC functions differently depending on rural or urban context, depending on whether or not groups have historically organized around the specific hunger issues in the past, and depending on the impetus for initial convening of community members and organizations, as well as numerous other factors.

In this section, we discuss considerations that coalitions take into account when convening local coalitions, and how the HFCs are addressing these considerations, as examples of what kinds of things impact good multisector partnerships. Next, we discuss the various ways coalitions might begin to take shape and how coalitions have developed their membership bases. Then, we conclude with case examples of successful coalition building.

Considerations for Community-Organizing Context

Urban and rural communities present distinct conditions for community organizing. In communities that are largely urban, the landscape of nonprofit and direct service organizations that are networked in some capacity is wider, and they will be working on a host of projects and issues that impact the community. Urban and rural communities are both rich environments for networking and community organizing, with unique opportunities and challenges.

A community organizer in the midsize city of Amarillo appreciated the dichotomous nature of facilitating a coalition in urban communities and rural communities. In order for the Amarillo HFC to find success, the community organizer believed that building a cohesive alliance with high structure and regularity was important. Because many of the stakeholders and community members in the HFC participate in numerous other groups and projects, efficiency is key: when momentum is lost, sustained member engagement is reduced.

In the rural areas, including Moore and Sherman Counties in Amarillo, a small-town sense of community, known as the panhandle spirit, underpins culture and social relationships. A sense of mutual reciprocity and neighborliness are community values because helping others' land helped one's own land. While trust is important in every community context, gaining trust in a rural community can be difficult for organizations because outsiders may be regarded with more skepticism. Schools and churches are central institutions in rural communities: the Amarillo community organizer emphasized that in rural communities, life often centers on high school football, for example. Attending to what is already central in small-town institutions is key when there can be fear in rural towns of big organizations "coming in and taking over." Working for the welfare of children is an important place to start—it is an issue many can rally around

Convening Groups

There is no one right way to convene a group to strategically address hunger. In fact, there are a variety of catalysts for initial group engagement. In Dallas and El Paso, the first major organizing activity was a regional summit because there were already many community members working in the antihunger space in some capacity. For others, community organizers traveled to communities on a regular basis to help organize preliminary meetings and strategically plan the HFC's next steps. Because education and awareness are key components in addressing hunger, film screenings were common avenues of bringing people together to learn, discuss, and network. A group of community members came together to view the documentary *A Place at the Table*, which follows the narratives of families who experience hunger, with a concluding panel discussion. In San Antonio, the screening of the film *Hunger in America*, which documents the reality of food insecurity in the United States, convened several stakeholders and interested community members for the purpose of showing viewers that the issue of hunger is largely unchanged since the 1960s, when the film was made.

Additionally, community assessments are initial catalysts and are especially important for groups that may be relatively new to the antihunger space or are still learning about the issue of hunger in the context of their community. The HFC in small-town Marlin began with community assessment and asset mapping tools to better understand the scope of the issue in their backyards. One of the questions on the assessment was whether there was a weekend backpack program. There was not, so the group decided to pursue its development. Funding opportunities are important catalysts. Some groups organized around prospective funding; one group in North Texas was inaugurated by both a community assessment and by the opportunity for grant funding from a nearby university.

Even so, there are many challenges to initially convening groups. Community organizers and their partners often report that bringing together groups of committed community members to address hunger takes time. In addition, bringing people together quickly makes it difficult to acknowledge and address differences in group dynamics, including differences in power, race, and educational background (Kadushin et al. 2005). Groups often start in one of two ways: as a desire to take immediate action or as a desire to talk about issues and priorities—known as "project-driven" and "concept-driven" groups, respectively.

The process of building a coalition requires strategic community-organizing skills that build trust, convene individuals who have been left out of the conversation, and effectively lead a group. Skills in community organizing include meeting with individuals one on one from the beginning and throughout the coalition-building process. In Dallas, community organizers serve both as leadership and as administrative support. A key component of this administrative support is meeting individually with HFC members on a regular basis to ascertain an understanding of their experience with the group, their hopes and dreams, and their plans for the future. During an important transition phase for the Dallas HFC, strategic one-on-ones took place so that HFC members were actively engaged in the strategic planning process of the group.

In the midsize city of San Angelo, community organizers met with representatives from the congregations to discuss their assets and capacity to address summer hunger in their community and, more specifically, how the representatives foresaw their congregations' involvement in the SMP. The community organizers supported the congregations' autonomy in decision making while providing guidance and facilitating coordination with the other congregations who agreed to be a part of the SMP. A common theme throughout these one-on-one conversations was listening and identifying participants' strengths.

Membership

HFCs comprise government and civic leaders, food security stakeholders, corporate representatives, people experiencing food insecurity, and volunteers from the community. And yet the diversity of membership extends beyond this definition: the number and variety of sectors represented by their members is exactly what upholds the integrity of the HFC mission. Some groups are more sector diverse than others, and some are more homogenous. While there advantages and disadvantages to each, ensuring inclusivity, harnessing a core group, and maintaining key external support are crucial for all groups.

Good community organizing espouses grassroots inclusivity and community-based ownership; however, because HFCs tend to be more professionally representative, they can indirectly discourage the involvement of community members who are experiencing food insecurity, even when community organizers intentionally employ strategies to include them. Another key to inclusivity is the degree of ownership. In order to avoid tokenism and only brief engagement by community members, a real sense of control is a key component for meaningful and sustained engagement. While HFCs engage community members from multiple sectors, the history and relationships within a community as well as the dynamics of power and privilege must be considered and analyzed. The structure of one HFC was professionally led; the group was largely made up of professionals within the community, and their group and subcommittees met in professional environments. Because the structure of the group from the beginning was more attuned to a group of people with professional, organizational interests, the unintentional exclusion of community members who had experience with hunger was deeply felt. This is why community-based leadership and ownership is key.

Outside support to the HFC includes external endorsements or support by key members in the community. External support for an HFC is crucial because it enables and sustains community buy-in and trust. It is not always practical to have every key player serve as a committed member on the HFC, and external support aids in legitimizing the HFC. In Amarillo, a community organizer made a presentation to the commissioner's court on how the community might collaborate around ensuring that food insecure families are able to access public benefits. The county commissioner was interested in the SMP, and the community organizer shared information on their efforts to form a coalition in Moore County on the SMP. Since that conversation, the county commissioner has been an instrumental supporter of the group as it continues to form. He holds crucial influence and power, and as a trusted insider he has helped to legitimize the group's work in the community by opening doors to the small, rural community. Building external relationships can be just as important as building and maintaining internal relationships.

Case Examples

Tom Green County Hunger Coalition of San Angelo, Texas, is where the SMP Kids Eat Free was developed by local congregations and community. The congregations provided volunteers, space, and food by coordinating the lunch program based on each congregation's resources and capacity, neighborhood location, and established relationships and networks. They now operate meal sites at area churches and an apartment complex during July and August; a variety of churches provide what they can out of their own resources, whether that means providing food and supplies, coordinating and leading activities at sites, distributing flyers about meal sites, or having Sunday school classes and youth groups serve meals (Nolen and Krey 2015).

A prime example of this kind of resource pooling is the partnership that churches and farmers in Tyler, Texas, have formed alongside the work of the local HFC. Community organizers connected local churches and farmers in Tyler, realizing that they could work together to help address summer hunger. They decided to start a weekly farmers' market coalition. The local churches pick up the leftover produce from the weekly farmers' market and distribute it to summer meal sites and to low-income seniors. Additionally, the HFC, in partnership with AgriLife, sought to expand the reach of the farmers' market by reaching out to other farmers' market associations.

The Dallas Coalition for Hunger Solutions' faith community action team developed the *Hunger Solutions Guide for the Faith Community*, which involves six programmatic solutions: serve as a site for community members to access public benefits; participate in SMP; partner with the local urban outreach ministry of a local church; engage in nutrition education; encourage congregants to support the Family Garden Initiative; and volunteer with Meals on Wheels.

Hunger is a winnable issue, one that most people and organizations can rally around. Consensus building through public-private partnerships is garnering momentum to address hunger and other issues of poverty across the nation. Through these partnerships, we are building a public-private infrastructure—one that can be sustainable and accountable even after specific partnerships and funding are exhausted. In this chapter, we have discussed three concepts for increasing collaboration: statewide organizing for increasing access to federal nutrition programs, organizing for policy change at the state and federal levels, and organizing in local communities through a coalition model. These collaborations are addressing the root causes, pooling resources, and shaping a system of accountability by creating space for consensus building. Finding common ground with unlikely political allies formed the lynchpin for providing school breakfast and engendered administrative policy changes. Working with local religious groups and organizations who know their neighbors developed solutions to hunger during the summer months. These examples demystify some of the art of community organizing and offer a structure for change making.

REFERENCES

Alinksy, S. 1971. *Rules for Radicals: A Practical Primer for Realistic Radicals.* New York: Vintage Books.

Bishaw, A. 2012. *Poverty: 2010 and 2011, American Community Survey Briefs.* Washington, DC: US Department of Commerce. Last modified September. *www.census.gov/prod/2012pubs/acsbr11–01.pdf.*

Granner, M., and P. Sharpe. 2004. "Evaluating Community Coalition Characteristics and Functioning: A Summary of Measurement Tools." *Health Education Research* 19 (5): 514–32.

Kadushin, C., M. Lindholm, D. Ryan, A. Brodsky, and L. Saxe. 2005. "Why Is It So Difficult to Form Effective Community Coalitions?" *City and Community* 4 (3) 255–75.

Kania, J., and M. Kramer. 2011. "Collective Impact." *Stanford Social Innovation Review. ssir.org/articles/entry/collective_impact.*

Marks, G. 2012. "What Salesforce.com Won't Tell You." *Forbes.* Last modified December 31. *www.forbes.com/sites/quickerbettertech/2012/12/31/what-salesforce-com-wont-tell-you.*

National Commission on Hunger. 2015. "Freedom from Hunger: An Achievable Goal for the United States of America." Recommendations of the National Commission on Hunger to Congress and the Secretary of the Department of Agriculture. *cybercemetery.unt.edu/archive/hungercommission/20151216222324/https://hungercommission.rti.org/Portals/0/SiteHtml/Activities/FinalReport/Hunger_Commission_Final_Report.pdf.*

Newman, C., and E. Scherpf. 2013. "Supplemental Nutrition Assistance Program (SNAP) Access at the State and County Levels: Evidence from Texas SNAP Administrative Records and the American Community Survey." Washington, DC: USDA. Last modified September. *www.ers.usda.gov/media/1199858/err-156_summary.pdf.*

Nolen, E., and K. Krey. 2015. "Addressing Summer Child Hunger in San Angelo, Texas: A Congregation-Based Case Study. *Journal of Family and Community Ministries* 28: 19–31.

Wolff, T. 2016. "Ten Places Where Collective Impact Gets It Wrong." Guest editorial. *Global Journal of Community Psychology Practice. www.gjcpp.org/en/resource.php?issue=21&resource=200.*

14

Race, Class, Privilege, and Bias in South Florida Food Movements

MARINA KARIDES AND PATRICIA WIDENER

> I am on this to create a voice for people. We are playing a political role. There is inherent inequalities, structural reasons for the reason the system is the way it is.

—Participant in a south Florida food policy council

> I would suggest the best thing we can do is provide a big umbrella that everyone can get under.

—Participant in a south Florida food policy council

The US public has become increasingly engaged with issues of food production, fresh food availability, and diet-related illnesses. In many regions, members of the white and middle class pursue a food movement that prioritizes fresh cooked, locally grown, seasonal, and organic foods in opposition to fast food and food produced through chemical-intensive agriculture (Alkon and Agyeman 2011; Desjardins 2010).[1] In contrast, lower-income neighborhoods and communities of color are often guided by food justice that seeks to secure local means of food production and the affordable distribution of fresh, unprocessed foods in marginalized communities (Alkon and Agyeman 2011; Desjardins 2010; Alkon and Norgaard 2009).

Our study explores a case of food activism in south Florida and is indicative of the deep and difficult work to integrate both food consumer movements and food justice movements into a single food movement. The few years we focus on (2010–2012) mark the inception of coordinating a food movement in south Florida. We consider the struggles of the south Florida community to organize a cohesive food platform through the formation of a regional food policy council (RFPC) and three Annual Greater Everglades Community Food Summits in these years.[2] Among the participants at the food summits and the almost monthly meetings of the RFPC, we identify differing perceptions of food activism and food justice—distinctions that point to the challenges in coordinating a single food movement in south Florida. We suggest that class and race privilege veils for some participants the breadth of problems faced by some groups in producing or attaining and preparing fresh, affordable foods. Privilege is often a hidden entitlement, not easily identified by groups who possesses it, who accrue more opportunities, more resources, and more advantages, while avoiding obstacles, resource scarcities, and disadvantage, due to such privilege (McIntosh 1989). In addition, we recognize that race, class, and gender privileges can intersect so advantages are compounded for individuals who fit simultaneously into categories given unearned favor in a society (Hill-Collins 1991).

Our research in south Florida on the efforts of various food-related interests to coalesce into a single food movement demonstrates that privilege mattered, including: (a) in the location of food activities and enterprises, with more challenges for those in poor and low-income neighborhoods; (b) for understanding the relationship between inequalities and access to fresh and affordable foods; and (c) in attempts to merge divergent food movement activities, where food activism, the goal of increasing the general availability of healthier foods, trumped food justice, the equitable distribution and access of healthy foods, as an overall goal.

In the last few decades, food policy councils (FPCs) have proliferated across the United States. Formed in Knoxville, Tennessee, in the 1980s, the first FPC was a nonregulatory advisory board to the city government. It consisted of community members and stakeholders engaged in securing access to fresh and healthier foods for low-income populations through free school meals and better public transit.

The recent revival of FPCs in the United States arrives with a growing consciousness of the possible toxicity and lower nutritional value related to industrial food production and processing (Patel 2012; Nestle 2007). These concerns have contributed to an emphasis on local food production for healthier and fresher produce, to reduce food miles and support local economies (Hess 2009). In addition, rising food insecurity, in which American households have had difficulty regularly meeting food needs (Scanlan, Jenkins, and Peterson 2010), and a national obesity epidemic, have contributed to the growth of FPCs. These diversified interests and understandings of contemporary food issues have resulted in the formation of FPCs with a range of organizational missions and goals.

Broadly, FPCs may serve some kind of advisory function to local, regional, or state government in an official capacity or informally to improve food policies such as extending zoning and permits for farming and farmers' markets, supporting public schools to secure healthier menus, and facilitating networks for an alternative or local food system. In some instances FPCs act as grassroots organizations coordinating efforts to reduce or stop the use of petrochemicals, to label genetically modified foods, and to challenge corporate encroachment in determining food availability. Finally, some FPCs address food insecurity and its root causes in economic and racial inequality and promote food justice by increasing the production, accessibility, and availability of fresh foods in poor and low-income areas and communities of color.

Given the range of food-related causes for FPCs to undertake, a diverse pool of actors are attracted to participate in their development. This may cause difficulty for new FPCs to establish an agenda within the flurry and competing goals of food movements. In our study, participants in the food summits and RFPC included community members and residents who had become concerned about food quality, food writers for local newspapers, local urban and rural farmers, food entrepreneurs interested in developing a niche of organic or specialty food items, health or local food restaurateurs, grassroots community activists focused on food poverty, university students, cultural-based organizations, government staff and employees, members of community organizations, and researchers like ourselves interested in the improved production of, access to, and affordability of healthy food.

Though we gathered to advance local, healthy food in the region, the diversity of participants and the plethora of goals that can be structured under a FPC contributed to the struggles that preoccupied the commencing of a south Florida FPC. Yet our analysis indicates that the difficulties in establishing the RFPC extend beyond a pluralism of possibilities and lie in the social locations and varied appreciations of class and racial privilege of participants. Our research supports arguments by Slocum (2006, 327), who states: "Whiteness enables the coherence of an alliance organized to promote community food security and sustainable farming. Unacknowledged white privilege gives the lie to the movement's rhetoric of justice, good intentions and sustainability. And yet it is clear that racism is an organizing process in the food system: people of color disproportionately experience food insecurity, lose their farms and face the dangerous work of food processing and agricultural labor."

Our chapter offers empirical fodder for Slocum's (2006) assessment. Despite the intent of many members who sought in general more local and healthy food for the greater region, bias and privilege based on race and class were revealed in the RFPC meetings. In the following section we present a brief overview of the south Florida agricultural, racial and ethnic, and economic context. We then turn to a chronological account of the development of the RFPC including: (a) meetings on location and participation and indecisiveness on determining the work and mission by the RFPC; (b) the closings of farmers' markets in Miami's poor African American neighborhoods; (c) how the RFPC came to respond to the closures; and (d) the ending of the RFPC and food summits. The story of RFPC demonstrates how white privilege and class advantage belie a clear understanding of the structural limits to producing and consuming local, healthy, affordable, and fresh foods and the kinds of interventions and approaches necessary to secure such food for everyone.

The first author attended and collected ethnographic data at approximately fifteen meetings of the RFPC between October 2010 and December 2012 and the three food summits (July 2010, October 2011, and October 2012). The second author attended two council meetings and two food summits and conducted interviews with a variety of alternative food enterprises in south Florida. Data consists of notes, documents, and observations collected at these meetings. Findings have also been informed by e-mail exchanges among participants, meetings and conversations with those involved in the RFPC, and news articles.

The South Florida Context

South Florida is both an agricultural and highly urbanized region. It is also more ethnically diverse than other regions in the United States, according to US Census Bureau data. Of the 2.617 million who reside in Miami–Dade County, approximately

60 percent of the population is Latino/a, 18 percent is African American, and approximately half are foreign born. In Broward County (whose largest city is Fort Lauderdale), about 25 percent of residents are African American, and another 25 percent are Latino/a. Approximately 30 percent of the 1.748 million residents of Broward County are foreign born.

The history of south Florida politics demonstrates severe marginalization of African Americans and a history of strong collective and grassroots resistance by African Americans (Mohl 2000; Portes and Stepick 1994). The "transformation of Miami" from an elite tourist destination and agricultural community to an ethnically diverse "global city" and financial center of Latin America altered the landscape of the entire region (Portes and Stepick 1994) and created the construction of various urban neighborhoods or ethnic enclaves including Little Haiti and Little Havana. Broward County is also one of the most racially and ethnically diverse counties in the United States, having become a "minority majority" county.

Economically, Florida shows a continuing rise in poverty and a decline in real wages, which have not improved since the recession in 2008–2009, and holds one of the highest levels of state income inequality in the United States. Miami and Fort Lauderdale both rank in the top ten places of highest income inequality, fourth and eighth respectively (RISUP 2012). The extreme of economic inequality, the racial and ethnic confluence, and the concentration and proximity of metropolitan and agricultural zones make the south Florida region sociologically striking.

Getting Started: The Privilege of Complaining

The RFPC was propelled by the first Greater Everglades Community Food Summit in July 2010. The vision for the first summit was to bring together for the first time "stakeholders seeking to advance the passion for South Florida's year 'round bounty" and to consider the "challenges and opportunities affecting local food consumers and producers" (participants quoted from first summit). With goals of including participants from diverse backgrounds, a food policy training facilitated by Mark Winne, a well-known proponent of the food policy councils, was included as one of the major events with a $25 fee (see also Burgan and Winne 2012; and Winne 2008). Of the three food summits that were organized, the first had a distinctly larger and more diverse attendance. About seventy-five registered participants represented a varied set of food-centered organizations, including food justice interests. Outreach included attracting "grassroots community groups and food activists" (according to participants) with the goals to construct a local food action plan. The continuation of the summit's plans and goals to propel a local food system was to be the responsibility of the RFPC.

The first RFPC meeting attended was in October 2010, during which approximately thirty-five people gathered to elect a board. The following meeting, in November 2010, was held on the top floor of a high-rise building in downtown Miami on the floor of an elite architectural firm. One of the architects that participated in the food policy council offered the location. This was very different from the first organizational meeting of the policy council held a month prior in distinctly more humble and community-centered circumstances. We later learned that the architectural firm was responsible for one of the major gentrification projects in midtown Miami that had forced the relocation of African American residents in the Overtown neighborhood.

Meeting location was a perpetual discussion of the food policy council. In this up-market high-rise, some participants who worked in marginalized communities made statement such as "We need a location that is more accessible" or "This might not be suitable for everyone," but they chose not to identify class or race as factors that might hinder persons from traveling to an isolated upscale locale and entering a private building.

In the second meeting, attendees, including new board members, were trying to find their feet. Distinctly dissimilar perspectives on what a food policy group should look like, and perhaps organize for, were present. In attendance were about fifteen participants, mostly white, but also including approximately three Latin Americans or Cubans, an African American woman from a large nonprofit, and an African American man who identified with a grassroots organization in a low-income African American neighborhood. Participants introduced themselves as being from "an organization for Haitian Youth"; as being from "a urban garden in Coral Gables"; as "interested"; as "a Montessori teacher interested in Edible South Florida"; as "a photographer that works with at-risk youth"; as "a carpenter"; as "a volunteer at a farm"; and as "a food and school gardener." Although some were active in the years of the RFPC, many of the elected board members never attended a single meeting.

Young white activists who held and expressed a critical political economic stance were regularly present, as were other citizens who had become disenchanted with the costs and quality of foods at the major grocery store chains in Florida. A few that attended the RFPC meetings somewhat regularly were local food entrepreneurs. Other participants referred to wanting and desiring to feed their children better foods, mentioning concerns with pesticides, herbicides, and fertilizers.

After complaints about supermarket produce were shared, one of the activists noted that for some neighborhoods in Miami that had only small convenience stores, a supermarket would be a welcomed addition. A member of Power U, a community activist organization in Overtown (a low-income community of color), highlighted the relationship between limited transportation access and fresh produce. He explained that for many Overtown residents shopping at a supermarket required a long and onerous commute and noted that the south Florida region was "notoriously hostile" to effective public transportation.

Although the activist organizer was highlighting limited access to grocery stores by some populations, he and other participants at the meeting were not necessarily advocating for increased corporate presence in the distribution of food. Most RFPC participants were seeking ways to develop farmers' markets and small urban farms, but the socioeconomic advantages of some groups hid the inequalities or the privilege of having a neighborhood grocery store that they could easily frequent. Despite or because food deserts and grocery store gaps are the outcomes of food distribution based on class and race privilege, food deserts remained physically and ideologically invisible to many who attended the RFPC meetings.

A central issue for the RFPC was that of location—not only the space and place of the meetings, which needed to be welcoming to all, but also the accessibility of fresh food—whether from farmers' markets or supermarkets. When discussions turned to the articulation of a mission statement for the organization, different and competing approaches and understandings and misunderstandings of the food system became even more evident.

Determining a Food Mission

Deciding the mission of the RFPC occupied most of the first six months of meetings and much of the organizational planning in the following year. The debates around defining the objectives of the RFPC exposed mismatched understandings of how and where an FPC should intervene and how inequalities shape south Florida's food system. While the first summit sought to attain a diverse constituency, it was not explicit in making food inequality rather than food quality a primary goal.

A white woman activist who organized a food-related nonprofit in one of the poorest areas of Miami-Dade explained at the November 2010 meeting, "We need to be clear that our goal is to have a voice in food policy and planning that has not existed." She also emphasized to a largely white group of attendees that part of the work of the RFPC would be to bring "people to the table who are missing." Another participant, a Latino, in support of this perspective, suggested that "the market has decided the food system that affects us all and not by democratic decision." In a meeting in early 2011, an older African American man, a somewhat regular attendant from an urban farming organization, in an unusually direct remark on the lack of diversity in the room, asked:

> Would you or anybody be willing to go to these groups? We have not reached out. We need a committee of just those people. It is a huge glaring camp, Roots in the City [a grassroots food justice organization in Overtown]; these are groups that want to turn the dirt, but the dirt can't be turned in these areas because it is illegal. . . . What do we have in common, and what would work for us? Everybody is facing different barriers. There are barriers to get representatives from different organization.

Another participant explained, "The struggle is to get the right people attending, and figuring out the role of this group, and not duplicate efforts of other organizations."

The statements above imply that who participates in the RFPC will shape the group's mandate. There is little indication as to why many from among the thirty-five who attended the first meeting stopped attending. In this framing "the right people" are those most disenfranchised by the food system. These comments and others in the meetings of the RFPC also indicate a recognition that those with least economic opportunities and the grassroots organizations built by these groups are most challenged in participating—though some of them may have tried to participate initially as indicated by the large size of the first meeting.

Other participants dismissed discussions on attendance and refused prioritizing the food needs of the poor and low-income sectors of south Florida. Their claims tended to suggest this would lead to a loss of neutrality. For example, in response to addressing food deserts and food insecurity, one white woman responded, "We don't want to start off adversarial. There is a lot of positive stuff. Local food has all these benefits. We are here to work with the public and private sectors." In another response, from a white woman from a wealthy neighborhood in Miami-Dade, said, "It's important that we be positive. The mission statement should be about goals not strategies."

These sorts of statements, such as "There is not one place that we celebrate all the local food activities of south Florida," seemed to sidestep the inequities of south Florida's distribution of food due to race and class. Instead of conceding to an interventionist role, one that such councils have played across the country, various suggestions were offered in its stead by members seeking to avert confrontation. For example, the RFPC might serve as a clearinghouse of information on how to buy local, or on farming opportunities, or it might play an educative role on local foods. Others identified as a worthy purpose finding properties that could be farmed, or supporting local farmers through a needs assessment survey. These activities might increase access to fresh foods, but they do not confront race, class, and food injustice.

By May 2011 the continued merry-go-round of identifying the correct objectives and constructing a reasonable mission statement seemed to have depleted many in the RFPC. Participants began making statements such as "If we had a clear topic, we would get a clear meeting," and "We are just struggling to exist, but I don't know how we would serve anyone," or "We need a purpose and direction." The group began to acknowledge its difficulty in agreeing to an orientation. Some participants opposed targeting food justice issues in low-income and African American neighborhoods as a central goal of the RFPC. They felt it would present the organization as "coming on strong" by making "value statements." Others in the RFPC, especially community members or activists located in poorer African American neighborhoods, wanted to politicize the inequalities of food policies and food systems.

Those who were most drawn to the RFPC becoming a large umbrella for local food consumption and production were unable to discern the different needs and goals of community gardens located in wealthier neighborhoods versus the pressing food needs of low-income and largely African American neighborhoods. A generalized interest in local foods undermined supporting communities spatially marginalized from fresh, affordable food (see Widener and Karides 2014).

Eventually the RFPC meetings changed locations, owing in part to pressures to increase access to a diverse constituency and because the availability of a meeting room and low usage fees. Meetings were held in a community center in a low-income, African American neighborhood. Racial and class biases among members were evident in statements made to the first author at the start or close of the meetings or in the parking lot. For example, one white woman member volunteered: "I wonder if the location inhibits attendance as well. I've come. I don't have a problem. But we don't know. . . . To be honest I did not tell my husband where I was going, but it is reasonably accessible, and there is parking." A Latina in the parking lot offered: "The first time it was a little bit of a mental challenge. We might not have people participate. It's safe once you are in the gate."

These statements reflect socioeconomic privilege that limits appreciation of community centers in underserved neighborhoods or perhaps veils the challenge of transportation for the low-income people in south Florida. Unlike the upscale high-rise in which meetings took place, the community centers in low-income neighborhoods are centrally located and easily accessed by the interstate. Yet despite the convenient location and availability of meeting rooms, the racial context and poverty of these neighborhoods appeared unwelcoming to privileged participants. Race and class privilege also shrouded understanding as to why meeting rooms in wealthier neighborhoods or upscale buildings might be disconcerting or uncomfortable for those who work with or live in poor neighborhoods of color.

Although the experience and awareness of poor food quality and corporate profits can develop into a critique of the entire food system or the economic organization of food production, it does not necessarily enable an understanding of food poverty, food insecurity, or food deserts as an outcome of institutional racism. Envisioning racial inequality of south Florida (as well as in other urban contexts) as explanation for the problematic production and distribution and quality of food would require FPC participants to recognize their relationship to food consumption as an unearned privilege.

Resolution by Reaction: The City Closes Local Farmers' Markets

In spring 2011, the city of Miami shut down two farmers' markets in the primarily low-income, African American communities of Liberty City and Overtown. Of the more than fifteen farmers' markets and local food enterprises known to the RFPC members at the time, local government interfered with only these two (Niño 2012). The first to attract government attention for not having "proper permits" was the Liberty City Farmers' Market, held at a community center under the City of Miami's jurisdiction. The market relocated to another community center in the same neighborhood that was in county not city jurisdiction with a permitting process that allowed the market to operate freely.

Roots in the City, a nonprofit coordinating the farmers' market in Overtown along with the support of other community members, also was served a notice of violation for the "illegal sale of fruits and merchandise from open stands and vacant lots" and a "failure to obtain a Class I special permit" and would incur a fine of $250 a day if they did not cease operation (Kanner 2011). The Overtown farmers' market was the first local market in south Florida to accept Electronic Benefit Transfers (EBTs), or food stamps, and doubled their value. The market also involved community members and youth in the farming and selling of produce along several blocks in urban Miami that had been secured from the city just a year before. Some of the funds supporting the farmers' market endeavor were drawn from the city's Community Redevelopment Authority (CRA), which is designated to develop areas determined to be underserved areas.

Community organizers and shoppers responded to the shutdown of the market by arriving at its usual market-day location to protest its closing. Vendors who had planned to sell that day gave away produce complying with the ban and showing their determination to support the community's access to fresh foods. Spokespersons from the city government attended as well, arguing that the market was not forced to close but that it needed to acquire the proper permitting. In various accounts of the event, city officials suggested that the problem was that markets needed to comply with existing regulations.

Yet the City of Miami held no existing license, permits, or ordinances specific to farmers' markets. Instead farmers' markets that operate on a weekly basis could apply only for a special events permit that could be obtained for a cost of $153.50 per event up to two times a year. The closing of the Overtown market drew significant media attention and community protest. Local media reported on some of the political doings of the city commissioner who was tied to the closing of both the Liberty City and Overtown markets (Rabin 2011). Through the closures what became evident to the media, public, and engaged community groups was that the city had no codes, rules, or legislation for the specific needs of farmers' markets.

In the city's interference with the operation of farmers' markets, the RFPC had found a pearl of consensus. At its mid-April 2011 meeting, the market closings, protests, and politics of the previous month galvanized the council. The group that had been floundering for over a half a year on a mission statement began to coalesce, and a fresh sense of purpose became evident. One participant enthusiastically expressed: "This group needs to be public about farmers' markets. And we need to be clear. The fact that these farmers' markets were shut down, this is a great first initiative to figure out. [We need to] sit with the commissioner's office to find out what it is that we need to happen to comply with, to put the farmers' markets up and running." Another member of the RFPC, in an inspired tempo, added: "We should shame the commissioner for closing down the farmers' markets. . . . [The commissioner] lied about the procedures. Each politician gives RITC [Roots in the City] another policy—they cannot find the right policy. Tell them to please be transparent about the process. No one has the staff process to run around the city to figure out the permitting process. It is unclear."

To this comment, one of the members with a more general food movement position quickly replied, "We shouldn't shame him; that's not a positive way." The tit for tat in approaching food distribution was still evident, but when another member, part of a nongovernmental food justice organization in Liberty City that had attended almost all RFPC meetings, stated, "Well, we should meet with him," the group began to forge a plan. One of the attendees stated: "There is nobody in the city of Miami to look at permitting for farmers' market. No laws. They are treating it similar to a flea market. To go through the process, there is nobody; there is nothing on the books for community gardens and nothing on farmers' markets on the books. Our job is to advise them on this." Another added: "We need to give them [city government] recommendations, and we can't be naive about politics in Miami. We are nobodies to the commissioner. What would make him make changes?" A politically judicious participant at the meeting stated: "I am not sure that an elected official does not zero in on something without some trigger. There is something that does not make political or policy sense. This could be an opportunity to resolve this, this action we might take. I would like to get to the bottom of what happened with these markets. Even this in itself, this is huge. . . . And what is the administrative piece? There has to be someone, something, somewhere, we need to figure out." The closure of the farmers' markets helped RFPC to discern its role. A meeting was planned with the commissioner. Other actions introduced to address the closures, such as distributing a petition or commenting to the media, were swept aside. RFPC members developed a document, a sample ordinance for the city to adopt, and those with entrée into government took advantage of their position to determine the correct language for it.

The outcome was the development of a Temporary Market Procedure that went into effect in 2011 (chapter 62, article 7 of the Miami City Code). The Neighborhood Enhancement Team (NET) of city government became the office responsible for issuing the licenses. The one-time fee for a farmers' market permit was $500 for profit-oriented markets and $250 for nonprofits and those that doubled the value of EBTs. According to the RFPC, the language for the city's formalized account of farmers' markets was very close to what they had proposed.

The closing of the farmers' markets in Liberty City and Overtown sparked organizational unity for the council by presenting a discrete mission for members to rally around. Yet in their preparations to address the absence of farmers' market policy in Miami, they glossed over how the two farmers' markets closed were in low-income African American neighborhoods with some of the highest levels of poverty and greatest healthy, affordable food needs. "The white farmers' markets [farmers' markets in white neighborhoods] are not being shut down," was one of the only statements made in this regard. Yet even those identifying as food justice activists were tactful it seems, limiting conversations on the intersections of race, class, and food.

Food for Thought: Race and Class in South Florida's Food Policy

Until the ordinance for a Temporary Market Procedure was passed, all farmers' markets operating in the City of Miami could apply only for a special event or special use certificate permit as there was no other form of permitting. Yet only those in low-income communities of color were challenged for using this loophole when the city held incoherent or nonexistent city policies for farmers' markets. The RFPC agreed that these closures served as a just cause for action but seemed do so with "unacknowledged white privilege" and without the recognition "that racism is an organizing process in the food system" (Slocum 2006, 327). RFPC never got to the bottom of how or why these markets were targeted.

Our research of the south Florida region confirms that a blindness of privilege exists in the development of alternative food systems. At the second Everglades Food Summit in fall 2011, there was more evidence to support the disinclination of those developing local food networks to identify race and class in the operation of food systems. Hanging on one of the walls in the central meeting location of the summit was a large poster board with the following handwritten statement:

> Whoever comes are the right people
> Whatever happens is the only thing that could happen
> Whenever it starts is the right time
> Whenever its over its over

This claim represents a very different approach from that of those who were concerned with getting marginalized groups at the table of the RFPC in its first year. In the main meeting room of the second summit was almost an entirely white or white

Latino/a set of participants. Some passing attention was directed to the statement by meeting organizers, but there was no direct challenge to it and what it might represent. The diversity of representation from different communities and race and ethnic groups had distinctly decreased from the first summit. During a session called "Envisioning Local Food Systems" at the second summit, the discussion that ensued primarily drew from a culture-of-poverty perspective that emphasizes "cultural" attributes for one's poverty, rather than systemic and structural factors, such as institutionalized privilege.

When considering how to create systems for accessible healthy food in Miami's central corridor (which includes African American neighborhoods and Little Haiti), one white young man stated: "It is hard to get through to them—you have to make things easy. You have to shove it in their hands for people to take it." A young Latina offered: "Not to get pessimistic, not to live in that, the other route is cheaper and easier, and they are used to it." No counterstatement was offered that recognized the limited physical access to fresh and healthy foods for these communities. Instead participants offered testimonies of their own choices to eat healthy, overlooking how race, class, and power shape opportunities and the distribution and consumption of food.

Despite the closure of the farmers' markets just several months prior, in the announcements, agendas, and workshops of the second Everglades Food Summit, race and class were absent. In the meetings and events attended there was not even a nominal evaluation of social context and historical inequities for why certain communities lack resources or opportunities to purchase fresh foods. The relationship between poverty, lack of transportation, or low-paid work and limited time to prepare cooked meals was left unacknowledged. In the following year, the main gathering for the third and final Greater Everglades Food Summit was held at a private university, was more costly to attend ($65 for a one-day event rather than $80 for the two-day events of the previous years) with a further reduced audience that lacked diversity.

Our position is that bias, discrimination, and privilege based on race and class must be directly engaged for the success of an alternative food system. The RFPC transformed into a Miami–Dade County specific FPC by the end of 2012. It appears that other counties have not been able to create their own FPCs. The new county-specific FPC's first meeting occurred in the same location of the first meeting of the RFPC, a downtown community-centered organization. The new FPC also adopted the original mission statement of the RFPC, which after much vetting did not take a food justice approach but broadly states: "This council works to ensure equal access to healthy, local, sustainable, and affordable food for all people by reducing barriers to the production, distribution, and consumption of such food."

The adopted mission statement avoids confrontation with racial unevenness in food distribution that characterizes south Florida as showcased in the closing of the two farmers' markets. It also fails to address how class interferes with access to affordable healthy food in the region.

Policy for Metro Regions: Race and Class First

In south Florida race and class bias were a subtext to conversations around the location for food policy meetings, explanation for poor diets, and the lengthy and fickle discussions over a mission statement for the RFPC. Conflicting perspectives on the duties of a food council were captured in the various positions on whether and how to politicize food, race, and class. For some, food justice is distinctly tied to social and economic inequality and challenging privileged access to food. For others, who identify as food activists, increasing local food production or networks and community gardens without addressing race or socioeconomic status is sufficient.

Replacing processed and conventional agriculture food items with fresh, whole, and local foods was the general interest of all groups and individuals who participated in the development of the FPC. Although this appears to be an innocuous guiding principle, the struggles in south Florida suggest that FPCs in metro regions, generally distinguished by diverse populations and economic inequalities, would be better off adopting principles of food justice from their inception. We suggest that while goals and strategies of various FPCs may vary, improving their effectiveness in metro regions requires that they be premised on the understanding that race or ethnic and economic inequalities fundamentally shape one's ability to produce, locate, and purchase fresher and healthier foods.

Often when economically privileged participants engage in food consumer movements it is because they want the privilege of fresher and healthier foods. What needs to be realized is that the availability of fresh and healthy foods is a right deserved by all regardless of economic status. By insisting on a food justice focus and recognizing uneven structural limitations to land, farmers' markets, and local foods, as well as grocery stores, new leaders can articulate that the means of success for growing an alternative food system in a metro region depends on equitable participation in it by those with and without resources and economic privilege. Given the outcomes of our case, we suggest that food councils and coalitions require a direct confrontation with structural racism and class inequality; otherwise the critical issue of food seems to descend into privileged outposts that lose momentum and desire for widening and making permanent accessibility to fresh, local, and healthy foods.

NOTES

1. We provide race information only when the person we quote self-identified. In some instances we use phrases such as wealthy neighborhoods rather than the name of the neighborhood to protect the anonymity of participants.
2. The specific name of this FPC is being protected.

REFERENCES

Alkon, Alison H., and Julian Agyeman. 2011. "Introduction: The Food Movement as Polyculture." In *Cultivating Food Justice: Race, Class, and Sustainability*, edited by Alison H. Alkon and Julian Agyman, 1–20. Cambridge MA: MIT Press.

Alkon, Alison H., and Kari Marie Norgaard. 2009. "Breaking the Food Chains: An Investigation of Food Justice Activism." *Sociological Inquiry* 79 (3): 289–305.

Burgan, Michael, and Mark Winne. 2012. "Doing Food Policy Council Right: A Guide to Development and Action." Mark Winne Associates. *www.markwinne.com/wp-content/uploads/2012/09/FPC-manual.pdf*.

Census of Agriculture. 2007. "United States Census of Agriculture Report." *www.agcensus.usda.gov/Publications/2007/Full_Report/*.

Desjardins, Ellen. 2010. "The Urban Food Desert: Spatial Inequality or Opportunity for Change?" In *Imagining Sustainable Food System*, edited by A. Blay-Palmer, 87–114. Surrey, UK: Ashgate.

Hassanein, Neva. 2003. "Practicing Food Democracy: A Pragmatic Politics of Transformation." *Journal of Rural Studies* 19: 77–86.

Hess, David. 2009. "Localist Movements in the Global Economy: Sustainability, Justice, and Urban Development in the US." Cambridge, MA: MIT Press.

Hill-Collins, Patricia. 1991. *Black Feminist Thought: Knowledge, Consciousness, and the Politics of Empowerment*. New York: Routledge.

Kanner, Ellen. 2011. "Meatless Mondays: Roots in the City, Growing More Than Green." *Huffington Post*, n.d., accessed May 12, 2015. *www.huffingtonpost.com/ellen-kanner/ meatless-monday-roots-in-_b_843500.html*.

McIntosh, Peggy. 1989. "White Privilege: Unpacking the Invisible Knapsack." *Peace and Freedom*, July/August.

Mohl, Raymond A. 2000. *South of the South: Jewish Activists and the Civil Rights Movement in Miami, 1945–1960*. Tallahassee: University of Florida Press.

Nestle, Marion. 2007. *Food Politics: How the Food Industry Influences Nutrition and Health*. Berkeley: University of California Press.

Niño, Paula. 2011. "City Crack Down on Overtown, Liberty City Farmers' Markets." *Miami New Times*, n.d., accessed April 8, 2011. *www.miaminewtimes.com/restaurants/ city-cracks-down-on-overtown-liberty-city-farmers'-markets-updated-6580514*.

Patel, Raj. 2012. "Stuffed and Starved: The Hidden Battle for the World Food System." Brooklyn, NY: Melville House.

Portes, Alejandro, and Alex Stepick. 1994. *City on the Edge: The Transformation of Miami*. Berkeley: University of California Press.

Rabin, Charles. 2011. "Miami Commissioner Dunn Denies Friendship with Chef Seeking Deal in His District." *Miami Herald*, n.d., accessed May 30, 2015. *www.miamiherald.com/ news/local/community/miamidade/article1937927.html*.

RISUP. 2012. "Florida Worse Off Than Other States in the Recovery." September 3. *www. risep-fiu.org/2012/09/florida-worse-off-than-other-states-in-the-recovery/*.

Scanlan, Stephan J., J. Craig Jenkins, and Lindsey Peterson. 2010. "The Scarcity Fallacy." *Contexts* 9 (1): 34–39.

Slocum, Rachel. 2006. "Anti-racist Practice and the Work of Community Food Organizations." *Antipode* 38 (2): 327–49.

Widener, Patricia, and Marina Karides. 2014. "Harvesting Food System Literacy to Engage Citizens and Consumers." *Journal of Food, Culture, and Society: An International Journal of Multidisciplinary Research* 17 (4): 665–87.

Winne, Mark. 2008. *Closing the Food Gap: Resetting the Table in the Land of Plenty*. Boston: Beacon.

15

Food Insecurity in Southeast Grand Rapids, Michigan

How Our Kitchen Table Is Building Food Justice in the Face of Profiteering and Exclusionary Practices

CHRISTY MELLO

Our Kitchen Table (OKT), a food justice group, addresses the structural inequality responsible for food insecurity in southeast Grand Rapids, Michigan. Here, the residents are disproportionately African American and low-income earners suffering from high rates of food insecurity and other health-related issues. As an applied anthropologist, I have worked closely with OKT, documenting their approach to food insecurity. I believe that OKT has developed a replicable model for other cities in the country where citizens are impacted by food insecurity and gentrification. In southeast Grand Rapids, a social network of different business stakeholders and nonprofit organizations are gentrifying these neighborhoods. They are doing this in the name of creating food security by instituting local food-related business ventures. These efforts are actually reinforcing food insecurity or, at the least, providing only Band-Aid solutions to this poverty-related issue. In part, OKT's activism challenges and critiques the hardship that these projects are creating for the southeast residents. Exploring the relationship between gentrification and food security work, this chapter situates the work of OKT within this broader context of power relations. It mainly provides an ethnographic account of how OKT attempts to put long-term solutions to food insecurity into practice as an alternative to development efforts.

During an interview, one of OKT's members shared the following excerpt of a longer narrative that details the connections that OKT participants and others form around growing food in the face of food insecurity and gentrification.

> There are several families and people in the area that we have developed relationships with over the years primarily because of gardening. So there's an older African American woman who grew up in Mississippi and moved here to get a job in the auto industry, so lots of people moved from the South in the '50s. She lives a couple

blocks from here and, because she's a senior citizen, has asked us to do a few things like trim trees for her. So I'd been going over to her house to help her. I realized she has a garden. We began sitting and having conversations about those kinds of things. I'd share plants with her and she with me, things we didn't have.

Then Mr. Williams around the corner was doing the same things, another elderly African American guy. Doesn't matter what day of the week, he wears bib overalls. I love him. The first strawberry plants we had were from him. He had a pretty good patch of strawberries and [it] got to be too much; they bent over to the ground because there was so much. He said, "If you want some, pick 'em and take a bunch." So for strawberries I got some, and we still have some from his batch from twenty years ago. He and his wife have both since passed.

Then there's a Mexican family around the corner from them. One year there was a vacant lot next to their house, and the neighborhood association planted a sort of small community garden for the residents. The one Mexican family, Raul and his family, participated and enjoyed it; then they were able to convince the city to sell them the lot, so now it's part of theirs, and they have a big garden there. He has a peach tree. We used to have them here, and we gave him the seedling.

So it's been that kind of relational thing. So when I walk the dog or I'm out and about, if I see him we stop and talk and invariably almost always about the garden because that was our topic of initiation of the relationship with the garden. "How's the tomatoes doing?" and that sort of thing. It's really fun.

As with other interviews, this interviewee described gardens as the basis of interaction between neighbors. Participants commonly expressed that they shared food, recipes, and seeds, some seeds dating more than thirty years ago.

The above story goes on to describe how development projects have been forcing working-class families out of the neighborhood as redevelopment (gentrification) has been attracting affluent and white residents to the adjacent neighborhoods. In contrast, my documentation of development projects that were premised on building food security does not include similar stories of relationship building. This, in part, is due to the fact that the input of actual community members, living in the southeast, was not included in the implementation and design of these projects. Developers' narratives concerning food security consist of data on projected economic growth and future plans for urban "revitalization."

How OKT's approach differs from other food insecurity approaches, targeting the southeast communities, provided the basis for my October 2009 to October 2010 ethnographic research. This chapter's description of OKT's work is based on my continued conversations with OKT's members and observations dating back to 2008. This is the year that I began my preliminary research and OKT developed the Food Diversity Project (FDP), a cooperative food-growing model that addresses the root causes of food insecurity as well as childhood lead poisoning. The principal organizer, Lisa Oliver-King (founding member), of OKT designed the FDP to be a community-led advocacy project that involves other activists, utilizes popular education activities, analyzes public policy, and mobilizes citizens to network as backyard and community gardeners. With funding support from the W. K. Kellogg Foundation, beginning in the late fall of 2010, the FDP includes capacity-building activities for teaching residents how to practice food justice in the face of food insecurity and gentrification. Food justice can be understood as owning the production and distribution of one's own food (Peck 2010). Our Kitchen Table and local food advocates in Grand Rapids define food insecurity as little to no access to fresh, healthy, culturally appropriate, or affordable food.

Observations were based on my methodology designed to document the values and practices of OKT, the southeast food growers, participants in other food security initiatives (i.e., farmers' markets, gardening youth programs, food council, community gardens, etc.), and those of economic development initiatives. I attended as many activities and committee meetings as possible that concerned local food security in the Grand Rapids area. I did this in order to meet people and decipher these connections. I asked people about whom they frequently interacted with concerning local food and suggestions for people to contact for my study.

I conducted a total of fifty interviews. I purposefully networked as a participant observation activity in order to identify social networks and sample interviewees. I stopped recruiting interviewees after I identified the major players in different initiatives, as well as OKT's most active members and gardening participants. Thirty of the respondents participated in different top-down initiatives that were targeting or claiming to target food insecurity in the southeast. A top-down approach is one that is imposed by an outside organization rather than one led by community members. I observed this major distinction during my preliminary research used to design this methodology. Examples of top-down initiatives ranged from neighborhood-based community gardens to formal organizations like the health department, community development corporations, and different constituents of the Downtown Market, the major case example in this chapter. The remaining twenty interviewees were involved with OKT and/or were food growers living in the southeast neighborhoods. Interview questions were designed to determine values, practices, and reasons for participation.

I informally asked interview questions and made structured observations during participant observant activities in which most of my interactions occurred. Research activities included gardening, attending the board or committee meetings of top-down organizers, and participating in community events organized by top-down initiatives that included farmers' markets, health fairs, film screenings, conferences, and plant giveaways. I spent a significant amount of time observing the work of OKT and assisting with OKT's Food Diversity Project (FDP). Participant observation activities also included conducting informal interviews on videotape over the course of a growing season for insights into what it meant to participate in a garden or food security initiative. I filmed many of OKT's public activities. I was able to capture the process of gentrification with images of blighted areas juxtaposed with new development and sites that were about to undergo development.

A Comparison between a Top-Down and a Grassroots Approach to Food Insecurity

In this chapter, I compare OKT's grassroots approach to food insecurity with that of one particular top-down initiative, the Downtown Market. I use this major development effort as an example because it highlights the gentrification happening in the area. Gentrification contributes to poverty, and, therefore, food insecurity. OKT's struggle to build food security is situated within this context of inequality.

It is commonly observed that development efforts result in gentrification. As noted by Low and Smith (2006), gentrification involves attracting suburban consumers to urban areas. Moreover, it occurs when wealthier business or property owners start up new businesses and buy up or rehab houses in order to renew blighted areas in urban cities. Gentrification is also evident in that the current lower-income residents, often people of color, are forced out of their neighborhoods. They can no longer compete with these businesses or afford the rising cost of living, including rent. Property taxes also increase. Following such a pattern, in southeast Grand Rapids, outsiders are buying up the cheap foreclosed housing and replacing the original African American–owned small businesses with trendy restaurants selling local food, boutiques, beauty salons, pubs, coffee bars, and art and home décor stores. Developers in Grand Rapids refer to this type of gentrification as "urban revitalization."

Much of the development is premised on the growing popularity of the local food movement in Grand Rapids and the major concern over food insecurity. Grand Rapids is a midsize US city now in rebirth after the auto industry collapse, and the 2007 onset of the housing market crisis in the United States. Business stakeholders in Grand Rapids have been advertising it as being a destination spot offering popular cultural activities, locally owned businesses, and locally made products. Local food is central to this growing cultural identity. In particular, these stakeholders are tapping into the popularity of the local food movement and claiming to address food insecurity in the southeast by providing access to local food through restaurants, organic food grocers, and the newly built Downtown Market. These new businesses offer fresh and healthy food grown on farms in the west Michigan area. Developers are increasingly funded through large grants and public dollars by proposing to reduce food insecurity for southeast residents. These for-profit solutions are embedded into stakeholders' plans to improve business zone corridors and build or rehabilitate housing. As a result, developers are gentrifying these neighborhoods in the name of creating food security.

The Downtown Market

The Downtown Market is located in an old furniture factory in the southeast that was converted into an upscale location. It opened over the summer of 2012. Based on information from my respondents, I learned that the Downtown Market was a $43 million project, financed with both public and private dollars. Its development was partially premised on a study put together by Local Initiatives Support Corporation (LISC) (Local Initiatives Support Corporation [LISC] MetroEdge 2012). Grand Action, responsible for building the Downtown Market, used the LISC data as a measurement of food insecurity and proposed to address it through their development project. With the use of this study, Grand Action was awarded funding to address food insecurity. This study also included data estimating that an additional $74 million in food and beverage sales, given the housing density and lack of grocers, could be generated in southeast Grand Rapids. As the director of a nonprofit business zone redevelopment organization told me in an interview, developers predicted much opportunity for profit from food sales in the southeast. Not all their funding was intended to address food insecurity. However, it remains unclear if the funding designated for this issue was used to address it in any sort of capacity.

Today, the Downtown Market is a popular tourist attraction including restaurants, an outdoor farmers' market, a greenhouse, a juice bar, meeting rooms, and rooms for classes such as yoga. There is a year-round indoor market offering items like fresh cut flowers and spices, as well as artisan breads and cheeses.

Early in its development stages, with a community advocate, I met with the consultant and cofounder of Grand Action to learn how they intended to address food insecurity. They told us that they were addressing food insecurity by offering a community kitchen for neighborhood residents. However, this community kitchen never came to completion. Instead, an incubator kitchen for nearby college students was built. During this meeting, the consultant reported that the Downtown Market would also address food insecurity by providing obese children with the opportunity "to touch and taste food." He reported that they received funding from the W. K. Kellogg Foundation for addressing childhood obesity and food insecurity. These statements were in response to our questions concerning their sources of funding. At the time, it did not appear as if they were addressing food insecurity

In its planning phase, the constituents of the Downtown Market formed a social network that included: (1) city officials; (2) Grand Action, a nonprofit group started by one of Grand Rapids' wealthiest men; (3) a privately and publicly funded regional nonprofit development group whose board members include the heads of local and nonlocal corporations, energy companies, members of Grand Rapids' wealthiest families, and representatives from nearby universities; (4) community development corporations; and (5) various nonprofit groups addressing social issues and food insecurity. Many of these participants sit on the same boards or have direct correspondence. I identified the constituents through interviews, attending board meetings, and using a social networking approach to identify "who knows who."

Based on my meetings with various stakeholders, I learned about the distribution of resources and that these projects initially lacked community input. City dollars and tax credits had been used for the Downtown Market. Between 40 and 50 percent of the money, at the time of my research, was anticipated to come from tax credits and foundation grants. Because Grand Action has a nonprofit status, they were able to use tax credits and grant money. To finance the predevelopment, the city's Downtown Development Authority (DDA) gifted $100,000 of Grand Rapids' residents' unapproved tax dollars to Grand Action. The DDA bought the property in 2007 for $2 million and sold this vacant building and surrounding property for $1 to Grand Action.

Stakeholders reported that the Downtown Market is an investment tool designed to boost nearby business sales by attracting tourists into the city (agrotourism). One of Grand Action's stakeholders explained at a meeting that they were purposefully constructing this atmosphere, a sense of place, in order to appeal to shoppers' desire for history and "diversity." He believed that the Downtown Market would extend downtown and "help revitalize this frontier." It is located near the historical railroad and near an abandoned furniture warehouse owned by one of the constituents. Grand Action hoped to use these buildings for housing and retail. This process of homogenization to attract suburban consumers is what Ferrell (2001) refers to as the "disneyfication" of urban space. This process involves experiencing urban life, as it must have been in the past.

Stakeholders, throughout downtown, continue to design the city to look and function as it did one hundred years ago, when residents lived, worked, and shopped within areas the size of a few blocks. They recreate these past spaces, for example, by building brick-laid streets and installing wrought-iron light posts. Thus, they create a marketable sense of place through this disneyfication of urban space. The Downtown Market is a made place (disneyfied) of exclusion and a contested space. For instance, there are those who believed that they were left out of the engineering plans because of their race. Those experiencing homelessness were pushed out. Finally, citizens were opposed to the spending of public dollars for private enterprise, especially without any of the southeast residents' input.

One of my interviewees—the director of a nonprofit organization concerned with preserving green space, involved in city politics, and actively involved in projects addressing local food—provided a summary of the Downtown Market's primary objective: "From Grand Action's perspective, it could be a public market this week, a soccer field next week, an amphitheater the week after that, and the rapids of the river the week after that. It doesn't really matter if it's a good project. They are concerned with economic development."

Overall, the Downtown Market is an investment tool for private investors who own nearby businesses and is partially funded by public money that includes tax credits and money granted from the city's Downtown Development Authority (DDA). The *New York Times* heralded the market and the city of Grand Rapids for its entrepreneurial nature:

> The Downtown Market, in effect, is the newest piece of civic equipment built here (Grand Rapids) since the mid-1990s to leverage the same urban economic trends of the 21st century—higher education, hospitals and health care, housing, entertainment, transit, and cleaner air and water—that are reviving most large American cities.
>
> Few small cities, and possibly none in the industrial Midwest, have been nearly as successful. One reason is the distinctive partnerships formed between this city's redevelopment agencies and wealthy industrialists and philanthropists. Hundreds of millions of private dollars have been raised here to build a downtown that encourages entrepreneurs, develops career-track jobs and attracts new residents. (Schneider 2012)

The *New York Times* article does point out the fact that there are partnerships between business stakeholders, redevelopment agencies, and philanthropists. To the general public, the development that is a result of these social networks appears to be a positive thing. However, it does not appear to address food insecurity for the southeast residents who are suffering from the effects of the gentrification, partially caused by those philanthropists and developers who are claiming to address food insecurity through providing local food.

Our Kitchen Table as an Organization and the Food Diversity Project

Contrasting the work of OKT with other local food security initiatives illustrates how a "food security" approach can build the capacity of a community of people, justify gentrification, or ignore the root causes of this issue. Top-down approaches, targeting the southeast, receive funding based on developing ways to change individuals' food choices. This is significant, because, rather than targeting individual behavior, OKT addresses the causes of food insecurity, one being poverty. Gentrification contributes to poverty, and, therefore, higher rates of food insecurity as people can no longer afford the rising cost of living in their neighborhoods. This is the paradox in which OKT's work is situated, and in which I made my observations.

Our Kitchen Table (OKT) was established in 2003 when the founding member, Lisa Oliver-King, began recruiting women who were frustrated with the disparate rates in health issues faced by other African American women and their children living in or having ties to the Baxter, Southtown, Garfield Park, and Eastown neighborhoods, located in southeast Grand Rapids. It is here that community advocates have identified the highest rates of food insecurity and childhood lead poisoning in Grand Rapids. OKT's core membership typically, but not always, consists of six to eight African American women over the age of thirty-five with school-aged children or older, from different socioeconomic statuses, and concerned with growing food, reducing health disparities, community activism, and politics. These women recognize that common interventions tend to target individual behaviors and blame victims while health issues persist in their communities.

Drawing on their members' expertise, OKT organizes in response to local individuals interested in building toxin-free neighborhoods and a self-sustaining food system. As revealed in community discussions hosted by OKT, residents feel ill equipped to grow food in their neighborhoods or to lead projects designed to address food security issues. This is particularly true for single women who earn low wages, are unemployed or underemployed, and/or are the primary caregivers of children who were school aged or younger.

In these neighborhoods, besides a couple of upscale organic food markets, the result of urban "revitalization," there is only one grocery store that offers fresh meat and produce. For many of those without or having limited transportation, they have access only to corner markets, liquor stores, and fast-food places. These individuals constitute those who are a part of the modern food system that Holt-Giménez and colleagues (2009) note as having left millions of people without access to healthy food. Further, they report, it is one of the leading reasons for the prevalence of diet-related diseases being highest among people of color. For example, African American women, nationwide, are 50 percent more likely to be obese than white women.

For all the above reasons, OKT began the Food Diversity Project (FDP) in the spring of 2008. This project offers educational activities around growing food in conjunction with avoiding environmental contaminants. Participants include both southeast residents and nonresidents who want to support the work of OKT. They include both experienced gardeners and beginning gardeners who are relying on support provided by OKT. Support includes gardening coaches and educational workshops, as well as resources such as starter plants and testing kits for detecting lead in the soil. Through the FDP, OKT encourages community members to take action by growing food to live semi-independent of the larger political economic system. This is a model whereby grassroots organizations can engage in what Levkoe (2006) refers to as the difference between those who act as democratically engaged citizens in their food production rather than as consumers dependent on larger corporations to supply their food.

During my study, I observed and extensively documented one of OKT's major goals, which is to have the novice gardeners become skilled gardeners who can, in turn, recruit others to garden and provide their new expertise with them. The overall objective is to strengthen a cooperative social network of gardeners and to identify community assets (i.e., growing knowledge and existing gardens) for growing and sharing food. Landman (1993) observes the importance of sharing and identifying food-related assets for building and strengthening communities. This is evident in the work of OKT, who refers to community building as capacity building. Compared to top-down approaches, the FDP is unique in that it builds capacity, meaning it provides support to the community for dealing with systemic problems and creating long-term change.

Activities are modeled after the Building Movement Project (BMP) (2006), which is based on Paulo Freire's (1970) "popular education" model. The goal of popular education is to develop people's capacity for social change through a collective problem-solving approach emphasizing participation, reflection, and critical analysis of social problems. The Michigan coordinator from the BMP advises OKT members on how to analyze the relationship between power and the inequality in their lives and communities. Participants are taught, as outlined by BMP, how to be agents in shaping social change through organizing others and identifying their own power (assets) in the community.

In accordance with the BMP, one of OKT's goals is to train a group of women who are conscious about the pervasive problems in their neighborhoods. These women's role is to establish strategies for building an infrastructure to address issues in the community and generate a cohort to serve either as peer educators or as organizers. The FDP recruits peer educators to serve as gardening coaches for those first learning how to grow food. Educators include community activists who are also food growers. Coaches include members of OKT and southeast household gardeners who already grow food. One member, Esther (pseudonym), often acts as a gardening coach and lives in one of the southeast neighborhoods, the Baxter neighborhood. Her expertise is a product of her childhood and agrarian roots in Alabama. She has also been trained as a master gardener and has managed a couple of small-venue farmers' markets, where she sells food from her backyard. Even though her vision of food insecurity does not always align with other members' notions around justice, she does share the common concern over diet-related illnesses in her community. She even delivers food to homes in the southeast neighborhoods, where she also shares herbal remedies for improved health.

Esther's concern regarding food insecurity began as atypical or apolitical compared to other members of OKT. During my research, she avoided the topic of racism and told other members of OKT that she did not want to address issues of injustice. Instead, she cared about targeting health on an individual basis. Several times, she told me that she never gets into discussions of politics or race. "I do not do politics. I am about helping the people and their health." However, after poor treatment from two different top-down agencies targeting food insecurity in the southeast, she began recalling different experiences with racism. On a couple of occasions, she spoke of being a youth in Alabama and when she truly first realized the existence of racism when former president John Kennedy sent in the National Guard to forcibly desegregate the University of Alabama in 1963. This is one example of how she began to incorporate her personal history and stories into OKT's activities that explicitly link food insecurity to structural issues such as racism.

Besides training gardeners, the FDP offers several capacity-building activities related to promoting food security, avoiding exposure to lead in the soil, and education on sustainable subsistence activities. Interactive workshops provide education on canning and seed saving, composting, starting plants from seeds, organic growing methods, growing winter crops, and selecting seeds for plant diversity. Walking and bicycle tour workshops are organized around both household gardens and naturally growing food in the neighborhoods. During these tours, examples of topics include lead in the soil; herbal gardening for health and culinary purposes; and urban foraging for edible fruit, nuts, and weeds that grow in public spaces within the city. Cooking demonstrations are another type of workshop, in which peer educators prepare food with both familiar and unfamiliar types of locally grown produce. Workshops encourage gardeners to grow and share food, and diversify their gardens. OKT also hosts a farmers' market and partners with nearby schools for gardening with the youth.

During many of these capacity-building activities, participants discuss different land use policies, including those that support publicly growing food using sustainable methods, as well as those that facilitate the gentrification occurring in the city. Realizing that long-lasting change is beyond targeting individual behaviors, OKT addresses public policy as a method to institute change. OKT's members actively discuss the impacts of policy on food insecurity such as the US Farm Bill, as well as city policy that blocks access to vacant spaces for growing food by giving preference to developers.

As evidenced by the dialogue that occurs during and outside of workshops, OKT's participants recognize the benefits and importance of growing local food in an environmentally sustainable manner. Sustainable, in this sense, is understood as preserving the Earth's resources for future generations by planting heirloom seeds to maintain biodiversity, preserving cultural knowledge around growing food, and not using chemicals that poison the land, air, water, and living species. Environmental toxins, especially lead, are a primary topic for discussing what it means to have a clean environment and to live sustainably in the city, and for discussing land use in an urban context.

Maintaining biodiversity is a major tenet of the FDP. OKT encourages gardeners to grow varieties of different plant species to preserve cultural heritage, as specific varieties of fruits, vegetables, and grains are used for traditional cuisines and healing modalities. Diverse groups of people have cultivated seeds for generations; these seeds—some centuries old—are part of their cultural heritage (Klindienst 2006). Several southeast gardeners who exhibit their gardens during the FDP's food garden tours speak about the link between their plants and their cultural or ancestral heritage. Many are involved in OKT's activities, and a few sell at OKT's farmers' market.

Many of the FDP' participants include southeast residents who are growing food in their yards, and some grow food in community gardens. I became acquainted with household and community gardeners through my involvement with OKT and the networking process of "who knows who" grows food. Gardens across the southeast vary in their appearance and are gardened by people with diverse backgrounds. Individuals' stories are quite eclectic, especially since the demographics of the southeast have diversified with the onset of gentrification. Many of the African American elders migrated from the South for industrial jobs in the North. Many of their children, several of my interviewees, are now gardeners. Besides these families, OKT's gardeners included college-age students and young families who have relocated to the city from the outlying suburbs of Grand Rapids.

During my interviews and conversations with OKT's gardeners, they shared similar values and reasons for growing food and why they started their garden. There were those who longed for a return to a simpler agrarian lifestyle; valued their health and the environment; desired to be self-sufficient during an economic crisis; sought to preserve cultural heritage; and felt a spiritual connection to the land. Overall, people expressed a need to connect to the land or each other, living or deceased. Gardeners keep a connection to a living sense of place as well as past places when they cultivate their land as well as grow and cook their own food. A sense of place is conjured as a means to communicate memories through a collective history. Often, gardeners would fondly recall memories of relatives and their childhood. Pete described how he felt close to his deceased grandfather whenever he works in his garden. "It's like my grandpa is standing right here with his rake looking over me and I'm back in my childhood and the garden, the land, and I feel safe." Several of the gardeners save seeds to grow and cook particular foods for maintaining continuity with past places and their ancestors. As illustrated by the gardeners, beyond the pragmatics of gardening to counter food insecurity and an ineffective food system, growing food lends deeper meaning to individuals' lives and defines the essence of the human experience.

OKT's food growers never listed a singular benefit. Rather, they always spoke of several motivating factors for why they gardened:

> I lose track of everything else. I can spend eight hours, and I'm oblivious to anything going on around me. It's quite nice. I don't think about radio, cable TV, bills, finances, anything else than what I'm doing, what's directly in front of me, and that's peaceful. I think that's how people were designed to be. At peace and doing one task in front of you at a time instead of trying to race around from one red light to the next to get nowhere, to be able to hurry and stand in line for something. That's the other thing I like, I don't have to stand in line and wait. I'm hungry, I walk out in the yard and grab something and I eat it. I don't have the hassles of getting in the car, driving to the store . . . that store has good tomatoes, bad oranges . . . this store has good strawberries . . . whatever. It's at my house. (Ms. Evelyn)

Implications for Food Security Advocates

In contrast to top-down efforts such as that of the Downtown Market, Our Kitchen Table's bottom-up grassroots approach to food insecurity is predicated on their fundamental principle of justice. OKT views justice as the changing of the conditions responsible for inequality in order for all citizens to be afforded the same rights of food security, safe environmental conditions, and social opportunities. OKT mobilizes community residents through community-building activities around gardens. OKT views food insecurity as not the problem of individuals but one of communities to restructure the food system. They encourage participants to tap into available resources and at the same time to avoid dependence on those organizations and top-down schemes that plan events on their behalf. OKT recognizes that these agendas are paternalistic and privilege the perspectives of "experts." According to Escobar (1995), as witnessed by OKT, "experts" often do not incorporate the needs of individuals of different age, ethnicity, religion, or gender.

As observed by OKT, marginalized groups often internalize the ideology that it is their responsibility to change unhealthy behaviors, and something is inherently wrong with them for living in impoverished conditions. OKT acknowledges citizens' agentive ability in pursuing healthy practices. However, members also educate their fellow neighborhood residents that the structural causes behind these conditions must be addressed in order to achieve any sort of long-term solutions to poverty-related issues.

The FDP, with its justice-oriented approach to food insecurity, was in its early development during the time of this research. My research documented the FDP in its infancy and contrasted it to top-down approaches such as that of the Downtown Market. Since the time of my research, OKT has increased the number of community members it has outreached. They now keep annual data on how many individuals participate in their project. There is no measurable data on how their work has reduced food insecurity, overall, in the southeast. Nonetheless, today's participants, as during the time of my research, speak to the positive impact that OKT has had on their lives in that their health status has improved. Positive outcomes, as reported by my interviewees, include the preservation of biodiversity, healthy diets, reduced food budgets, and the maintenance of cultural heritage and identity. Future research could further document the FDP's positive impact in the community.

Despite OKT's efforts, food insecurity will continue in the southeast as long as the voices of actual community members are excluded from food security initiatives and development projects. OKT believes that many top-down efforts provide Band-Aid solutions to food insecurity and are further gentrifying the southeast. These efforts drive up the cost of living, and, therefore, increase food insecurity. OKT's approach to building food security, however, is an alternative to those outside of top-down organized agencies. OKT trains community residents on the basic tenets of justice and has equipped them with the tools, skills, and knowledge for living in a sustainable and self-sufficient manner. This movement continues to grow and ultimately has impacted food insecurity more so than efforts such as those of the Downtown Market.

Overall, my research is a documentation of the experiences and methods of a social justice movement that possesses substantive tenets and tactics on which other food sovereignty projects can model themselves and take part in exchanges of dialogue in how to grow in solidarity across the nation. Residents are autonomously supplying their own local food in an environmentally sustainable and affordable way. Food growers are also connecting to the intangible elements of life; gardening as an activity provides a sense of place as well as community. Food was once fully integral to humans' social, economic, and political lives. Efforts such as OKT's FDP seek to restore our relationship with food as a fundamental human right.

REFERENCES

Building Movement Project. 2006. *Social Service and Social Change: A Process Guide.* New York: Building Movement Project.

Escobar, Arturo. 1995. *Encountering Development: The Making and Unmaking of the Third World.* Princeton, NJ: Princeton University Press.

Ferrell, Jeff. 2001. *Tearing Down the Streets: Adventures in Urban Anarchy.* New York: Palgrave.

Freire, Paulo. 1970. *Pedagogy of the Oppressed.* New York: Herder and Herder.

Holt-Giménez, Eric, Raj Patel, and Annie Shattuck. 2009. *Food Rebellions: Crisis and Hunger for Justice.* Oxford: Pambazuka.

Johnson Center at Grand Valley State University. 2011. "The Neighborhoods of Grand Rapids." Community Research Institute. *cridata.org/Neighb_GR.aspx.*

Klindienst, Patricia. 2006. *The Earth Knows My Name: Food, Culture and Sustainability in the Gardens of Ethnic Americans.* Boston: Beacon.

Landman, R. H. 1993. *Creating Community in the City: Cooperatives and Community Gardens in Washington, D.C.* Westport, CT: Bergin and Garvey.

Levkoe, Charles. 2006. "Learning Democracy through Food Justice Movements." *Agriculture and Human Values* 23 (1): 89–98.

Local Initiatives Support Corporation (LISC) MetroEdge. 2012. "LISC 'MetroEdge' Profiles Highlight Grand Rapid's Urban Markets." *www.instituteccd.org/MetroEdge/MetroEdge-News/LISC-MetroEdge-Profiles-Highlight-Grand-Rapid-s-Urban-Markets.html.*

Low, Setha, and Neil Smith. 2006. "How Private Interests Take Over Public Space: Zoning, Taxes, and Incorporation of Gated Communities." In *The Politics of Public Space*, edited by Setha Low and Neil Smith, 81–105. New York: Routledge.

Peck, John. 2010. "You Are What You Eat: The Food Sovereignty Struggle within the Global Justice Movement." In *Uses of a Whirlwind: Movement, Movements, and Contemporary Radical Currents in the United States*, edited by Team Colors Collective, 125–33. Edinburgh: AK Press.

Schneider, Keith. 2012. "A Michigan City Bets on Food for Its Growth." *New York Times*, n.d., accessed November 13, 2012. *ww.nytimes.com/2012/11/14/realestate/commercial/grand-rapids-mich-bets-on-a-food-market-for-growth.html?_r=0.*

16

Community Leadership and Participation to Increase Food Access and Quality

Notes from the Field

AMEENA BATADA AND OLUFEMI LEWIS

As you drive past the food bank headquarters on the outskirts of town, a large truck is perpetually parked so that passersby can see the picture and writing on the side. The picture is of a brown-skinned family at a dining table, and above them is the statement, "Working Together for Hunger Relief." Prominent are the food bank and corporate sponsor logos. The statement declares a solution; however, for us, it raises more questions than it answers. What is "hunger relief"? *Who* specifically is included in the "together"? And, how do the *ways* we seek hunger relief matter, if at all? We don't know if we'll ever have definitive answers to these questions, but they are worth considering if we are to address societal challenges.

The *what, who,* and *how* of eliminating hunger and food insecurity matter. In this chapter, we argue that traditional approaches to addressing food insecurity are problematic and that alternative approaches should have a clear emphasis on including program participants as stakeholders. In order for us to have a future that is food secure and just, we argue that leadership from within communities is necessary, in particular leadership by community members living in lower-wealth communities and communities of color. In the final section of this chapter, we provide several examples of such leadership from around the country, and we focus on how such leadership exists and continues to be negotiated in Asheville, North Carolina, a city where contemporary foodie trends and food security efforts intersect. Finally, we offer several recommendations for building a food sovereign community, based on many of our lessons learned and observed.

The question of *what* hunger and food insecurity are have been discussed in previous sections of this book. *How* we use terms related to hunger and food insecurity in our approaches to addressing these challenges, however, may be problematic (People's Institute for Survival and Beyond n.d.). Most appeals to Americans focus on alleviating hunger rather than promoting food security. Focusing on hunger puts a face to the issue, which may make it more attractive as a charitable cause. The food banks and corporations and the millions of people who donate food and money to provide foods to those in need believe that they are saving the mostly low-wealth and brown and black people who live in households that are food insecure. The *saving* of these populations means that they will forever be indebted, locked in a power structure that limits their own agency and perpetuates cycles of oppression and poverty. Moreover, the face of hunger removes the structural frame, diffusing responsibility and maintaining the focus on individual approaches over institutional change. *Food insecurity*, on the other hand, is more often framed as a problem with systems. Until those systemic problems are addressed, food insecurity likely will persist.

The Food Bank Conundrum

The majority of community-based efforts that provide food directly to community members are considered *traditional* approaches to alleviating hunger and often include food banks, food pantries, food drives, backpack programs, farmers' markets programs, and fund-raisers (Roncarolo et al. 2015). Government agencies, such as the Department of Health and Human Services (DHHS) and local school districts, also provide food assistance to individuals and families. These efforts and services, while meeting immediate needs, may not be as inclusive of communities experiencing food insecurity and/or may draw attention and resources from longer-term solutions.

Traditional, direct-to-community approaches to reducing hunger are helpful for addressing short-term immediate needs of individuals and families. However, many recognize that they are not the solution to our long-term problems. Temporary food assistance also may be related to dependency on programs (Kicinski 2012). According to Feeding America spokesperson Maura Daly, "the majority of our clients are receiving food assistance for six months or longer" (Korkki 2012). As Erik Talkin (2012), CEO of the Foodbank of Santa Barbara, writes in his blog *From Hunger to Health*, "As food banks grew . . . this did not translate into an eradication or significant shrinkage of the problems they were trying to address."

Yet, there is a reluctance to shift the focus of food banks and other large organizations because their limited funding inhibits their ability to move beyond their core mission of food provision (Korkki 2012). Another challenge of limited funding for these organizations is the variability in nutritional quality of foods provided through temporary assistance programs. While some programs provide fresh fruits and vegetables and other nutrient-dense foods to recipients, much of the food is packaged, low in positive nutrients, and processed. For example, a report on the Feeding America backpack program indicated that the average nutrition score of the bags sent home was 64 out of 100 (Harnack, Hearst, and Harrison 2012).

When organizations partner with corporations to raise additional funds it also raises questions about the root causes of food insecurity. As Erik Talkin (2012) says, "In fact, the need seems to have grown in a way that can be linked to the ability to meet that need. . . . The success of the network in obtaining food has also helped grow the opportunity for agencies and individuals to receive support. . . . I have to ask where are we going with all this. Do we keep growing and growing the numbers we serve, giving a get out clause to companies who want to avoid paying a living wage and providing real benefits? What is the way out of this dilemma?"

Nonprofit traditional programming to address hunger has become competitive, often with larger, established organizations obtaining large grants and corporate sponsorships. Herein lies several problems. First, large national- and state-level organizations often are well established in structure and approach, which makes them part of a system that race and social activist bell hooks (2013, 32) describes as "an imperialist white supremacist culture of domination." These organizations are adept at garnering funds for their programs and providing services to communities, and to the knowledge of the current authors, they rarely work in deep collaboration with local communities so that interventions are co-owned by people who themselves have experienced hunger and the day-to-day challenges of living in poverty. As such, there is a perpetuation of the lines between those who have and feed others and those who are constantly without basic needs. Second, the constant demand for hunger alleviation resources diverts attention and support from the longer-term, institutional changes that are necessary for sustainable change. Not only do companies create a "halo" effect by sponsoring hunger-free events and programs in lieu of paying a living wage or providing benefits to their workers; the American public is lulled into thinking that they are helping people by donating food or money, or attending a special event that both entertains them and contributes to a social good.

Fishing in Polluted Ponds

As food insecurity, poverty, illness, and other problems increase for certain segments of society, we are reminded of a fishing analogy that has evolved over time. As the idiom goes, *Give a man a fish and you feed him for a day; teach a man to fish and you feed him for a lifetime.* Contemporary social justice advocates challenge this notion however, recognizing that the focus is on the individual when the focus should be placed on the system (McCraig 2014). What is the point of knowing how to fish when the pond in which your fish are swimming, perhaps even the place where you are located, is polluted? What is the point of supporting people from lower-wealth communities to move out of poverty so they become food secure when the majority of available food is of poor nutritional quality (McCraig 2014)? These areas have come to be known as "food swamps," where "unhealthy foods are more readily available than healthy foods" (Johns Hopkins n.d.).

Some activists also extend the pond analogy to highlight the segmentation and fragmentation of our social service systems. When programs provide food assistance, unemployment benefits, health care services, insurance subsidies, and other services, they often address specific problems, but at the same time, they may create additional problems for populations, increasing the need for additional services. For example, when food assistance programs provide unhealthy foods to communities of lower wealth and/or communities of color, community members are more likely to develop nutrition-related health problems such as overweight status and diabetes. These health problems result in an increased need for health care services, represented by another pond. In effect, problems are just transmitted from pond to pond, rather than the entire water system being cleaned up. The problems associated with food and poverty are so deeply embedded in our institutions and societal structures that it takes shifts in power and leadership to truly strengthen our approaches. As Holt-Giménez and Wang (2011, 98) state in their article on the role of food justice in the US food movement, "solving the food crisis requires dismantling racism and classism in the food system and transforming the food regime. . . . This pivotal praxis may yet produce a new, powerful food movement narrative: the narrative of liberation."

Alternative Approaches

Beyond traditional approaches, *alternative* approaches may hold promise (Tarasuk 2011). Collective kitchens and community gardens are examples of alternative interventions, with their focus on nurturing solidarity and creativity among diverse populations, particularly those living in poverty and with limited access to healthy foods. Collective kitchens bring small groups of community members together to cook in bulk for sharing and distribution, and community gardens bring together residents to grow and harvest food on separate or joint plots on land in their own neighborhoods.

Ultimately, alternative interventions seek to empower participants and thereby reduce dependency on services and to address social inequalities (Roncarolo et al. 2015). While these alternative approaches have potential to engage diverse communities in long-term solutions, research and practice suggest that attracting and retaining the most affected populations remains difficult (Tarasuk 2011).

For approaches to work toward Gottlieb and Joshi's (2013, 7) vision in their book *Food Justice*, communities must "prioritize the need to address inequities while seeking to change the system as a whole integrated into other social movements"; community members must not only be participants but leaders in their own food security, economic, political and other social efforts. Thus, the *who* of food security and justice matters.

Community Members as Leaders

At the local level, power and decision making among community members can transform social systems for long-term changes. Community mobilization, grassroots organizing, and community-participatory research and action all describe models of community leadership. Approaches in which community members lead or colead interventions are beneficial because they bring perspectives and expertise of potential program participants, which is useful in designing culturally relevant activities; they help to build trust with community members and thereby increase the likelihood of intervention acceptance and utilization; and they build technical capacities of community members and infrastructure to address ongoing and possible new needs (Minkler and Wallerstein 2008).

Paynter and colleagues (2011, 53) also recommend locally informed and led approaches, stating, "we firmly believe that any course of action will fail without a clear understanding of the nature and extent of the problem"; and "based on our previous research, we believe the most effective hunger programs will result from collaborative solutions born of holistic groups of stakeholders rather than from individual units. . . . In short, effective hunger policies will arise when all the stakeholders join at one table." For these reasons, it may not only be recommended that community members participate as leaders in food security solutions; as Brazilian education activist Paulo Freire (1974, 46) insisted: "It is absolutely essential that the oppressed participate in the revolutionary process with an increasing critical awareness of their role as subject of the transformation."

Just Approaches

Community food systems—in which "neighborhood stakeholders are the ones growing the food, moving it around, and in control of land tenure or wherever soil-, food-, and Earth-based materials are being grown" (Allen 2010, 3)—gained prominence nationally in the 1990s. One early example from this movement is Nuestras Raices (Our Roots) in South Holyoke, Massachusetts, where in 1992, a group of migrant farmers from Puerto Rico turned an abandoned lot into the city's first community garden. The initiative inspired more community gardens throughout the city and became a model for developing culturally relevant sustainable agriculture. The garden network also provided a way to organize community members around many issues, and today the organization is known for its ongoing economic and environmental contributions in the area.

One of the most widely known community food programs continues to be Growing Power, started in Milwaukee, Wisconsin. Growing Power is "a national organization and land trust supporting people from diverse backgrounds, and the environments in which they live, by helping to provide equal access to healthy, high-quality, safe and affordable food for people in all communities" (*www.growingpower.org*). Established in 1993, Growing Power provides training, demonstrations, outreach, and technical assistance to develop community food systems from cultivation to distribution. As Growing Power's founder and chief executive officer, Will Allen, states, "if people can grow safe, healthy, affordable food, if they have access to land and clean water, this is transformative on every level in a community. I believe we cannot have healthy communities without a healthy food system" (*www.growingpower.org*).

What Will Allen describes may be considered food sovereignty. While food security is a social condition and food justice a progressive movement, the term *food sovereignty* refers to an approach to reclaiming people's land, food, livelihoods, and identities in the face of industrial food system monopolies (Alkon and Agyeman 2011). Food sovereignty is a response to racist and classist food and social projects and systems, and the resulting food insecurity, and is an approach gaining recognition throughout North America. One southern city, Asheville, North Carolina, is engaging in efforts to alleviate hunger, promote food security and food justice, and work toward more food sovereignty.

Redefining Foodtopia: A Case Study in Food Justice

Asheville, North Carolina, is a midsized city of approximately eighty-seven thousand people (US Census Bureau 2015), nestled within mountain ranges and close to the borders of Georgia, Tennessee, and Virginia. The city is a popular tourist destination for its arts and crafts, music, and food, and it is known informally as Foodtopia because of the eclectic, local, and trendy food and beer scene. Among its many foodie accolades, Asheville was among TripAdvisor's Top 10 Destinations for Food and Wine in 2011. Paradoxically, Asheville also ranks among the most food insecure regions of the country. The Food Research and Action Center (FRAC) (2013) listed the Asheville metropolitan area as the ninth-hungriest city in the United States in 2012. Within Asheville city limits, there are several food deserts, populated primarily by public housing communities and other communities of lower wealth (US Department of Agriculture Economic Research Service 2015).

Asheville also harbors many of the racial and economic challenges facing cities across the nation. Though unemployment is lower than in most of the state, communities are highly segregated by race, and income levels vary widely. Gentrification of the downtown and river arts districts and a shortage of affordable housing is pushing long-time residents of color out of the city (Judson 2010). In addition, the public housing structure recently shifted to a Rental Assistance Demonstration, which privatizes properties and provides section 8 vouchers to community members with lower income levels, and many fear that the shift might accelerate gentrification (Forbes 2014). With one in five people experiencing food hardship in this food-rich area (Food Action and Research Center 2013), the potential for interventions rooted in community development and empowerment is great and is being realized. A network of organizations, communities, and individuals is working in various ways to build capacities, support multisectoral change, and encourage food sovereign communities.

Asheville is the site of many traditional approaches to addressing hunger and food insecurity, such as the MANNA Food Bank, with its multiple food assistance, educational, mobile, and advocacy efforts; church-, school- and other community organization–based food pantries and programs; government programs such as SNAP and WIC assistance; and incentives for SNAP beneficiaries at farmers' markets. There also are gleaning programs, which engage community members with time to harvest food from farms after the growing season is complete, and then take the produce to local organizations such as shelters/safe havens with kitchens on-site. One recently developed program, the Food Connection, provides a taxicab and a community-based organization to callers who report that they have leftover food from an event.

Beyond short-term food assistance, the alternative approaches to addressing hunger and food insecurity in Asheville range from programs to engage communities in gardening to policy advocacy. One of the most promising approaches is through black-organized and/or owned agriculture, which is important because of the discrimination and disproportionate impact of food insecurity in black communities (Giancatarino and Noor 2014), and because of the value of the historical and continued involvement of black communities in agriculture in the region.

Black-Organized Agriculture

Black-organized agriculture in the communities of lower wealth in Asheville may be the most promising and most challenged approach to increasing food sovereignty in the area. In 2007, Robert White and Lucia Daugherty established the Pisgah View Community Peace Garden on an abandoned baseball field next to their home in Pisgah

View Apartments (PVA), a public housing community in west Asheville (Sezak-Blatt 2010). The peace garden produces organic vegetables, fruits, herbs, and eggs and has provided food for community food banks, sold food to local businesses, and vended food at farmers' markets. The garden provides opportunities for residents to learn about and get involved in urban agriculture and their local food system and, at a small scale, to engage in economic activities. As Daugherty explains, "Personally, the project has been rewarding because it is resident-driven." She notes, "So often, nonprofits come into our community to 'save' us, but in this case we are creating our own destiny—saving our own neighborhood" (Sezak-Blatt 2010).

The work of White and Daugherty has been expanded by others at PVA, including Sir Charles Gardner and Carl Johnson, and has been connected with other gardens, such as the Burton Street Peace Garden and the Hillcrest Community Garden. At PVA, Sir Charles remarks, "I work here because I want to empower my community and I want to give my community a chance to eat healthy at decent costs" (Etheredge 2014).

Members of the historically African American Burton Street Community, activists DeWayne Barton and Safi Mahaba created the garden in 2003 as an organic community garden network, a space for growing, learning, and outdoor art. They also revived the regional Black Agricultural Fair, which took place annually from 1913 to 1947. The Burton Street Community hosted the first fair, which was organized by Burton Street Community founder E. W. Pearson. According to the Burton Street Community website (Burtonstreet 2011), "Pearson deeply understood the power of self-reliance when it comes to engaging and building community, especially a community of people facing social barriers most of us have only read or heard about." With regard to black involvement in the local foods movements, the web page author goes on to say, "Our modern-culture's recent return to a love of all things 'local' rides on the shoulders of communities like Burton Street who, out of necessity and the delight of true community, relied on themselves and each other to build slow, simple, and profoundly rich lives."

In 2008, Barton cofounded Green Opportunities (GO!), which "helps youth and adults living in poverty get and keep jobs that support their families and improve community and environmental health" (*greenopportunities.org*). Over the years, GO! has developed several job training programs and its GO! Ready Kitchen provides culinary arts training, and its teaching kitchen offers a daily lunch to public housing residents for free and to all on a sliding scale. The GO! training programs and the kitchen demonstrate a model for how efforts to feed people can be created and sustained within community.

GO! also received funding to support farmers at PVA and Hillcrest communities to create Gardens United, a network of urban agriculturalists in communities of lower wealth. Olufemi Lewis (a coauthor of this chapter) and gardeners from the low-income public housing communities were part of the network. However, when the grant money was exhausted, the group no longer was able to sustain the efforts.

Another model of a community-developed and community-owned project is the Ujamaa Freedom Market, a worker-owned cooperative mobile market started by Olufemi Lewis and Ayanfe Free. The market's tagline is "Liberation through cooperation," and its mission is to "feed and nourish the whole community through access to healthy, fresh food" (*www.ujamaafreedommarket.wordpress.com*). Now led by local food activist Calvin Allen, Ujamaa Freedom Market sells affordable produce obtained through donations by nearby gardens to residents of several communities in Asheville. Their main clientele are residents of communities of lower wealth, where access to healthy food is very limited, thereby promoting "social, economic, environmental, and food justice by serving as a model for self-sufficiency while inspiring healthy relationships with food in order to strengthen the quality of life, health and wellbeing of the community."

Asheville's oldest African American community, Shiloh, also recently started a community garden, inspired by college students who had been working with the community association. Over the past three years, Shiloh Community Association members and students from the University of North Carolina–Asheville and Warren Wilson College have created a garden and amphitheater on a plot of land across from the community center and are currently working on a trail next to a creek on the land. Every Saturday the team works on the garden, inviting residents to join them in tilling, planting, harvesting, cooking on the fire, and eating in community.

Cultivating and sustaining resident ownership of gardens in communities of lower wealth and communities of color in Asheville can be challenging. In many communities of lower wealth, residents have multiple jobs and responsibilities, limiting available time to contribute. Further, most people rent rather than own, and combined with the lack of upkeep by the housing administration, there is low emotional investment in community spaces. Generally, people are disconnected from the food they eat, and people with limited incomes and people of color may feel disenfranchised from the current food movements (Alkon and McCullen 2011). For example, though African Americans played a significant role in the agricultural foundations of this country, particularly in the South, it is the history of enslavement on the land that can cause many African Americans to be averse to farming or gardening. Funding for community-owned projects also is limited, with funders less likely to give money to individuals or community associations than to issue-based organizations. As is the case with some projects led by community leaders, leveraging the structure of community-based organizations can be beneficial. In addition, community member engagement and leadership in community organizations can enhance the work of these institutions.

Leveraging Engagement

Since 2000, the Asheville-based nonprofit organization Bountiful Cities has partnered "with community groups, focusing on dialogue, trust and community needs, to create urban agricultural spaces . . . [emphasizing] social justice, access to education, sustainability and economic viability" (*www.bountifulcities.org*) in Asheville. Their vision is "abundance and food sovereign communities." Bountiful Cities works with communities to grow food from seed, trains and employs community members to provide urban agriculture expertise to paying clients, and advocates for accessible healthy food systems. The advisory board for Bountiful Cities includes members of local communities and institutions, who represent a range of life experiences, cultural and racial backgrounds, and income levels. The organization has been a leader for community-led collaborations locally, brokering an important partnership with the UNC–Asheville and initiating the local food policy council.

Started in 2011, the Asheville-Buncombe Food Policy Council (ABFPC) is one of a handful of food policy councils in the state of North Carolina. The council, made up of members from a range of occupations, sectors, neighborhoods, and life experiences, came together because they "recognized a need for a localized structure that would address issues of the sustainability of, and access to, the food system in the Asheville area" (Feldman and Kujawa 2012, 2). The ABFPC's mission is "to identify and propose innovative solutions to improve local food systems, spur local economic development and make food systems environmentally sustainable and socially just" (*www.abfoodpolicycouncil.org*), and to this end the council uses a consensus model for decision making. The ABFPC also includes local businesses, such as the French Broad Food Co-op, and Short Street Cakes, which are committed to making healthy, just food accessible to all. The ABFPC developed and advocated for the Food Action Plan, which was adopted by the Asheville city council in 2013. The first of the plan's five goals is to "improve the quality of life for those in need by increasing access to food for people who experience food insecurity" (see Appendix). In 2017, the ABFPC presented an updated Food Action Policy Strategy.

Community development organizations also play an important role in supporting communities to organize and advocate for food and social justice. Local examples include the Women's Wellbeing Development Fund (WWD-F), Just Economics, and the Center for Participatory Change (CPC). The Women's Wellbeing Development Fund works with residents in the Hillcrest community to increase access to career development, health programming, and social services. Just Economics advocates for a living wage through employer recognition and policy change. The Center for Participatory Change conducts antiracism training for people in the school system and other agencies, providing opportunities for people to identify their own biases and take steps to address them. With the support of these and other local organizations, many community groups are able to gain the technical expertise and/or resources to kick-start their leadership across multiple important dimensions and to exercise their sovereignty across issues.

In 2015, five local organizations began an alliance to "address root causes of poverty, injustice, and inequity within the local food system while utilizing a collective impact framework" called the Urban Agriculture Alliance (UAA) (Urban Agriculture Alliance n.d.). The UAA organizations identified four areas of shared work: agriculture education; economic opportunity; relationships and resources; and revolutionary food systems; and they are utilizing a collective impact approach to work together to develop a set of shared goals and strategies, including identifying sustainable sources of funding and support for the alliance and its work.

Increasingly, local colleges also are getting more involved in supporting community food security efforts. UNC–Asheville recently started a collaborative on food security and well-being, to explore ways to support the ABFPC and other organizations' efforts. Students engage in volunteer work, service learning, internship, and other opportunities to provide assistance with community research and interventions. In 2012, faculty, students, and community organizations and members engaged in a research project called Exploring Food. The purpose of the project was to gather information about decision making around healthy eating among local community members in lower-wealth communities, utilizing a community-centered approach to identifying and gathering data. Exploring Food represents a model of campus-community partnership that attempts to minimize power dynamics and leverage the expertise and relationships built in and among local communities.

In 2016, Bountiful Cities and Dig In!, a Yancey County garden that gives, invited UNC Asheville to become involved in the second phase of the Appalachian Foodshed Project (AFP). The initial AFP was a tristate (North Carolina, West Virginia, and Virginia) project funded by the US Department of Agriculture, which envisioned "a place-based food system that is resilient, accessible, affordable, and healthy for Appalachian communities" (Eshleman, Schroeder-Moreno, and Cruz 2016, 18). The next phase of the AFP will strengthen the community-based participatory model at the core of the collaborative work. There are additional examples involving UNC Asheville, as well as Warren Wilson College, Mars Hill College, and other higher education institutions in the area.

The efforts in Asheville demonstrate the potential for the coming together of multisectoral stakeholders to consider and to tailor to local needs in the areas of food and social and economic well-being. There also are many lessons. Based on these experiences, we recommend the following strategies for cultivating food sovereignty:

Organizations and Institutions

Provide only healthier items in all food distribution (see the Feeding America's Foods to Encourage guidance (Feeding America 2015)).

Accept donations, contributions, sponsorships, or partnerships only with organizations, businesses, or institutions that provide adequate wages and benefits to their employees (Just Economics in Asheville conducts a Living Wage certification for local businesses).

Engage communities as collaborators in intervention design of community-based organizations by working with residents' associations, holding public forums, and connecting with organizations that already include participatory methods.

Share financial, training, and other resources with communities where members are devoting their time and energy outside of their regular work and commitments by ensuring that community members' time is incorporated into grant budgets, for example.

Encourage anchor institutions, such as hospitals, schools, and churches, to identify specific individuals within the organizations to devote time to addressing food insecurity.

Pay equally across racial/ethnic, gender, and class lines as well as across job descriptions.

Policy Makers

Adopt policies that support urban agriculture, living wage, and community development that does not displace residents (Sanders and Shattuck [2011] present several model policies in their resource guide for local foods policy makers and practitioners).

Create programs that allocate and prioritize grants to communities of lower wealth, and incorporate technical assistance and evaluation assistance.

Individuals

Plant a garden at your home.

Work in a community garden and in relationship with others.

Participate in racial and other equity training programs.

Support businesses and policies that pay a living wage, source local foods, and
limit waste.

Ultimately, the question of outcomes remains. While the efforts are well documented in this case example and more broadly in Asheville, we are still in the early stages of measuring the impact. Whether local efforts will lead to elimination of food insecurity is unclear, or, as Philip McMichael (2014, 358) concludes in the final chapter of *Globalization and Food Sovereignty*, we will come to see that "localization of food markets is a necessary but not sufficient condition for food sovereignty."

Recently, Robert Gottleib described food justice as "where, how, and what we eat" (Gottleib and Joshi 2013, 7). We assert that the *who* also greatly matters. We believe and have seen that leadership in communities that are most affected by food insecurity and other injustices is critical to their own liberation and to the liberation of all of us. If evidence is required, perhaps we can only look at what has happened to our communities in the absence of community leadership and ownership of food and other systems. Maybe the real result we are looking for is a day when Foodtopia is a place where community garden signs are bigger than parked food-relief trucks.

Appendix

Asheville City Food Action Plan
Goals:

The City of Asheville commits to participating in the Asheville Buncombe Food Policy Council efforts and supports the following shared goals:

1.   Improve the quality of life for those in need by increasing access to food for people who experience food insecurity.
2.   Continue growing a robust regional food economy by increasing production and consumption of regional food and food products.
3.   Strive to meet all nutritional needs of the community with regionally produced foods.
4.   Work to prepare for short-term food emergencies and long-term food security.
5.   Collaborate with regional partners to achieve all food policy goals.

Provisions:

1.   Utilize the Unified Development Ordinance (UDO) as a tool to support food policy goals by amending the UDO as needed to remove barriers to local food production and distribution. For example, but not limited to, priorities such as community gardens, urban agriculture, and use of mobile markets in residentially zoned districts under certain circumstances such as farmers' markets.
2.   Optimize permitting and regulatory services for farmers' markets.

3. Prioritize partnering to find a long term permanent location for the Asheville City Market.

4. Pursue establishing local food purchasing policies for the City of Asheville through clarity on existing state legislation as well as state enabling legislation where needed.

5. Seek partnerships to incorporate regional food and beverage options into the US Cellular Center concessions, as well as city-run events.

6. Create a public private partnership for implementing a citywide curbside composting program that complements trash and recycling services. A successful partnership would improve regional economic development and provide compost regionally to support healthy ecological soil systems.

7. Include use of edible landscaping as a priority for public property such as parks, greenways and/or right of ways. In support of this, foster relationships with strong community partners who wish to access edible landscaping and/or use underutilized public land for food production.

8. Encourage partnerships for food production that supports organic and permaculture principles by identifying arable underutilized city-owned land for lease or sale. Pursue methods to make information about such land available to the public.

9. Update the city recommended plant list for developers to include edible plants and remove exotic and invasive species.

10. Include safe and convenient pedestrian, bicycle, and transit connections between residential neighborhoods and community gardens, food banks, grocery stores and farmers' markets as a priority when evaluating transportation projects.

11. Include achieving food policy goals as a priority when allocating Community Development Block Grants.

12. Support Asheville Buncombe Food Policy Council efforts to set baselines and metrics for achieving food policy goals. Play an active role in providing access to existing city data when needed.

13. Encourage food distribution by engaging underserved communities who live in food deserts. Support community efforts by co-designing incentives that establish neighborhood based markets that provide healthy food.

REFERENCES

Alkon, Alison Hope, and Julian Agyeman. 2011. *Cultivating Food Justice: Race, Class, and Sustainability*. Boston: MIT Press.

Alkon, Alison Hope, and Christie Grace McCullen. 2011. "Whiteness and Farmers Markets: Performances, Perpetuations . . . Contestations?" *Antipode* 43 (4): 937–59.

Allen, Erika. 2010. *Growing Community Food Systems*. Healdsburg, CA: Watershed Media. *library.uniteddiversity.coop/Cooperatives/Food/Growing_Community_Food_Systems-Post_Carbon_Reader.pdf; www.postcarbon.org/publications/growing-community-food-systems/.*

Burtonstreet. 2011. "E. W. Pearson and Local Self-Reliance." *Burtonstreet* (blog). *burtonstreet.org/e-w-pearson-local-self-reliance/.*

Eshleman, John T., Michelle Schroeder-Moreno, and Angel Cruz. 2016. *The Western North Carolina Appalachian Foodshed Project Community Food Security Assessment.* *www.appalachianfoodshedproject.org/documents/AFP_WNC%20CFSA_Final.pdf.*

Etheredge, George. 2014. "Sunday Frame: Pisgah View Peace Garden." *Asheville Citizen-Times: Behind the Frame,* July 11. *blogs2.citizen-times.com/photography/2014/07/11/sunday-frame-pisgah-view-peace-gardens/.*

Feeding America. 2015. *Feeding America's Foods to Encourage Background. hungerandhealth. feedingamerica.org/wp-content/uploads/legacy/mp/files/tool_and_resources/files/f2e-background-detail.v1.pdf.*

Feldman, Amanda, and Emily Kujawa. 2012. *Asheville-Buncombe Food Policy Council: Year One Snapshot. abfoodpolicy.org/wp-content/uploads/2012/12/AB-FPC_report_11–15–12.pdf*

Food Action and Research Center (FRAC). 2013. *Food Hardship in America 2012 Data for the Nation, States, 100 MSAs, and Every Congressional District. frac.org/pdf/food_hardship_2012.pdf.*

Forbes, David. 2014. "Asheville Public Housing Agency, Residents Facing Unprecedented Overhaul." *Carolina Public Press,* June 24. *www.carolinapublicpress.org/19592/asheville-public-housing-agency-residents-facing-unprecedented-overhaul.*

Freire, Paulo. 1974. *Pedagogy of the Oppressed.* New York: Seabury.

Giancatarino, Anthony, and Simran Noor. 2014. "Building the Case for Racial Equity in the Food System." W. K. Kellogg Foundation. *www.centerforsocialinclusion.org/wp-content/uploads/2014/07/Building-the-Case-for-Racial-Equity-in-the-Food-System.pdf.*

Gottlieb, Richard, and Anupama Joshi. 2013. *Food Justice.* Boston: MIT Press.

Guthman, Julie. 2011. "'If They Only Knew': The Unbearable Whiteness of Alternative Food." In *Cultivating Food Justice: Race, Class, and Sustainability,* edited by A. H. Alkon and J. Agyeman, 264–81. Boston: MIT Press.

Harnack, Lisa, Mary Hearst, and Megan Harrison. 2012. *Report to Feeding America: Evaluation of the Nutritional Quality of Back Pack Program Menus.* St. Paul: University of Minnesota Press.

Holt Giménez, Eric, and Yi Wang. 2011. "Reform or Transformation? The Pivotal Role of Food Justice in the US Food Movement." *Race/Ethnicity* 5 (1): 83–102.

hooks, bell. 2012. *Writing beyond Race: Living Theory and Practice.* New York: Routledge.

Johns Hopkins Center for a Livable Future. N.d. "Baltimore City Food Swamps." *mdfoodsystemmap.org/wp-content/uploads/2013/01/Atlas_CLF-Food-Swamp_final.pdf.*

Judson, Sarah M. 2010. "Twilight of a Neighborhood." *Crossroads* 14 (1): 1–16.

Kicinski, Leah R. 2012. "Characteristics of Short and Long-Term Food Pantry Users." *Michigan Sociological Review* 26: 58–74.

Korkki, Phyllis. 2012. "Food Banks Expand beyond Hunger." *New York Times,* November 8.

McCraig, Wendy. 2014. "Power and Poverty—Race Dialog Part 2." *Wendy McCraig* (blog). *wendymccaig.com/2014/12/01/power-and-poverty-%E2%80%93-race-dialog-part-2/.*

McMahon, Martha. 2014. *Local Food: Food Sovereignty or Myth of Alternative Consumer Sovereignty.* Toronto: University of Toronto Press.

McMichael, Philip. 2014. "The Food Sovereignty Lens." In *Globalization and Food Sovereignty: Global and Local Change in the New Politics of Food,* edited by P. Andrée, J. Ayres, M. J. Bosia, and J.-M. Massicottee. Toronto: University of Toronto Press.

Minkler, Meredith, and Nina Wallerstein 2008. *Community-Based Participatory Research for Health: From Process to Outcomes.* San Francisco: Jossey-Bass.

Paynter, Sharon, Maureen Berner, and Emily Anderson. 2011. "When Even the 'Dollar Value Meal' Costs Too Much: Food Insecurity and Long-Term Dependence on Food Pantry Assistance." *Public Administration Quarterly* 35 (1): 53.

People's Institute for Survival and Beyond (PISAB). N.d. "Who We Are." *www.pisab.org/who-we-are.*

Ratcliffe, Caroline, Signe-Mary McKernan, and Sisi Zhang. 2011. "How Much Does the Supplemental Nutrition Assistance Program Reduce Food Insecurity?" *American Journal of Agricultural Economics* 93 (4): 1082–98.

Roncarolo, Federico, Caroline Adam, Sherri Bisset, and Louise Potvin. 2015. "Traditional and Alternative Community Food Security Interventions In Montreal, Quebec: Different Practices, Different People." *Journal of Community Health* 40: 200.

Sanders, Beth, and Annie Shattuck. 2011. *Cutting through the Red Tape: A Resource Guide for Local Food Policy Practitioners and Organizers. foodfirst.org/wp-content/uploads/2013/12/PB19-Cutting_Through_the_Red_Tape.pdf.*

Sezak-Blatt, Ariyanna. 2010. "Sowing Deeper Seeds." *Mountain Express*, August 3. *mountainx.com/living/farm-garden/080410sowing_deeper_seeds/.*

Shaefer, H. Luke, and Kathryn Edin 2013. "Rising Extreme Poverty in the United States and the Response of Federal Means-Tested Transfer Programs." University of Michigan, National Poverty Center.

Talkin, Erik. 2012. "Food Banks—Today and Tomorrow." *From Hunger to Health* (blog). *hungerintohealth.com/.*

Tarasuk, Valerie. 2011. "A Critical Examination of Community-Based Responses to Household Food Insecurity in Canada." *Health Education and Behavior* 28 (4): 487–99.

TripAdvisor. 2011. "TripAdvisor Presents 2011 Travelers' Choice Food and Wine Destinations Award." *www.tripadvisor.com/PressCenter-i4859-c1-Press_Releases.html.*

US Census Bureau. 2015. "State and County QuickFacts: Asheville (City), North Carolina." *quickfacts.census.gov/qfd/states/37/3702140.html.*

Urban Agriculture Alliance. N.d. Urban Alliance Facebook page. *facebook.com/pg/UrbanAgricultureAlliance/about/?ref=page_internal.*

US Department of Agriculture Economic Research Service. 2015. "Food Access Research Atlas." *www.ers.usda.gov/data-products/food-access-research-atlas/go-to-the-atlas.aspx.*

17

Hunger in the Land of Plenty
Local Responses to Food Insecurity in Iowa

GABRIELLE ROESCH-MCNALLY, JACQUELINE NESTER, ANDREA
BASCHE, ERIC CHRISTIANSON, AND EMILY ZIMMERMAN

> The answer to poverty is not cheap food, but rather, livable wages. Working for a wage should not be the only thing you do; we must build community through school gardens and reinvigorating food into all we do. People are empowered to eat food with dignity. Food at First here in Ames is a great example of this.
>
> —*Flora and Roesch-McNally 2014, 4*

Story County (estimated population 92,406 in 2013) lies in the heart of central Iowa, a state renowned for its remarkable agricultural productivity. Iowa leads all states for production of corn, soybean, and hogs. Revenues from agricultural products in Iowa total more than $30 billion annually according the 2012 Agricultural Census (USDA-NASS 2014). This productivity stems from a favorable natural and political environment. The temperate climate, productive soils, and gentle topography are ideal for our production system of commodity agriculture facilitated by federal policies, which include subsidized crop insurance and commodity payments (Horrigan, Lawrence, and Walker 2002). Despite this productivity and political support for commodity production, a very small amount of acreage in Iowa produces food crops such as fruits and vegetables. Within Story County, the amount of cropland dedicated to fruit, vegetable, and nut production per one thousand residents is 2.4 acres, compared to 3.7 acres statewide, which is much lower than the US average of 32 acres per one thousand residents (ISUEO 2014).

Paradoxically, in this land so perfectly suited for agriculture, there is an increasing demand for food assistance. Iowa State University Extension and Outreach (ISUEO) estimates 16,366 people live in poverty in Story County, a 20.1 percent poverty rate, compared to a statewide average of 12.2 percent (2014). ISUEO further estimates that 15.2 percent of Story County residents are food insecure, representing nearly 14,000 individuals. Comparatively, the statewide rate is 12.7 percent (ISUEO 2014).

Compounding the problem, 45 percent of people who are food insecure in Story County do not qualify for direct government assistance because their income is above the economic threshold set for federal food assistance, and so they depend on charitable efforts to meet their needs. According to Feeding America's statistics, Story County is the most food insecure county in Iowa (Gundersen, Engelhard, and Waxman 2015). The juxtaposition of a productive agricultural system with persistent hunger and need for food assistance is widely apparent in Story County and has inspired community-based efforts to address food needs.

Through this chapter, we analyze the work of Food at First (FAF), a nonprofit that has emerged in response to the need for food assistance in Story County. Their work addresses the food needs of Story County residents by providing a daily free meal program and market as well as the recent development of a community garden. We illustrate the benefits of the FAF effort dedicated to building community-based solutions to hunger and food insecurity through a form of food democracy. We also explore key challenges associated with doing this work, including pragmatic issues of retaining and engaging volunteers. Further, we examine limitations of this model by exploring the underlying causes of food insecurity and how this organization contests as well as perpetuates a neoliberal model of food assistance. This neoliberal focus emphasizes individual responsibility and corporate charitable donations rather than collective, and/or government-level, responsibility for community food insecurity. We hope to raise important questions about how this community-driven work critically improves food security and a broader sense of community while still falling short of addressing poverty and inequality, the underlying reason for food insecurity in Ames and across the country.

Food at First: Feeding Folks, "No Questions Asked"

Food at First, a 501(c)(3) organization, began operation in 2004. This food assistance program distributes food to those in need through a daily free meal program and four weekly market distributions (see Table 17.1). Rather than adopting the title of a "soup kitchen" or "food pantry," the program emphasizes a community meal program and market that welcomes everyone to participate as recipients, preparers, and growers of food. Food at First exists entirely through the work of hundreds of volunteers who prepare meals and organize food distributions, with only one part-time paid staff member. According to FAF director Chris Martin, twenty-five thousand volunteer hours per year keep FAF functioning. This volunteer time equals twelve full-time paid staff working forty hours per week, providing a value of nearly $600,000 per year in employee wages.[1] Martin notes that FAF's proximity to Iowa State University (ISU) shapes its success, noting, "Every student that comes to ISU has to do some kind of service along the way."

Food at First is unique in Story County because it does not require socioeconomic information or photo identification from customers.[2] All FAF services are open to everyone, and no questions are asked regarding income, employment, or other socioeconomic details. FAF is one of sixteen food assistance programs in Story County (Mid-Iowa Community Action 2014) and is the only food assistance program in the region that does not require photo identification or place constraints on the number of visits. This approach is a less stigmatizing food intervention approach; research on this topic has found that in general, creating less social distance between volunteers and customers can reduce

TABLE 17.1. Highlights of Food at First food security strategies implemented as part of its effort to address hunger in Story County, Iowa

FAF Food Security Strategies	Highlights
Accessible Food	• Anyone can utilize FAF services, no questions asked • Customers can go to as many food distributions and/or meals • Market supports ~40,000 individuals who received food items. Meals: ranges from 30-130 people daily, up to 300-500 for holidays, approximately 24,000 individual meals annually (2014 estimates).
Decentralized Food Sourcing	• Volunteers pickup surplus food from local businesses, such as Iowa State University, local grocery stores and multinational corporations (e.g., Walmart) • Volunteer run community garden dedicated to growing fresh food for FAF • Local farmers and gardeners donate surplus fruits and vegetables
Diversity of Foods	• Perishable and non-perishable items donated (over 200 tons of food a year, worth nearly $1 million USD) • Staple items include canned food items, frozen meats, frozen processed foods, rice, pasta, and prepared desserts • Fresh fruits and vegetables from diverse sources
Committed Volunteers	• Estimated 25,000 annual hours of volunteer labor (Equivalent to 12 full-time employees) • Blurred lines between volunteers and customers • Diverse group of volunteers (churches, schools, friends, families, etc.)
Community Emphasis	• Volunteers are encouraged to eat/mingle with customers • People come to meals for companionship • Diverse mix of community members who join in at meals and free market

the stigma associated with food banks and other forms of emergency food aid (Molnar et al. 2001; Poppendieck 1999). This finding is supported by our conversations with FAF customers and volunteers, who repeatedly refer to FAF as a family and a community. This is in part because the "no questions asked" policy creates less division between the recipients and volunteers. FAF does not require volunteers to wear T-shirts, nametags, or other identifying materials while working with customers; therefore, there is no clear delineation between those who are serving and those who are being served. As we will explore, these blurred boundaries between volunteer and customer strengthens FAF's impact. The "no questions asked" policy provides flexibility to deliver emergency assistance in instances of both temporary economic hardships and more protracted poverty, without the barriers of access to formal government food assistance.

Food at First collects no demographic or socioeconomic data from customers, but volunteers do count participation at every meal and market distribution. Daily meal attendance ranges from 30 to 130 customers, with popular community holiday meals reaching over three hundred people. At market distributions, where FAF customers shop for dry goods and perishables that include fresh vegetables and fruit, attendees are asked how many people are in their household to estimate the number of individuals being served. Attendance at the market, open four times a week, has been steadily increasing, from approximately sixteen thousand individuals in 2011 to forty thousand in 2014. We further estimate from average meal attendance that in 2014 FAF provided twenty-four thousand meals. Because FAF does not require photo identification to participate and does not keep track of "unique" visitors, it is difficult to estimate how many of the food insecure within Ames and Story County are reached. However, these figures offer a picture of the overall need among those using FAF's services.

Food at First has fully integrated gleaned food into their kitchen and pantry, making significant impact in reducing food waste in our community. With entirely volunteer labor, FAF uses two hundred tons of gleaned food (food sourced from many locations that would otherwise go to waste) per year, an estimated US$1 million in retail annually, for meals and groceries for thousands of people in need (Chris Martin, FAF director, personal communication, May 2, 2015). The type of food available from gleaning highlights the paradox of our food system, in which systematized overproduction and protracted food insecurity exist side by side. More specifically, a tour of the FAF market reveals the kind of food produced in large abundance in the US food system. Much of what is available at FAF is often heavily processed, nutrient-poor, and calorie-rich foods, including large amounts of meat products, as well as bread, pasta, or other carbohydrates. More nutritionally dense options, including fresh and canned produce, are available sporadically. Some of the major food donations come from local grocery stores, which include Walmart, HyVee, Aldi's, Sam's Club, and food services at Iowa State University.

Food at First does not have an explicit mission statement. However, from our collective volunteer work with the organization and discussions with key leaders and customers, we see FAF operating within two paradigms, one encompassing community building that values greater food democratization and the other perpetuating a charity-based model that emphasizes a neoliberal approach to emergency food security. In this chapter we refer to neoliberalism as the idea that food insecurity can be managed by charity-driven efforts of private citizens and nongovernmental institutions, which often benefit for-profit corporations through tax deductible surplus food donations. This connects to the broader ideals of neoliberalism that emphasize "a shrinking state mandate, deregulation and privatization," which prioritizes individual freedom and responsibility (Trnka and Trundle 2014). Food democracy as a concept can take many forms; however, for the purposes of this analysis we recognize it as "the fulfillment of the human right to safe, nutritious food that has been justly [with regard to farmworkers' rights] produced" (Pesticide Action Network 2015). While we observe that FAF takes both a neoliberal and a food democratization approach to food insecurity, we recognize that neither of these approaches fully describes what FAF is and does.

A tension exists between the goals of the emergency food system that works to manage surplus food and give it away, versus a more systemic challenge of addressing food insecurity and poverty. Food at First is a small actor in a much larger emergency food system, but they do fill a gap in emergency food provision and serve a need for free food while minimizing food waste. Nonetheless, this effort does not fundamentally contest the current neoliberal paradigm because it does not address more systemic causes of hunger and poverty or consistently provide fresh and nutritionally adequate food for those in need at all times of the year. In this chapter we highlight the work of our student group, the Sustainable Agriculture Student Association (SASA), with FAF and the inherent contradictions associated with food insecurity efforts in the heart of the US Corn Belt, where the merits of the food system are regularly purported to be feeding the world (Olmstead 2011).

The efforts presented in this chapter represent our critical reflections as both Food at First volunteers (in meal preparation, food distribution, and garden development) and scholars in the field of sustainable agriculture. As part of this analysis, we conducted semistructured interviews with eleven FAF customers who regularly attend market distributions and/or daily meal service, three FAF board members, and volunteer executive director Chris Martin. We reached out to a broad group of FAF customers and board members who self-selected to speak with us at distributions and meals. We intentionally sought out one board member who has been critical to the success of the FAF garden project and the executive director. It is important to note that the FAF board consists of actively engaged members of the FAF volunteer workforce and also includes people who utilize the free market distribution and/or meals. We seek to analyze our participation in the culture and organization of FAF as active volunteer participants while bringing additional data, analysis, and literature to our exploration of the topic (Ellis, Adams, and Bochner 2011). We acknowledge that we have privilege that sets us apart from many FAF customers and volunteers due to our class membership (primarily middle and upper middle class), our race (we all identify as white), and our academic standing as current and former graduate students at Iowa State University. In order to create transparency in our analysis, we shared our preliminary analysis with the FAF board of directors, who are key stakeholders involved in the day-to-day operations of FAF, in an effort to broaden FAF's impacts in the community.

Context for the Emergency Food System

Food is recognized as one of the basic necessities for life and has been recognized as a human right.[3] Nonetheless, US food production is embedded in a commodity-oriented food system that is largely focused on national and international markets rather than ensuring local food needs, which is clearly evident right here in Story County, Iowa. For example, approximately one-third of the state's agricultural products, an estimated $10.4 billion, went to international export in 2013 (USDA-ERS). An estimated 90 percent of all food in Iowa is imported via national and international markets (Tagtow 2008). Thus, to help provide food to the needy without circumventing the market, the government's response has been federal programming to help people purchase food with programs such as Supplemental Nutrition Assistance Program (SNAP),

Supplemental Nutrition for Women, Infants, and Children (WIC), Child nutrition programs, nutrition programs for seniors, and food distribution programs. Over the last few decades these federal programs have experienced extensive benefit cuts and changes in restrictions, resulting in greater need for private sources of food assistance, such as food banks, food pantries, and soup kitchens.

Though private food assistance programs are serving a need, some argue they take the responsibility away from the government to provide a more comprehensive food safety net (Riches 2002). In 2014, the largest network of food banks and pantries, known as Feeding America, diverted and distributed 2.5 billion pounds of otherwise to be disposed of food. Some argue that food waste reduction has become the main focus of food banks, while feeding people in need has become a secondary priority (Tarasuk and Eakin 2005; Winne 2005). Recently, private emergency food systems, such as Food at First, have experienced large increases in demand from the continuing effects of the Great Recession from 2007 to 2009. In the case of FAF, customers coming to the free market distribution from 2011 to 2014 increased 183 percent, from 5,305 in 2011 (representing 16,326 individuals) to 14,993 in 2014 (representing 39,632 individuals). As noted by the director, Chris Martin, "as the number [of people seeking assistance] goes up—and [before] we went from one distribution to two, to three, to four—if those numbers get too high and it's not manageable, we'll add a day, and another day" (personal communication, May 2, 2015).

Organizations like Food at First fill a unique gap by helping people who do not qualify or who do not choose to apply for federal programs, as well as those who have experienced cuts in their federal food assistance. Feeding America estimates that 58 percent of their users also receive federal food assistance, suggesting the current federal food assistance benefit level is inadequate (Feeding America 2014). Of note is the timeliness and ability of the private emergency system to adapt to local demand in times of economic change. For instance, between 2006 and 2010, Feeding America noted there was a "46% increase in requests from emergency food assistance" due to the Great Recession ("Feeding America Concerned" 2011, 1). FAF, like other food pantries, is a private charitable response to inadequate public food assistance. In absence of public intervention, FAF helps to address community food insecurity as well as providing additional community benefits.

Benefits of the Food at First Model

> The staff here is really nice. They don't make you feel like you're poor. Sometimes you can go to places, and it's like, "Oh, why are you here?" And I mean everyone has their needs. They never ask questions, and they treat you like a human, and that's nice.
>
> —*FAF participant, personal communication, 2015*

Nationally, the emergency food system is trending toward centralization, as food distribution becomes concentrated into large and efficient warehousing systems (Campbell et al. 2013). These systems serve as wholesalers between industrial donors and the smaller food pantries, who actually deliver food to users. This centralization creates a parallel food system that mirrors the same industrial food system that has failed to eliminate hunger, even in the most productive agricultural areas of the Global North, such as central Iowa. One effort that illustrates a community group coming together to produce food locally, rather than through centralization, is the Food at First garden. The garden is a partnership between FAF, the Sustainable Agriculture Student Association (SASA), Trinity Christian Reformed Church, and other community partners. SASA is a student-led organization of graduate students at Iowa State University (ISU) in the Graduate Program in Sustainable Agriculture. The FAF garden, which started in 2013, provides a venue to connect students in sustainable agriculture with local food production and food insecure community members.

The Food at First garden produces a diverse set of fresh fruits and vegetables to widen the types of food available to FAF recipients. Approximately ten active SASA members and a few community members actively manage the FAF garden. Over sixty people, including other students and community members, participate in weekly workdays in the spring, summer, and fall to maintain the garden. Produce is harvested and used at FAF market distributions once a week, hosted at the church where the garden is located. Prior to the 2015 growing season, SASA members surveyed FAF customers to identify their perceptions of the garden, perceived benefits and challenges, and preferences for produce. The goal was to democratize the selection of produce and to try to include more FAF customers in the work of the garden in an effort to build more buy-in. Many customers spoke about their interest in healthy and nutritional eating, including increasing the availability of fresh vegetables. One participant noted, "I am trying to eat more healthy, a healthier diet, even more fruits and vegetables," and another recalled the garden produce from previous seasons saying, "Well, the tomatoes, cucumbers, and peppers, I used all of those, and the onions. . . . I remember walking out and looking at the garden last year." FAF customers often share appreciation for the fresh fruits and vegetables at the monthly meals prepared by SASA.

Food at First is challenging the tendency toward centralization of food support systems by providing a diversity of sources of food and by deliberately involving community partners in the production, distribution, and preparation of food and meals. A large amount of food still comes from the mainstream agricultural/food sector but is accessed through community-based relationships between FAF volunteers and businesses within the community. In addition to partnerships with these businesses, community members bring vegetables from home gardens, and local farmers and community-supported agriculture (CSA) programs donate boxes of produce, and other partners grow food specifically for donation to the program. This diversity of sourcing and involvement of community partners is an attempt to build on the tenets of food democracy via a more locally controlled approach to food acquisition and a more democratized emergency food supply. Additionally, this effort integrates a diverse group of community members into the efforts of FAF, ranging from local larger-scale farmers bringing truckloads of sweet potatoes and sweet corn, to smaller-scale organic farmers dropping off leftover vegetables from the farmers' market.

Community development offered by Food at First is derived from building more local food security through a diversified food-provisioning system, run by a large group of volunteers, with a policy of "no questions asked." One of the biggest successes of

FAF is the power of volunteer work shared by a large but disparate group of local community members, from college students and church leaders to FAF recipients who also volunteer for the organization. Volunteers simply sign up to prepare and cook meals with little top-down management or oversight. Chris Martin, FAF director, noting the success of the community of volunteers, said: "So, you're taking all that food [estimated at two hundred tons], serving all those people [estimated at forty thousand], with basically 99.9 percent volunteer labor. That's a success. . . . It's a hodgepodge of different groups, churches, and service clubs, and you guys [graduate students], and random people off the street that come together and get it done, single-mindedly" (personal communication, May 2, 2015).

Though individuals from organizations (e.g., fraternities, churches, etc.) frequently sign up together, other partnerships often form for a single meal. Our graduate student club has often been joined by other graduate student groups, churches, and undergraduates who assist with preparing and serving meals. This bottom-up approach to preparing and cooking a meal embodies food democracy and community building by creating partnerships and relationships among volunteers and their organizations. Martin, emphasizes the true community among volunteers, stating:

> I believe that volunteers get almost as much out of it, if not more, than the shoppers and diners do. I think FAF is filling a need for volunteers, a big need. It did for me. And I'm not alone in that, you know. We all need to be needed and appreciated, need to be valued. . . . You've got sort of a family at those meals in the dining room, but you also have a family in the back [with volunteers]. . . . And people are committed to it like its family, in terms of not giving up and so on. (personal communication, May 2, 2015)

In addition to building community among volunteers and partner organizations, Food at First has created a space for community among its clients. This is further evidence of FAF's role in creating food democracy not only around food access but also around shared experiences, friendships, and support networks. Chris Martin highlighted the importance of this community for customers, saying, "I think a lot of people at the meals come for companionship. We have lots of regulars. It's like a family. It *is* a family" (personal communication, May 2, 2015). A FAF board member and frequent client echoed Martin's observation, stating, "When you're old and when your family's gone and you have no relatives, you have nothing. This [FAF] was always home for me." Interviews with clients confirmed these sentiments; one interviewee stated, "That is a big thing, I think friendliness of people, and gosh, when I started, the people who were doing this were just so friendly, and they still are, I mean the volunteers and all, but slowly everyone else has gotten more and more friendly too, I think. It is like we have a community here. We call ourselves a family." Another interviewee noted, "I think the food is part of it. The social is also part of it. . . . It saves me the issue of, it is not just money, it saves me the issue of having to buy and having to cook every night alone."

Evocative words used by clients, such as "family" or "community" provide evidence to the inclusiveness and openness that Food at First has successfully cultivated by creating an culture of dignity around food access. Because FAF has fostered such an environment, most people feel welcomed, accepted, and most importantly, respected and valued as whole human beings at FAF. One client noted that FAF provides support for people with diverse and complicated financial situations, saying, "So I don't like this idea that you are either terribly poor or you can afford it, you know what I mean. It is not black and white; there is a lot of gray in there, and that is one of the reasons why accepting everyone [at FAF] is the only right approach." Another echoed this by saying, "[The FAF way] is the only way to do it with dignity because you cannot discriminate; you can't say 'you are poor, you are not.' You know? It just doesn't work that way." Finally, another market customer suggested that FAF fills an important gap for food needs among those with middle-income situations: "I'm not poor, but I've got two kids in college. You take those college expenses out, you don't have money left over for yourself. Just knowing that it doesn't matter, you know . . . I don't have to walk in dirty and grimy and unemployed. I can still come in as a middle-class person and be respected for that."

The ability of Food at First to be comprehensive in providing food access to all people, no questions asked, is an important facet of the program's success. But that is not and should not be the only metric by which this effort is judged. Importantly, by providing a valuable, locally controlled community resource, FAF is actively cultivating and advocating for an increasingly democratic food system through its alliances with local farms, its volunteers and partners, and its customers.

Challenges and Limitations of the Food at First Model

> The food industry will make its endless abundance available to food banks only if it can link its waste removal and food surplus utilization needs to its donations. And rather than take the bold steps necessary to end poverty, food insecurity's ultimate cause, we use our large and complex network of public and private anti-hunger and nutrition programs to manage poverty instead.
>
> —Winne 2008, 175

We have illustrated benefits of the Food at First model for providing access to freshly cooked meals, market distributions, and fresh produce from our community garden, all of which provide food and meet social needs for the Ames community. These connections are powerful and help create the building blocks of community food security (Fisher 2002) in a more democratic manner. However, there are challenges associated with this food security model, the first being pragmatic issues with retaining and engaging volunteers in the ongoing efforts to increase access to healthy foods for those who are food insecure. While the power of the volunteer method is wonderful, Chris Martin has noted that it is "a double-edged sword [because] it's all volunteer. The problem with volunteers is that you can't boss them around. They're not employees; they are there of their own free will. So it's kind of like herding cats." Additionally, many of the people that we spoke to suggested that a gap remains in engaging more of the FAF customers in more empowering, and potentially skill-building, roles, including meal preparation, market distributions, or garden work. We and others (e.g., local shelters, Iowa State University Extension and Outreach, etc.) have attempted several events (e.g., cooking and nutrition classes, food processing and preservation events, etc.), but consistent and reliable volunteers remain difficult to identify and retain. It may be unreasonable to expect that many of the people who use the FAF services would also want to garden with us. Many of them struggle with health and disability issues, and most, from our experience, are members of the working poor and as a result have limited time, and perhaps desire, to garden in their free time.

One challenge, as much as opportunity, is the effort to build community engagement with Food at First, particularly inspiring sustained volunteer effort rather than variable and occasional volunteering. In particular, we have struggled with maintaining volunteers in our garden with only a small group of individuals taking leadership roles. To build greater community buy-in we have created community events including garden tours, cooking classes, and help with distribution days at Trinity Christian Reformed Church on Saturdays in the summer to give out vegetables and encourage FAF customers to come to the garden. However, there is a real tension among volunteers, who, according to a FAF board member, "are [normally] flying by the seat of their pants," to complete extra projects that require additional time, planning, and outreach, because the core volunteer group, including board members, are stretched very thin.

This tension is not unique to our efforts, as other community gardens have also struggled with being relevant to communities (Wright and Middendorf 2008; Ogawa 2009), particularly as food insecure members of the community did not create the FAF garden. We have struggled with creating a space where the efforts for growth and development are not coming from a top-down group of volunteers but rather are informed by the community in a way that is nonhierarchical and participatory. We worry that our efforts will not be sustainable if we cannot find others, particularly those who are not students, to carry on this work that we have personally seen such great value in.

One reason that grassroots volunteer efforts are difficult is because many Americans have individualized the causes and solutions of hunger and food insecurity. This individualization drives a more neoliberal approach to volunteerism, often associated with a charity model of giving back to the community by offering money or limited time rather than committing to the larger effort of addressing the food gap. Mark Winne suggests quite appropriately that "community gardens can help people fill the food gap only when they are motivated and encouraged to do the hard work that forms the building blocks of community" (2008, 66). As we explored in the section above, Food at First has helped to create a sense of community and in many ways a sense of family, but there are challenges that remain with engaging more people in sustained volunteerism. One ray of light is this idea that through the vehicle of FAF, many people, especially young people who volunteer through the local college or high school, gain an appreciation for volunteerism: "It's possible that that sense of volunteerism can be instilled in that person [who volunteers for FAF]. And it's possible that that person will go through the rest of their life with the volunteerism mentality. And that's a good thing. They can teach their kids that, tell their friends about it" (Chris Martin, personal communication, May 2, 2015).

Another challenge for the sustainability of the Food at First model is the reliance on donations from large corporations. These companies donate a tremendous amount of food, including meat and other fresh foods that would otherwise be destined for the dumpster. These companies utilize the free volunteer labor force of FAF to move that food to market distribution and meal preparation while receiving a tax break for their donations, which requires FAF volunteers to do daily pickups and deliveries of gleaned food. Although many for-profit companies donate immense amounts of food to organizations like FAF, many, particularly Walmart, are infamous for their low wages and propensity toward offering part-time work, making it difficult for families and individuals to transition out of poverty (Goetz and Swaminathan 2006). According to research by Americans for Tax Fairness, Walmart employees in Iowa receive more than $73 million in annual public assistance (2014).

There is a notable paradox here when corporations can choose to pay their workers low wages, in part because their employees can and often do rely on social safety nets such as Food at First; meanwhile these same corporations receive a tax break for their charitable donation of food waste. In 2013, Walmart donated 1.3 percent of their pretax profits, and while their donations of cash have declined, their donations of food have increased (Frostenson and O'Neil 2013). Ultimately FAF is "at the mercy of what we are given, [and] we don't have a big budget; we have a very small budget" (FAF board member, personal communication, April 29, 2015). This reliance on what FAF is given by large corporations means a lot of what is donated consists of processed foods with little nutritional value, especially in the winter months, when there are few fresh fruits and vegetables, and instead includes processed canned goods high in sodium and sugar. This reliance on surplus food waste, generated by the market structure, is what runs the emergency food system. This is ultimately a liability because it places organizations like FAF at the whim of corporations and institutions. This situation is a challenge to building greater food democracy and may provide further obstacles for organizations to expose and address root causes of food insecurity and poverty.

Poverty Alleviation and Food Insecurity

> I think it's a sad commentary on society that we have to do what we are doing. It's ridiculous we have to have a community meal program and food pantries. You know? . . . It's a stopgap measure; it's not solving a problem. It's a Band-Aid, which is great: people need Band-Aids. But you know there are bigger societal issues at play that we can't really do anything about.
>
> —*Chris Martin, personal communication, May 2, 2015*

More critically, perhaps, than the challenges of engaging volunteers and recipients more meaningfully in the efforts of Food at First is the crisis model of food assistance that is focused on the symptoms of a much larger problem, which is poverty and inequality. This represents a core tension between our efforts at building a more democratically managed and decentralized emergency food response and the limitations of a more neoliberal model of food assistance that emphasizes a charity-based approach. Food systems experts such as Mark Winne claim that "we must seriously examine the role of food banking, which requires that we no longer praise its growth as a sign of our generosity and charity, but instead recognize it as a symbol of our society's failure to hold government accountable for hunger, food insecurity, and poverty" (2008, 184).

Poverty alleviation is a complex task and one that will require systemic changes to many aspects of our society. Food banks are in a special position to promote a larger conversation about hunger and its root causes (Winne 2008). After being involved in Food at First, we recognize there is a great deal of work that goes into the work of putting a Band-Aid on a broken food system; this includes hours spent picking up food that would otherwise be thrown away, growing the food, preparing it, and sharing it with those who need it. The larger task of empowering people to get out of poverty through job training programs, mental health services, and community efforts to raise awareness about poverty and food insecurity takes time and resources not always available. Empowerment efforts are not easily measured because they cannot be counted in pounds of food or number of meals served, and it takes significantly more time to assess their success. Working at the policy level takes specific skills, abilities, and resources that not all organizations have. There is no one policy solution to end poverty and hunger but rather a combination of many efforts such as addressing the tax code, unequal wage distribution, and entrenched poverty in communities with few jobs or opportunities for livable wages. While many FAF board members acknowledge these challenges, there is hesitancy in addressing these systemic problems because of how overextended volunteers already are. Nonetheless, Food at First has started to rethink the notion of feeding the hungry by focused on finding strategies to improve the types of food available, including fresh fruits and vegetables, by developing a garden space for diverse produce to extend the growing season. The FAF policy of creating less of a division between the "haves" and the "have nots" is another strategy for transforming the traditional charity-based model. The organization fiercely defends its ability to minimize the amount of red tape required of customers so that they can remain a free market, which "should be free in all aspects. . . . [Having to ask questions of customers] to justify [giving out] this food that would otherwise be wasted or thrown out is just ridiculous; it is silly; it is stupid; it is embarrassing" (FAF board member, personal communication, April 29, 2015).

Concluding Reflections

> [I think] anyone at FAF would love to not have a FAF. You know, to be put out of business would be a fantastic thing. To solve the problem, to not be needed would be great, but until then, somebody has to help out.
>
> —*FAF board member, personal communication, April 29, 2015*

Work still needs to be done to address the root causes of hunger and food insecurity in our community rather than solely celebrating charity-based models that are attempting to meet emergency food needs of food insecure Americans. This case study of Food at First finds that a volunteer-based model, although successful on many levels, does not provide a sustainable solution to chronic food insecurity in this paradoxically rich agricultural region. As we have delved into in this work we have learned more about the challenges associated with nutrition and creating greater access to healthy food, which is essential given the current challenges with obesity, particularly among those who receive food assistance (ISUEO 2014; USDA-FNS 2015).

We have described several instances where the Food at First model counteracts some of the more neoliberal tendencies in the private emergency food system. We realize that these characteristics—such as the "no questions asked" policy, blurred division between customers and volunteers, and emphasis on acquiring food from several different organizations—may not be sustained in the long run. Economic downturns or a continued increase in customers may require Food at First leaders to seek food from governmental sources such as the Food Bank of Iowa, which does require the collection of socioeconomic information from recipients. Additionally, the efforts associated with managing food donations from a broad set of sources, as well as the work that is required of a volunteer-based organization where demand only seems to be increasing, begs the question of where and when poverty alleviation work can be done and whether it can be accomplished by leaders and volunteers who are already working hard to make food available to those in need, no questions asked. This raises the question of not only who should be doing that work, but also the capacity of established organizations like Food at First to expand their operation. Should organizations with limited time and resources, which serve an immediate need in the community, focus more efforts on poverty alleviation? Or is there room for existing and perhaps new organizations to address these complex set of factors? This idea is best articulated by Chris Martin, who said, "More and more I think poverty is the root problem of all of this. . . . It comes down to lack of money, lack of opportunity, lack of resources, lack of education; and then you get into this cyclical, multigenerational hole that people can't get out of. And so, what's FAF doing about that? Not really anything" (Personal Communication, May 2, 2015).

Importantly, Martin and the board of directors clearly recognize that Food at First is treating a symptom rather than a root cause; nonetheless, when presented with our analysis and reflections on expanding their vision and operation to more directly address poverty alleviation, Martin and the board of directors were largely defensive. This tension is reflective of a larger challenge associated with a certain amount of path dependency (e.g., doing the same thing because it is what you have always done) that impacts many organizations. This path dependency was reflected in our conversation with board members though language such as "It's all we can do," or "It's what we've always done." For Food at First, the pragmatic task of feeding people by managing a large amount of food waste, with limited volunteer hours, ultimately limits the capacity of the organization to develop innovative approaches or address more systemic causes of hunger because they are caught up in the busy day-to-day work of running the organization. We acknowledge the very real difficulty of actively engaging in the difficult work of meeting community food security needs while also extending a vision for solving much bigger challenges that come with addressing the root causes of hunger.

Despite these critiques and ongoing challenges, Food at First is working to build greater food democracy in the heart of the Corn Belt and has provided an opportunity for many to confront the complexity of the paradox of hunger in the land of plenty. More work must be done, but the lessons learned about building community with a shared purpose of meeting the food and social needs of many in Story County, Iowa, offer insight on what can be done elsewhere and what still needs to be done across the region and beyond; perhaps efforts such Food at First's will eventually be "complemented by a comprehensive national food program" that enshrines the right to food and adequate nutrition for all Americans (Powers 2015, 69).

This chapter is dedicated to Sonia Kendrick, a mother, veteran, farmer, and tireless advocate for a more just and accessible food system. She started this work in her backyard and went on to build a local food movement in Cedar Rapids, Iowa, which has left an indelible mark on our awareness of and commitment to a more just food system.

NOTES

1. The Independent Sector assessed the value of volunteer labor at $24.14 per hour in 2016. *www.independentsector.org/resource/the-value-of-volunteer-time/.*
2. Throughout this chapter we refer to the recipients of FAF meals and free food market distributions as customers. Food at First makes a concerted effort to refer to these individuals as customers rather than recipients to minimize social stigma associated with those who use emergency food services.
3. The United Nations Commission on Human Rights has written extensively on the human right to adequate and culturally appropriate food: *www.ohchr.org/EN/Issues/Food/Pages/FoodIndex.aspx.*

REFERENCES

Americans for Tax Fairness. 2014. "Walmart on Tax Day: How Taxpayers Subsidize America's Biggest Employer and Richest Family." Last modified April, 2015. *www.americansfortaxfairness.org/files/Walmart-on-Tax-Day-Americans-for-Tax-Fairness-1.pdf.*

Campbell, Elizabeth Catherine, Michelle Ross, and Karen L. Webb. 2013. "Improving the Nutritional Quality of Emergency Food: A Study of Food Bank Organizational Culture, Capacity, and Practices." *Journal of Hunger and Environmental Nutrition* 8 (3): 261–80.

Daponte, Beth Osborne, and Shannon Bade. 2006. "How the Private Food Assistance Network Evolved: Interactions between Public and Private Responses to Hunger." *Nonprofit and Voluntary Sector Quarterly* 35 (4): 668–90.

Ellis, Carolyn, Tony E. Adams, and Arthur P. Bochner. 2011. "Autoethnography: An Overview." *Historical Social Research/Historische Sozialforschung* 12 (1): 273–90.

Feeding America. 2014. "2014 Annual Report." *www.feedingamerica.org/our-response/about-us/annual-report/2014-annual-report.pdf.*

"Feeding America Concerned That Proposed Budget Cuts Could Lead to Increased Food Insecurity." 2011. Feeding America. *www.feedingamerica.org/hunger-in-america/news-and-updates/press-room/press-releases/feeding-america-concerned-that-proposed-budget-cuts-could-lead-to-increased-food-insecurity-in-the-us.html.*

Fisher, Andrew. 2002. "Community Food Security: A Promising Alternative to the Global Food System." *Community Food Security News,* 5.

Flora, Cornelia, and Gabrielle Elan Roesch-McNally. 2014. "Sustainable Agriculture and Social Justice: A Conversation with Dr. Cornelia Flora." *Journal of Critical Thought and Praxis* 3 (1): 3.

Frostenson, S., and M. O'Neil. 2013. "10 Companies That Gave the Most Cash in 2013." *Chronicle of Philanthropy. www.philanthropy.com/article/10-Companies-That-Gave-the/150507.*

Goetz, S. J., and H. Swaminathan. 2006. "Walmart and County Wide Poverty." *Social Science Quarterly* 87 (2): 211.

Gundersen, Craig, Emily Engelhard, and Elaine Waxman. 2015. "Map the Meal Gap 2015: Overall Food Insecurity in Iowa by County in 2013." Feeding America. *www. feedingamerica.org/hunger-in-america/our-research/map-the-meal-gap/2013/IA_AllCounties_ CDs_MMG_2013.pdf.*

Horrigan, Leo, Robert S. Lawrence, and Polly Walker. 2002. "How Sustainable Agriculture Can Address the Environmental and Human Health Harms of Industrial Agriculture." *Environmental Health Perspectives* 110 (5): 445.

ISUEO. 2014. "Poverty and Food Needs: Story County, Iowa." Iowa State University Extension and Outreach. *www.icip.iastate.edu/sites/default/files/poverty/poverty_19169.pdf.*

Mid-Iowa Community Action. 2014. "Story County Resource Guide." *www.uwstory.org/sites/ uwstory.oneeach.org/files/2014%20Resource%20Guide.pdf.*

Molnar, Joseph J., Patricia A. Duffy, La Toya Claxton, and Conner Bailey. 2001. "Private Food Assistance in a Small Metropolitan Area: Urban Resources and Rural Needs." *Journal of Sociology and Social Welfare* 28 (3): 187–209.

Ogawa, Tomoko. 2009. "Looking at Community Gardens through Neoliberal Lenses." Master's thesis, Iowa State University.

Olmstead, J. 2011. "Feeding the World? Twelve Years Later, US Grain Exports Are Up, So Too Is Hunger." Institute for Agriculture and Trade Policy, Minneapolis. *www.foodmyths.org/reports-resources/feeding-the-world-twelve-years-later-u-s-grain- exports-are-up-so-too-is-hunger/.*

Pesticide Action Network. 2015. "Food Democracy." *www.panna.org/issues/food-agriculture/ food-democracy.*

Poppendieck, J. 1999. *Sweet Charity? Emergency Food and the End of Entitlement.* New York: Penguin.

Powers, J. 2015. "The Right to Food in the US: The Need to Move Away from Charity and Advance towards a Human Rights Approach." *Right to Food and Nutrition Watch* 7: 68–69. *www.righttofoodandnutrition.org/files/Watch_2015_Article_11_eng_ %20The%20 Right%20to%20Food%20in%20the%20US.pdf.*

Riches, Graham. 2002. "Food Banks and Food Security: Welfare Reform, Human Rights and Social Policy. Lessons from Canada?" *Social Policy and Administration* 36 (6): 648–63.

Tagtow, Angie. 2008. "A Vision for 'Good Food' for Iowa: Linking Community Based Food Systems to Healthy Iowans and Healthy Communities." A report for the Leopold Center for Sustainable Agriculture.

Tarasuk, Valerie, and Joan M. Eakin. 2005. "Food Assistance through 'Surplus' Food: Insights from an Ethnographic Study of Food Bank Work." *Agriculture and Human Values* 22 (2): 177–86.

Trnka, Susanna, and Catherine Trundle. 2014. "Competing Responsibilities: Moving beyond Neoliberal Responsibilisation." *Anthropological Forum* 24 (2): 136–53.

USDA-ERS. 2015. "Definitions of Food Security." *www.ers.usda.gov/topics/food-nutrition- assistance/food-security-in-the-us/definitions-of-food-security.aspx.*

USDA-FNS. 2015. "Diet Quality of Americans by SNAP Participation Status: Data from the National Health and Nutrition Examination Survey, 2007–2010—Summary." USDA Food and Nutrition Service. *www.fns.usda.gov/sites/default/files/ops/NHANES-SNAP07–10- Summary.pdf.*

USDA-NASS. 2014. "2014 State Agriculture Overview: Iowa." Last modified May 20, 2015. *www.nass.usda.gov/Quick_Stats/Ag_Overview/stateOverview.php?state=IOWA.*

Winne, Mark. 2005. "Waste Not, Want Not?" *Agriculture and Human Values* 22 (2): 203–5.

———. 2008. *Closing the Food Gap: Resetting the Table in the Land of Plenty.* Boston: Beacon.

Wright, Wynne, and Gerard Middendorf, eds. 2008. *The Fight over Food: Producers, Consumers, and Activists Challenge the Global Food System.* Penn State Press.

18

Food Pantries on College and University Campuses

An Emerging Solution to Food Insecurity

CARMEL E. PRICE AND NATALIE R. SAMPSON

The National Center for Education Statistics (2015) reports that the costs of college (i.e., tuition and room and board) for undergraduate programs at public institutions in the United States rose 40 percent in the ten years between the 2001–2002 and 2011–2012 academic years. These increasing costs, combined with the effects of the Great Recession beginning in 2007, have resulted in increased numbers of college students experiencing food insecurity. In response, since 2010, over six hundred colleges in the United States have established a food pantry to serve their student populations, and in 2012, leaders in this movement established the College and University Food Bank Alliance (CUFBA).[1] The media have drawn some attention to food insecurity and food pantries on college campuses (Jordan 2015). However, there is a dearth of academic research on campus food pantries. To fill this void, we interviewed eight food pantry directors from campuses across the United States and six food pantry clients from a four-year public university in the Midwest. We also conducted a thorough document review of 141 campus pantries currently registered with CUFBA.[2] This chapter examines the emergence of campus food pantries in the United States and helps to develop an understanding of why they are needed. In addition, we describe the experiences of pantry directors and clients and, based on their experiences, offer best practices for the implementation of campus food pantries.

Economic and Food Insecurity among College Students

Although American culture perpetuates the myth that college students are classless, class differences on college campuses are very real and have lasting effects (Hurst 2012). The current annual price for an undergraduate program is estimated to be $14,300 at public and $37,800 at private institutions respectively, which amounts to a total of $57,200 and $151,200 for four-year degrees. Several programs have been developed to help low-income, working-class, and first-generation college students access higher education. Given public criticism over rising costs, many colleges have pondered how they can open their doors to more students from disadvantaged backgrounds (Simons 2003). However, few programs are helping low-income and working-class students cope with daily expenses after they arrive on campus, such as the costs of food or transportation (Hurst 2010). Meanwhile, the majority of students from working-class and low-income families are working part- or full-time jobs while pursuing a postsecondary degree (Hurst 2012). In contrast, students from middle- and upper-class families are using their time to develop marketable skills and professional networks through unpaid internships and research opportunities. These variances lead to well-documented differential outcomes upon graduation and beyond (Armstrong and Hamilton 2013). Essentially, college, which is often thought of as the great equalizer, exacerbates class differences (Hurst 2012).

Food insecurity on campuses has not been studied systematically, but various reports illustrate the concerning scale of this issue. A 2011 internal study by the City University of New York (CUNY) found slightly under 40 percent or roughly one hundred thousand CUNY students had experienced food insecurity while in college (Freudenberg et al. 2011). Furthermore, the CUNY study found that students who were either financially supporting themselves or working more than twenty hours a week were more likely to experience food insecurity than students who did not support themselves. A 2014 study found that 59 percent of students attending a rural midsized university in Oregon had experienced food insecurity while in college (Patton-Lopez et al. 2014). Feeding America's 2014 national report estimates that 10 percent of community food pantry clients are college students (Weinfield et al. 2014). And, according to a 2015 policy report from the Wisconsin HOPE Lab, "half of all community college students are struggling with food insecurity or housing insecurity" (Goldrick-Rab et al. 2015, 2). It is unclear if food insecurity on campuses is a new issue or just newly recognized.

Threats to food security are exacerbated on campuses because many college students do not qualify for food assistance benefits. The Supplemental Nutrition Assistance Program (SNAP) is the primary US program providing nutrition assistance to eligible low-income persons and families. Unfortunately, as the US Department of Agriculture (USDA) website explains, "Most able-bodied students ages 18 through 49 who are enrolled in college or other institutions of higher education at least half time are not eligible for SNAP benefits" (US Department of Agriculture: Food and Nutrition Service 2014b). Many undergraduate students are ineligible because they are claimed as dependents on their parents' tax returns, placing them in a higher income bracket than if they filed their taxes independently. However, even nontraditional students and graduate students, who might be more likely to file their taxes independently and thus meet SNAP income requirements, still experience eligibility problems and/or receive reduced SNAP benefits once deciding to return to school. This is because, in general, full-time students are considered ineligible for SNAP benefits. There are a few exceptions. For example, students are eligible if they are working at least twenty paid hours per week; taking care of a dependent under the age of six; or part of a state or federally financed work study program. One food pantry client we interviewed explained that her SNAP benefits were reduced from $400 to $63 a month when she enrolled in college. Another food pantry client reported that her SNAP benefits are frequently reduced, and each time she must remind her caseworker that she is an *eligible* student because she meets the exception clauses. Nevertheless, some schools are encouraging students to apply for SNAP benefits to help with the financial burdens of college. For example, in addition to its campus food pantry, Portland State University has a page on their website headed "Nutrition, it's a SNAP!" where the SNAP application process and eligibility requirements are explained.

Furthermore, if college students are able to receive SNAP benefits, they typically cannot use their benefits on campus. Despite increased awareness of food insecurity on college campuses and wider acceptance of SNAP (e.g., farmers' markets have begun to accept SNAP benefits), our research indicates that campus food vendors typically do not accept SNAP assistance as a valid form of payment. In addition, SNAP cannot be used on hot or prepared food and is instead designed to be spent on raw ingredients that will be prepared in the home (US Department of Agriculture: Food and Nutrition Service 2014b). This is problematic for students with limited mobility. For example, one pantry client reported that because she lacks reliable transportation and SNAP is not accepted on campus, she frequently spends her SNAP benefits at a gas station, where food items are often unhealthy. Goldrick-Rab and colleagues (2015) provide eleven recommendations for reducing food and housing insecurity among college students, one of which is for campus food vending services to accept SNAP benefits.

Campus Food Pantries: An Emerging Reality

A detailed document review of 141 campus food pantries that are registered with CUFBA suggests that food pantries on college campuses are both plentiful and diverse.[3] For example, there are college-based food pantry programs in thirty-nine states including both urban and rural locales. The size of the schools where these pantries are located range from 221 to 59,589 students. The majority of food pantry programs, 101 out of 141, are located at four-year public institutions. Thus, just under 29 percent (or 40 out of 141) of the food pantry programs are housed at two-year public institutions. Students from low-income or working-class families, as well as first-generation college students—who may be most prone to food insecurity—are more likely to attend a two-year or for-profit college than students from middle- and upper-class families (Hurst 2012). Of the 141 campuses with CUFBA-registered food pantries, two-year public schools have an average of 52 percent of students receiving federal Pell grants, whereas the four-year public schools have an average of 39 percent of students receiving federal Pell grants. Only two food pantry programs are located at for-profit colleges, both interestingly at art institutes.

Integrating Food Pantries into College Life

Food pantry directors offer important context about how campus pantries function. Eight pantry directors at two- and four-year public universities across the United States participated in semistructured interviews where they outlined their experiences developing and implementing campus food pantries.[4] Key themes from these interviews, as well as our thorough document review of pantries, are shared here.

Most food pantries have emerged organically out of a recognition of need, most often through student-led initiatives and sometimes through staff and faculty efforts. Need has been observed through both formal data collection processes and anecdotal evidence. At one large West Coast public university, for example, a formal needs assessment was conducted, and an unmet need on campus was discovered. This led to a proposal written by students to start a food pantry on that campus. At another Midwest public university, a pantry director told the following story:

> We were noticing that there were students who were sort of in the halls, outside of meetings, stalking, kind of walking back and forth waiting for the meetings to let out because they knew there was food in there . . . so, if lunch was being served, maybe a buffet, right? And, even to the point to where one time I was in a meeting and a student came in, and I jumped up and ran back, and I said, "Can I help you?" And she said, "Oh, I was just going to grab some lunch," or something to that nature. And I was like, "Well, no, this is a private meeting, and that's why the doors were shut, you know?" I said, "We'll be out of here at two. If there is any food remaining, you know, you can have some." She was like, "Oh, okay." She kind of just stood there. So I thought that I would go back to my seat to indicate that she should, you know, head to the exit. So I get back to my seat, and I turn around, and she is scooping food out the chafing dishes with her hands. You know, just absolutely just trying to, to eat, which was really unsettling to everyone in the room to see someone who was legitimately hungry.

At the same school, a reputable student, who served as a campus math tutor, was seen eating the leftovers from other students' plates in the cafeteria. As student hunger became increasingly visible, particularly to the Office of Student Engagement, students and staff members felt compelled to respond. Similarly, another pantry director shared stories of faculty providing students with lunch money. Some campuses even began to recognize homelessness. It is important to note that the homeless population and student population are not mutually exclusive groups; some students are homeless (Goldrick-Rab et al. 2015). Multiple students who were interviewed about their participation in campus food pantries reported living in shelters, transitional housing, and federally subsidized housing. In addition, one food pantry director described how his pantry emerged after faculty observed students sleeping in their cars.

There may not be a one-size-fits-all approach to institutionalizing campus pantries, and not all campus pantries follow the same model. Pantries may be established in various administrative units from health centers to student governments, from counseling services to student life. For example, at NYU Stony Brook, the pantry is a joint project of the Division of Campus Residences and the School of Health Technology and Management. At the University of Kentucky, the Big Blue Pantry is housed within the Center for Community Outreach. Virginia Commonwealth University's RamPantry is a collaborative effort of various faith-based student groups and staff at the Division of Student Affairs. Where the program is housed does not necessarily influence student use or the success of the program; the location reflects how the program was developed and what makes institutional sense for each particular college.

The integration of food pantries into campus life occurs in diverse ways. Pantries may act as a gateway to other campus and community resources such as career and counseling services. Pantry directors described using pantry spaces to advertise for other resources, such as community food pantries or free and reduced-price health services. Some faculty develop coursework around the pantry. On several campuses, for instance, students enrolled in nutrition and dietetic programs create health education materials or workshops to accompany food distribution. Multiple pantry directors described a relationship with their college English department, where students write about food insecurity. A variety of service-learning courses have also been developed to support campus and community pantries.

Colleges have developed other innovative strategies for addressing food insecurity and supporting their pantries. At the University of Nevada–Las Vegas and the University of Michigan–Dearborn, faculty and staff can choose to donate to the campus pantry through a payroll deduction. Some institutions with residential housing and corresponding meal plans, including the University of Nevada–Reno, have systems in place for students to donate their excess meals to eligible students. Oregon State University provides small food subsidies to low-income commuter students through the Mealbux meal card program.[5] They also partner with their University Housing and Dining Services to bring in donations, and they offer a three-dollar nutritionally balanced meal. Many schools, such as University of North Carolina–Pembroke, partner with their athletic department to bring in donations; one popular event is to encourage each fan to bring a food donation with them to an athletic event (sometimes in exchange for admission to the event).

Pantries are typically not expected to be the only source of food for students. Most pantry directors explained that their pantry was meant to be "supplemental" and "to kind of help alleviate some of their challenges—not to really have it as a place where they are going to come and grocery shop every day." Campus food pantries consider themselves to be supplemental in part because they rely heavily on inconsistent donations and because they want to stretch their resources to meet the demand. One pantry organizer stated that his biggest challenge was keeping the pantry stocked and that his largest role was fund-raising. Some campus pantries solicit money, instead of product donations, as a strategy to better meet their clients' needs. This is because: (1) pantries can purchase food cheaper through their community partnerships than individuals can buy it themselves, and (2) pantries have an intimate knowledge of students' needs. As one pantry director describes, people tend to donate their leftovers: "The reality of donations is that people look in their cabinet and say, 'Ah, we didn't make chili this winter and, you know what, now that it's sixty [degrees outside] I don't want to make chili.' So they blow the dust off the two cans of chili beans that they had in their pantry. I've never seen so many beans in my life." This results in less variety for the students: "We're up to our eyeballs in canned green beans!" notes another pantry director. However, donors may prefer giving products to giving money, and campus pantries embrace this fact. One pantry has developed a strategy to steer donations toward best meeting students' needs: "It's really hard to put together a meal when all you have is beans, pasta, and mashed potatoes. . . . I've learned over time to ask, when I'm asking folks for donations and [they] say what do you need at the store? Instead of saying "Oh, we love pasta." I Say "if you're going to get three things get me pasta, spaghetti sauce, and a vegetable." So something that will make a meal as opposed to getting me five things of pasta." To run their pantries in the most cost-effective way, directors must communicate their needs to donors and those coordinating food drives.

Because student clients may be sensitive about their food insecurity, pantry directors, staff, and student volunteers seek to provide them anonymity and respect. Pantry directors explained ways that they have been thoughtful about the pantry location and its entry points to relieve students from traversing busy spaces where they may be seen accessing the pantry. In addition, campuses are sensitive to the types of bags clients use to carry the food from the pantry. For example, one pantry lets student clients use a bag of their choice, including book bags; another provides students with bags that are donated by faculty after attending academic conferences; and another uses bags donated by the campus bookstore embellished with the university's logo. Furthermore, although most pantries collect client information for evaluation purposes or as a requirement of their affiliated food banks, many choose to do so in a very minimal way. This is another effort to make accessing the pantry a confidential and respectful process. On the campuses that receive USDA food, pantry staff and volunteers are required to participate in USDA civil rights training, and many campuses have developed similar trainings. Other campuses carefully consider the promotional messages they develop and how they speak to students. One pantry director explained:

> We're very open about the fact that we have a food pantry on our campus, and our advertising is really meant to try and normalize it. . . . You know, our advertising does not have photos that . . . sometimes services will put pictures of people looking sad, looking broken, looking down with language that implies a deficit, implies something that makes people feel like, "Wow, that is how you see me?" And, instead, our advertising does not—we do not put images of people on our advertising because we do not want to reinforce stereotypes.

On a large public university campus on the West Coast, students come to an auditorium space for their food pickup, and staff work to create a comfortable space:

> We show YouTube videos so there is a little bit of noise. They can have a conversation if they want. They don't have to sit there in silence. We create YouTube playlists. So, for example, we'll put on recipes, and we'll have cooking shows for the whole time. Or, we'll do nature videos or whatever . . . so that people can come and hang out in an environment that is relaxed. It's comfortable. . . . A lot of the practices we have in place now are directly focused on confidentiality and privacy for our clients, as well as creating a sense of comfort while they are there with us, which allows them to feel less ashamed.

Many pantries devise ways to let their clients self-select their items so they do not feel they are "being watched" or "under scrutiny." This may mean shopping by preselecting items from a list or going through the pantry as if at a grocery store to select items. Each pantry approaches issues of confidentiality and client respect differently, and a list of these strategies is reported in Appendix 1.

Student Perspectives: Balancing Need, Health, and Well-Being

Food pantry staff and volunteers offer important context about how campus pantries function; the clients also provide vital perspectives on their pantry experiences. Six students at a four-year public university in the Midwest provided their perspectives through semistructured interviews (see Appendix 2).

All six expressed extreme gratitude for their campus pantry. One student explained the impact of the pantry when her husband lost his income:

> Food. I can't cut that, you know? I still gotta feed my kids. And, um, this program was just, you know, it's a blessing. It was one less thing. I mean—you don't know how much. I said I wouldn't cry, but [wipes tears], um, I want to share, I want to share . . . um, but like you don't know how much of a ninety-nine-cent pack of spaghetti or pasta means to someone when they're struggling. And, um, this pantry, just having it on the shelves, and they say, you know, come get what you need. It was just, you know, it was a blessing to me. That's how I describe it.

In addition, the students expressed appreciation for the university's investment in their success and well-being. As one student stated: "It's a huge impact on the school. . . . It feels like the campus cares about their students when they're creating programs like this. The university doesn't have to house this [food pantry]." In fact, several students were so grateful that they reported their reluctance to provide critical feedback on their campus pantry program.

Students learned about the food pantry program from other students, transfer orientation, the Women's Resource Center, and a campus outreach program designed to support nontraditional students. Most of the students reported using the food pantry once a week (the maximum amount allowed), but some reported using it every other week or once a month. One student reported that 80 percent of her household food comes from food banks or food pantries, including the campus pantry.

All six students reported that they liked the campus pantry model because of the anonymity, discretion, respect, and privacy afforded to students. A few students reported an initial reluctance to use the pantry but have been pleasantly surprised by the dignity with which they have been treated. For example, one student commented on how nice it is not being watched while shopping for food and not feeling like a beggar. In comparison, a student reported being uncomfortable with some of the local church pantries because of the invasion of privacy and, as they explained, the requirement to attend church in order to receive food. Students generally appreciated that the campus pantry did not require an application nor the verification of need. Students also preferred the shopping model.

Students overwhelmingly reported their gratefulness for toiletries and personal hygiene products, paper products, and cleaning supplies like laundry detergent found at the pantry. Nonfood items may not be purchased with SNAP,[6] and they are infrequently found at other food pantries (because they go so quickly). One student simply stated: "I don't purchase any cleaning supplies; I cannot afford it." Another student described a family of five living with one roll of toilet paper per week. One student described her reaction at finding shampoo in the pantry: "It's indescribable, like, I seen it on the shelf, and it was gold. My gosh they have Herbal Essence, like it's amazing." In addition, students appreciated finding school supplies, winter gloves and hats, and holiday treats like Thanksgiving turkeys, Easter baskets, and Christmas toys.

The food students reported getting from their pantries included canned vegetables, boxed macaroni and cheese, spaghetti and other pastas, spaghetti sauce, canned ravioli and soups, rice, and peanut butter. Students most desired foods that could be used for dinners or meals. Similarly, the most frequent criticism about the food available is that, apart from spaghetti and spaghetti sauce, most of the food represents side items, not actual meals. As many of the pantry clients explained, their children get free and reduced-price breakfast and lunch at school, so their primary concern is dinner. Not surprisingly, the food pantry wish list for all six students interviewed included meats, fresh fruits and vegetables, breads, milk, cheese, and eggs. As one student stated, "Anything fresh would be absolutely wonderful." Another student described fresh food as "beautiful." Students also provided a wish list of items that are perhaps more attainable, such as 100 percent fruit juice, more whole grain pasta, a greater variety of products, more dinner products, and canned fruits and canned tuna, both of which are occasionally found in the pantry but reportedly move off the shelf quickly.

Use of the food pantry and the foods available appear to significantly affect the health of pantry clients and their families.[7] For example, several students indicated a positive outcome:

> Yes it does. It does affect [our health]. Uh, because before, when I go like to stretch my food stamps, before I buy junk food because it's a little bit cheaper. Um, and makes them feel full sometimes, like chips or things like that, for dinner, just to keep them quiet. But now when we start this program, so I have all the cans, spaghetti, and sauce from here. I don't purchase it from [the store], and the money I stretch it to buy more food. Fruits and vegetables. So it helps so much. It changes so much; it's healthier.

Many students reported that before using the pantry, they would run out of SNAP benefits before the end of the month, but the pantry helps them stretch their SNAP benefits and use them wisely. Another mom described a situation where on the weekends, before the campus pantry began, she would encourage her children to sleep late so that they would be able to skip a meal. She would feed her children breakfast at lunchtime, skip lunch altogether, and then feed her children dinner in the evening. Since she began using the pantry, her children no longer have to skip a meal. Clearly, eating less junk food and having enough food throughout the day are meaningful and healthful outcomes for food pantry clients.

Food pantry clients often find themselves in a predicament where they are choosing between heavily processed food and no food at all. For example, as one student explained: "You know, when it comes to a pantry, you [are] kind of limited as a diabetic; you take the lesser of two evils; they don't really want you to eat canned anything, but you can't put fresh in a pantry. So you just have to do what you have to do."

This student explained that she has a difficult time finding whole wheat or whole grain pasta in the pantry, which is preferred by her doctors if she eats pasta at all. Another student simply stated: "If you're where I'm at, financially, it is either processed food or nothing." In an effort to combat the highly processed pantry foods, some students lean on other resources. For example, students buy meats, fruits, and vegetables with their limited SNAP benefits to supplement the canned and boxed items available in the pantry. Other students reported leaning on community food banks outside of the campus. One student described a local food bank that provided meat, fresh fruit, vegetables, bread, and dairy products. However, it has a one-day-a-week pickup time (probably to avoid storage issues that accompany providing fresh food) that may be challenging for students. This student scheduled her classes around the pickup time but was unable to avoid the conflict one semester. Another student reported that she was turned away from a community-based food bank because of her student status.

Students faced additional challenges when using campus pantries. One student explained that she does not use the pantry as much as she would like because she takes the bus, and it is a challenge to lug around a heavy bag of food. Another student described how exhausting it is to carry a bag of canned foods, tomato sauce, peanut butter, and rice all day long. Furthermore, the quantity and quality of the pantry food ebbs and flows unpredictability. Although pantry patrons recognized that this is because pantries rely heavily on donations, it still created challenges for them. For example, one student was frustrated about expending gas money for special trips to visit the campus pantry only to find a low food supply. Another student described a moral dilemma: "It feels a little bad when you go to the pantry and there is only one left, and, you know, you don't want to be the one to take it, you know. So it feels a little, you know, at least for me, it's, I feel a little more at ease if I'm taking not the last can of soup."

However, the biggest challenge occurred when the pantry was closed. The campus pantry is closed over the summer (May through August) and on holidays (including winter/Christmas break, Thanksgiving, and spring break). As one student explained, her family "struggles the most" in summer because her children are not being provided free or reduced-price breakfast and lunch at school and the campus pantry is closed. The students were, however, very grateful that the pantry recognized this need. The pantry lets students take an extra bag before holiday breaks. The number one recommendation for improvement from the students interviewed was to open the pantry over the summer. Students also requested educational materials including recipes; information about nutrition, diabetes, and other health and wellness topics; and lists of community-based resources (such as clothing banks) that would serve students.

Best Practices for Campus Food Pantries

Based on our interviews with campus pantry directors and clients, as well as an online document review of 141 campus pantries, we found that the success of campus pantries largely relies on three factors: (1) a data-driven approach to assessing program need and effectiveness, (2) the appropriate combination of staff and student leadership and support from administration and faculty, and (3) the development of a program that respects students and allows them to receive assistance with anonymity and dignity.

Many campus pantries start by collecting data to document food insecurity among their student population. When a director from a large West Coast public university pantry was asked to offer advice to new pantries, she explained: "My recommendation is to be data driven. To look and try to truly assess need. And, you know, I always tell folks to check out the USDA food security module. There is a, like a six-question questionnaire [US Department of Agriculture: Economic Research Service 2014] that can be used to see what your need is." These data help schools justify the need for a pantry to donors and administrators. The data also help develop community partnerships and are important for meeting any regulatory or funding requirements.

Campus pantries need a balance of both student and staff leadership for their success. As pantry directors explained, "students are the champions of the program," "they have tremendous energy to kick start things," and "they bring incredible creativity to campus initiatives." However, "students graduate," so there is great value in having staff with institutional knowledge to facilitate administrative processes and long-range strategic planning for the pantry. Furthermore, although faculty involvement is not necessary to having a campus food pantry, pantries that are able to integrate their food pantry into their larger educational mission seem to be thriving. Many of the schools view their food pantry as vital to student success and as an integral part of the academic institution. For example, Norwalk Community College uses the motto "Feeding Student Success" for their pantry. Similarly, Northeastern Illinois University states that their initiatives to address food insecurity are part of an effort to enhance their "learning environment and better support student success and retention."

Every campus pantry we studied placed an emphasis on privacy and respect. For example, campus pantries tend not to require students to justify their financial need; we did not find any discourse about deserving and undeserving recipients; and campus pantries have very few protections in place for fraud—all of which affords students their dignity. Many pantry directors reported that they do not worry about individuals taking advantage of their program. The fact that students are hungry is blatantly obvious; pantry directors know they are meeting a legitimate need. Among directors interviewed, there was consensus that "there is no one face of food insecurity on campus." However, they were concerned about the pervasive myths of food insecurity on college campuses. For example, some believe that poverty is part of the college experience, or that college students are rich, or that students rely on parents to support their basic needs. Pantry directors take it on themselves to dispel these myths and to protect the students using their campus pantries.

Campus pantries have spurred the development of new resources, including CUFBA's online network and the Oregon Food Bank's guide, *So You Want to Start a Campus Food Pantry: A How-to Manual* (Cunningham and Johnson 2011). However, new research and resources are needed to identify and share best practices for decreasing food insecurity on campuses. In particular, a nationwide survey may help colleges and local and federal agencies better understand the need for campus pantries. This type of large-scale, aggregate information may be useful for planning future food assistance programs targeting young adults and nontraditional students experiencing food insecurity.

Food insecurity is a threat to the health and success of college students in the United States, and significant numbers of students are vulnerable. The emergence of food pantries on campuses is one strategy to reduce this threat, whereas other federal or state food assistance programs may be unable to address student needs. Pantries may not fully counter the economic disparities that exist when low-income students enter college, but they may provide essential resources that begin to equalize the opportunities that higher education is meant to provide. Furthermore, they may support student retention, providing relief for students who would otherwise need to choose between their education and basic needs. Much variation exists in the form and function of campus pantries. However, commonality exists in the goal of most pantries—to provide a respectful, confidential experience for students who encounter food insecurity.

Appendix 1

Strategies for Ensuring Confidentiality and Respect for Clients of Campus Food Pantries Derived from Thematic Analyses of Interviews with Pantry Directors and Clients

- Selecting a discreet location for the pantry
- Providing or allowing students to use nondescript bags to carry food
- Collecting minimally required information about the student and his or her economic status on intake forms or other documentation
- Creating safe spaces at the pantry for students to wait or interact with staff and volunteers
- Advertising the pantry in ways that support the diversity of students who may experience food insecurity and do not perpetuate stereotypes
- Requiring staff and volunteer training on food insecurity, confidentiality, and respectful communication at the pantry
- Determining processes that allow for a comfortable shopping experience

Appendix 2

Interviewees were invited to participate through the use of flyers at their campus pantry, which also led to a snowball sampling approach to recruit additional participants. They were provided $25 incentives for their time and contributions. All six of the students interviewed were nontraditional, undergraduate, adult students. All six students were female, and five out of six had dependent children currently living with them (ranging from one to four children). One student was married, there were three white and three nonwhite students, and most were working part- or full-time jobs in addition to going to school.

Guiding Questions for Student Interviews

1. How did you learn about your campus's food pantry?
2. What types of items do you get from the food pantry?

3. How often do you go to the food pantry?
4. How much of your daily diet do you get from the food pantry?
5. Do you access other free or reduced services on campus or in your community? Please explain.
6. Had you been to a food pantry or bank before visiting the one on campus? Please explain.
7. What are one or two ways the food pantry could serve students better?
8. Does your use of the food pantry affect your personal health or well-being? Please explain.

NOTES

1. CUFBA was established as a clearinghouse of resources and an active network for campus food pantries. For more information see *sites.temple.edu/cufba/*.
2. If information for this research project was gained through publicly accessible documents and resources, then the university remains identified; if information was gained through private, Institutional Review Board–approved interviews, then the university is deidentified.
3. To gather basic information about the colleges with food pantries in the United States, a database was established using a list of schools registered with CUFBA. A simple Google search was conducted to systematically review the campus food pantries, as information was available online (typically via the websites for the colleges, websites for the campus pantries, and/or local news stories about the campus pantries). Information gathered included: location, year of establishment, history, leadership (e.g., student, staff, faculty), organizational structure, hours of operation, frequency of use, and other relevant information about the program, its processes, or evaluation. Additional information was gathered about each campus from the National Center for Education Statistics regarding the type (e.g., two-/four-year, public/private), size of the school by student population, and percentage Pell grant eligible.

   As of April 2015 (during the writing of this chapter) there were 141 campus food pantries registered with CUFBA. As of May 2018 there were 640 campus food pantries registered with CUFBA, which underscores the growing emergence of campus food pantries and the importance of researching food insecurity among college students.
4. Interviewees were invited to participate through the CUFBA network via direct e-mail contact and a listserv announcement. Interviewees represented colleges in eight different states from diverse regions.

   Sample guiding questions for pantry director interviews: 1. Tell us about your campus food pantry. How/why did it start? How is it managed? Who on campus is involved in its implementation? 2. Can you describe the students who use your food pantry? 3. Are there eligibility requirements for using the campus food pantry? If so, how do you verify if someone is eligible? 4. How do you communicate your programs to students? 5. What are the types of items you provide at your food pantry? 6. Are there other related interventions that you implement in addition to food distribution? 7. Do you work with local community food banks or other local food programs? 8. What legal or regulatory issues do you have to consider? How do you negotiate these?
5. For more information on the Mealbux program, visit the Mealbux fact page on OSU's website: *studentlife.oregonstate.edu/hsrc/food-security/food-assistance-funds/faqs*.
6. Three out of six students interviewed were receiving SNAP benefits. One student said that she did not qualify; the other two students were unsure if they were eligible.

7. Evaluation of off-campus pantries generally show that they are effective at reducing food insecurity, increasing access to nutritious foods, and improving health (Kaiser and Hermsen 2015).

REFERENCES

Armstrong, Elizabeth A., and Laura Hamilton. 2013. *Paying for the Party: How College Maintains Inequality.* Cambridge, MA: Harvard University Press.

Cunningham, Sarah E., and Dana M. Johnson. 2011. *So You Want to Start a Campus Food Pantry: A How-to Manual.* Corvallis: Oregon Food Bank.

Freudenberg, Nicholas, Luis Manzo, Hollie Jones, Amy Kwan, Emma Tsui, and Monica Gagnon. 2011. "Food Insecurity at CUNY: Results from a Survey of CUNY Undergraduate Students." Healthy CUNY Initiative, City University of New York.

Goldrick-Rab, Sara, Katharine Broton, and Daniel Eisenberg. 2015. *Hungry to Learn: Addressing Food and Housing Insecurity among Undergraduates.* Wisconsin HOPE Lab Report.

Hurst, Allison. 2010. *The Burden of Academic Success: Managing Working Class Identities in College.* Lanham, MD: Lexington Books.

———. 2012. *College and the Working Class: What It Takes to Make It.* Rotterdam: Sense.

Institute for College Access and Success. 2015. "Project on Student Debt." *ticas.org/posd/map-state-data#.*

Jordan, Miriam. 2015. "Colleges Launch Food Pantries to Help Low-Income Students." *Wall Street Journal,* April 7. *www.wsj.com/articles/colleges-launch-food-pantries-to-help-low-income-students-1428408001.*

Kaiser, Michelle, and Joan Hermsen. 2015. "Food Acquisition Strategies, Food Security, and Health Status among Families with Children Using Food Pantries." *Families in Society: The Journal of Contemporary Social Services* 96 (2): 83–90.

National Center for Education Statistics. 2015. Washington, DC: US Department of Education. *nces.ed.gov/collegenavigator/.*

Patton-Lopez, M., D. F. Lopez-Cevallos, D. Cancel-Tirdao, and L. Vazquez. 2014. "Prevalence and Correlates of Food Insecurity among Students Attending a Midsize Rural University in Oregon." *Journal of Nutrition Education and Behavior* 46 (3): 209–14.

Simons, Gary, ed. 2003. *Be the Dream: Prep for Prep Graduates Share Their Stories.* Chapel Hill, NC: Algonquin Books.

US Department of Agriculture: Economic Research Service. 2014. "Survey Tools." *www.ers.usda.gov/topics/food-nutrition-assistance/food-security-in-the-us/survey-tools.aspx.*

US Department of Agriculture: Food and Nutrition Service. 2014a. "Civil Rights Training Requirements for Volunteers." *www.fns.usda.gov/civil-rights-training-requirements-volunteers-0.*

———. 2014b. "Supplemental Nutrition Assistance Program (SNAP)." *www.fns.usda.gov/snap/facts-about-snap.*

Weinfield, Nancy S., Gregory Mills, Christine Borger, Maeve Gearing, Theodore Macaluso, Jill Montaquila, and Sheila Zedlewski. 2014. *Hunger in America, 2014.* Chicago: Feeding America. *help.feedingamerica.org/HungerInAmerica/hunger-in-america-2014-full-report.pdf?s_src=Y15XP1B1X&s_keyword=feeding%20america&s_subsrc=feeding%20america&_ga=1.19841585.82608726.1430928896.*

CONTRIBUTORS

Andrea Basche is an assistant professor of agronomy and horticulture at the University of Nebraska–Lincoln.

Ameena Batada is a faculty member in the Department of Health and Wellness at the University of North Carolina–Asheville.

Maureen Berner is a professor of public administration and government at the School of Government at the University of North Carolina–Chapel Hill.

Jennifer W. Bouek is a graduate student in the Department of Sociology at Brown University.

Kaitland M. Byrd is an instructor in the Department of Sociology at Virginia Tech.

W. Carson Byrd is an assistant professor in the Department of Pan African Studies at the University of Louisville.

Raphaël Charron-Chénier is an assistant professor in the School of Social Transformation at Arizona State University.

Eric Christianson is a field specialist for Iowa State University Extension in Community and Economic Development in Cedar Rapids, Iowa.

Samuel R. Cook is an associate professor in the Department of Sociology at Virginia Tech.

Mark Edwards is a professor of sociology in the School of Public Policy at Oregon State University.

Linda English is a clinical assistant professor in the Department of Economics at Baylor University.

Jeremy Everett is the founding director of the Texas Hunger Initiative at Baylor University.

Kevin M. Fitzpatrick, University Professor and Jones Chair in Community in the Department of Sociology at the University of Arkansas, is a coauthor of *Unhealthy Cities* and a co-editor, with Don Willis, of the 2015 book *A Place-Based Perspective of Food in Society*.

Michael D. Gillespie is associate professor of sociology at Eastern Illinois University.

Marie C. Gualtieri is currently a doctoral candidate at North Carolina State University in the Department of Sociology and Anthropology.

Leslie H. Hossfeld is a professor and head of the Sociology Department at Mississippi State University and is a local food systems researcher and advocate. She has twice presented her research to the US Congress on rural economic decline and poverty alleviation and economic development projects.

Michael Jindra is a visiting scholar at the Institute on Culture, Religion and World Affairs at Boston University. His forthcoming book is on the clash of lifestyle diversity and equality.

Marina Karides is an associate professor of sociology at the University of Hawai'i at Hilo on Hawai'i island. She is a coauthor of *Global Democracy and the World Social Forums* (2015).

E. Brooke Kelly is a professor of sociology in the Department of Sociology and Criminal Justice at the University of North Carolina–Pembroke.

Kathy Krey is an assistant research professor and the director of the Texas Hunger Initiative at Baylor University.

Nicolas Larchet is an associate professor of sociology at the University Le Havre Normandie and a research associate at the Center for Urban Cultures and Societies (CRESPPA-CSU, CNRS–University of Paris 8–University Paris Nanterre).

Olufemi Lewis is an active mother, daughter, and food warrior and has personally experienced hunger and homelessness, which is why she is resilient and self-determined to be part of building an equitable food system for communities most affected by food insecurity.

Doug McDurham is the Texas Hunger Initiative's director of strategic initiatives, as well as affiliate faculty in the Diana R. Garland School of Social Work.

Christy Mello is an applied cultural anthropologist and assistant professor of anthropology at the University of Hawai'i–West O'ahu. She completed her PhD in anthropology at the University of New Mexico.

Jacqueline Nester is a planner for Monroe County government, in Bloomington, Indiana.

Erin Nolen is the assistant director of research for the Texas Hunger Initiative at Baylor University.

Myriam Paredes is an associate professor in the Department of Desarrollo, Ambiente y Territorio (Development, Environment and Territory) at Facultad Latinoamericana de Ciencias Sociales (Latin American Social Science Faculty) in Quito, Ecuador.

Carmel E. Price is an assistant professor of sociology at the University of Michigan–Dearborn.

Sam Regas is a PhD student in the Indiana University Department of Sociology.

Gabrielle Roesch-McNally is a postdoctoral fellow with the US Department of Agriculture Northwest Climate Hub in Corvallis, Oregon.

Gloria Ross completed her PhD in the history and sociology of technology and science at Georgia Tech. She is currently a researcher for the federal government.

Natalie R. Sampson is an assistant professor of public health at the University of Michigan–Dearborn.

Stephen J. Scanlan is an associate professor of sociology at Ohio University. He has contributed chapters to *Environment and Sustainable Development in Asia* (edited by Jieli Li, 2014) and *Mountains of Injustice* (edited by Michele Morrone and Geoffrey L. Buckley, 2011).

Alexander Vazquez earned his master's in public administration from the School of Government at the University of North Carolina–Chapel Hill. He currently works as a management fellow in the City of Raleigh.

Julia F. Waity is an assistant professor of sociology in the Department of Sociology and Criminology at the University of North Carolina–Wilmington.

Patricia Widener is an associate professor of sociology at Florida Atlantic University. She is the author of *Oil Injustice: Resisting and Conceding a Pipeline in Ecuador* (2011).

Rachel Wilkerson studies statistics at the University of Warwick. She worked as a data scientist for the Texas Hunger Initiative at Baylor University.

Don Willis, Huggins Fellow and graduate instructor in the Department of Sociology at the University of Missouri, is a coeditor of the 2015 book *A Place-Based Perspective of Food in Society*.

Bill Winders is an associate professor at Georgia Tech and the author of *Grains* and *The Politics of Food Supply*.

Emily Zimmerman is a lecturer at Iowa State University in the Department of Horticulture and a doctoral candidate in the Graduate Program in Sustainable Agriculture and Environmental Science at Iowa State University in Ames, Iowa.

INDEX